W9-BXV-797

lonely planet

Cyprus

Paul Hellander

LONELY PLANET PUBLICATIONS
Melbourne • Oakland • London • Paris

CYPRUS

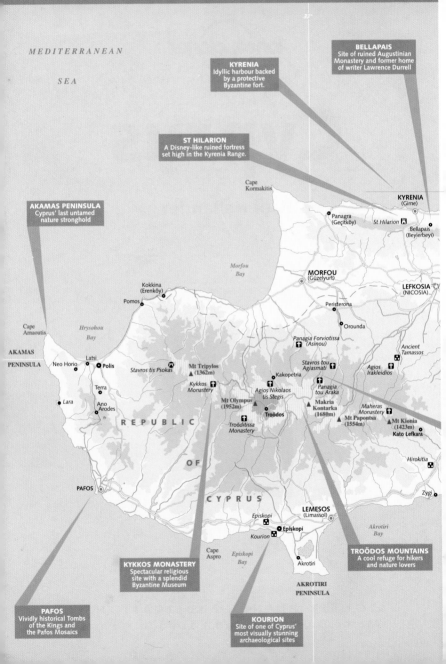

MEDITERRANEAN

SEA

KYRENIA
Idyllic harbour backed by a protective Byzantine fort.

BELLAPAIS
Site of ruined Augustinian Monastery and former home of writer Lawrence Durrell

ST HILARION
A Disney-like ruined fortress set high in the Kyrenia Range.

Cape Kormakitis

KYRENIA
(Girne)

AKAMAS PENINSULA
Cyprus' last untamed nature stronghold

Panagra
(Geçitköy) *St Hilarion*

Bellapais
(Beylerbeyi)

Kokkina
(Erenköy)

Morfou Bay

MORFOU
(Güzelyurt)

LEFKOSIA
(NICOSIA)

Pomos

Cape Arnaoutis

Hrysohou Bay

Peristerona

Orounda

AKAMAS PENINSULA

Neo Horio   Latsi
●Polis

Stavros tis Psokas

▲ Mt Tripylos
(1362m)

Panagia Forviotissa (Asinou)

Kakopetria

Stavros tou Agiasmati

Ancient Tamassos

Agios Irakleidios

Terra

Kykkos Monastery

Agios Nikolaos tís Stegis

Panagia tou Araka

Lara

Ano Arodes

R E P U B L I C

Mt Olympus
(1952m) ▲
Troödos

Makria Kontarka
(1680m)

Maheras Monastery

▲ Mt Kionia
(1423m)

Kato Lefkara

O F

Troöditissa Monastery

▲ Mt Papontsa
(1554m)

Hirokitia

PAFOS

C Y P R U S

Episkopi

Akrotiri Bay

Zygi

Episkopi ●

LEMESOS
(Limassol)

Kourion

KYKKOS MONASTERY
Spectacular religious site with a splendid Byzantine Museum

Cape Aspro

Episkopi Bay

Akrotiri

TROÖDOS MOUNTAINS
A cool refuge for hikers and nature lovers

AKROTIRI PENINSULA

PAFOS
Vividly historical Tombs of the Kings and the Pafos Mosaics

KOURION
Site of one of Cyprus' most visually stunning archaeological sites

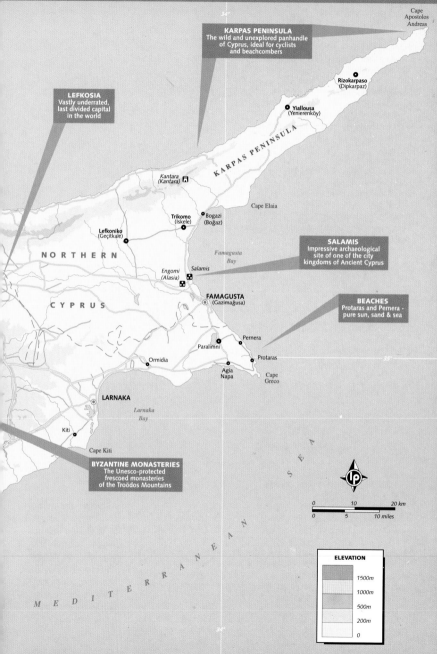

CYPRUS

KARPAS PENINSULA
The wild and unexplored panhandle of Cyprus, ideal for cyclists and beachcombers

LEFKOSIA
Vastly underrated, last divided capital in the world

SALAMIS
Impressive archaeological site of one of the city kingdoms of Ancient Cyprus

BEACHES
Protaras and Pernera - pure sun, sand & sea

BYZANTINE MONASTERIES
The Unesco-protected frescoed monasteries of the Troödos Mountains

Cape Apostolos Andreas

Rizokarpaso
(Dipkarpaz)

Yiallousa
(Yenierenköy)

KARPAS PENINSULA

Cape Elaia

Kantara
(Kantara)

Trikomo
(İskele)

Bogazi
(Boğaz)

Lefkoniko
(Geçitkale)

NORTHERN

*Famagusta
Bay*

Engomi
(Alasia)

Salamis

FAMAGUSTA
(Gazimağusa)

CYPRUS

Pernera

Paralimni

Ormidia

Protaras

Agia
Napa

Cape
Greco

LARNAKA

*Larnaka
Bay*

Kiti

Cape Kiti

S E A

0   10   20 km
0   5   10 miles

M E D I T E R R A N E A N   S E A

ELEVATION

1500m

1000m

500m

200m

0

Cyprus
1st edition – May 2000

Published by
Lonely Planet Publications Pty Ltd A.C.N. 005 607 983
192 Burwood Rd, Hawthorn, Victoria 3122, Australia

Lonely Planet Offices
Australia PO Box 617, Hawthorn, Victoria 3122
USA 150 Linden St, Oakland, CA 94607
UK 10a Spring Place, London NW5 3BH
France 1 rue du Dahomey, 75011 Paris

Photographs
Many of the images in this guide are available for licensing from
Lonely Planet Images.
email: lpi@lonelyplanet.com.au

Front cover photograph
Pera, one of the timeless villages of the Mesaoria, Republic of Cyprus.
(Paul Hellander)

ISBN 1 86450 075 1

Contents – Text

LEMESOS & THE SOUTH COAST 102

THE TROÖDOS MASSIF 117

LARNAKA & THE EAST 132

PAFOS & THE WEST 155

NORTHERN CYPRUS

NORTH NICOSIA   179

KYRENIA & THE NORTH COAST   193

FAMAGUSTA & THE KARPAS PENINSULA   204

LANGUAGE   219

GLOSSARY   227

INDEX   235

MAP LEGEND   back page

METRIC CONVERSION   inside back cover

Contents – Maps

MAP INDEX

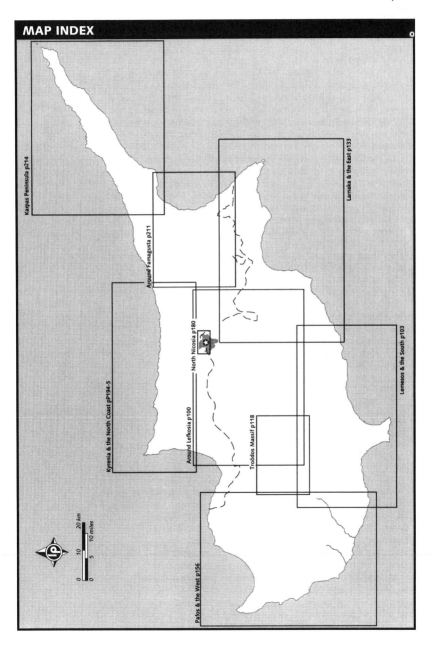

Karpas Peninsula p214

Around Famagusta p211

Larnaka & the East p133

Kyrenia & the North Coast pP194-5

North Nicosia p180

Around Lefkosia p100

Lemesos & the South p103

Troödos Massif p118

Pafos & the West p156

0   5   10 miles
0   10   20 km

The Author

Paul Hellander

Paul has never really stopped travelling since he was born in England to a Norwegian father and English mother. He graduated with a degree in Ancient, Byzantine and Modern Greek before arriving in Australia in 1977, via Greece and 30 other countries. He subsequently taught Modern Greek and trained interpreters and translators for 13 years before throwing it all away for a life as a travel writer.

Paul joined Lonely Planet in 1994 and wrote LP's *Greek phrasebook* before being assigned to *Greece* and *Eastern Europe* where he has covered Albania, Bulgaria, the Former Yugoslav Republic of Macedonia and Yugoslavia. Paul has also worked on *Singapore*, *Malaysia, Singapore & Brunei* and *South-East Asia*. Paul recently worked on updates of *Israel & the Palestinian Territories*, *Jerusalem* and *Middle East*. He can usually be found in cyberspace at paul@planetmail.net. When not travelling, he resides in Adelaide, South Australia, where he studies the history of espionage, listens to Neil Young, cooks Thai food and grows hot chillies. He was last spotted eying up yet more Nikkor lenses before heading off to write about and photograph the South of France and tropical Honduras.

From the Author

Global events and ethnopolitics contrived to make covering Cyprus in its entirety a challenging task. The long hot summer of '99, biting insects and dusty, winding roads contributed equally to the challenge, but I wouldn't have missed it. A number of people made my task easier. Among these I count Savvas and Panagiota Venizelou as friends to whom I am most indebted. I thank them for their house in Agia Marina Xyliatou and their fellow villagers for their hospitality and warmth. Special thanks to Geoff Harvey and Driveaway of Sydney and Peugeot of Paris for making possible the longest and least worrisome fly-drive program I have ever undertaken, and to Salamis Lines for smooth sailing to and from Cyprus.

Thanks also to the Cyprus Tourism Organisation and the North Cyprus Tourist Organisation for their unstinting assistance. Among individuals in Cyprus that I must mention are Christos Moustras, Orhan Tolun, Vasso and Sotiris Kokkotis, Mehmet Chavuš, Ruth Keshishian, Havva Sonay Bartutçu, Takis and Tasoula Christodoulidis for their assistance in a variety of ways and Hikmet Uluçam and Andreas Demetropoulos for their wild flower photos. Thanks also to Brendan O'Malley for sharing some of Cyprus' secrets, Charlotte Hindle for her groundwork, Louiza Maragozidis for proofreading and to Stella Hellander for more proofreading and her excellent photographic work in Cyprus with me. Thanks also to Yvonne Byron, Csanád Csutoros and Yvonne Bischofberger at Lonely Planet for making a book out of my script and maps. Marcus and Byron Hellander – this one is for you too.

This Book

From the Publisher

The 1st edition of *Cyprus* was produced in the Melbourne office and was coordinated by Yvonne Byron (editorial) and Csanád Csutoros (mapping and design). Helen Yeates and Miriam Cannell assisted with editing and proofing, and Yvonne Bischofberger, Paul Dawson, Piotr Czajkowski, Celia Wood and Mark Germanchis assisted with mapping. Jenny Jones compiled the colour wraps and Paul Dawson put together the special section. Rachel Imeson, Katie Cody, Chris Wyness and Mark Griffiths assisted with layout. Thanks also to Tim Uden and Paul Dawson for Quark support and Dan Levin and Rowan McKinnon who grappled with character fonts. Lindsay Brown supplied advice on wildlife of Cyprus.

Illustrations were supplied by Matt King, Quentin Frayne prepared the Language section and the cover was designed by Tamsin Wilson. Photographs were supplied by Fiona Croyden at Lonely Planet Images. Special thanks to Rachel Imeson, Tony Davidson, Katie Cody, Mark Griffiths and Carolyn Bain for their guidance.

Foreword

ABOUT LONELY PLANET GUIDEBOOKS

The story begins with a classic travel adventure: Tony and Maureen Wheeler's 1972 journey across Europe and Asia to Australia. Useful information about the overland trail did not exist at that time, so Tony and Maureen published the first Lonely Planet guidebook to meet a growing need.

From a kitchen table, then from a tiny office in Melbourne (Australia), Lonely Planet has become the largest independent travel publisher in the world, an international company with offices in Melbourne, Oakland (USA), London (UK) and Paris (France).

Today Lonely Planet guidebooks cover the globe. There is an ever-growing list of books and there's information in a variety of forms and media. Some things haven't changed. The main aim is still to help make it possible for adventurous travellers to get out there – to explore and better understand the world.

At Lonely Planet we believe travellers can make a positive contribution to the countries they visit – if they respect their host communities and spend their money wisely. Since 1986 a percentage of the income from each book has been donated to aid projects and human rights campaigns.

Updates Lonely Planet thoroughly updates each guidebook as often as possible. This usually means there are around two years between editions, although for more unusual or more stable destinations the gap can be longer. Check the imprint page (following the colour map at the beginning of the book) for publication dates.

Between editions up-to-date information is available in two free newsletters – the paper *Planet Talk* and email *Comet* (to subscribe, contact any Lonely Planet office) – and on our Web site at www.lonelyplanet.com. The *Upgrades* section of the Web site covers a number of important and volatile destinations and is regularly updated by Lonely Planet authors. *Scoop* covers news and current affairs relevant to travellers. And, lastly, the *Thorn Tree* bulletin board and *Postcards* section of the site carry unverified, but fascinating, reports from travellers.

Correspondence The process of creating new editions begins with the letters, postcards and emails received from travellers. This correspondence often includes suggestions, criticisms and comments about the current editions. Interesting excerpts are immediately passed on via newsletters and the Web site, and everything goes to our authors to be verified when they're researching on the road. We're keen to get more feedback from organisations or individuals who represent communities visited by travellers.

Lonely Planet gathers information for everyone who's curious about the planet – and especially for those who explore it first-hand. Through guidebooks, phrasebooks, activity guides, maps, literature, newsletters, image library, TV series and Web site we act as an information exchange for a worldwide community of travellers.

Research Authors aim to gather sufficient practical information to enable travellers to make informed choices and to make the mechanics of a journey run smoothly. They also research historical and cultural background to help enrich the travel experience and allow travellers to understand and respond appropriately to cultural and environmental issues.

Authors don't stay in every hotel because that would mean spending a couple of months in each medium-sized city and, no, they don't eat at every restaurant because that would mean stretching belts beyond capacity. They do visit hotels and restaurants to check standards and prices, but feedback based on readers' direct experiences can be very helpful.

Many of our authors work undercover, others aren't so secretive. None of them accept freebies in exchange for positive write-ups. And none of our guidebooks contain any advertising.

Production Authors submit their raw manuscripts and maps to offices in Australia, USA, UK or France. Editors and cartographers – all experienced travellers themselves – then begin the process of assembling the pieces. When the book finally hits the shops, some things are already out of date, we start getting feedback from readers and the process begins again …

WARNING & REQUEST

Things change – prices go up, schedules change, good places go bad and bad places go bankrupt – nothing stays the same. So, if you find things better or worse, recently opened or long since closed, please tell us and help make the next edition even more accurate and useful. We genuinely value all the feedback we receive. Julie Young coordinates a well travelled team that reads and acknowledges every letter, postcard and email and ensures that every morsel of information finds its way to the appropriate authors, editors and cartographers for verification.

Everyone who writes to us will find their name in the next edition of the appropriate guidebook. They will also receive the latest issue of *Planet Talk*, our quarterly printed newsletter, or *Comet*, our monthly email newsletter. Subscriptions to both newsletters are free. The very best contributions will be rewarded with a free guidebook.

Excerpts from your correspondence may appear in new editions of Lonely Planet guidebooks, the Lonely Planet Web site, *Planet Talk* or *Comet*, so please let us know if you *don't* want your letter published or your name acknowledged.

Send all correspondence to the Lonely Planet office closest to you:

Australia: PO Box 617, Hawthorn, Victoria 3122
USA: 150 Linden St, Oakland, CA 94607
UK: 10A Spring Place, London NW5 3BH
France: 1 rue du Dahomey, 75011 Paris

Or email us at: talk2us@lonelyplanet.com.au

For news, views and updates see our Web site: www.lonelyplanet.com

HOW TO USE A LONELY PLANET GUIDEBOOK

The best way to use a Lonely Planet guidebook is any way you choose. At Lonely Planet we believe the most memorable travel experiences are often those that are unexpected, and the finest discoveries are those you make yourself. Guidebooks are not intended to be used as if they provide a detailed set of infallible instructions!

Contents All Lonely Planet guidebooks follow roughly the same format. The Facts about the Destination chapters or sections give background information ranging from history to weather. Facts for the Visitor gives practical information on issues like visas and health. Getting There & Away gives a brief starting point for researching travel to and from the destination. Getting Around gives an overview of the transport options when you arrive.

The peculiar demands of each destination determine how subsequent chapters are broken up, but some things remain constant. We always start with background, then proceed to sights, places to stay, places to eat, entertainment, getting there and away, and getting around information – in that order.

Heading Hierarchy Lonely Planet headings are used in a strict hierarchical structure that can be visualised as a set of Russian dolls. Each heading (and its following text) is encompassed by any preceding heading that is higher on the hierarchical ladder.

Entry Points We do not assume guidebooks will be read from beginning to end, but that people will dip into them. The traditional entry points are the list of contents and the index. In addition, however, some books have a complete list of maps and an index map illustrating map coverage.

There may also be a colour map that shows highlights. These highlights are dealt with in greater detail in the Facts for the Visitor chapter, along with planning questions and suggested itineraries. Each chapter covering a geographical region usually begins with a locator map and another list of highlights. Once you find something of interest in a list of highlights, turn to the index.

Maps Maps play a crucial role in Lonely Planet guidebooks and include a huge amount of information. A legend is printed on the back page. We seek to have complete consistency between maps and text, and to have every important place in the text captured on a map. Map key numbers usually start in the top left corner.

Although inclusion in a guidebook usually implies a recommendation we cannot list every good place. Exclusion does not necessarily imply criticism. In fact there are a number of reasons why we might exclude a place – sometimes it is simply inappropriate to encourage an influx of travellers.

Introduction

Independent as an integral nation for only 14 years of its long history, Cyprus today is both an enigmatic and enticing destination for the traveller. Culturally European yet geographically Asian, Cyprus nonetheless shares a close history with its Levantine neighbours along the Mediterranean littoral.

Both Turkish and Greek, Cyprus is a bi-cultural nation with disparate monotheistic religions which, although often cause for division and strife, share a closer inheritance than many would care to admit. Cyprus is off the beaten track yet easily accessible – unless you wish to travel between the Greek and Turkish communities. Vaguely recalled school-day images of Aphrodite and the implied eroticism that accompanied her worship imbue a subtle sense of excitement in a visit to the island. Could this be why Cyprus entices so many young people to its sun and fun lifestyle?

The island of Cyprus has seen turbulent times in its illustrious and occasionally che-quered past. It was settled in Palaeolithic times and ever since has been fought over and subsequently settled by Ancient Greeks, Romans, Lusignans, Venetians, Genoese, Ottomans and the British. Some would argue that in recent times the So-viets, Greeks, Americans and Turks have all fought over hegemony.

Cyprus has remained a divided island since 1974, when its two communities were forcibly partitioned by outside powers. This division has been a bitter pill for its people to swallow. As Cyprus enters the new millennium, its destiny remains unfulfilled and uncertain and its resilient people are still divided by local politics and global interests. Cyprus is destined to play an important role in its position as keystone to the Middle Eastern region. Yet, while the globalisation of economies and cultures has become widespread and the undeclared Cold War no longer poses a threat to humanity, the country looks set to shoulder the troubled legacy it inherited in the 20th century well into the 21st.

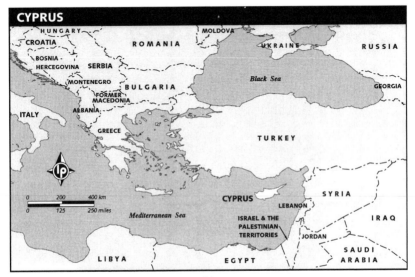

CYPRUS

Today's image of Cyprus is muddled in the minds of many. The word evokes images of sun and sand, yet few people realise that you can ski in the morning and swim at one of the many beaches in the afternoon. Cyprus is inextricably linked with invasion and bloodshed, yet the tranquil valleys of the Troödos Mountains shelter humble Byzantine monasteries and churches with some of the most exquisite frescoes found in Orthodox Christendom.

For many visitors Cyprus means riotous hedonism and overindulgence in eating and drinking – Aphrodite would no doubt be impressed – yet the island is home to a great legacy of archaeological treasures. Nature lovers perhaps don't realise that Cyprus supports a rich and varied ecosystem of endemic and imported flora and fauna. The spring wild flowers of the island are in total contrast to the grey-brown aridity of its summer months.

In contrast to other nations in the region, Cyprus is a small and compact country – the third largest island in the Mediterranean, yet only half the size of the island of Tasmania in Australia and smaller than the Netherlands or the US state of New Jersey. The Republic of Cyprus is an economic dynamo in the region with one of the highest standards of living in the Mediterranean basin. The Turkish-dominated Northern Cyprus, in contrast, languishes in economic dependence on its sponsor and guarantor Turkey, neither recognised nor seemingly wanted by the rest of the world community.

Despite its adversity and division, Cyprus is an excellent destination for independent travellers and package tourists. The infrastructure is good, English is spoken widely, the food is excellent, the Cypriots are welcoming, the climate is warm year-round – Cyprus awaits discovery. One proud Greek Cypriot summed it up succinctly when asked to describe his country he said, 'Cyprus is like a Greece that works'. He was not far wrong.

Facts about Cyprus

HISTORY

Situated at the maritime crossroads of the eastern Mediterranean basin, Cyprus has a rich and varied history. Many invaders, conquerors, settlers and immigrants have come to Cyprus and the island has seen Greeks, Romans, Byzantines, Lusignans, Genoese, Venetians, Ottomans, British and Turks in turn seek to take a part of Cyprus for themselves.

Cypriots, whether Greek or Turkish, are rightly proud of their nation and feel a strong sense of national identity. The division of their island in 1974 is viewed by many as a temporary setback and Cypriots look to the day when Cyprus will be a united island once again.

Neolithic & Chalcolithic Cyprus

Human habitation of Cyprus can be traced back with any certainty to around 6000 BC when the Neolithic settlement of Hirokitia in the south of the island flourished and prospered. This remarkable community is considered by archaeologists to be representative of one of the most distinct periods of settlement in Neolithic Europe. Hirokitia was a small village of some 2000 inhabitants who lived in well-built round houses made of stone in an organised and protected settlement. Finds of obsidian, a stone not native to Cyprus, indicate that the Hirokitians must have had contact with other cultures outside Cyprus. This community lasted for perhaps only a few hundred years and there is a gap in knowledge about the area until the beginning of the next period of habitation known as the Sotira culture which dated from 4500 to 4000 BC.

Small villages near Sotira in the South and in the Kyrenia Ranges in the North flourished and produced the earliest examples of pottery in Cyprus. Copper began to be used towards the end of the Sotira culture. The Chalcolithic Age followed (3000–2500 BC) where copper implements were being used alongside traditional stone implements and tools. Today two sites mark the pinnacle of Chalcolithic Cyprus – at Erimi near Lemesos and at Lemba and Kisonerga near Pafos.

The Bronze Ages

Early Bronze Age Copper was discovered relatively late in Cyprus, despite the island having abundant resources that subsequently fuelled a flourishing economy for many years. The first Bronze Age period is considered to have lasted from 2400 to 1900 BC during which exceptionally well-detailed vessels appear, commonly decorated with motifs of animals or humans.

Middle Bronze Age The second phase extended from 1900 to 1600 BC and artefacts discovered demonstrate an accomplished art culture. Imported items from Crete, Anatolia, Egypt and Syria indicate that external trade had already started. The settlement of Engomi (Alasia) near Famagusta flourished during this time.

Late Bronze Age The final phase lasted from 1600 to 1050 BC and is considered to be one of the most important periods in the cultural and historical development of Cyprus. Extensive foreign trade with places as far away as Egypt and the Aegean Sea characterised the era. Most importantly, writing in the form of a linear script known as Cypro-Minoan was adapted from Crete. Fine jewellery, ivory carvings and delicate pottery were produced during this time and from around 1400 BC there is a notable increase in the amount of Mycenaean pottery imported from mainland Greece.

Greek Immigration With the collapse of Mycenaean civilisation sometime after 1200 BC, there appears to have been a wave of mass migration to Cyprus, principally from the Peloponnese. It is about this time that the Greek language begins to dominate the scene and the dialect of the time, known

The Cypriot Syllabary

Writing came to Cyprus quite early in its history. The indigenous pre-Greek Cypriots used a syllabic form of writing – a syllabary – to represent the spoken language. A syllabary is a set of written symbols used to represent the syllables of the words of a language – for example, *ka, ke, ki, ko* or *ku*. Syllabaries are a form of writing that bridged the gap between earlier pictographic systems and later fully alphabetic writing systems.

The Cypriot Syllabary was used in Cyprus between the 6th and the 3rd centuries BC. It consists of 56 separate symbols, each of which represented a different syllable. Although most inscriptions found are in the Greek language, the syllabary was originally designed to record the indigenous pre-Greek language of Cyprus, which linguists called Eteo-Cypriot. Unfortunately we have no written record of this language form.

The classical Cypriot syllabary is most likely a late development of the Cypro-Minoan script which has not yet been deciphered. This script consisted of 63 symbols and was found on clay tablets in both Cyprus and Syria. It in turn is thought to have evolved from the early Cretan scripts know as Linear-A and Linear-B.

as Arcado-Cyprian. This confirms the link between early Greek migrants and Arcadia in the Peloponnese.

Archaic & Classical Cyprus

The City Kingdoms The first Greeks established a series of city kingdoms at Kourion, Pafos, Marion (Polis), Soloi, Lapithos, Tamassos and Salamis. Two more were later established at Kition and Amathous. These kingdoms enjoyed a period of advancing civilisation and prosperity between 750 and 475 BC, as shown in evidence found at the Royal Tombs near Salamis. These extensive tombs contained sumptuous examples of wealth and also closely matched the description of Mycenaean burials described by Homer in *The Iliad*.

During this time Cyprus was ruled in turn by Assyrians, Egyptians and Persians as the fortunes of these various empires waxed and waned and when they encompassed Cyprus as part of their own territorial expansions.

Classical Age Cyprus' Classical Age coincides with that of mainland Greece (475–325 BC) and during this period Cypriot art came under strong Attic influence. Zenon of Kition, the founder of the Stoic philosophy movement, was born during this time. Evagoras, king of Salamis maintained strong links with the Hellenic mainland and extended Greek influence over most of the island, despite Persian hegemony. However, he was finally overcome by the Persians in 381 BC and assassinated seven years later. His death effectively brought the Classical Age to an end.

Hellenistic & Roman Cyprus

Alexander the Great, following his victory over the last Persian ruler Darius III at Issus in 333 BC, took control of the city kingdoms of Cyprus and ushered in a new era. While giving the kingdoms essential autonomy he refuted their right to make coins. When Alexander died 10 years later in 323 BC, Cyprus was ceded to Ptolemy I of Egypt who further suppressed the city kingdoms, eventually causing the last king of Salamis, Nikokreon, to commit suicide. For 250 years Cyprus remained a Ptolemaic colony languishing under the rule of an appointed governor-general.

Cyprus was annexed by the expanding Roman Empire in 58 BC and became a Roman province. Orator and writer Cicero was one of Cyprus' first proconsuls. Despite being briefly given to Cleopatra VII of Egypt and subsequently handed back to Roman control, Cyprus enjoyed some 600 years of relative peace and prosperity under Roman rule. Many public buildings and works date from this time, noteworthy among them were the theatre at Kourion, the colonnaded gymnasium at Salamis and the Sanctuary of Apollon Ylatis.

Christianity in Cyprus It was during this period that Christianity made its early appearance on the island in around AD 45. Barnabas (later to become St Barnabas – Agios Varnavas in Greek), a native of Salamis, accompanied the Apostle Paul and preached on Cyprus. Among his first conversions was Sergius Paulus the Roman proconsul. Christianity flourished in Cyprus so, by the time of Constantine the Great, paganism had almost completely been supplanted and Christianity was dominant on the island.

The Byzantine Empire

The Roman Empire was divided in 395 with its eastern variant, the Byzantine Empire, based in Constantinople and still retaining hegemony over Cyprus. However, Cyprus retained a considerable degree of ecclesiastical autonomy from Constantinople and in 488 the archbishop was granted the right to carry a sceptre instead of an archbishop's crosier and the authority to write his signature in imperial purple ink. This practice is carried on to this day.

Arab Raids The expansion of Islam at around this time had adverse effects on Cyprus. A series of disastrous Arab raids starting in 647 caused great depredation and suffering. Salamis was sacked and never recovered, Kourion declined and coastal settlers moved inland to escape the repeated warring and pillaging. In 688 a kind of truce was called when Justinian II and the Arab caliph Abd-al-Malik signed an agreement giving joint condominium of Cyprus. This agreement lasted until 965 when the Emperor Nikiforos II Fokas regained Cyprus completely for the Byzantines.

Lusignan, Genoese & Venetian Cyprus

Byzantine rule might well have continued in Cyprus had renegade Governor Isaak Komninos not decided to proclaim himself Emperor of Cyprus and take on the might of the Crusader king Richard the Lionheart of England in 1191. Richard took possession of Cyprus and subsequently sold it to the Knights Templar. They were unable to afford the upkeep and sold it in turn to the by

now dispossessed king of Jerusalem, Guy de Lusignan.

The French-speaking new Lord of Cyprus established a lengthy dynasty that brought mixed fortunes to the island. He invited families who had lost property in the Holy Lands to settle in Cyprus and for some time they involved themselves in the affairs of the diminished territories that still belonged to the kingdom of Jerusalem. This proved an economic strain on Cyprus until the kingdom finally fell with the fall of Acre (Akko) in 1291.

For a hundred years or so thereafter Cyprus enjoyed a period of immense wealth and prosperity, with Famagusta being the centre of unrivalled commercial activity and trade. Many fine buildings and churches were completed, some of which are still visible in North Nicosia, Bellapais and Famagusta. Cyprus' prosperity reached its zenith under King Peter I (1359–69), who mounted an unsuccessful crusade in 1365 that only managed to achieve the sacking of Alexandria.

Meantime, Orthodox Greeks, while nominally free to practise their religion independently, were becoming more and more restless at being obliged to show obeisance to a Latin ecclesiastical administration. Many clerics retreated to the mountains and quietly and unobtrusively built simple churches and monasteries and decorated them with some of the finest frescoes ever painted in the Orthodox world.

The fortunes of the Lusignans were to take a turn for the worse after the accession to power of Peter I's heir and son, Peter II. Each eying Cyprus' wealth and strategic position as entrepot, Genoa and Venice jostled for control. This led to Genoa seizing Famagusta which it held for the next 100 years. Both Famagusta and Cyprus declined as a result. The last Lusignan king was James II (1460–73). He managed to expel the Genoese from Famagusta and married a Venetian noblewoman, Caterina Cornaro, who succeeded James and became Queen of Cyprus – becoming the last royal personage of the Lusignan dynasty. Under pressure she ceded Cyprus to Venice.

The Venetians ruled Cyprus from 1489 to 1571, but their control was characterised by indifference and torpor. Corruption and inefficiency marked the administration and the Greek peasantry fared no better under their new overlords than under their previous masters. In the meantime the Ottoman Empire was expanding and, in anticipation of attack from the North, the Venetians fortified Nicosia (Lefkosia) with immense circular walls and built massive fortifications around Famagusta. Neither measures held back the Ottoman onslaught and in 1570 Nicosia fell to the Turks. Almost a year later, after a long siege, Famagusta was taken by the Ottomans.

The Ottoman Empire

The newly arrived Ottomans suppressed the Latin Church and restored the Orthodox hierarchy. The peasantry who had hitherto suffered under a feudal tenancy system were granted inalienable and hereditary rights to land. Taxes were initially reduced but later increased, often arbitrarily, with the Orthodox archbishop now being responsible for their collection. Some 20,000 Turks were settled on Cyprus following its capture, but the island was not high in the priorities of the ruling sultans.

Indolence, corruption and sloth marked the Ottoman rule and dissent was frequently put down by oppression. In 1821 the Orthodox archbishop was hanged on suspicion of supporting the then growing Greek revolution in mainland Greece. Edicts issued by the sultan had progressively less effect on the restive populace as it became harder to implement the regulations. Ottoman rule lasted 300 years, until another foreign power sought influence in the region.

British Rule

In 1878 Turkey and Britain signed an agreement whereby Turkey would retain sovereignty of the languishing colony, while Britain would shoulder the responsibility for administering the island. Britain's aim was to secure a strategic outpost in the Middle East from where it could monitor military and commercial movements in the Levant and the Caucasus. As part of the agreement Britain would protect the sultan's Asian territories from threat by Russia.

In 1914 the parties were at war so Britain assumed outright sovereignty of Cyprus. Turkey's recognition of the annexation of its territory was not ratified until the 1923 Treaty of Lausanne, under which it also regularised territorial claims with its long-time subject and now newly independent Greece.

British control of Cyprus was initially welcomed by its mostly Greek population, since it was assumed that Britain would ultimately work with them to achieve *enosis,* union with Greece. Turkish Cypriots were less than enthusiastic at the prospect. The British had offered to unite Cyprus with Greece as early as 1915 on condition that Greece fulfilled its treaty obligations towards Serbia when attacked by Bulgaria. The Greek government refused and the offer was never repeated again.

Pro-enosis riots broke out in 1931 but it wasn't until the 1950s that the enosis movement really began to gather steam. Energy was generated by a Cypriot lieutenant colonel by the name of Georgos 'Digenis' Grivas who founded the National Organisation for the Cypriot Struggle (EOKA). Between 1955 and 1958 EOKA launched a series of covert attacks on the British administration and military and on anyone who was seen as being against enosis. The British came up with various proposals for limited home rule, but all were rejected. The 17% minority Turkish Cypriots became increasingly alarmed at the prospect of being forcibly incorporated into Greece.

The respective governments in both Greece and Turkey began to take an active interest in developments in Cyprus and, while Greek Cypriots called for enosis, the Turkish Cypriots demanded either retrocession to Turkey, or *taksim* (partition). In 1959 Greek Cypriot ethnarch and religious leader Archbishop Makarios and Turkish Cypriot leader Faisal Küçük met in Zurich with Greek and Turkish leaders, as well as representatives of the British government. They came to ratify a previously agreed plan whereby independence would be granted to Cyprus under conditions that would satisfy all sides. The British were to retain two bases and various other military sites as part of the agreement. Cyprus wouldn't enter into a political or economic union with Turkey or Greece, nor agree to be partitioned. Political power was to be shared on a proportional basis, though with less than 20% of the total population the Turkish Cypriots were granted 30% of civil service positions, 33% of seats in the House of Representatives and 40% of positions in the army.

Ominously, Britain, Turkey and Greece were to be named as 'guarantor powers' which gave any nation the right to intervene in the affairs of Cyprus should it be believed that the terms of the independence agreement were being breached in any way.

The Republic of Cyprus

The birth of the new independent Republic of Cyprus was realised on 16 August 1960. Transition from colony to an independent nation was not without growing pains and sporadic violence and agitation continued. The unrest culminated in serious sectarian violence in 1963 which further divided the Greek and Turkish communities. The Turkish Cypriots retreated to ghettos and enclaves as a means of protecting themselves against Greek harassment and aggression.

The Cold War was at its peak and Cyprus' strategic value as a radar listening post became vitally important to the British and the militarily stronger Americans. Both nations relied on Cyprus in order to monitor Soviet nuclear missile testing in Central Asia. The British maintained an air force garrison on its Akrotiri base that included a nuclear arsenal.

Archbishop Makarios, the President of Cyprus, played an increasingly risky game of political non-alignment while seeking arms and support from communist nations like the Soviet Union and Czechoslovakia. He also covertly supported further calls for enosis with Greece. Turkey and Turkish Cypriots became increasingly uneasy at the thought of a possible communist-dominated government in Cyprus and the Americans

and their British allies felt concern at the possibility of another Cuba crisis – this time in the Mediterranean.

Discussions on the possibility of segregation of the two communities began to take on a greater tempo. In 1967 a coup in Greece installed a right-wing military junta in power. Relations with Cyprus cooled while the US cosied up to the more accommodating colonels in Athens. Cyprus under Makarios became a less and less attractive option for both the Greeks and the Americans. On 15 July 1974 a CIA-sponsored and Greek-organised coup took place in Cyprus with the intention of eliminating Makarios and installing a more pro-west government.

Fearing that the next step would be enosis with Greece, the Turks launched a preemptive invasion of northern Cyprus five days later. After a brief hiatus in the fighting, the Turkish mainland army occupied the northern 37% of the island. Cyprus was finally divided. While the arrival of the Turkish army was seen as a Godsend by hitherto harried and harassed Turkish Cypriots, it was viewed as an enormous disaster by the 200,000 Greek Cypriots who then lived in the northern third of Cyprus. Many were caught up in the onslaught and killed, most were evacuated or fled to the South. Similarly, some 100,000 Turkish Cypriots from the South fled, or were forcibly evacuated to the North.

Cyprus Today

The division of Cyprus in 1974 has remained to this day. In the aftermath of the invasion huge numbers of refugees from both North and South fled to their respective sides of the island. The cost to Cyprus in terms of its economy and stability was enormous. The now-truncated Greek Republic of Cyprus was deprived of some of its best land, two major towns, its lucrative citrus industry and the bulk of its tourist infrastructure.

While the forced division of Cyprus served certain short-term military and political purposes and Turkish Cypriots received protection from their mainland brothers, the final result was ultimately a Pyrrhic victory for the Turks. Makarios escaped assassination by the coup plotters, the military junta in Greece ceded power to civilian rule and the idea of enosis dissipated.

The declaration of a Turkish Republic of Northern Cyprus (TRNC – KKTC in Turkish) by President Rauf Denktaş in 1983 was recognised by no nation other than Turkey and this nonstatus remains to this day. The Cold War came to an end in 1990, by which time half the population of native Turkish Cypriots had fled the island for lives in the UK, Canada and Australia. Known by most foreigners simply as 'Northern Cyprus' and by Greeks as the 'Occupied Territories' *(ta katehomena)*, the northern segment of Cyprus defies logic and continues to survive and develop, supported in no little way by its client and sponsor nation Turkey.

The Greek Cypriots quickly regrouped and put their energies into rebuilding their shattered nation. Within a few years the economy was on the mend and the Republic of Cyprus continues to enjoy international recognition as the sole legitimate representative of the nation of Cyprus. The economy is booming, the Cyprus Stock Exchange opened in mid-1999 and has absorbed vast amounts of surplus private funds, which Greek Cypriots have managed to accumulate despite the odds, and tourism is on a high.

Talks to reunite Cyprus have taken place sporadically since 1974 but little ground has been gained, both sides presenting an entrenched and uncompromising point of view. The United Nations has maintained peace along the Green Line since 1964, and in 1974 was called upon to patrol and monitor the ceasefire line, now called the Attila Line, running almost the length of the country. Whether the applications of Turkey and the Republic of Cyprus for accession to the European Union (EU) can be linked to a final solution to the Cypriot problem is anyone's guess. For the moment it looks like the only light at the end of a very long and dark tunnel.

GEOGRAPHY

The saucepan shape of Cyprus is a result of its topography, which in turn reflects its geology. In the North a 100km-long mountain chain known as the Kyrenia Range runs more or less parallel to the northern coastline. It is the southernmost range of the great Alpine-Himalaya chain in the eastern Mediterranean and is made up of thrust masses of Mesozoic limestone.

South of the Kyrenia Range lies a vast plain known as the Mesaoria (or Mesarya). It stretches from Morfou (Güzelyurt) in the west to Famagusta (Gazimağusa) in the east. The capital Lefkosia (Lefkoşa) lies more or less in the middle of the plain. The Mesaoria is the island's principal grain-growing area. Around 50% of its 188,385 hectares is irrigated; the remainder is given over to dryland farming.

The south of the island is dominated by the Troödos Massif, a vast bulky mountain range towered over by Mt Olympus (1951m). To the east is a small, lower plateau where most of the South's tourist industry is now based.

GEOLOGY

The Troödos Massif are of particular interest to geologists who have concluded that the range is made up of igneous rock and was originally formed from molten rock beneath the deep ocean (Tethys) that once separated the continents of Eurasia and Afro-Arabia. Since antiquity the mountain range has been particularly rich in minerals with abundant resources of copper and asbestos. Other natural resources include chromite, gypsum and iron pyrite. Marble has also been mined since antiquity.

CLIMATE

Cyprus enjoys an intense Mediterranean climate with a typically strongly marked seasonal rhythm. Summers are hot and dry and last from June until September. Winters are changeable, with cold and warmer weather alternating, and conditions also vary with the elevation. The Troödos Mountains usually receive snow in winter. Autumn in October and spring in April and May are short and the transition between winter and summer is rapid. Rain falls mainly in autumn and winter and outside

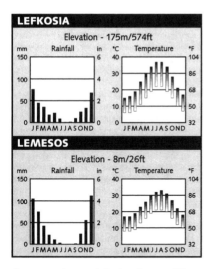

these months precipitation is rare. Water shortages can be a real problem in Cyprus.

Average summer daily temperatures in Lefkosia are between 22° and 37°C but often reach 40°C or more. From December to March the night temperature in the Troödos is often below freezing for several weeks.

ECOLOGY & ENVIRONMENT

Like most modern nations today, Cyprus is feeling the pinch in matters relating to urban encroachment, water and air pollution, erosion and deforestation. Significant urban encroachment took place in the South after 1974 when vast hotel complexes were built on pristine or undersettled coastal areas, particularly near Lemesos and Agia Napa. While many would argue that saturation point has been reached, new hotel complexes are still being built to soak up more of the tourist dollar. These complexes use up considerable amounts of energy and particularly water, which is in permanent short supply.

In the North, where authorities have not yet experienced the advantages and disadvantages of mass tourism, they have had the chance to monitor encroachment more carefully. In some large areas – notably the Karpas Peninsula – large scale development is now banned.

Overall, authorities in the North and the South are now belatedly taking a more cautious approach to conservation and there are small but active conservationist groups making waves in the country. Visitors should be aware that the tourist presence does have an impact on the country and should, wherever possible, make sure that their presence is as unobtrusive as possible. (See also Responsible Tourism in the Facts for the Visitor chapter.)

FLORA

The diversity of Cyprus' flora is not immediately obvious to first-time visitors. In summer the island is arid and the vegetation dry, but springtime sees an explosion of colour from its endemic flora – particularly its wild flowers. The island is home to some 1800 species and subspecies of plants of which about 128 or 7% are indigenous to Cyprus.

Plants can be found in the five major habitats that characterise Cyprus' flora profile: pine forests, gariques and maquis, rocky areas, coastal areas and wetlands. The main areas for endemic or indigenous plant species are the Troödos Mountains and their western extension the Pafos Forest, the Karpas Peninsula and the northern coastal strip, and the southern strip of the Cape Greco Peninsula in the south-east. (See also the special colour section 'Wild Flowers of Cyprus'.)

FAUNA

Birds travelling between Africa and Europe use Cyprus as a stepping stone on their migratory path. Bird-watchers have an excellent window, not only onto more exotic migratory species, but also local birds such as griffon vultures, falcons and kestrels. Mammals to be found on the island include fruit bats, foxes, hares and hedgehogs. There are a few snake species in Cyprus and, although you are unlikely to cross their paths, it is worth noting that the Montpellier snake and blunt-nosed viper are poisonous and can inflict nasty bites. Lizards are the most obvious of Cyprus' fauna species and they are literally everywhere. Don't be afraid of the pretty geckos in your hotel room; they come out at night to feed on insects.

Endangered Species

The moufflon is Cyprus' best known endangered species. It is an indigenous wild sheep that used to be abundant throughout the Pafos Forest on the western flank of the Troödos Mountains. Wide-scale shooting by farmers and hobby hunters over the years has reduced their numbers drastically to a degree that they are rarely, if ever, spotted wild in the Pafos Forest. A small herd is kept under protection at the Stavros tis Psokas forest station in the Pafos Forest. It is estimated that from near extinction in the early part of the 20th century, the current moufflon population is just over 2000. Cyprus Airways uses a stylised logo version of the moufflon on all its aircraft.

Green and Loggerhead turtles breed and live on the beaches. These endangered animals enjoy some protection in Cyprus and conservation programs in the North and the South are in place to ensure their continuing survival.

NATIONAL PARKS

This previously neglected area is now receiving some serious attention. In the South, the areas under study include the Akamas Peninsula, the Akrotiri Salt Lake and Fassouri Marsh and the Platys Valley. Two forest nature reserves have already been established at Tripylos – which includes Cedar Valley – and at Troödos. There is one marine reserve, the Lara-Toxeftra Reserve on the west coast, which was established to protect marine turtles and their nesting beaches. There are also six national forest parks that have been set up in recent years.

In the North plans are afoot to declare the far eastern section of the Karpas Peninsula as a nature reserve. Marine turtles nest on beaches on the north and south sides of the peninsula.

GOVERNMENT & POLITICS

The partition of Cyprus has resulted in two de facto political administrations. The government of the Republic of Cyprus is recognised internationally while the government of Northern Cyprus is officially recognised only by Turkey.

In 1960 Cyprus was declared an independent sovereign republic with a presidential system of government. Under the 1960 constitution, executive power is vested in the president of the Republic, elected by universal suffrage for a five-year term. The president exercises his executive power

MARTIN HARRIS

A small population of the rare Mediterranean monk seal can be found off the coast of Cyprus.

through a council of ministers appointed by him. Each minister is the head of his ministry and exercises executive power over all subjects within that ministry's domain. The president is both chief of state and head of government. Under the 1960 constitution, the post of vice president is allocated to a Turkish Cypriot but has been vacant since 1974. Glafkos Kliridis is the current president and has held the post since 1993.

Parliament (House of Representatives) is currently led by the National Unity Party – a coalition of the Democratic Rally (DESY) and the Liberal Party who hold 20 seats. Other parties in parliament include the Progressive Party of the Working People (AKEL), Communist Party with 19 seats, the Democratic Party (DIKO) holding 10 seats, the Socialist Party (EDEK) that holds five seats and the Free Democrats (KED) with two seats. The president of the house is Spyros Kyprianou.

Presidential and parliamentary elections are held independently every five years. The next presidential elections are scheduled for 2003 and the next parliamentary elections for 2001. For further details, look on the Internet at www.pio.gov.cy for the Public Information Office Web site.

In February 1975, Rauf Denktaş declared North Cyprus the independent Turkish Federated State of Cyprus, with himself as president. In 1983 he renamed North Cyprus the Turkish Republic of Northern Cyprus (TRNC, or KKTC in Turkish). Only Turkey recognises this self-styled nation. Denktaş leads a coalition of the National Unity Party and the Democrat Party. He has been president of the Turkish Cypriot administration since 1995 with runner-up Dervis Erog taking the post of prime minister in the government in 1996. A council of ministers is appointed by the president. The next presidential elections are due to be held in April .

Political parties active in the North's administration include the National Unity Party (UBD) under the leadership of Dervis Erog, the Communal Liberation Party (TKP) headed by Mustafa Akinci, the Republican Turkish Party (CTP) led by Mehmet Ali Talat, the Democratic Party

Rauf Denktaş – Portrait of a Renegade

Viewed as the bane of Cypriot society by Greeks and saviour of the nation by Turks, Rauf Denktaş provokes strong feelings either way among Cypriots. President of a self-proclaimed independent republic, this one-time lawyer is a mercurial character, matched in resilience and political longevity by few of his neighbouring Middle Eastern political leaders. He has used charisma and stubbornness to lead the Turkish Cypriot community from well before the forced division of Cyprus in 1974 and still shows no signs of passing on the baton of leadership to a younger protege.

Rauf Denktaş, 76 years old at the turn of the century, was born near Pafos in the South and trained as a barrister in London before commencing his long political career in Cyprus. As leader of the Turkish Communal Chamber from 1960, he was in and out of the spotlight – and trouble – until 1974, whereupon he became leader of the partitioned Turkish Cypriots.

Denktaş is known in political circles for his persistence and perceived intransigence in seeking a solution for the Cyprus issue. He dodges and weaves, teases and tests the will of both the South's political leadership and that of the intermediary nations or organisations who have vainly attempted to broker numerous peace deals.

His willingness to seek a mutually acceptable solution to the political impasse is compromised by petty quibbles. At talks held in New York in late 1999 he initially refused to participate unless addressed as 'Mr President'. He later compromised when he – and the Republic's President Glafkos Clerides – both agreed to be addressed as 'His Excellency'. Whether these talks will bear any fruit, only time will tell. Sceptics are weary of the stalemate and can only hope that a new leader will bring new optimism to a problem that has been unresolved for far too long.

(DP) of Serdar Denktaş and Arif Salih Kirdag's Unity and Sovereign Party (BEP). Look at the Web site of the TRNC at kktc.pu binfo.gov.nc.tr for further information.

ECONOMY

Reflecting yet again the division that characterises present-day Cyprus, the economy of the country presents two diverse pictures. That of the South is generally buoyant, but highly susceptible to external shocks. Erratic growth rates in the 1990s reflect the economy's vulnerability to swings in tourist arrivals. These in turn are caused by perceived political instability as well as fluctuations in economic conditions in Western Europe. Economic policies in the South are geared to meeting the criteria laid down for accession to the EU. Other than from tourism, the South generates income from export commodities such as citrus fruits, potatoes, grapes, wine, cement, clothing and shoes.

The economy of the North hasn't fared as well as that in the South. Export commodities such as citrus fruits, potatoes and textiles supplement income generated from a modest but growing tourist industry. The economy here generates only about one-third of the per capita GDP of the South but, because the North is not recognised internationally, it has had difficulty in securing foreign investment and overseas financing. The economy therefore relies heavily on the government service, which employs about 50% of the workforce, and agriculture. Difficulties are compounded by the use of the Turkish lira (TL) as legal tender, a currency that suffers repeated and almost daily inflation. Turkey ultimately provides direct and indirect aid to nearly every sector in order to keep the sputtering economy fuelled.

POPULATION & PEOPLE

Cyprus is made up primarily of Greek and Turkish Cypriots who together constitute a total population of 754,064 (July 1999). The Greeks are descendants of the early settlers who intermingled with the indigenous population around 1100 BC and subsequent settlers who came to Cyprus up to the 16th century. The Turkish Cypriots descend from Ottoman settlers who first arrived on Cyprus in 1570 following the Ottoman conquest of the island.

Around 18% (135,730) of the population are Turkish Cypriots. Turkish immigrants from the mainland are thought to make up about 50% of that total. Many Turkish Cypriots have left the island since 1974 to seek residence elsewhere, mainly in Canada, the UK and Australia. A large number of Greek Cypriots left Cyprus as refugees in 1974, but many have since chosen to return permanently to the South.

EDUCATION

Education is given a high priority in both sectors of Cyprus and literacy and numeracy levels are high. Education systems in the North and the South are administered separately, but follow similar patterns. Six grades of free and compulsory education are provided for children from age five. At least three years of the five-year secondary education programs are free and all secondary education at technical schools is free. Post secondary educational facilities include university, teacher training colleges, technical schools, hotel and catering training, nursing and midwifery. Cyprus' university system is relatively new and still cannot absorb the demand of graduating secondary students, many of whom choose to study abroad in Greece, Turkey, the UK or the USA.

ARTS
Dance

The origin of Cypriot folk dancing is very old. It may even be said to be related to shamanistic ceremonies and early religious and incantational worship. Different characteristics may be noticed because of geographical and local features. In the Republic musical and dance traditions also follow those of mainland Greece to some degree. The folk dances of today derive from the ritual dances performed in ancient Greek temples. One of these dances, the circular *syrtos*, is depicted on ancient Greek vases, and there are references to dances in

Homer's works. Many Greek folk dances, including the syrtos, are performed in a circular formation; in ancient times, dancers formed a circle in order to seal themselves off from evil influences.

One dance you'll see performed everywhere is the *kalamatianos*, originally from Kalamata in Greece, where dancers stand in a row with their hands on one another's shoulders. Two solo dances, ostensibly for men and women alternatively, are the *zeïmbekikos* and the *tsiftiteli* – though these days the differentiation is rather blurred. The zeïmbekikos is a slow, stylised and usually improvised blues solo dance performed a man. It is generally accompanied by hand-clapping from friends kneeling nearby on one knee and is characterised by introspective slow twirling and spontaneous high leaps when the mood or music takes an appropriate turn. For their part women dance the tsiftiteli, a spirited belly dance often performed on the table if the emotion of the moment leads to it.

There is of course a wide range of indigenous Cypriot dances, but it would be fair to say that you would only see them performed these days at folk festivals or specially staged dance performances. The most famous of these is the *kartzilamas*, in effect a suite of up to five different dances, that usually ends with the more familiar, syrtos dance or zeïmbekikos. Cypriot dances are commonly 'confronted pair' dances of two couples, or vigorous solo men's dances in which the dancer often holds an object such as a sickle, a knife, a sieve or a tumbler. Show dances at popular tourist restaurants frequently feature a dance called a *datsia* where the dancer balances a stack of glasses full of wine on a sieve. Another is a contrived dance in which diners are invited to try to light the tail – usually a rolled-up newspaper – of the solo male dancer who will attempt to dance and bob his way out of being set alight.

Dances in the North share very similar patterns of development and execution as those in the South, the only real difference being the names. Thus the kartzilamas is the North's *karşilama* and the tsifteteli is the *ciftetelli*. In addition there is the *testi*, the *kozan* and the *kaşikli oyunları* – a dance performed with wooden spoons. However, it is unlikely you will come across many occasions of Turkish dancing unless you happen upon sporadic summer folk festivals at either Kyrenia or Famagusta, or the harvest festivals that occasionally take place in country towns and villages. Restaurants with floor shows are most likely your best opportunity to sample some of the northern variants of Cypriot dancing.

Music

Greek Cypriots have tended to follow the history of music as it has been played out on mainland Greece. The mainland musical preferences are almost exactly reflected in what you hear in the Republic of Cyprus today. Conversely Cyprus has also produced some of its own home-grown musicians who have made a successful career in Greece as well as in their homeland.

The *bouzouki*, which you will hear all over Cyprus, is a mandolin-like instrument similar to the Turkish *saz* and *baglama*. It is one of the main instruments of *rembetika* music

MARGARET JUNG

The bouzouki was traditionally used for dancing and entertainment at social gatherings.

– the Greek equivalent of American Blues. The name rembetika may come from the Turkish word *rembet* which means outlaw. Opinions differ as to the origins of rembetika, but it is probably a hybrid of several different types of music. One source was the music that emerged in the 1870s in the 'low-life' cafes, called *tekedes* (hashish dens), in urban areas and especially around ports like Piraeus in Greece. Another source was the Arabo-Persian music played in sophisticated Middle Eastern music cafes *(amanedes)* in the 19th century. Rembetika was popularised originally in Greece by the refugees from Asia Minor and was subsequently exported to Cyprus.

Censorship of rembetika music by Greek authorities meant that themes like hashish, prison and gambling disappeared from recordings of rembetika in the late 1930s, but continued clandestinely in some tekedes. This polarised the music and the recordings, stripped of their challenging themes and language, became insipid and bourgeois; recorded rembetika even adopted another name – *laïko tragoudi* (popular song) – to disassociate it from its illegal roots. Although WWII brought a halt to recording, a number of composers emerged at this time, including Apostolos Kaldaras, Yiannis Papaïoanou, Georgos Mitsakis and Manolis Hiotis. One of the greatest female rembetika singers, Sotiria Bellou, appeared at this time.

Today's music scene in Cyprus is a mix of old and new – traditional and modern. Young Greek Cypriots are equally as happy with rembetika or demotic (folk) songs as they are with contemporary Greek rock music. Among artists to look out for are Pelagia Kyriakou and in particular her contribution to two albums known as the *Paralimnitika 1 & 2,* a superb collection of Cypriot demotic songs from the beginning of the 19th century and sung in the original Cypriot dialect. Mihalis Violaris is an exponent of folk and modern songs and was especially popular during the 1970s and 1980s. Two popular songs he made famous and that you will inevitably hear somewhere in Cyprus are *Ta Rialia* (Money) and *Tillyrkotissa* (Girl from Tillyria), again sung in Cypriot dialect.

Of the more modern singers, Anna Vissi sings contemporary Greek music and has appeared on albums released by top Greek singer Georgos Dalaras, as well as producing her own albums. Alkinoos Ioannides is a young Lefkosian who sings emotional ballads of his own composition that occasionally border on rap and rock and he has released three excellent albums. His first , *O Dromos o Hronos kai o Ponos* (The Road, the Time and the Pain), is worth picking up for an introduction to this talented Cypriot.

Georgos Dalaras, while not a Cypriot himself, has devoted much time and energy to the Cypriot cause. His album *Es Gin Enalian Kypron* (To Sea-Girt Cyprus) is a poignant tribute to the trials and tribulations of modern-day Cyprus, set to the music of Cypriot composer Mihalis Hristodoulidis. Finally, Cypriot singer and lyricist Evagoras Karageorgis has produced some excellent music, best represented on a fine album that is little-known outside of Cyprus called *Topi se Hroma Loulaki* (Places Painted in Violet), which is definitely worth seeking out for your CD collection. It is a nostalgic and painful look at the lost villages of the North sung in a mixture of Cypriot dialect and standard Greek accompanied by traditional and contemporary musical instruments.

In the North musical trends tend to mirror those of mainland Turkey, although Greek music is still admired and quietly listened to on radio broadcasts from the South – radio thankfully knows no boundaries and both cultures share a remarkable overlap in sounds and instrumentation. Among Turkish Cypriot musical personalities, Yiltan Tasci has made something of a name for himself locally and helped create and play in such bands as *Golgeler*, *Ozgurler*, *Kalender5* and *Letul*. Tasci's first recording, *Bana Seviyorum De*, came out in March 1995 and it contains seven songs that he composed and performed.

Literature

Cyprus has produced a sprinkling of literary illuminati and the literature scene is actively promoted and encouraged by the government of the Republic with competitions and accompanying awards being organised annually. Little Cypriot literature however is available in translation and, where it is available, its circulation is limited and usually restricted to Cyprus. Home-grown talent of the 20th century includes Cypriot Loukis Akritas (1932–65) who made his mark mainly in Greece as a journalist and writer, while later championing the cause of Cypriot independence through letters rather than violence. His literary works include novels, plays, short stories and essays.

Theodosis Pierides (1908–67), who wrote actively from 1928 onwards, can be considered among Cyprus' national and most respected poets. His *Cypriot Symphony* is regarded to be the 'finest most powerful epic written by a Greek poet about Cyprus', according to contemporary and fellow poet Tefkros Anthias (1903–68). Anthias himself was excommunicated by the Orthodox Church and ultimately internally exiled by the British administration in 1931 for his poetry collection *The Second Coming*. He was arrested during the liberation struggle of 1955–59 and imprisoned. While in prison he wrote a collection of poems called *The Diary of the CDP* which was published in 1956.

His literary legacy is considered important by contemporary critics. He wrote over 40 substantial works and was regarded a keystone in the history of Cypriot letters and intelligentsia. He was a teacher, intellectual fighter, journalist, writer and poet all rolled into one. His legacy is still being emulated by younger Cypriot writers.

The North supports a small but healthy literary scene with over 30 'name' personages. Nese Yasin (1959–) is a writer, journalist and poet in Northern Cyprus and was one of the founding members of a movement known as the '74 Generation Poetry Movement. This was a post-division literary wave of writers that sought inspiration from the climate generated after Cyprus was divided. Yasin's poems have been translated and published in magazines, newspapers, anthologies and books in Cyprus, Turkey, Greece, Yugoslavia, Hungary, Holland, Germany and England. One of her poems, *Which Half?*, has been used as lyrics in a composition by Greek composer Marios Tokas. She has published two collections of poetry, *Sumbul ile Nergis* (1978) and *Savasların Gozyasları* (1979). In 1978, when only 19, she was awarded the Special Arts and Culture Prize by the Republic of Cyprus government. This was the first time that such an award has been received by a Turkish Cypriot artist.

Hakki Yucel (1952–) is a poet, literary researcher and eye specialist. His poems and essays have been published in magazines and newspapers in Cyprus, Turkey, the UK and Hungary. He is one of the leading members of the '74 Generation Poetry Movement. He has been active in the promotion of Cypriot culture and literature in Turkey. His first collection of poems, *Aci Surgun* (Bitter Exile, 1986), is published by Yasemin Publications. He is now working on a novel and publication of a magazine on Turkish Cypriot arts.

Painting

Painting enjoys a healthy patronage in the South and one of the more famous exponents of the art neither runs a gallery nor attends art festivals. He is Father Kallinikos Stavrovounis, the aged priest of the Monastery of Stavrovouni, between the cities of Lefkosia and Lemesos. Father Kallinikos is regarded as the most superb contemporary icon painter of the Orthodox Church. He has been painting Byzantine religious icons for 50 years and, despite ailing health, does not seem ready to hang up his brushes just yet. Icons are made to order and money received is ploughed back into the Orthodox Church for the upkeep of the Stavrovouni and other monasteries.

Athos Agapitos is a contemporary Greek Cypriot painter who was born in Lefkosia in 1957. His art portfolio runs the gamut from realism and naive painting to expressionism in more recent years, with a predilection for themes encompassing elements from Greek and Egyptian civilisation, mythology and mysticism. His work was exhibited at the

Florence Biennale of International Contemporary Art in 1999.

Another contemporary artist is Panikos Tsangaras, originally from Trikomo in Northern Cyprus but now resident in Lemesos, whose works are being widely recognised. Savella Mihail is a female painter whose work is influenced by American abstract expressionism and who is beginning to make waves on the art scene.

Sculpture

Sculpture is another active area of art with a small but growing pool of practitioners. Among the foremost sculptors is Fylaktis Ieridis whose talent finds its most natural expression in the bronze medium. A chiropractor by vocation, his exposure to the human anatomy has given him an unusual insight into his subject and his interaction with people on a day-to-day professional basis has allowed him to lend a stark realism to his works which consist mainly of human figures. He has been commissioned to complete several busts and reliefs for heroes' monuments.

Folk Art

Cyprus is particularly well developed in the area of folk art, with lace and basketry being prominent among items produced. Lefkara lace, from the village of the same name in the South Troödos foothills, is one of Cyprus' most famous folk art export commodities. Large, woven bread baskets are on sale all over Cyprus and are characterised by their intricate and multicoloured patterns. Silver and copperware are also popular folk art items made throughout the country and are always of high quality and fine design.

The Cyprus Handicraft Service (CHS) in the South has been instrumental in promoting and preserving these arts which, without the support of the service, may well have taken the road to oblivion as have folk arts in other industrialising nations. It runs shops in the major towns and sells the wares of the artists that it supports. Items bought in these shops are guaranteed to be the genuine article. Look out for decorated

gourd flasks, objects that are becoming increasingly rare with the advent of modern packaging, as well as ornate bridal chests (sendouki), which are seen less and less these days at wedding celebrations. The town of Lapithos (Lapta) in the North used to be the island's centre for sendouki-making but that industry has taken a downturn following the events of 1974. Weaving used to be widespread throughout Cyprus, though you are unlikely to see looms, other than in remote villages or at the CHS where they are in regular use.

Chair-making in Cyprus, once a busy and lucrative trade that produced wonderfully durable and eye-pleasing items, has sadly given way to the 'plastic fantastic' culture. Restaurants and cafes invariably have replaced the wonderful wickerwork of yore with ghastly white plastic mouldings that truly blight what once was a much more aesthetic sight. If you come across a traditional wicker chair-maker and can get an order in for a chair or two to send home, do so now because this is a dying art that may not last much longer.

Pottery

Well-made and often highly decorative pottery is produced in Cyprus and is worth seeking out. You can hardly miss the enormous earthenware storage jars, called pitharia which are often used as decorative plant pots outside rural houses. Originally used for storing water, oil or wine they have fallen victim to more convenient methods of storage and packaging. Their sheer size and volume render them all but impossible to take home as souvenirs or as working artefacts. The village of Kornos between Lemesos and Larnaka is still an active pottery-making community, as is the Pafos region where, in Pafos town, you will find shops selling all kinds and sizes of multicoloured, functional as well as decorative pottery pieces.

Cinema

Cinema in Cyprus is a relatively recent phenomenon – hardly surprising perhaps, given the turbulent and disruptive nature of recent

Cypriot history. At the end of the 1940s the British colonial government started to train Cypriot film makers in the Colonial Film Unit. With the impetus created by the arrival of television in Cyprus in 1957, the first home-grown cinema productions began. These were mainly documentaries and the first independent production was called *Roots*. The Cyprus Broadcasting Corporation sponsored most productions over the next two decades, with a 1963 production by Ninos Fenwick Mikellidis called *Cyprus, Ordained to Me* winning a prize at the Karlóvy Vari Festival in Czechoslovakia. George Lanitis' film *Communication* won first prize for a short foreign film at the Thessaloniki Festival in 1970.

Further prizes were awarded in 1985 to Cypriot film makers Hristos Siopahas, at the Moscow Film Festival for his film *The Descent of the Nine,* and Andreas Pantazis, at the Thessaloniki Film Festival for his depiction of the Turkish invasion of Cyprus entitled *The Rape of Aphrodite*. Both film makers were honoured 10 years later at the Thessaloniki Film Festival for their works *The Wing of the Fly* (by Siopahas) and *The Slaughter of the Cock* (by Pantazis), both dealing with the invasion of Cyprus.

The recent upsurge in film production in Cyprus since 1974 is due primarily to newly found support from the state, which is keen to support young film directors. Since 1983 an enlightenment committee has been particularly active in the area of cinematography with a view to projecting the Cypriot problem to a wider international audience.

The North does not support a domestic film-making scene; its supply of cinematographic culture is supplied entirely from mainland Turkey. Both parts of Cyprus support a cinema industry geared to showing the latest Hollywood blockbusters in English with Greek or Turkish subtitles.

Theatre

Theatre in the South is a flourishing industry, with the Cyprus University Theatre Group (THEPAK) being very active in the performance of Cypriot- and Greek-written works. One of their more memorable recent

performances was a theatrical representation of a Middle Ages Cypriot chronicle by Lenities Maher, *Recital Concerning the Sweet Land of Cyprus – 1423–1431*. This adaptation of Maher's analysis of medieval political circumstances was a critical look at Cyprus towards the end of the Lusignan regime and was accompanied by the music of Cretan musician Antonis Xylouris Psarantonis and the songs of Cypriot composer Evagoras Karageorgis (see the Music section earlier in this chapter).

The biannual Kypria Festival regularly sees performances from a variety of domestic theatre groups. Tthe Cyprus Theatre Organisation performed Aristophanes' *Peace* and the Eleftheria Theatre of Cyprus presenting Euripides' *Bacchae* at the 1998 Kypria Festival. The stage production, choreography and music for both these plays were undertaken entirely by Cypriots.

Theatre in the North can be said to have started with the arrival of the Ottomans in 1570 and with the importation from the Turkish mainland of the *Karagöz* puppet shadow theatre. This theatre tradition is shared by the Greeks, which they call *Karagiozis*. Sadly Karagöz is performed rarely in the North these days (or even in the South for that matter) and is relegated to television shows and live performances during feasts such as Bayram. Theatre in the modern contemporary sense started on the island with British influence after 1878, but only really took off after independence in 1960 with amateur theatre groups being established in most Turkish Cypriot communities.

A new generation of playwrights proliferated, such as Hilmi Özen, Üner Ulutug and Ayla Haşmat. In 1964, the Department of Education provided the Atatürk Ilkokulu salon for the use of the Turkish Cypriot Theatre. The works that were performed at this venue, under the name of *First Stage,* continued to receive the admiration and support of audiences. As a result the theatre received official status as the Turkish Cypriot Theatre. Since then, and now renamed the Turkish Cypriot State Theatre, the company has performed nearly 85 plays with success.

After 1974, the State Theatre moved into new premises in Yenişehir, North Nicosia, and performs regularly in this venue, as well as in other cities and towns in Northern Cyprus. It also travels once a year to perform to Turkish Cypriots living abroad, notably in the UK and Turkey. Turkish Cypriot theatre has met with some success, due to a radio theatre production called *Alikko & Caher* in which the characters spoke in a rough dialect with which Turkish Cypriots closely identified.

The Kyrenia Amateur Dramatics Society is an English-language, amateur theatre group formed by British and local residents of Kyrenia, and produces a few plays (all in English) during the year. Look around Kyrenia noticeboards for possible productions that may be on when you visit.

The Turkish Cypriot Theatres have also produced a small number of celebrity actresses, among them Mine Senhuy, who stars in the popular television series *Bizimkiler*, on Turkish television, and Ayhatun Atesin, who is famous for her successful performance in the one-person play *One Woman: Shirley Valentine* by Willy Russel in 1993.

Whether you find yourself in the North or the South, plays are normally in Greek or Turkish and, unless you understand the languages, enjoyment of the performances will be limited by your linguistic skills. You may, however, wish to enjoy a purely visual theatrical experience per se.

SOCIETY & CONDUCT

The 1974 division of Cyprus has sadly polarised Cypriot cultural life as much as it has its political scene and demographic borders. When asked, both Turks and Greeks will still claim a common sense of Cypriot identity. They are Cypriots first and Greek or Turkish second. Both communities have been influenced by the cultures of the previous overlords of Cyprus. In more recent times Greeks and Turks have shared colonisation of their country by the British. While the British domination of the scene was understandably rejected by Cypriots in the late 1950s, there is a lingering 'Britishness' about Cyprus in the North and the

South. This impression is perhaps reinforced by cars that drive on the left and people that keep to appointed times for meetings.

Since 1974, however, there has been a creeping Turkification of the North. Greek place names have all been converted to Turkish names so that anyone familiar with the previous names may find it difficult to find their way around the North without a Turkish-language map. Greek road and wall signs of any description have completely disappeared from the North and visitors cannot help but feel that they are in a district of Turkey.

Likewise there has been a near-total Hellenisation of the South. Even the former city names of Nicosia, Limassol and Paphos have been officially changed to their Greek versions, something that may catch out the unaware traveller. Other than in the UN-controlled village of Pyla (see the Pyla section in the Larnaka and the East chapter), where one can see Turkish and Greek Cypriots still living together, there are few signs of the Turkish language or culture anywhere in the South.

On both sides of the Green Line, Cypriots are friendly, hospitable and courteous. Don't listen to disparaging comments by one community about the other. While in times of war and strife many atrocities have been committed in Cyprus – and haven't they elsewhere? – Cypriots are just as eager to pursue peaceful coexistence as any other nation. Family and social unity feature high on any Cypriot's list of priorities; strife and division are low on the list.

For visitors Cyprus is a very safe place. Cypriots regularly leave cars and houses unlocked and your personal safety is pretty well guaranteed. Petty thievery and crime may be on the increase in urban centres, but you are more likely to encounter trouble from fellow tourists than locals. Cyprus is a stable, westernised country and would-be travellers should show no particular concern about visiting.

Traditional Culture

Despite its overt Western outlook, Cyprus is steeped in traditional customs. Name

What's in a Name?

The issue of names is a thorny one in Cyprus, pregnant as it is with political, cultural and linguistic overtones and potential pitfalls. To avoid treading on too many peoples' toes we have adopted a few basic ground rules to make navigating this maze a little easier.

In general we have adopted the naming scheme that existed prior to 1974 when the Turkish army invaded the northern third of Cyprus. Since that time many of the Greek town and village names have been changed to Turkish. While we acknowledge the Turkish Cypriots' right to call a town or village by a Turkish name, this can lead to problems for a publication like this guide where many of the former Greek villages of the North are still known internationally by their Greek names and are still shown as such on maps.

The self-declared Turkish Republic of Northern Cyprus has never been recognised by any other authority than itself and its sponsor state, Turkey. It is not LP's intent to 'recognise' states as such and thus confer implied legality on them, but to describe a given situation as fairly as possible and allow readers to make their own conclusions. In this book we refer to Northern Cyprus as the territory currently occupied by the Turkish military and to the Republic of Cyprus, or Southern Cyprus, as the territory not occupied by the Turkish army.

In the North we have given Greek names of towns and villages followed by the Turkish where appropriate. This occurs more out of a need to assist travellers to navigate Turkish-language destination signs than to make a political statement. Without this knowledge and with Greek-only place names in our guide, navigating the North would be totally unfeasible.

In the South we have used the new, approved Hellenised place names for cities and towns. Thus, Nicosia is known as Lefkosia; Limassol as Lemesos; Paphos as Pafos and Larnaca as Larnaka. Road signs these days tend to use the new names though you will occasionally see the old names being used on older signs.

days, weddings and funerals all have great significance. Weddings are highly festive occasions, with dancing, feasting and drinking sometimes continuing for days. In Cypriot villages it is common for the whole village to be invited to the wedding.

Greek Cypriots tend to be superstitious. Tuesday is considered an unlucky day because on that day the Byzantine Empire fell to the Ottomans. Many Greek Cypriots will not sign an important transaction, get married or begin a trip on a Tuesday. Greek Cypriots also believe in the 'evil eye', a superstition prevalent in many Middle Eastern countries. If someone is the victim of the evil eye, then bad luck will befall them. The bad luck is the result of someone's envy, so one should avoid being too complimentary about things of beauty, especially newborn babies. To ward off the evil eye, Cypriots often wear a piece of blue glass, resembling an eye, on a chain around their necks.

Turkish Cypriots are noted for their seemingly excessive politeness – vestiges of a state of mind that dates back to the royal courts of the Ottoman Empires. The Turkish language has a series of rigid greeting formulas (polite phrases) which are often repeated on cue several times daily. This sometimes translates into English as stereotyped small talk and should be viewed in light of its original linguistic context. It might help if you go along with it, perhaps by joining in the banter with similar talk on your part.

It is considered by Greek and Turkish Cypriots as a compliment to their culture and a sign of respect if you can speak some Greek or Turkish, or at least if you make an attempt to say a few phrases. Never assume that someone will speak English, though English *is* widely spoken in Cyprus.

Dos & Don'ts

The Cypriot reputation for hospitality is well known. Cyprus is one of the few countries in Europe where you may be invited into a stranger's home for coffee, a meal or even to spend the night. This can often lead to a feeling of uneasiness if the host is poor, but to offer money is considered offensive. The most acceptable way of saying thank you is through a gift, perhaps to a child in the family. A similar situation arises if you go out for a meal with Cypriots; the bill is not shared as in Western European countries, but paid by the host.

When drinking wine it is the custom to only half fill the glass. It is impolite to empty the glass, so it must be constantly replenished. When visiting someone you will be offered coffee and it is bad manners to refuse. You will also be given a glass of water and perhaps a small serve of preserves. It is the custom to drink the water, then eat the preserves and then drink the coffee.

Cypriots are a little more formal in their interpersonal relations than their mainland brethren. People are commonly addressed as Mr 'so-and-so', eg, 'Kyrie Kosta' or 'Orhan Bey', and the use of first names alone is considered to be too familiar. Appointments are usually kept to the agreed time and in the villages it is not unusual for villagers to phone each other before visiting even if they live next door to each other.

You may have come to Cyprus for sun, sand and sea, but if you want to bare all, other than on a designated nude beach, remember that Cyprus is a traditional country, so take care not to offend the locals.

When visiting churches or mosques remember that they are primarily places of worship not tourist sights. Dress conservatively and avoid prayer times or church services if possible. Don't take flash photos and if you must speak, then do so quietly.

Some taboos to avoid in the Turkish community are pointing your finger directly at someone, showing the sole of your shoe or foot to anyone, blowing your nose loudly, picking your teeth and being overtly affectionate with someone in public.

While politics are discussed widely on both sides of the Green Line, the 'Cypriot problem' is a very sensitive issue – particularly for Greek Cypriots – and should be approached with tact and understanding. Both Greek and Turkish Cypriots can nonetheless be quiet frank and forthright in discussing the issue, but it is better to let them make the running rather than for you to initiate a discussion.

If you are of Greek extraction, or even have a Greek surname, it would be better to avoid trying to visit the North without making prior arrangements. You may be barred from entering or detained for questioning.

RELIGION

About 78% of Cypriots belong to the Greek Orthodox Church, 18% are Muslims and the remaining 4% are Maronite, Armenian Apostolic and other Christian denominations. These days the Muslims live mainly in the North and the Greek Orthodox in the South. The Maronites have traditionally been centred on the village of Kormakitis (Koruçam) in the North and there are small non-Orthodox Christian communities in both the North and the South.

The Greek Orthodox Church is closely related to the Russian Orthodox Church and together with it forms the third-largest branch of Christianity. Orthodoxy, meaning 'right belief', was founded in the 4th century by Constantine the Great, who was converted to Christianity by a vision of the Cross.

Religion is still integral to life for Greek Cypriots, and the Greek year is centred on the festivals of the church calendar. Most Greeks, when they have a problem, will go into a church and light a candle to the saint they feel is most likely to help. Sunday afternoons are popular times for visiting monasteries, and the frescoed Byzantine churches in the Troödos Mountains can often become packed with elderly weekend pilgrims.

Turkish Cypriots are for the most part Sunni Muslims and, while religion plays an important part in Turkish Cypriot culture, the conservatism of Islamic culture elsewhere in the Middle East and rural Turkey is not so obvious in Cyprus. Alcohol, for example, is widely available and frequently consumed by Turkish Cypriots. Turkish Cypriot women dress more casually than their Turkish mainland counterparts.

LANGUAGE

Most Cypriots in the Republic speak English and many road signs are in Greek and English. In North Cyprus this is not the case outside the tourist areas and you'll have to brush up on your Turkish. In both areas, the spelling of place and street names varies enormously.

Since mid-1995 the Republic has converted all place names into Latin characters according to the official system of Greek transliteration. As a result, Nicosia has become Lefkosia, Limassol is now Lemesos, Famagusta is Ammohostos and Kyrenia is Keryneia. Throughout this book the new names are given since the old ones are being phased out on all tourist maps and road signs. The new Greek names for Famagusta and Kyrenia in Northern Cyprus have not been used.

The Turkish names for North Nicosia, Famagusta and Kyrenia are Lefkoşa, Gazimağusa and Girne.

See the Turkish and Greek language guides at the back of the book as well as the boxed text 'Talking Cypriot' for pronunciation guidelines and useful words and phrases.

Talking Cypriot

Visitors to Cyprus are unlikely to encounter any serious language difficulties since many people in the North and the South speak English as a matter of course. However, if you have a smattering of Greek or Turkish and wish to fine tune your linguistic skills, there are a few pointers you should be aware of. Talking Cypriot is not as simple as it might seem.

In the South the Cypriots speak Greek, but it's not the same as you will hear in Greece. To an ear familiar with the standard language, Cypriot Greek sounds harsh and even incomprehensible. Consonants are palatalised so that the guttural 'ch' becomes 'sh', 'k' becomes 'tch' and the vocalised 'b' becomes 'p'. Many other phonetic variations distinguish Cypriot Greek. The vocabulary has its own set of words not heard outside Cyprus, though both standard Greek terms as well as Cypriot versions will be familiar to most Cypriots. Speakers of Greek from the mainland are known as *kalamarades* or penpushers – a hangover from the days when the only educated speakers of the language in Cyprus were from Greece.

Turkish Cypriots have their own Cypriot dialect, which is distinguished from Turkish spoken on the mainland by a number of peculiarities. These include a slurred, lazy mode of articulation, and the use of verb forms not used in standard Turkish, as well as a whole lexicon of Cyprus-specific words.

Neither Greek nor Turkish Cypriots will expect a visitor to be able to speak their respective languages – let alone the Cypriot variants. However, an hour or so spent practising the contents of the short language section in this book will go a long way to breaking the ice and to demonstrating to your new Cypriot friends your interest in their country.

Facts for the Visitor

HIGHLIGHTS
Republic of Cyprus
If it's sun, sand and fun you are looking for, there's plenty of it in the south of Cyprus. The economy of the Republic of Cyprus relies heavily on the tourist industry and for the most part that means organised tourism. There are beaches, resort hotels, water sports, wining and dining to rival the best in the world. It's well organised, easily accessible and relatively inexpensive.

If it's culture, history, archaeology, walking or cycling you prefer the Republic caters for you too. Nine of the frescoed Byzantine churches in the Troödos Massif are on Unesco's World Heritage List and a visit to at least some is worth the effort. Pafos is home to the Tombs of the Kings – an impressive underground necropolis dating back to the 3rd century BC – while nearby the Pafos Mosaics draw fascinated visitors who gaze upon works of art almost as fresh as the day they were created.

For hikers and cyclists the Troödos Mountains offer cool respite from the heat of the plains and some energetic cycling circuits for those keen enough to tour the Cyprus highlands on two wheels.

Northern Cyprus
Northern Cyprus offers a refreshing antidote to the sometimes frenetic hype of the South's tourist scene. The pace is slower, people are more prepared to give you their time, the beaches are among the best in Cyprus and food and accommodation are on a par with the finest of the Mediterranean.

Kyrenia (Girne) is the North's jewel and the hub of the compact tourist industry. With its horseshoe-shaped harbour, medieval castle, waterfront restaurants, bars and sea excursions, Kyrenia is the first port of call for most visitors to the North. The proudly Greek ruins of Salamis near Famagusta (Gazimağusa) bear testimony to a splendid city state that flourished in Cyprus during the 11th century BC.

The deserted Karpas (Kirpaz) Peninsula, the 'panhandle' of Cyprus, tempts cyclists, walkers, lovers of solitude and beachcombers alike. The country's most magnificent beach is here and remains totally unspoiled, protected as it is by a newly established national park.

SUGGESTED ITINERARIES
Republic of Cyprus
Depending on the length of your stay, you might want to see and do the following things:

One week Allow two days for Lefkosia, two days for Pafos, one day for exploring the ancient coastal sites between Pafos and Lemesos, and the rest in the Troödos Massif.

Two weeks As above but make two trips into Northern Cyprus, add Polis and the Akamas Peninsula (beaches and walks), and have a steam bath and/or massage at the Hammam in Lemesos.

Northern Cyprus
One week Allow one day for North Nicosia, one day for Famagusta, half a day for Salamis, and spend the rest staying in Kyrenia and visiting the castles in the Kyrenia Mountains.

Two weeks As above but have a Turkish bath in North Nicosia and spend some time exploring the near-deserted Karpas Peninsula and its archaeological sites.

PLANNING
When to Go
The beach and sea scene runs from early April to late October. At any time during that period you can be guaranteed fine weather. July and August are considerably hotter and are at the peak of Cyprus' tourist season. Avoid this period if you don't like the heat or the crowds.

October to April is the best time to see Cyprus' wild flowers, to walk the Troödos Mountains or the Akamas Peninsula or to cycle the Karpas Peninsula in the North. You can ski on Mt Olympus in the South from early January to mid-March.

WILD FLOWERS OF CYPRUS

In the heat and aridity of midsummer travellers to Cyprus could easily be forgiven for believing that the island is bereft of flora. The dry, maquis-covered and rock-strewn hills present little evidence that Cyprus is home to a wide variety of wild flowers and plants, many of which are to be found in no other country. Visitors in spring and late autumn, on the other hand, will confront a riotous blossoming of colour, with carpets of poppies, buttercups and anemones stretching as far as the eye can see, while the Troödos Mountains and Kyrenia Range are home to spectacular orchids and other rare endemic species.

Of the 20,000 or so orchids known to botanists, some 45 species are to be found in Cyprus and one of these – Kotschy's bee orchid – is unique to the island. Cyprus boasts some 130 endemic plants of which 45 are found only on the high slopes of the Troödos Mountains. A further 19 endemic species are found only in Northern Cyprus, with Casey's Larkspur perhaps the rarest plant on the whole island.

Cyprus' Flora Profile

The country's flora profile is a result of the catastrophic ice ages when much of the flora of northern and Central Europe was covered in ice sheets and glaciers, while the Mediterranean basin escaped unscathed and provided a haven for the further evolution of plant life. As an island, isolated from the mainland, Cyprus became rich in endemic flora and home to a large number of varied species that are typical of the Mediterranean area as a whole.

The country can be divided into six basic vegetation zones each of which supports its own set of flowers, shrubs, bushes and trees. Pine forests used to cover most of Cyprus, but shipbuilding in antiquity and the unabated use of wood for charcoal has destroyed much of the original forest cover. Forests are now mainly limited to the western

Left: Kotschy's bee orchid (endemic), *Ophrys Kotschyi*.
Right: Troödos helle-borine, *Epipactis troodi*.
Inset detail: The three-coloured chamomile (photo by Hikmet Oluçam).

slopes of Mt Olympus in the Troödos Mountains. Gariques and maquis are widespread areas of man-induced erosion where forest once stood and now only low bushes survive. Rocky areas comprise a variety of habitats and are commonly found in exposed mountain settings such as the Kyrenia Range. Coastal areas cover a narrow belt of some 50 to 100m along the coast which, with one or two exceptions, encompass the full girt of Cyprus. Cultivated land includes agricultural areas as well as fallow land and constitutes the largest geographical area of the island, yet hosts the fewest number of flower species. Wetlands constitute a marginal sector of the flora distribution. They are characterised by stream beds, salt lakes, marshy areas and artificial lakes.

When and Where to Go

The best time to see Cyprus' wild flowers is in early spring (February and March) when most of the species enjoy a short period of blossoming and take advantage of the usually moist climate at this time of the year. There is a second period in late autumn (October and November) when flowers can also be enjoyed. During the arid summer months only a few hardy flowers, found chiefly in the mountain regions, and colourful thistle plants on the Mesaoria/Mesarya

Top left: Troödos Anatolian orchid, *Orchis anatolica vat Troodi.*
Top right: Pyramidal orchid, *Anacamptis pyramidalis.*
Bottom left: Woodcock orchid (endemic), *Ophrys lapethica.*
Bottom right: Cyprus crocus, *Crocus cyprius.*

Plain provide any relief from what to the unobservant eye can seem like a botanical desert.

The main areas for flower spotting are the slopes and summit region of the Troödos Mountains, the northern aspects of the Kyrenia Range and the Akamas Peninsula. The isolated Karpas Peninsula is rich in specimens and the coastal strip east of Larnaka Bay is also exceptional for spotting endemic flora. In order to get the best out of flower spotting, enthusiasts will need to spend plenty of time walking and searching carefully since many species are limited to small geographical areas, sometimes to only a few hundred square metres.

What to Spot

Orchids are the most popular wild flowers for enthusiasts. The one endemic orchid – Kotschy's bee orchid – is an exquisite species, looking much like a bee both in its shape and patterning. It is fairly rare yet can be found in a variety of habitats all over the island. The Troödos helleborine, while not endemic, grows mainly on the slopes of Mt Olympus. Other orchid varieties include the slender, pink-coloured Troödos Anatolian orchid, the cone-shaped pyramidal orchid, the giant orchid and the colourful woodcock orchid.

Top left: Cyprus tulip (endemic), *Tulipa cypria*.
Top right: Troödos golden drop (endemic), *Onosma troodi*.
Bottom left: St Hilarion cabbage (endemic), *Brassica Hilarionis*.
Bottom right: Three-coloured chamomile (endemic), *Anthemis tricolor*.

HIKMET OLUÇAM
ANDREAS DEMETROPOULOS
HIKMET OLUÇAM
HIKMET OLUÇAM

The delicate white and yellow Cyprus crocus from the Iris family is an endangered species protected by law and is found commonly at high altitudes in the Troödos Mountains. The delicate, dark red Cyprus tulip is another rare species also protected by law and is today restricted to the Akamas and Kormakitis (Koruçam) Peninsulas and parts of the Pentadaktylos (Beşparmak) Range. A member of the borage family is the endemic Troödos golden drop, a small yellow, bell-shaped flower appearing in leafy clusters. This endangered species is confined to the highest peaks of the Troödos Mountains.

In the North, the unlikely sounding St Hilarion cabbage is found mainly on rocky outcrops near St Hilarion Castle. This large endemic cabbage flower grows to 1m in height and has spikes of creamy white flowers. Growing also near St Hilarion is Casey's larkspur, a late-flowering species that carries a dozen or more deep violet, long-spurred flowers atop a slender stem. Its habitat is limited to the northern tip of one small rocky outcrop 1.5km south-west of St Hilarion. Less spectacular but still uniquely Cypriot flowers are the three-coloured chamomile, the purple rock cress and the hard-to-miss Cyprus cotton thistle, which makes its appearance during the long hot summer months.

Tips for Spotters

While it is not possible to scratch more than the surface in this brief introduction to the wild flowers of Cyprus, there are some good publications available for the seriously botanically minded (see recommended reading). When looking for wild flowers, travel light and on foot. Take only photos of the flowers you spot, leave the flowers themselves; their existence may be tenuous at best. Others will no doubt want to enjoy their beauty as well.

Recommended reading: *Flora of Cyprus*, R Desmond Meikle; *The Endemic Plants of Cyprus*, Takis Tsintides & Loizos Kourtellarides; *Cyprus Trees and Shrubs*, E. F. Chapman; *Flowers of Cyprus*, Christos Georgiades; *Wildflowers of Cyprus*, George Sfikas.

HIKMET OLUÇAM HIKMET OLUÇAM

Left: Purple rock cress (endemic), *Arabis purparea*.
Right: Cyprus cotton thistle (endemic), *Onopordum cyprium*.

What Kind of Trip

You have two main choices here. Come on a package or do it yourself as a solo traveller. Both options have advantages and disadvantages. Packages take the worry out of travel arrangements yet leave you some flexibility to hire a car or a motorcycle to see Cyprus at your own pace when you are tired of the hotel pool or karaoke nights. A package holiday can often work out cheaper than solo travel, but you are usually locked into fixed arrival and departure dates and you normally only stay in one hotel, which rarely gives you the chance to sample the 'real' Cyprus.

Solo travel is an ideal way to see Cyprus and, while backpacker hostels and even a backpacker culture are still limited, options for budget accommodation are growing. An expanding chain of agrotourist hostels and pensions can be found around the country. Public transport is generally good, though a stout mountain bike or hired car or motorcycle are going to be necessary to get to some of the more off-the-beaten-track sights in the Troödos Mountains or the Karpas Peninsula.

Solo travellers can easily include Cyprus as a stopover between the Middle East and Greece, or as a value add-on to a round-Turkey loop. However, do note that you cannot use Cyprus as a stepping stone between Turkey and Greece or Israel, or vice versa. Regional politics still make travel tricky in some directions. See the Getting There and Away chapter for more details.

Maps

The free country and city maps available from the Cyprus Tourism Organisation (CTO) for the Republic of Cyprus are quite adequate for getting around. Do check however, the publication dates of the maps (in the right hand lower corner). These maps are not available commercially outside Cyprus other than from CTO offices overseas. Some older editions are still in circulation and are inaccurate in some cases.

The North Cyprus Tourism Organisation (NCTO) also produces a few free maps – a regional map and city maps of North Nicosia, Famagusta and Kyrenia. While adequate for most purposes, they are fairly skimpy and cheaply produced but do cover a wider urban area than the equivalent city maps in this book. Similarly, these maps are only available in Northern Cyprus, or from NCTO outlets overseas (see the following Tourist Offices Abroad section).

Predeparture planners might want to look at the Kyriakou Travel Maps' *Cyprus Road & Town Maps* which is possibly available in your bookshop. Collins *Cyprus Holiday Map* offers less overall detail but good local maps, while the Kümmerly+Frey *Cyprus Traveller's Map* is similar to the Collins product. The nifty pocket-sized and laminated Insight Map *Cyprus* is handy for quick references and folds very easily – a boon when you are on a bus or in a taxi. All of them are available internationally.

All maps cover Northern Cyprus, though only the Kümmerly+Frey map attempts to provide Turkish names as well as Greek ones – an essential detail if you are going to tour the North by car where road signs list only Turkish names of the towns and villages.

What to Bring

If you are coming on a package tour, bring whatever you like as long as it is within your baggage allowance. If you are going solo, bring only what you are prepared to carry around with you for the duration of your stay in Cyprus.

Bring clothes made with light-coloured and lightweight fabrics, that are easy to wash and require little ironing. You will not need heavier clothing or footwear unless you come in winter, or you plan to do some bush bashing in the Troödos Mountains or Kyrenia Range. Bring a warm jacket if you plan to visit the coastal regions in winter. It can still get chilly, despite the country's southerly latitude.

Water sports gear can be hired easily in Cyprus. Leave it at home unless you have a good reason to bring it along. Bring a small medical kit (see the Health section in this chapter for suggested items) and plenty of high factor sunscreen for Cyprus' unmerciful summer sun.

RESPONSIBLE TOURISM

Some might argue that hoteliers and tourist operators have gone overboard and have not acted responsibly in the race to develop (in the South at least). However, there is no reason for travellers to adopt this same attitude that thankfully, with one or two notable exceptions, is now beginning to wane.

Travelling light, lean and green is the way to go – in Cyprus as much as anywhere. Water is scarce in this country so use it sparingly, even in a big hotel. Ordinary Cypriots at home may be on water rations if a drought is biting. Take your rubbish with you when you have finished walking the Troödos Mountains or the Karpas Peninsula. Locals take pride in their countryside so follow their example. Don't pick the wild flowers in spring, others may want to enjoy them too. Spread your spending money around; support small businesses and local artists. Visit village taverns, not just hotel restaurants. Get to know Cyprus – not just your hotel pool.

TOURIST OFFICES

The Cyprus Tourism Organisation (CTO) is the main organisation responsible for assisting visitors to the south of the island. It has offices in major towns in the Republic. Its leaflets and free maps are excellent. The Cyprus Tourism Organisation (CTO) headquarters (☎ 02-337 715, fax 331 644) is at Leoforos Lemesou 19, Lefkosia, in the New Town on the road to Larnaka and Lemesos. The head office should only be approached for written inquiries.

The North Cyprus Tourist Office (NCTO) maintains tourist offices in North Nicosia (Lefkoşa), Famagusta (Gazimağusa), Yiallousa (Yenierenköy) and Kyrenia (Girne) which have free country and town maps plus an increasing number of brochures. The main office (☎ 228 1057, fax 228 5625) is on Bedrettin Demirel Caddesi in North Nicosia. There are also branch offices at Kyrenia Gate and at the Ledra Palace Hotel crossing point in North Nicosia.

Local Tourist Offices

The CTO has offices in the major towns in Cyprus where brochures and assistance can be found easily. CTO offices are in the following locations:

Agia Napa (☎ 03-721 796) Leoforos Kryou Nerou 12, CY-530
Lefkosia (☎ 02-674 264) Aristokyprou 11, Laïki Yitonia, CY-1011
Lemesos (☎ 05-362 756) Spyrou Araouzou 15, CY-3036
(☎ 05-323 211) Georgiou A' 22a, Germasoyia CY-4040
(☎ 05-343 868) Passenger Terminal, Lemesos Port
Larnaka (☎ 04-654 322) Plateia Vasileos Pavlou, CY-6023
(☎ 04-643 000) International Airport (24-hour service)
Pafos (☎ 06-232 841) Gladstonos 3, CY-7130
(☎ 06-4222 833) International Airport (services all flights)
Polis (☎ 06-322 468) Agiou Nikolaou 2, CY-8820
Platres (☎ 05-421 316) Platres, CY-4820

Tourist Offices Abroad

The CTO has branches in most European countries, the USA, Russia, Israel and Japan. Addresses and contact details for some of these offices are:

Belgium (☎ 02-735 0621, fax 735 6607, @ cyprus@glo.be) Boulevard Clovislaan 2, B-1000 Brussels
France (☎ 01-42 61 42 49, fax 42 61 65 13, @ CTO.CHYPRE.PARIS@wanadoo.fr) 15 Rue de la Paix, F-75002 Paris
Germany (☎ 069-251 919, fax 250 288, @ CTO_FRA@t-online.de) Kaiserstrasse 50, D-60329, Frankfurt am Main
Greece (☎ 01-361 0178, fax 364 4798, @ cto-athens@ath.forthnet.gr) Voukourestiou 36, GR-106 73, Athens
Holland (☎ 020-624 4358, fax 638 3369, @ cyprus.sun@wxs.nl) Prinsengracht 600, NL-1017 KS, Amsterdam
Israel (☎ 03-525 7442, fax 525 7443, @ cto@netvision.net.il) Top Tower, Dizengof Centre, 14th Floor, 50 Dizengoff St, Tel Aviv 64332
Italy (☎ 0258303328, fax 0258303375, @ turismo_cipro@cube.it) Via Santa Sofia 6, I-20122 Milano
Sweden (☎ 08-10 50 25, fax 10 64 14, @ cypern.tur.info.cto@stockholm.mail.telia .com) PO Box 7050, S-10386 Stockholm

UK (☎ 020-7569 8800, fax 7499 4935,
  @ ctolon@ctolon.demon.co.uk) 17 Hanover
  St, London W1R 0HB
USA (☎ 212-683 5280, fax 683 5282,
  @ gocyprus@aol.com) 13 East 40th St, New
  York, NY-10016

North Cyprus Tourist Offices can be found
in the UK, Belgium, the USA, Pakistan and
Turkey; otherwise inquiries are handled by
Turkish tourist offices.

VISAS & DOCUMENTS
Passport
You will need a valid passport to enter
Cyprus or, for EU nationals, an identity
card with a photo is sufficient. You will
need to produce your passport or ID card
every time you check into a hotel in Cyprus
and to conduct banking transactions.

As a foreigner it is a good idea to carry
your passport or ID card with you at all
times; you may be stopped by the police or
the military for routine checks. Keep a
photocopy of the details of your passport or
ID card separately, in case of loss or theft.

Visas
In both the Republic of Cyprus and Northern Cyprus, nationals of the USA, Australia, Canada, New Zealand, Singapore and
EU countries can enter and stay for up to
three months without a visa. Citizens of
South Africa may enter for up to 30 days
without a visa.

If you have a Northern Cyprus stamp in
your passport you can still visit the Republic, but it will be deleted by customs on
entry. This will not, however, prevent you
from visiting Greece. Despite this, it is advisable to get immigration to stamp a separate piece of paper instead of your passport
when entering Northern Cyprus. When you
enter the North from the South on day trips,
Turkish Cypriot officials issue you with a
day pass only and do not stamp your passport. There is no cost for the day pass.

Travel insurance
A travel insurance policy to cover theft, loss
and medical problems is a good idea. Some

policies offer a range of medical-expense
options; the more expensive ones are chiefly
for countries such as the USA, which have
extremely high medical costs. There is a
wide variety of policies available, so check
the small print. Cyprus will normally be
covered under 'European Countries'.

Some policies specifically exclude
'dangerous activities', which can include
scuba diving, motorcycling, even trekking.
A locally acquired motorcycle licence is not
valid under some policies.

You may prefer a policy that pays doctors or hospitals directly rather than you
having to pay on the spot and claim later. If
you have to claim later make sure you keep
all documentation. Some policies ask you to
call back (reverse charges) to a centre in
your home country where an immediate
assessment of your problem is made.

Check that the policy covers ambulances
or an emergency flight home.

Driving Licence & Permits
Driving Licence For citizens of the EU
your home driving licence is sufficient for
use in Northern and Southern Cyprus. As
with your passport or ID card, keep a photocopy of the main details separate from the
licence itself.

International Driving Permit Citizens
from outside the EU may not be expressly
required to hold an International Driving
Permit (IDP) in the North or the South, but
it is a good idea to obtain one in any case.
They are obtained easily and quickly from
your home country's motoring association
for a minimum charge. You will normally
need to provide only your regular driving
licence and a photo in order to obtain an
IDP.

If you are driving to Cyprus through
countries that do not have clearly defined
agreements regarding the recognition of
your home country's driving licence, an
IDP is strongly recommended. This is particularly so in the case of possible traffic
accidents or infringements when the non-
provision of an IDP may cause unforeseen
delays.

Vehicle Documents When entering the Republic of Cyprus from Greece or Israel the customs authorities are keen to see the vehicle registration book that clearly shows the vehicle's chassis number. Make sure you can easily link the chassis number with its identifying paperwork. The second key document the authorities will want to see is your 'Green Card' – an international extension of your home vehicle insurance policy. It must be specifically endorsed to cover the Republic of Cyprus. Make sure the CY international code for Cyprus is listed among the countries endorsed on your Green Card. If it is not listed, you will be required to purchase Cypriot insurance on the spot before being allowed to enter.

In the North, you will be almost certainly requested to purchase additional Northern Cyprus insurance, irrespective of what your Green Card or insurer may tell you. This currently costs around CY£2 (or equivalent thereof) per day or about CY£4 for 5 days. This applies equally to vehicles entering via the ports of Kyrenia and Famagusta or the Ledra Palace Hotel land crossing in Lefkosia.

Hostel Cards

A Hostelling International (HI) card is not mandatory for a stay in any of Cyprus' youth hostels, though it may get you a 10% discount.

Student & Youth Cards

The most well-known and easily obtainable student ID card is the International Student Identity Card (ISIC). This is available from your home educational institution before you depart. Its only real advantage in Cyprus is to obtain student discount rates for entries to museums and archaeological sites. There is no real student discount travel scene and no special student concessions on bus travel within Cyprus.

Other Documents

Your passport is without question your most valuable form of identification and security when you are travelling. If you lose it or have it stolen, replacing it can take time and effort and ruin the best-laid plans. In order to replace it more quickly, it's recommended that you take along a copy of your birth certificate and any other document that identifies you as a resident of your home country. A tax return certificate is a good example.

If you are thinking about looking for employment, take with you any educational or trade certificates that you may have earned. It is also handy to have a set of passport-sized photos of yourself.

Copies

All important documents (passport data page and visa page, credit cards, travel insurance policy, air/bus/train tickets, driving licence etc) should be photocopied before you leave home. Leave one copy with someone at home and keep another with you, separate from the originals.

It's also a good idea to store details of your vital travel documents in Lonely Planet's free online Travel Vault in case you lose the photocopies or can't be bothered with them. Your password-protected Travel Vault is accessible online from anywhere in the world – create it at www.ekno.lonelyplanet.com.

EMBASSIES & CONSULATES
Your Own Embassy

It's important to realise what your own embassy – the embassy of the country of which you are a citizen – can and can't do to help you if you get into trouble.

Generally speaking, it won't be much help in emergencies if the trouble is remotely your own fault. Remember that you are bound by the laws of the country you are visiting. Your embassy will not be sympathetic if you end up in jail after committing a crime locally, even if such actions are legal in your own country.

In genuine emergencies you might get some assistance, but only if other channels have been exhausted. For example, if you need to get home urgently, a free ticket is exceedingly unlikely – the embassy would expect you to have insurance. If you have all your money and documents stolen, it might assist with getting a new passport, but a loan for onward travel is out of the question.

Some embassies used to keep letters for travellers or have a small reading room with home newspapers, but these days the mail holding service is not common and even newspapers tend to be out of date.

Cypriot Embassies & High Commissions

The Republic of Cyprus has diplomatic representation in 26 countries, including:

Australia (☎ 02-6281 0832, fax 6281 0860) 30 Beale Crescent, Deakin, ACT 2600
France (☎ 01-47 20 86 28, fax 40 70 13 44) 23 Rue Galillée, F-75116 Paris
Germany (☎ 0228-367 980, fax 353 626) Kronprinzenstrasse 58, D-53173 Bonn
Greece (☎ 01-723 2727, fax 723 1927) Irodotou 16, GR-106 75, Athens
Ireland (☎ 01-676 3060, fax 676 3099) 71 Lower Leeson St, Dublin 2
Israel (☎ 03-525 0212, fax 629 0535) 50 Dizengoff St, 14th floor, Top Tower, Dizengoff Centre, 64322 Tel Aviv
Netherlands (☎ 070-346 6499, fax 392 4024) Surinamestraat 15, NL-2585 GG, Den Haag
UK (☎ 020-7499 8272, fax 7491 0691) 93 Park St, London W1Y 4ET
USA (☎ 202-462 5772, fax 483 6710) 2211 R St North West, Washington, DC 20008

The Northern Cyprus Administration has offices in:

Australia (☎ 02-2897 3114, fax 2682 4164) 295 Clyde St, Granville South, NSW 2142
Canada (☎ 905-731 4000) 328 Highway 7 East, Suite 308, Richmond Hill, Ontario L4B 3P7
France (☎ 01-40 50 01 77, fax 46 47 68 68) 4 rue André Colledebousuf, F-75016 Paris
Germany (☎ 0268-332 748, fax 331 723) Auf Dem Platz 3, D-53577 Neustadt Wied-Neschen
Italy (☎ 06-841 2353, fax 841 2354) Viale Gorizia 14, I-00198, Rome
Turkey (☎ 0312-437 6030, fax 446 5238) Rabat Sokak 20, Gaziosmanpaşa 06700, Ankara
UK (☎ 020-7631 1920, fax 7631 1948) 26 Bedford Sq, London WC1B 3EG
USA (☎ 212-687 2350, fax 949 6872) 821 United Nations Plaza, 6th floor, New York, NY 10017

Embassies & High Commissions in Cyprus

Countries with diplomatic representation in the Republic of Cyprus include:

Australia (☎ 02-473 001, fax 366 486) Corner Leoforos Stasinou & Annis Komninis 4, CY-1060 Lefkosia
France (☎ 02-779 910, fax 771 052) Ploutarhou 6, CY-2406 Engomi
Germany (☎ 02-664 362, fax 665 694) Nikitara 10, CY-1080 Lefkosia
Greece (☎ 02-441 880, fax 511 290) Leoforos Vyronos 8–10, CY-1513 Lefkosia
Israel (☎ 02-445 195, fax 453 486) Grypari 4, CY-1500 Lefkosia
UK (☎ 02-771 131, fax 777 198) Alexandrou Palli St, CY-1587 Lefkosia
USA (☎ 02-776 400, fax 780 944) Corner Metohiou & Ploutarhou, CY-2406 Engomi, Lefkosia

Countries with diplomatic representation in Northern Cyprus include:

Australia (☎ 227 7332) Güner Türkmen 20, Köşklüçiftlik, Lefkoşa
Germany (☎ 227 5161) Kasım 15, Lefkoşa
Turkey (☎ 227 2314, fax 228 2209) Bedrettin Demirel Caddesi, Lefkoşa
UK (☎ 228 3861) Mehmet Akif Caddesi 29, Köşklüçiftlik, Lefkoşa
USA (☎ 227 8295) Saran 6, Küçük Kaymaklı, Lefkoşa

Mail to any of the above addresses in Lefkoşa must be suffixed by Mersin 10, Turkey, *not* Northern Cyprus.

CUSTOMS

Items which can be imported duty-free into the Republic are 250g of tobacco or the equivalent in cigarettes, 2L of wine or 1L of spirits, and one bottle of perfume not exceeding 600mL. In Northern Cyprus it is 500g of tobacco or 400 cigarettes, and 1L of spirits or 1L of wine.

The importation of agricultural products or propagating stock such as fruit, vegetables, cut flowers, dried nuts, seeds, bulbs and cuttings etc are subject to strict quarantine control and should not be attempted without prior approval of the Ministry of Agriculture and Natural Resources. Such items should be declared upon arrival and will be subjected to inspection by agricultural ministry inspectors.

The importation of drugs or any psychotropic substances is strictly forbidden, as well as firearms, ammunition, explosives, ~~flick knives, daggers, swords, obscene ma-~~ terial and animals. Transgressors will be prosecuted.

MONEY
Currency

The Republic's unit of currency is the Cyprus pound (CY£), divided into 100 cents. There are coins of one, two, five, 10, 20 and 50 cents and notes to the value of one, five, 10 and 20 pounds. There is no limit on the amount of Cyprus pounds you can bring into the country, but foreign currency equivalent to US$1000 or above must be declared. You can leave Cyprus with CY£100 or the amount with you brought in, but exchanging Cypriot pounds into other currencies may be difficult except in Greece and perhaps neighbouring Mediterranean countries such as Lebanon, Syria, Israel and Egypt that have close commercial and tourist ties with Cyprus.

The unit of currency in Northern Cyprus is the Turkish lira (TL), and there are no restrictions on import or export. There are no coins and notes are issued in denominations of 100,000, 200,000, 500,000, 1 million, 5 million and 10 million.

Banks in Cyprus exchange all major currencies in either cash or travellers cheques. Most shops, hotels etc in Northern Cyprus accept CY pounds and hard currencies. UK pounds and Deutschmarks are commonly accepted. Starting in January 2002 EU currencies will be replaced by the euro (except in the UK, Greece, Sweden and Denmark).

In the Republic you can get a cash advance on Visa, MasterCard, Diners Club, Eurocard and American Express at a number of banks, and there are plenty of ATMs. In Northern Cyprus cash advances are given on Visa cards at the Vakiflar and Kooperatif banks in Lefkoşa and Kyrenia; major banks such as the İş Bank in large towns will have ATMs.

Exchange Rates

Exchange rates for the Turkish lira are subject to fluctuations due to a high inflation rate (80% in 1999) and will most likely not be valid by the time you read this. For current Turkish lira exchange rates refer to the Web site www.xe.net/ucc. All prices quoted in the Northern Cyprus section are either in US dollars for hotels or UK pounds for restaurants and excursions. Restaurants tend quote UK pounds on menus and hotels list rooms in US dollars. Museum entry fees and other sundry fees are given in Turkish lira.

At the time of going to print, the exchange rates for the Cyprus pound and Turkish lira against other major foreign currencies were:

country	unit		Cyprus pound	Turkish lira
Australia	A$1	=	0.38	364,087
Canada	C$1	=	0.39	378,261
euro	€1	=	0.58	556,482
France	10FF	=	0.88	848,351
Germany	DM1	=	0.29	284,520
Greece	GRD100	=	0.17	168,049
Ireland	IEP1	=	0.73	706,560
Israel	NIS1	=	0.14	133,839
Italy	L1000	=	0.30	287,388
Netherlands	f1	=	0.26	252,515
New Zealand	NZ$1	=	0.29	280,989
UK	UK£1	=	0.93	904,886
USA	US$1	=	0.57	547,000

Exchanging Money

Cash Cash is always a fail-safe way to carry money around from one country to another. It is also the least safe method of resource management. Once you lose it, it's gone. It's a good idea to only carry as much cash as you need for three days or so. However, a safety stash of about US$50 sewn into your backpack or suitcase will see you through a temporary cash flow problem.

Foreign currency notes may be OK in major tourist centres in Cyprus, but not much use in Troödos Mountain villages, or in a Lefkosia hypermarket. In the North, foreign currency is more likely to be widely accepted in lieu of Turkish lira.

If you carry little cash, you will find yourself working around banking hours and weekend bank closures, so plan your exchange transactions ahead so as not be to be caught short. Currency exchange bureaus in tourist centres do at least operate over extended hours and most weekends, so you are never likely to be far from a source of cash.

Travellers Cheques & Eurocheques

This once-popular method of carrying cash seems to be becoming less preferred by travellers. Restrictions on their use are naturally greater, though many hotels and larger establishments accept travellers cheques readily. Eurocheques are accepted by banks and exchange bureaus but are not commonly used in Cyprus.

Of the two, Eurocheques are nominally safer, since the user defines the amount of money to be cashed and the cheques are of no use to the finder if lost. Traveller cheques are almost as valuable as cash – each cheque being worth its declared face value – but their saving grace is that they are replaceable if declared lost.

ATMs More and more travellers are relying on fast cash pulled out of a hole in the wall. Automatic teller machines (ATMs) are as popular among Cypriots as they are among international visitors. They are a generally fail-safe way to get cash at any time of the day and the safest way to store your hardearned dollars, pounds or francs until you need them.

However, travellers should be aware of a few pointers. Credit your bank account before you leave home. Credit cards will allow you to draw up to your agreed limit and the ATM card check is immediate. No credit – no cash. Your home bank may charge you a large premium to make overseas ATM withdrawals. Check before you depart. Take at least two varieties of plastic in case you lose one and find yourself cut off from funds.

You will find ATMs in most towns and even some villages throughout Cyprus. In the North ATMs are currently limited to Nicosia, Famagusta and Kyrenia. In the South they are everywhere. The newish Hellenic Bank has a particularly good network of easy-to-spot 24-hour ATMs scattered throughout the South. See the listings of each city or town for the locations of ATMs.

Credit Cards Credit cards are equally as popular as ATMs and can be used in stores, restaurants, supermarkets and petrol stations. In the latter, you can even buy petrol after hours with your credit card from automatic dispensers. Most credit card transactions are conducted online, so if your credit is looking dodgy, don't attempt to use your card.

Using your credit card for big ticket items such as airline tickets and hotel bills may also help you clock up some useful frequent flyer points, if your credit card company is in partnership with your favourite airline. Check it out before you go. You may be eligible for frequent flyer points without knowing it.

The Republic of Cyprus is more credit card-friendly than the North, though the main restaurants, hotels and car-hire companies will happily take plastic.

International Transfers International transfers are possible from your home bank to any of Cyprus' major banks. While this method is reliable, it is usually slow – taking a week or more – and not helpful if you need a cash infusion quickly. Telegraphic transfers are nominally quicker – and cost more – but can still take up to three working days to come through.

The method is to nominate a Cypriot bank of your choice and advise your home bank of the details. If you can nominate a Cypriot bank account so much the better. When your money arrives you can collect it upon presentation of a passport or ID card. In practice, and if you have a credit card, it is far more convenient to get your home bank to credit your card directly and withdraw cash as soon as it is available from a suitable local ATM.

Security

Security and personal safety levels are good in Cyprus. As a traveller you run few risks of personal loss or harm. Cypriots regularly leave cars and houses unlocked, though travellers are advised to lock hotel rooms and keep personal belongings secure. The main risk here is from fellow travellers or even other foreigners, not usually Cypriots.

Costs

Prices in Cyprus are reasonable in comparison to most Western European countries. The cost of tourist commodities in the North and the South tend to be similar, though the North is better value when it comes to eating out and also at the budget end of accommodation options. Items in supermarkets are probably more expensive than you will be used to paying back home. Fruit and vegetables in local markets however will also be considerably cheaper than at home.

Accommodation in agrotourism houses in the South can cost as little as CY£12 per person per day and a meal with wine or beer in a local restaurant around CY£18. In the North bank on around US$20 to US$30 for a single room in a mid-range hotel and around UK£5 to UK£6 for a filling meal. Accommodation and general tourist services on both sides of Cyprus increase in price in July and August.

In the South public transport costs – bus and service taxis – are low, though taxis are not such a bargain. Access to museums and archaeological sites never exceeds CY£1.50. However, entrance to such sites in the North is comparatively more expensive with the average museum entry fee being around TL2 million.

Tipping & Bargaining

In both parts of the island a 10% service charge is sometimes added to a restaurant bill; if not, then a tip of a similar percentage is expected. Taxi drivers and hotel porters always appreciate a small tip. Bargaining is not normally part of the shopping scene in Cyprus – neither in the North nor the South.

Taxes & Refunds

Cyprus has an 8% value-added tax (VAT) which is automatically added to the cost of more or less all services provided. In the South there is currently no provision for the refund of VAT to travellers departing the country with goods on which tax has been paid.

An additional rate of between 2% and 10% is added to goods and services in Northern Cyprus. This is also not refundable to travellers upon departure.

POST & COMMUNICATIONS
Post

In the Republic of Cyprus, postal rates for cards and letters are between 25 and 41 cents. There are poste restante services in Lefkosia, Larnaka, Pafos and Lemesos.

In Northern Cyprus, rates are between UK£0.39 and UK£0.45. There are poste restante services in North Nicosia, Kyrenia and Famagusta. All mail addresses must be followed by Mersin 10, Turkey, *not* Northern Cyprus.

Telephone

In the Republic, you can make overseas calls from any public telephone box. There are two types: those that accept prepaid telecards and others that accept coins. The latter are similar to coin-operated phones found in the UK. They take two, five, 10 and 20 cent coins. Telecard-operated phones have explanations in English and Greek. Telecards to the value of CY£3, CY£5 and CY£10 can be purchased from banks, post offices, souvenir shops, street kiosks and from Cyprus Telecommunications Authority (CYTA) offices in all towns.

At peak times, a three-minute call to the USA will cost CY£2.90, and 21 cents during off-peak periods (10 pm to 8 am and all day Sunday). The Republic's country code is ☎ 357.

Lonely Planet's eKno Communication Card is aimed specifically at independent travellers and provides budget international calls, a range of messaging services, free email and travel information – for local calls,you are usually better off with a local card. You can join online at www.ekno .lonelyplanet.com, or by telephone from the Republic of Cyprus by dialling ☎ 0809 6251. Once you have joined, to use eKno from the Republic of Cyprus, you need to dial ☎ 0809 6248.

Check the eKno Web site for joining and access numbers from other countries and updates on super budget local access numbers and new features.

In Northern Cyprus public telephone boxes take phonecards bought at a Turkish Telecom administration office. A peak three-minute call to the USA will set you back UK£1.35 and off-peak UK£0.90. The eKno service is not yet available from Northern Cyprus because the telephone service operates through the Turkey.

To call Northern Cyprus from abroad dial ☎ 90 (Turkey), the country code ☎ 392, and then the local number. Area codes must be used when calling locally (codes have been incorporated into all phone numbers in the Northern Cyprus section).

In the North and the South many people now use mobile phones. If you have an international GSM-equipped phone, arrange global roaming with your home service provider. Assuming it has reciprocal arrangements with both sides of Cyprus you should be able to tune your mobile to any of the GSM services currently operating in both parts of the country (see the boxed text 'North-South Dialogue').

Fax

There are no public fax facilities available in the South, but most hotels will permit their guests to use the hotel fax facilities. Some stationers or high street shops advertising fax services may be alternative places from which to send faxes.

In the North you may send faxes from the Turkish Telecom administration offices or from high street stationers.

In either the North or the South you may consider ducking into an Internet cafe and sending a fax via the user-pays Faxaway

North-South Dialogue

In a country where the northern and southern halves share only one public utility – the sewerage system – it is not hard to imagine that communication between the two sides of the Attila Line is fraught with difficulty and frustration. This is no better illustrated than with the telephone service.

Calls to Northern Cyprus are all routed through Turkey. That means you must first dial Turkey (international access code 90), then the regional code for the whole of Northern Cyprus (392) and finally the local numbers. This means in effect that a call from the southern side of Lefkosia to the north side is an international call – even for a distance of perhaps a few hundred metres. That is if you can get a line. Lines are few and far between and would-be callers on either side of the Line are nervous that their calls may be monitored. They haven't got all that much to talk about in the first place, so North-South calls are consequently very rare occurrences.

If you have a mobile phone brought in from outside Cyprus there is a very simple way around this, should you have a need to call either direction. (This assumes you have made global roaming arrangements with your home mobile service provider and that your provider has reciprocal arrangements with both sides of Cyprus.) You simply tune your phone to either of the networks in the North, or the one network in the South. In the south you will invariably tune to CYTAGSM. In the North your GSM-equipped phone will pick up either TURKCELL or TELSIM GSM.

You must also have line of sight with either Turkish Cypriot or Greek Cypriot transmission towers – this most conveniently occurs if you are in the central Mesaoria/Mesarya Plain. Lefkosia/Lefkoşa is the best place to make such calls. In this way a call to the North from the South in effect becomes a local mobile call within the North. The same applies with calls to the South from the North.

There is of course the Internet. Both sides of the line have well-developed infrastructures for Internet communications. There are Internet cafes without restrictions such as those that apply to phone communications between the two communities. Where there's a will, there's a way and technology certainly makes it a lot easier.

network (www.faxaway.com), or the free email to fax services provided to many countries via TPC (www-usa.tpc.int). This is normally only good for text-based faxes unless you are adept at attaching postcript files of your formatted document or graphic. See the Web site for full instructions.

Email & Internet Access

Travelling with a portable computer is a great way to stay in touch with life back home, but there are potential problems. If you plan to carry your notebook or palmtop computer with you, remember that the power supply voltage in the countries you visit may vary from that at home, risking damage to your equipment. A universal AC adaptor for your appliance will enable you to plug it in anywhere without frying the innards.

Your PC-card modem may not work once you leave your home country – and you won't know for sure until you try. The safest option is to buy a reputable 'global' modem before you leave home, or buy a local PC-card modem if you're spending extended time in any one country. Telephone sockets vary between countries, so ensure that you have at least a US RJ-11 telephone adaptor that works with your modem. You can almost always find an adaptor that will convert from RJ-11 to the local variety. Phone plugs in Cyprus are of the flat modular kind such as those used in the UK. Adaptors are easy to find in major towns. For more information on travelling with a portable computer, see the Web sites www.teleadapt.com or www.warrior.com.

Major Internet service providers such as IBM Net (www.ibm.net) have dial-in nodes throughout Europe and Australia's Big Pond Internet service (www.bigpond.com) also has a wide range of overseas coverage for customers who wish to be able to access their ISP while roaming overseas. It's best to download a list of the dial-in numbers for all countries you plan to visit before you leave home. If you access your Internet email account at home through a smaller ISP or your office or school network, your best option is either to open an account with a global ISP, like those mentioned above, or

rely on cybercafes and other public access points to collect your mail.

If you do intend to rely on cybercafes, you'll need to carry three pieces of information with you in order to access your Internet mail account: your incoming (POP or IMAP) mail server name, account name and password. Your ISP or network supervisor will be able to give you these. With this information, you should be able to access your Internet mail account from any net-connected machine in the world, provided it runs some kind of email software (remember that Netscape and Internet Explorer both have mail modules). Become familiar with the process for doing this before you leave home. A final option to collect mail through cyber-cafes is to open a free Web-based email account such as HotMail (www.hotmail.com) or Yahoo! Mail (mail.yahoo.com). You can then access your mail from anywhere in the world from any net-connected machine running a standard Web browser.

You'll find cybercafes throughout Cyprus; for a recent list check out the Web site www.netcafeguide.com, though it doesn't contain every cybercafe in Cyprus. You may also find public net access in hostels or hotels.

There are Internet cafes in all main towns in South Cyprus and several in the North. The majority open late, close in the early hours of the morning and have become real social centres. They all charge in the region of CY£2.50 for the first hour and CY£1 for subsequent hours. A growing number of tourist facilities (accommodation, restaurants etc) now have email addresses.

If you plan to spend any time in Cyprus, it may be worthwhile taking out a temporary account with one of the country's Internet providers. SpiderNet (☎ 02-844 855, fax 669 470), 4th Floor, Isao's 1, CY-1082, Lefkosia, in the South can provide temporary accounts for as little as CY£10 (plus CY£10 initial registration fee) a month. Connection is immediate and dial-up access – providing you have a fast modem or fax/modem card – can be as fast as 42,000 bps, thanks to good digital connections in most parts of the country. You can apply for an account online by going directly to the Web site www.spidernet.net.

In the North, Cypronet is the main Internet service provider. Accounts for a minimum of three months can be taken out for US$80. This gives you a guaranteed 42,000 bps access speed. Accounts can be opened at Kyrenia's C@fe Net Internet cafe, or you can approach Mahir Bilgisayar (☎ 228 6537, ✆ mahir@northcyprus.net) in North Nicosia. A three-month account can be taken out for US$80.

INTERNET RESOURCES

The World Wide Web is a rich resource for travellers. You can research your trip, hunt down bargain air fares, book hotels, check on weather conditions or chat with locals and other travellers about the best places to visit (or avoid!).

There's no better place to start your Web explorations than the Lonely Planet Web site (www.lonelyplanet.com). Here you'll find succinct summaries on travelling to most places on earth, postcards from other travellers and the Thorn Tree bulletin board, where you can ask questions before you go or dispense advice when you get back. You can also find travel news and updates to many of our most popular guidebooks, and the subWWWay section links you to the most useful travel resources elsewhere on the Web.

Try the Web site www2.spidernet.net/web /~iacinfo/cypisp.html if you are looking for an Internet service provider in Cyprus. This link gives you the lowdown on all current providers in the country.

Places to search on the Internet to obtain a guide to and extensive information on Cyprus include:

Window on Cyprus Provides information on
the Republic of Cyprus, including useful leads
for independent travellers.
www.windowoncyprus.com
North Cyprus Home Page Most comprehensive site on Northern Cyprus including environmental issues.
www.cypnet.com/cyradise/cyradise.html
Kopiaste – Welcome to Cyprus Detailed
coverage of the South with information on

everything from history and the economy to hiking trails and where to rent cars.
http://www.cosmosnet.net/azias/cyprus/
c-main.html
Welcome to Cyprus (under construction)
Complete guide with information ranging
from doing business in Cyprus to the daily
weather.
www.welcometocyprus.com

Another good place to look for information is on the NetNews discussion group rec .travel.europe or even rec.travel.asia. Here you can set filters in your News reader program to highlight Cyprus-related topics that attract your attention. Your Web browser will normally have a utility to read Net-News.

BOOKS

Most books are published in different editions by different publishers in different countries. As a result, a book might be a hardcover rarity in one country while it's readily available in paperback in another. Fortunately, bookshops and libraries search by title or author, so your local bookshop or library is best placed to advise you on the availability of the recommendations.

Lonely Planet

Lonely Planet's *Greek phrasebook* is a handy volume to help you with possible language difficulties in the South while Lonely Planet's *Turkish phrasebook* will steer you round difficulties and perhaps open doors in the North.

The *Mediterranean Europe* guide covers most of the countries along the Mediterranean littoral, including a short section on Cyprus. If you are heading farther east, *Middle East* is a good general guide to the region. Individual Lonely Planet country guides exist also for Greece, Turkey, Syria, Lebanon, Jordan and Israel; all these countries have direct transport links with Cyprus.

Guidebooks

Blue Guide's *Cyprus* by Bernard MacDonagh and Ian Robertson is an archaeology-oriented title from this well-known publishing company. Strong on historical detail with less emphasis on practicalities, this book will suit travellers with a desire to know more about history. Insight Guides' *Cyprus,* by a band of contributing authors, is beautifully illustrated and photographed and makes a good coffee table publication for armchair travellers. There is a good balance of practical advice, but it is pitched mainly at the traveller on an organised tour.

The Cyprus Tourism Organisation produces a handy pocket-sized 150-page booklet called *Cyprus Travellers Handbook.* It is an alphabetically organised, free publication and contains a wide range of potted data and information on the Republic of Cyprus. It is available from any CTO office.

Windrush Island Guides produces one of the few dedicated books on the North called *Northern Cyprus* by John and Margaret Goulding. It is a reasonably detailed book, strong on descriptions, but less informative on traveller practicalities.

Travel

Lawrence Durrell's *Bitter Lemons of Cyprus* is a great first point of call for a look at the once idyllic but later troubled Cyprus of the mid-1950s. Durrell lived in the village of Bellapais in Northern Cyprus and describes, in his inimitable style, life in Cyprus from the local point of view and from that of a willing expat colonial administrator.

Colin Thubron's *Journey Into Cyprus* was the last significant travelogue of the once undivided Cyprus, written following an amazing almost 1000km walk undertaken in the spring and summer of 1972. Sprinkled with stories from the road and historical insight this book is a must for anyone contemplating an extended visit to Cyprus.

History & Politics

For the absolute latest version of events on the Cyprus debacle since the 1950s up to the coup and invasion of 1974, *The Cyprus Conspiracy* (1999) by Brendan O'Malley and Ian Craig is by far the best book on the market. In this meticulously researched work the two authors seek to shed light on the real role of the British government, the

CIA, Archbishop Makarios and the Junta colonels of Greece in events that led to the fateful summer of 1974.

Christopher Hitchens' *Hostage to History* (1998) is another honest and at times brutally frank account of events in Cyprus' more recent history. The book was initially written in 1984, but this latest version contains an updated preface. A somewhat drier and more academic perspective on the whole train of events from the Turkish Cypriot viewpoint, is Clemet H Dodd's *The Cyprus Imbroglio.* Compiled from a series of discussion papers written by this specialist in Middle Eastern politics, the book is a thought-provoking review of recent Cypriot politics.

Another 1999 release is *Cyprus: Ethnic Conflict and International Politics* by Joseph S Joseph. This work also examines the Cyprus problem and its implications in light of the ethnopolitics of the region and super powers.

CD ROMS

A clutch of CD ROMS released in late 1999 may be of interest to historians and butterfly or bird spotters. *The History of Cyprus* by Andreas Pavlides has more than 3000 pages of text, photos and video animation and theme presentations on Cypriot history. It costs CY£25. *The Butterflies of Cyprus* and *Migratory Birds of Cyprus* by Vassos Pentelas are a couple of fauna-oriented publications that may interest nature lovers. They both cost CY£12.

NEWSPAPERS

The Republic's English-language papers are the *Cyprus Mail* and the *Cyprus Weekly.* The Northern Cyprus publications are the *Turkish Daily News* and *Cyprus Today.* You can read the *Cyprus Mail* online at www.cynews.com.

UK papers and international versions of various English-language newspapers are available widely in the South, less so in the North.

RADIO & TV

CyBC (Cyprus Broadcasting Corporation) has programs and news bulletins in English on Radio 2 (FM 91 to 1MHz) at 10 am, 2 and 8 pm. BFBS 1 (British Forces Broadcasting Services) broadcasts 24 hours a day in English on 99.6 FM (East), 92.1 FM (West) and 89.7 FM (Lefkosia); BFBS 2 broadcasts on 95.3 FM (East), 89.9 FM (West) and 91.9 FM (Lefkosia). The BBC World Service is picked up 24 hours a day on 1323 AM.

CyBC TV has news in English at 8 pm on Channel 2. Satellite dishes are very common, so many hotels have CNN, BBC, SKY or NBC.

VIDEO SYSTEMS

Cyprus' TV and video system is PAL such as is used in the UK, Australia and New Zealand and most of Western Europe. Any video tapes bought in either Northern or Southern Cyprus will only be playable on equipment that caters for PAL playback. Owners of North American or Japanese (NTSC) video systems or French/Eastern European SECAM systems may not be able to view PAL-coded tapes.

PHOTOGRAPHY & VIDEO

Cyprus is an ideal place to take pictures or to make amateur videos. The weather will almost never spoil your plans. Your equipment will necessarily reflect your budget and interest level and good results are almost guaranteed as long as you follow some basic rules and tips.

Film & Equipment

Thanks to abundant quality light in Cyprus, photography can be a sheer pleasure. All makes of cameras and film are catered for in Cyprus, though technical services may be more limited in the North. Slide duplications, for example, need to be sent off to İstanbul. Same day or even same hour film development of prints is available in both the North and the South, while slide development will take up to three days.

The cost of a 36-exposure print film is CY£2.50 in the South and TL1.5 million in the North. To develop a 36-exposure print film will cost you CY£5 and TL5 million respectively.

It is probably a better idea to bring your own film and video tapes with you, especially if you can buy them at duty free rates before or as you leave home.

Technical Tips

The best time for photography in Cyprus is from dawn to 9 am and from 5 pm until sunset. Outside those times the light is generally too strong and images will look washed out. If you must photograph during the day, consider using a polarising filter. Bear in mind that landscape shots in midsummer – especially when looking from the Troödos Mountains down to the plains – may be disappointing due to a commonly persistent heat haze. Really clear days in summer are rare. The best time for these kind of shots is winter or spring.

When shooting archaeological or other sites, think light! Figure out whether your subject will be better illuminated by an early morning (east) light or late afternoon (west) light. Afternoon shots tend to be bathed in a warm iridescent red glow, while morning shots have a cooler, blue, sharp feel to them.

At all times, store your equipment carefully. Summer temperatures in Cyprus are usually very high. Keep your camera out of the sun when stored and keep exposed and unexposed film in a refrigerator, if you have one available.

Restrictions

In general you can photograph anywhere in Cyprus, with some fairly obvious exceptions. You cannot normally photograph anywhere near the Attila and Green Lines. In practice this is rarely monitored other than on both sides of the Green Line in Lefkosia, where sensitivities run high. Warning signs are normally displayed prominently so look out for them and heed them.

Military camps are another no-go area and, while there are military installations in both parts of Cyprus, you will be more aware of them in the North. Do not even pretend to photograph if you see a warning sign, which is commonly a diagram of an old-style bellows camera with a line through it.

Airports, ports and other government installations are normally touchy photo subjects so you are advised to keep your camera out of sight if you are in the proximity of such. If in doubt – don't photograph.

Museums do not normally allow you to photograph their exhibits unless you have a licence. Churches with icons do not allow the use of a flash and, depending on the potential commercial value of the photographs you take, may not even allow photos at all.

It is not culturally appropriate to take photographs in mosques when people are praying or when a service is in progress. However outside of these restrictions it is usually OK to take a photograph. It is less intrusive without a flash (and draws less attention to yourself), so use a fast film or fast lens whenever possible.

Photographing People
People the world over like to have their photos taken and Cypriots are no different in that respect. When handled correctly, Cypriots make engaging and often very willing subjects. However, it is bad form to point a camera in someone's face without at least acknowledging the existence of your subject. A simple *'kalimera'* or *'merhaba'* or a just a smile may be all that is required to break the ice and set up a potential portrait scene. Men in the kafenio, priests looking after monasteries and churches and women on donkeys in the villages often make some of the most photogenic 'folkloric' shots. If you promise to send a copy of the photos to your subjects, make sure you take their address and send the picture when you get home.

When initially approaching someone to seek their permission to photograph them, keep your camera down and out of the way. Use a zoom or telephoto lens wherever possible for portrait shots. Use a very wide angle (say 20mm) lens in order to make an effective group shot. You can often include people in the scene this way without them feeling uncomfortable since you will not appear to be pointing the camera directly at them.

Airport Security
Predeparture security checks in Cyprus tend to be less stringent than what you may have witnessed in other regional airports such as Tel Aviv's Ben Gurion or even Heathrow in London. While your luggage will be screened, as in airports the world over, you will not be subjected to any foreseeable delays. However, do not leave your bags unattended anywhere in the airport and naturally be wary of other peoples' unattended bags.

TIME
Cyprus is normally two hours ahead of GMT/UTC, but does adopt a system of summer time or daylight saving during the summer months. Clocks go forward one hour on the last weekend in March and back one hour on the last weekend in October.

ELECTRICITY
Voltages & Cycles
The electric current is 240V, 50Hz.

Plugs and Sockets
Plugs are large with three square pins as in the UK. Multi-plug adaptors are available cheaply in supermarkets, electrical and grocery stores, though it's always a good idea to bring your own adaptors with you. Hotels can usually supply adaptors upon request.

WEIGHTS & MEASURES
Cyprus uses the metric system.

LAUNDRY
There are plenty of dry cleaners to be found in all major towns and prices are reasonable. Laundrettes are less common and can be found only in major tourist centres. Where available, laundrettes are either self-service or the service is provided for you. The cost of the latter is usually more expensive, while a self-service wash and dry will normally cost around CY£2. Hotels often provide a laundry service, though prices tend to be on the high side. The above information applies to both the North and the South. However, self-service laundrettes are more or less non-existent in the North.

TOILETS

There are public toilets in the main towns and at tourist sites. They are almost always clean and western style, although in Northern Cyprus you sometimes come across dirtier ones or those of the squat variety. When stuck for choice, duck into a restaurant or cafe and discreetly use the facilities. You could then sit down for a beer or a coffee afterwards.

HEALTH

Travel health depends on your predeparture preparations, your daily health care while travelling and how you handle any medical problem that does develop. While the potential dangers can seem quite frightening, in reality few travellers experience anything more than an upset stomach.

Predeparture planning

Health Insurance Make sure that you have adequate health insurance. For details see Travel Insurance under the Visas & Documents section earlier in this chapter.

Foreigners do not receive free health care in either part of Cyprus.

Other Preparations Make sure you're healthy before you start travelling. If you are going on a long trip make sure your teeth are OK. If you wear glasses take a spare pair and your prescription.

If you require a particular medication take an adequate supply, as it may not be available locally. Take along the part of the packaging showing the generic name rather than the brand, which will make replacement easier. To avoid any problems it's a good idea to have a legible prescription or letter from your doctor to show that you legally use the medication.

Immunisations

Plan ahead for getting your vaccinations; some of them require more than one injection, while some should not be given together. Note that some vaccinations should not be given during pregnancy or to people with allergies – discuss with your doctor.

It is recommended that you seek medical advice at least six weeks before travel. Be

---

Medical Kit Check List

Following is a list of items you should consider including in your medical kit – consult your pharmacist for brands available in your country.

- [ ] **Aspirin or paracetamol (acetaminophen in the USA)** – for pain or fever
- [ ] **Antihistamine** – for allergies, eg, hay fever; to ease the itch from insect bites or stings; and to prevent motion sickness
- [ ] **Cold and flu tablets, throat lozenges and nasal decongestant**
- [ ] **Multivitamins** – consider for long trips, when dietary vitamin intake may be inadequate
- [ ] **Antibiotics** – consider including these if you're travelling well off the beaten track; see your doctor, as they must be prescribed, and carry the prescription with you
- [ ] **Loperamide or diphenoxylate** –'blockers' for diarrhoea
- [ ] **Prochlorperazine or metaclopramide** – for nausea and vomiting
- [ ] **Rehydration mixture** – to prevent dehydration, which may occur, for example, during bouts of diarrhoea; particularly important when travelling with children
- [ ] **Insect repellent, sunscreen, lip balm and eye drops**
- [ ] **Calamine lotion, sting relief spray or aloe vera** – to ease irritation from sunburn and insect bites or stings
- [ ] **Antifungal cream or powder** – for fungal skin infections and thrush
- [ ] **Antiseptic (such as povidone-iodine)** – for cuts and grazes
- [ ] **Bandages, Band-Aids (plasters) and other wound dressings**
- [ ] **Water purification tablets or iodine**
- [ ] **Scissors, tweezers and a thermometer** – note that mercury thermometers are prohibited by airlines
- [ ] **Syringes and needles** – in case you need injections in a country with medical hygiene problems; ask your doctor for a note explaining why you have them

aware that there is often a greater risk of disease with children and during pregnancy. Discuss your specific requirements with your doctor, but bear in mind that Cyprus enjoys a high standard of health and not all vaccinations will be absolutely necessary.

Diphtheria & Tetanus Vaccinations for these two diseases are usually combined and are recommended for everyone. After an initial course of three injections (usually given in childhood), boosters are necessary every 10 years.

Polio Everyone should keep up to date with this vaccination, which is normally given in childhood. A booster every 10 years maintains immunity.

Hepatitis A Hepatitis A vaccine (eg, Avaxim, Havrix 1440 or VAQTA) provides long-term immunity (possibly more than 10 years) after an initial injection and a booster at six to 12 months.

Alternatively, an injection of gamma globulin can provide short-term protection against hepatitis A – two to six months, depending on the dose. It is not a vaccine, but is a ready-made antibody collected from blood donations. It is reasonably effective and, unlike the vaccine, it is effective immediately, but because it is a blood product, there are current concerns about its long-term safety.

Hepatitis A vaccine is also available in a combined form, Twinrix, with hepatitis B vaccine. Three injections over a six-month period are required, the first two providing substantial protection against hepatitis A.

Typhoid Vaccination against typhoid may be required if you are travelling for more than a couple of weeks in most parts of Asia, Africa, Central and South America and Central and Eastern Europe. It is now available either as an injection or as capsules to be taken orally.

Hepatitis B Travellers who should consider vaccination against hepatitis B include those on a long trip, and those visiting countries where there are high levels of hepatitis B infection, where blood transfusions may not be adequately screened or where sexual contact or needle sharing is a possibility. Vaccination involves three injections, with a booster at 12 months. More rapid courses are available if necessary.

Travel Health Guides If you are planning to be away or travelling in remote areas for a long period of time, you may like to consider taking a more detailed health guide. The *CDC's Complete Guide to Healthy Travel* (1997) has recommendations for international travel from the US Centers for Disease Control & Prevention. *Travel with Children* from Lonely Planet includes essential information on travel health for younger children.

There is also a number of excellent travel health sites on the Internet. From the Lonely Planet home page there are links at www.lonelyplanet.com/weblinks/wlprep .htm to the World Health Organization and the US Centers for Disease Control & Prevention.

Basic Rules

Food There is an old adage that says, 'If you can cook it, boil it or peel it you can eat it ... otherwise forget it'. Vegetables and fruit should be washed with purified water or peeled where possible. Beware of ice cream which is sold in the street or anywhere it might have melted and been refrozen; if there's any doubt (eg, a power cut in the last day or two), steer well clear. Shellfish such as mussels, oysters and clams should be avoided as well as undercooked meat, particularly in the form of mince (ground beef). Steaming does not make shellfish safe for eating.

If a place looks clean and well run and the vendor also looks clean and healthy, then the food is probably safe. In general, places that are packed with locals or travellers will be fine, while empty restaurants are questionable. The food in busy restaurants is cooked and eaten quite quickly with little standing around and is probably not reheated.

Water Water in Cyprus is a precious commodity. In general tap water is perfectly safe to drink, though it may have a slightly salty flavour in some cities where the water has been reclaimed from the sea through desalination. In periods of drought water supplies may be restricted, but this does not usually affect major hotels.

Bottled drinking water is widely available and very popular. The Pedoulas spring water – from the village of the same name – is among the more well-known brands. In the Troödos Mountains you will often come across people filling their water bottles or even large containers from roadside springs. You might wish to take advantage of free spring water to replenish your supplies.

Medical Problems & Treatment

Self-diagnosis and treatment can be risky, so you should always seek medical help. An embassy, consulate or five-star hotel can usually recommend a local doctor or clinic. Although we do give drug dosages in this section, they are for emergency use only. Correct diagnosis is vital. In this section we have used the generic names for medications – check with a pharmacist for brands available locally.

Antibiotics should ideally be administered only under medical supervision. Take only the recommended dose at the prescribed intervals and use the whole course, even if the illness seems to be cured earlier. Stop immediately if there are any reactions and don't use the antibiotic at all unless you are sure it is the correct one. Some people are allergic to commonly prescribed antibiotics such as penicillin; carry this information (eg, on a bracelet) when travelling.

Environmental Hazards

Heat Exhaustion Cyprus can get very hot in the summer with inland temperatures commonly passing 40° (100° F). Dehydration and salt deficiency can cause heat exhaustion. Make sure you take time to acclimatise to high temperatures, drink sufficient liquids and do not do anything too physically demanding. Salt deficiency is characterised by fatigue, lethargy,

headaches, giddiness and muscle cramps. Salt tablets may help, but adding extra salt to your food is better.

Anhidrotic heat exhaustion is a rare form that is caused by an inability to sweat. It tends to affect people who have been in a hot climate for some time, rather than newcomers. It can progress to heatstroke. Treatment involves removal to a cooler climate.

Heatstroke This serious, occasionally fatal, condition can occur if the body's heat-regulating mechanism breaks down and the body temperature rises to dangerous levels. Long, continuous periods of exposure to high temperatures and insufficient fluids can leave you vulnerable to heatstroke.

The symptoms are feeling unwell, not sweating very much (or at all) and a high body temperature (39° to 41°C or 102° to 106°F). Where sweating has ceased, the skin becomes flushed and red. Severe, throbbing headaches and lack of coordination will also occur, and the sufferer may be confused or aggressive. Eventually the victim will become delirious or convulse. Hospitalisation is essential but, in the interim, get victims out of the sun, remove their clothing, cover them with a wet sheet or towel and then fan them continually. Give fluids if they are conscious.

Jet Lag Jet lag is experienced when travelling by air across more than three time zones (each zone usually represents a one-hour time difference). It occurs because many of the functions of the human body (eg, temperature, pulse rate, bladder and bowels) are regulated by internal 24-hour cycles. After rapid long distance travel, our bodies take time to adjust to the 'new time' of our destination, and we may experience fatigue, disorientation, insomnia, anxiety, impaired concentration and loss of appetite. These effects will usually be gone within three days of arrival, but to minimise the impact of jet lag try the following:

• Rest for a couple of days prior to departure.
• Try to select flight schedules that minimise sleep deprivation; arriving late in the day

means you can go to sleep soon after you arrive. For very long flights, try to organise a stopover.

- Avoid excessive eating (which bloats the stomach) and alcohol (which causes dehydration) during the flight. Instead, drink plenty of noncarbonated, nonalcoholic drinks such as fruit juice or water.
- Avoid smoking.
- Make yourself comfortable by wearing loose-fitting clothes and perhaps bring an eye mask and ear plugs to help you sleep.
- Try to sleep at the appropriate time for the time zone of your destination.

Motion Sickness Eating lightly before and during a trip will reduce the chances of motion sickness. If you are prone to motion sickness try to find a place that minimises movement – near the wing on aircraft, close to midships on boats, near the centre on buses. Fresh air usually helps; reading and cigarette smoke don't. Commercial motion-sickness preparations, which can cause drowsiness, have to be taken before the trip commences. Ginger (available in capsule form) and peppermint (including mint-flavoured sweets) are natural preventatives.

Prickly Heat Prickly heat is an itchy rash caused by excessive perspiration trapped under the skin. It usually strikes people who have just arrived in a hot climate. Keeping cool, bathing often, drying the skin and using a mild talcum or prickly heat powder or resorting to air-conditioning may help.

Sunburn In the tropics, the desert or at high altitude you can get sunburnt surprisingly quickly, even through cloud. Use a sunscreen, a hat, and a barrier cream for your nose and lips. Calamine lotion or a commercial after-sun preparation is good for mild sunburn. Protect your eyes with good quality sunglasses, particularly if you will be near water, sand or snow.

Insects Cyprus is home to some particularly nasty biting insects. Mosquitoes are very common as are biting flies and midges in rural areas. Fair-skinned people seem to be more prone to attack, though the development of a suntan may reduce susceptibility. While the mosquitoes are not malarial, the varieties found can be hard to spot and avoid and may cause severe skin reactions due to multiple bites.

The best way to avoid being bitten is to choose air-conditioned accommodation, apply insect repellent to exposed skin and use a chemical insect repellent such as mosquito coils or plug-in zappers. The Cypriots themselves recommend one fail-safe solution – cover yourself in a thin application of kerosene! This is guaranteed to keep not only insects away, but probably most of your friends too.

Infectious Diseases

You are less likely to pick up a disease that is endemic to Cyprus, than to catch something inadvertently from a fellow traveller or at best, suffer a stomach upset as a result of your body being unaccustomed to local food and water. Nonetheless it is a good idea to be alerted to the following possibilities that may make your stay uncomfortable.

Diarrhoea Simple things like a change of water, food or climate can all cause a mild bout of diarrhoea, but a few rushed toilet trips with no other symptoms is not indicative of a major problem.

Dehydration is the main danger with any diarrhoea, particularly in children or in the elderly, as dehydration can occur quite quickly. Under all circumstances *fluid replacement* is the most important thing to remember. Weak black tea with a little sugar, soda water and soft drink allowed to go flat and diluted 50% with clean water are all good. With severe diarrhoea a rehydrating solution is preferable to replace minerals and salts lost. Commercially available oral rehydration salts (ORS) are very useful; add them to boiled or bottled water. In an emergency you can make up a solution of six teaspoons of sugar and a half teaspoon of salt to a litre of boiled or bottled water. You need to drink at least the same volume of fluid that you are losing in bowel movements and vomiting. Urine is the best guide to the adequacy of replacement – if you have small amounts of concentrated urine, you need to drink more. Keep drinking small amounts often. Stick to a bland diet as you recover.

Gut-paralysing drugs such as loperamide or diphenoxylate can be used to bring relief from the symptoms, although they do not actually cure the problem. Only use these drugs if you do not have access to toilets, eg, if you *must* travel. Note that these drugs are not recommended for children under 12 years.

In certain situations antibiotics may be required: diarrhoea with blood or mucus (dysentery), any diarrhoea with fever, profuse watery diarrhoea, persistent diarrhoea not improving after 48 hours and severe diarrhoea. These suggest a more serious cause and in these situations gut-paralysing drugs should be avoided.

A stool test may be necessary to diagnose the cause of your diarrhoea, so you should seek medical help urgently. Where this is not possible the recommended drugs for bacterial diarrhoea (the most likely cause of severe diarrhoea in travellers) are norfloxacin 400mg twice daily for three days or ciprofloxacin 500mg twice daily for five days. These are not recommended for children or pregnant women. The drug of choice for children is co-trimoxazole with dosage dependent on weight. A five-day course is given. Ampicillin or amoxycillin may be given in pregnancy, but medical care is necessary.

Two other causes of persistent diarrhoea in travellers are giardiasis and amoebic dysentery.

Fungal Infections Fungal infections occur more commonly in hot weather and are usually found on the scalp, between the toes (athlete's foot) or fingers, in the groin and on the body (ringworm). You get ringworm (a fungal infection, not a worm) from infected animals or other people. Moisture encourages these infections.

To prevent fungal infections wear loose, comfortable clothes, avoid artificial fibres, wash frequently and dry yourself carefully. If you do get an infection, wash the infected area at least daily with a disinfectant or medicated soap and water, and rinse and dry well. Apply an antifungal cream or powder like tolnaftate. Try to expose the infected area to air or sunlight as much as possible and wash all towels and underwear in hot water, change them often and let them dry in the sun.

Hepatitis Hepatitis is a general term for inflammation of the liver. It is a common disease worldwide. There are several different viruses that cause hepatitis, and they differ in the way that they are transmitted. The symptoms are similar in all forms of the illness, and include fever, chills, headache, fatigue, feelings of weakness and aches and pains, followed by loss of appetite, nausea, vomiting, abdominal pain, dark urine, light-coloured faeces, jaundiced (yellow) skin and yellowing of the whites of the eyes. People who have had hepatitis should avoid alcohol for some time after the illness, as the liver needs time to recover.

Hepatitis A is transmitted by contaminated food and drinking water. You should seek medical advice, but there is not much you can do apart from resting, drinking lots of fluids, eating lightly and avoiding fatty foods. Hepatitis E is transmitted in the same way as hepatitis A; it can be particularly serious in pregnant women.

There are almost 300 million chronic carriers of hepatitis B in the world. It is spread through contact with infected blood, blood products or body fluids, for example, through sexual contact, unsterilised needles and blood transfusions, or contact with blood via small breaks in the skin. Other risk situations include having a shave, tattoo or body piercing with contaminated equipment. The symptoms of hepatitis B may be more severe than type A and the disease can lead to long-term problems such as chronic liver damage, liver cancer or a long-term carrier state. Hepatitis C and D are spread in the same way as hepatitis B and can also lead to long-term complications.

There are vaccines against hepatitis A and B, but there are currently no vaccines against the other types of hepatitis (see Vaccinations earlier in this section). Following the basic rules about food and water (hepatitis A and E) and avoiding risk situations (hepatitis B, C and D) are important preventative measures.

HIV & AIDS Infection with the human immunodeficiency virus (HIV) may lead to acquired immune deficiency syndrome (AIDS), which is a fatal disease. Any exposure to blood, blood products or body fluids may put the individual at risk. The disease is often transmitted through sexual contact or dirty needles – vaccinations, acupuncture, tattooing and body piercing can be potentially as dangerous as intravenous drug use. HIV/AIDS can also be spread through infected blood transfusions, though the high standards of medicine in Cyprus make this event extremely unlikely.

If you do need an injection, ask to see the syringe unwrapped in front of you, or take a needle and syringe pack with you.

Fear of HIV infection should never preclude treatment for serious medical conditions.

Intestinal Worms These parasites are most common in rural, tropical areas. The different worms have different ways of infecting people. Some may be ingested on food such as undercooked meat (eg, tapeworms) and some enter through your skin (eg, hookworms). Infestations may not show up for some time and, although they are generally not serious, if left untreated some can cause severe health problems later. Consider having a stool test when you return home to check for these and determine the appropriate treatment.

Sexually Transmitted Diseases HIV /AIDS and hepatitis B can be transmitted through sexual contact (see the relevant sections earlier in this chapter for more details). Other STDs include gonorrhoea, herpes and syphilis; sores, blisters or rashes around the genitals and discharges or pain when urinating are common symptoms. In some STDs, such as wart virus or chlamydia, symptoms may be less marked or not observed at all, especially in women. Chlamydia infection can cause infertility in both men and women before any symptoms have been noticed. Syphilis symptoms eventually disappear completely but the disease continues and can cause severe problems in later years. While abstinence from sexual contact is the only 100% effective prevention, using condoms is also effective. The treatment of gonorrhoea and syphilis is with antibiotics. The different sexually transmitted diseases each require specific antibiotics.

Typhoid Typhoid fever is a dangerous gut infection caused by contaminated water and food. Medical help must be sought.

In its early stages sufferers may feel they have a bad cold or flu on the way, as early symptoms are a headache, body aches and a fever which rises a little each day until it is around 40°C (104°F) or more. A victim's pulse is often slow relative to the degree of fever present – unlike a normal fever where the pulse increases. There may also be vomiting, abdominal pain, diarrhoea or constipation.

In the second week the high fever and slow pulse continue and a few pink spots may appear on the body; trembling, delirium, weakness, weight loss and dehydration may occur. Complications such as pneumonia, perforated bowel or meningitis may occur.

Insect-Borne Diseases
While mosquitoes and midges can be a real nuisance in Cyprus, particularly in rural areas (see Insects in Medical Problems & Treatment section earlier in this chapter), they are not disease- or malaria-carrying. The most serious reaction is likely to be an outbreak of unsightly skin lesions which may require medical attention in more severe cases.

Cuts, Bites & Stings
See the section on Less Common Diseases later in this chapter for details of rabies, which is passed through animal bites.

Cuts & Scratches Wash well and treat any cut with an antiseptic such as povidone-iodine. Where possible avoid bandages and Band-Aids, which can keep wounds wet. Coral cuts are notoriously slow to heal and if they are not adequately cleaned, small pieces of coral can become embedded in the wound.

Bedbugs & Lice Bedbugs live in various places, but particularly in dirty mattresses and bedding, evidenced by spots of blood on bedclothes or on the wall. Bedbugs leave itchy bites in neat rows. Calamine lotion or a sting relief spray may help.

All lice cause itching and discomfort. They make themselves at home in your hair (head lice), your clothing (body lice) or in your pubic hair (crabs). You catch lice through direct contact with infected people or by sharing combs, clothing and the like. Powder or shampoo treatment will kill the lice and infected clothing should then be washed in very hot, soapy water and left in the sun to dry.

Bites & Stings Bee and wasp stings are usually more painful rather than dangerous. However, in people who are allergic to them severe breathing difficulties may occur and require urgent medical care. Calamine lotion or a sting relief spray will give relief and ice packs will reduce the pain and swelling. There are some spiders with dangerous bites but antivenins are usually available. Scorpion stings are notoriously painful but in Cyprus are not fatal unless the sting causes an unexpected allergic reaction.

Snakes To minimise your chances of being bitten always wear boots, socks and long trousers when walking through undergrowth where snakes may be present. Don't put your hands into holes and crevices, and be careful when collecting firewood.

Snake bites do not cause instantaneous death and antivenins are usually available. Immediately wrap the bitten limb tightly, as you would for a sprained ankle, and attach a splint to immobilise it. Keep the victim still and seek medical help, if possible with the dead snake for identification. Don't attempt to catch the snake if there is a possibility of being bitten again. Tourniquets and sucking out the poison are now comprehensively discredited.

Women's Health
Gynaecological Problems Antibiotic use, synthetic underwear, sweating and contraceptive pills can lead to fungal vaginal infections, especially when travelling in hot climates. Fungal infections are characterised by a rash, itch and discharge and can be treated with a vinegar or lemon-juice douche, or with yogurt. Nystatin, miconazole or clotrimazole pessaries or vaginal cream are the usual treatment. Maintaining good personal hygiene and wearing loose-fitting clothes and cotton underwear may help prevent these infections.

Sexually transmitted diseases are a major cause of vaginal problems. Symptoms include a smelly discharge, painful intercourse and sometimes a burning sensation when urinating. Medical attention should be sought and male sexual partners must also be treated. For more details see the section on Sexually Transmitted Diseases earlier in this chapter. Besides abstinence, the best thing is to practise safer sex by using condoms.

Pregnancy It is not advisable to travel to some places while pregnant as some vaccinations normally used to prevent serious diseases (eg, yellow fever) are not advisable during pregnancy. In addition, some diseases (eg, malaria) are much more serious for the mother (and may increase the risk of a stillborn child) in pregnancy.

Most miscarriages occur during the first three months of pregnancy. Miscarriage is not uncommon and can occasionally lead to severe bleeding. The last three months should also be spent within reasonable distance of good medical care. A baby born as early as 24 weeks stands a chance of survival, but only in a good modern hospital. Pregnant women should avoid all unnecessary medication, although vaccinations and malarial prophylactics should still be taken where needed. Special care should be taken to prevent illness and particular attention paid to diet and nutrition. Alcohol and nicotine, for example, should be avoided.

Less Common Diseases

The following diseases pose a small risk to travellers, and so are only mentioned in passing. Seek medical advice if you think you may have any of these diseases.

Cholera This is the worst of the watery diarrhoeas and medical help should be sought. Outbreaks of cholera are generally widely reported, so you can avoid such problem areas. *Fluid replacement is the most vital treatment* – the risk of dehydration is severe as you may lose up to 20L of fluid a day. If there is a delay in getting to hospital, then begin taking tetracycline. The adult dose is 250mg four times daily. It is not recommended for children under nine years or for pregnant women. Tetracycline may help shorten the illness, but adequate fluids are required to save lives.

Rabies This fatal viral infection is found in many countries. Many animals can be infected (such as dogs, cats, bats and monkeys) and it is their saliva that is infectious. Any bite, scratch or even lick from an animal should be cleaned immediately and thoroughly. Scrub with soap and running water, and then apply alcohol or iodine solution. Medical help should be sought promptly to receive a course of injections to prevent the onset of symptoms and death.

Tetanus This disease is caused by a germ that lives in soil and in the faeces of horses and other animals. It enters the body via breaks in the skin. The first symptom may be discomfort in swallowing or stiffening of the jaw and neck; this is followed by painful convulsions of the jaw and whole body. The disease can be fatal. It can be prevented by vaccination.

Tuberculosis (TB) TB is a bacterial infection and is usually transmitted from person to person by coughing but which may be contracted through consumption of unpasteurised milk. Milk that has been boiled is safe to drink, and the souring of milk to make yogurt or cheese also kills the bacilli. Travellers are usually not at great risk as close household contact with the infected person is usually required before the disease is passed on. You may need to have a TB test before you travel as this can help diagnose the disease later if you become ill.

Typhus This disease is spread by ticks, mites or lice. It begins with fever, chills, headache and muscle pains followed a few days later by a body rash. There is often a large painful sore at the site of the bite and nearby lymph nodes are swollen and painful. Typhus can be treated under medical supervision. Seek local advice on areas where ticks pose a danger and always check your skin carefully for ticks after walking in a danger area such as a tropical forest. An insect repellent can help, and walkers in tick-infested areas should consider having their boots and trousers impregnated with benzyl benzoate and dibutylphthalate.

Everyday Health

Normal body temperature is up to 37°C (98.6°F); more than 2°C (4°F) higher indicates a high fever. The normal adult pulse rate is 60 to 100 per minute (children 80 to 100, babies 100 to 140). As a general rule the pulse increases about 20 beats per minute for each 1°C (2°F) rise in fever.

Respiration (breathing) rate is another indicator of illness. Count the number of breaths per minute; between 12 and 20 is normal for adults and older children (up to 30 for younger children, 40 for babies). People with a high fever or serious respiratory illness breathe more quickly than normal. More than 40 shallow breaths a minute may indicate pneumonia.

In Cyprus tap water is safe to drink everywhere, though it tends to be slightly brackish in Lefkosia because a percentage has been desalinated. Bottled mineral water is widely available. The greatest health risk comes from the sun, so take care against sunstroke, heat exhaustion and dehydration. Use a high plus factor sun block (32+ and upwards if at all possible) and try to avoid walking around in the sun between 11 am and 3 pm, when it is at its strongest. The temperature in Lefkosia in July and August regularly tops 37°C (100°F) so plan your sightseeing carefully.

Minor stomach upsets can be expected if you are not used to Mediterranean cuisine. Your digestive tract may not be accustomed to naturally occurring microbes in food and your surroundings that you probably would not find back home.

WOMEN TRAVELLERS

Women travellers will encounter little sexual harassment, although it is worth steering clear of any red-light areas and some of the cheaper hotels because they may double as brothels. In both parts of Cyprus, however, women may be subject to good-natured verbal sparring in the form of corny pick-up lines. This is common for both foreign and Cypriot women, though foreign women merit particular attention from these verbal Romeos. While some may find this offensive, it is part of the male culture and is best handled good-naturedly – usually by ignoring the perpetrator.

GAY & LESBIAN TRAVELLERS

Homosexuality is legal in the Republic and the Gay Liberation Movement (☎ 02-443 346) can be contacted at PO Box 1947, Lefkosia.

In Northern Cyprus homosexuality is technically illegal but, in practice, police maintain a generally liberal attitude – essentially in relation to foreigners, who will not be arrested unless caught in flagrante delicto. There are no organised support groups for gays or lesbians in Northern Cyprus.

DISABLED TRAVELLERS

Any CTO can send you the *What the Disabled Visitor Needs to Know about Cyprus* factsheet, which lists some useful organisations. The Republic's airports have truck-lifts to assist disabled travellers. Some of the hotels have facilities for the disabled, but there's little help at sites or museums. In Northern Cyprus there are few facilities for the disabled visitor.

SENIOR TRAVELLERS

Older visitors will find travelling around both the Republic and Northern Cyprus fairly easy. In general, no concessions exist for seniors. The only real discomfort may be the usually extreme weather conditions that prevail in July and August.

TRAVEL WITH CHILDREN

Visiting Cyprus with junior travellers is very easy. Children are the focal point of family life for all Cypriots and will always be received very warmly. Children are welcome in restaurants and bars and can be seen running around way past midnight at the many weddings that take place around the country during the summer.

Restaurants will often have high chairs for children and hotels should normally be able to supply cots if requested in advance. Hire cars will not normally supply child safety seats, so check with the company beforehand if you consider it necessary. Hotels often provide child-minding facilities. Again check before you book.

While large grassy playgrounds are few and far between in the main towns, there are several water theme parks around the country to keep kids occupied for the best part of a day and there are usually video games and rides available at most tourist centres. That said, there are always the beaches – most of them very safe with shallow water – and associated water activities to keep them amused all day.

For a full run-down on how to amuse children on holiday read Maureen Wheeler's *Travel With Children*, also published by Lonely Planet.

DANGERS & ANNOYANCES

In general, Cyprus is a very safe place to travel, both for locals and for tourists. The crime rate is minimal, people commonly leave cars and houses unlocked and violent personal crimes, such as theft or mugging, are almost unknown. This applies equally to both the Republic and Northern Cyprus. The greatest risk will often come from fellow travellers in resorts with a high concentration of tourists, where petty theft is the most likely annoyance to be encountered.

Care, however, must be exercised when travelling in the area of the Attila and Green Lines that divide the North from the South. The dividing line between the two communities is normally clearly visible and identifiable by barbed wire, sentry boxes and UN watchtowers. Despite this, there have been documented cases of people inadvertently straying across the Line towards the North whereupon they have been arrested and detained. The delineation between North and South is less clearly marked within the Dekelia British Sovereign Base Area in the east where there is no UN buffer zone as such. Extra care must be exercised here.

There are occasional demonstrations and gatherings by Greek Cypriots at various points along the Attila Line and tensions can run very high. In August 1996 two Greek Cypriots were murdered by Northern Cypriot counter-demonstrators. Some Greek demonstrators and several foreigners were injured by gunshots following clashes at Deryneia close to Famagusta.

To avoid possible problems, travellers should not linger near military bases in the North or the South and should obey prominent signs prohibiting photography.

Discrimination

Cypriots are very tolerant people – they would have to be, having endured occupation and colonisation for most of their history. You are not likely to find any racial discrimination of any kind on either side of the island.

If you are Greek or have a Greek surname and attempt to enter Northern Cyprus without a pre-arranged visa you will be given special attention and most likely turned back. If you make it to the North as a Greek you will be treated with a mixture of curiosity and deference. Remember, Turkish Cypriots under the age of 25 have no experience of living with Greeks and probably do not carry the first-hand resentment towards Greeks still harboured by their elders. However, some Turkish Cypriots, particularly those who once lived in the

south, will be delighted to meet you and may even speak Greek.

If you are Turkish or have a Turkish surname you will be allowed into the South and will be treated with deference and respect, though you will be an object of curiosity for some. Many Turkish Cypriots still work in construction industries in the South, crossing unhindered each day from the North via the Dekelia British Sovereign Base.

BUSINESS HOURS

In the South shopping hours are determined by season. In summer (1 June to 14 September) shops open at around 8.30 am and close at around 7.30 pm. In the major cities there is also an afternoon break from 1 to 4 pm. In the spring/autumn periods (1 April to 31 May and 15 September to 31 October) shops close at 7 pm and in the winter period (1 November to 31 March) at 6 pm. On Wednesday and Saturday early closing is at 2 pm and shops do not open on Sundays.

Banks maintain somewhat shorter hours: 8.30 am to 12.30 pm, Monday to Friday as well as 3.15 to 4.45 pm on Monday. In July and August banks open 15 minutes earlier. Centrally positioned banks also offer afternoon tourist services. Banks that offer this service post notices on their doors. Currency exchange bureaus operate over more extended hours and are often open until late in the evening.

Petrol stations have slightly different opening schedules. They open at 6 am and close at 7 pm (6 pm from 1 October to 31 March). On Wednesday in the Lefkosia district they close early at 2 pm; elsewhere early closing is 2 pm on Tuesday. Saturday opening times are 6 am to 3 pm and on Sunday they are closed. In rural areas, many petrol stations remain open on weekends and holidays.

Out of hours many petrol stations have automatic vending machines that take both cash and credit cards. Instructions are in English and Greek.

Finally, public service hours are 7.30 am to 2.30 pm (Monday to Friday) and additionally 3 to 6 pm (Thursday) from 1 September to 30 June and 7.30 am to 2.30

pm (Monday to Friday) from 1 July to 31 August.

In the North banks are open 8 am to noon and 2 to 5 pm in winter and from 8 am to 1.30 pm and 2.30 pm to 5 pm in summer, Monday to Friday. Shops are open 7.30 am to 2 pm in summer and 8 am to 1 pm and 2 to 5 pm in winter, Monday to Friday. There is also late opening on Monday from 3.30 to 6 pm.

PUBLIC HOLIDAYS & SPECIAL EVENTS

Holidays in the Republic are the same as in Greece, with the addition of Greek Cypriot Day (1 April) and Cyprus Independence Day (1 October). Greek public holidays are:

New Year's Day	1 January
Epiphany	6 January
First Sunday in Lent	February
Greek Independence Day	25 March
Good Friday	March/April
(Orthodox) Easter Sunday	March/April
Spring Festival/Labour Day	1 May
Feast of the Assumption	15 August
Ohi Day	28 October
Christmas Day	25 December
St Stephen's Day	26 December

Easter is the most important religious festival and just about everything stops. Fifty days before this is carnival time. A useful publication is the *Diary of Events* available from any CTO.

Northern Cyprus observes Muslim holidays, including the month of Ramadan, which means the North can sometimes shut down for periods of up to a week. It also observes New Year's Day (January 1), Peace & Freedom Day (July 20), Victory Day (30 August) and the Proclamation of the Turkish Republic of Northern Cyprus (15 November).

ACTIVITIES

There are outdoor activities to suit most tastes in Cyprus. Some activities are better suited to the cooler months, including cycling, skiing and hiking. Organised water-based activities in general run from mid-March to late October, though if you have your own equipment there is nothing to prevent you from enjoying your preferred activity at any time of the year.

Cycling

The Cyprus Tourist Organisation produces a helpful brochure called *Cycling in Cyprus,* which lists a number of recommended mountain bike trails utilising both regular surfaced and unsurfaced roads and off-road trails. This should be available from most CTO offices, but if its unavailable you can obtain a copy from the CTO head office in Lefkosia. The NCTO does not yet produce a similar cycling guide.

Overall, cycling in Cyprus is quite easy and not yet overrun by foreign long-haul cyclists due to the island's relative isolation from the Asian and European mainland. The distances are relatively short and regular roads exist in parallel to the busy motorways that connect Lefkosia, Larnaka, Lemesos and eventually Pafos. Cyclists may use the wide hard shoulder of the two-lane motorways, but the scenery of passing vehicles is less enticing than that found on the less busy regular roads.

Cyclists in the Troödos Mountains in the South will find some of the most scenic travelling, but bikes with a good range of gears are necessary to cope with the long, though not necessarily steep, gradients that lead up and down the mountains. Mountain bikes can be hired in Troödos should you not relish the idea of riding your own bike uphill.

In the North cyclists will find the relatively untrafficked roads of the Karpas (Kirpaz) Peninsula the most rewarding. Only the short-lived and narrow Kyrenia Range of mountains will provide any real obstacle to movement between the north coast and the interior plains.

Skiing

The Troödos Mountains enjoy a brief but often vigorous skiing season and the sport is fairly popular for those that have the equipment and energy to get up to the slopes of Mt Olympus from early January to mid-March. There are four ski runs close to

Troödos and these are operated and maintained by the Cyprus Ski Club. There are also two runs on the north face of Mt Olympus. One is 350m long and the other 500m long. There are two more 150m runs in 'Sun Valley' on the south side of Olympus. For further information contact the Cyprus Ski Club (☎ 02-365 340), PO Box 22185, CY-1518 Lefkosia, or request the CTO leaflet *Skiing in Cyprus*. There is no skiing in Northern Cyprus.

Hiking

Hiking in Cyprus is very popular except in the months of July and August when the weather can get too hot. Organised and well-marked trails have been set up and maintained by the CTO. The most popular trails are in the Troödos Mountains which sport at least four excellent and relatively easy trails around and close to Mt Olympus.

Other trails include a series of overland treks in the Pitsylia region immediately east of Mt Olympus. These normally require a drop off and pick up arrangement for walkers. The hiking trails of the Akamas Peninsula in the far north-west are circular as are a couple of trails in the Stavros tis Psokas park to the immediate south of the Tillyrian wilderness in the north-west of the country. Get a copy of the CTO brochure *Cyprus – Nature Trails* for details on all the organised trails in the South.

The North has some excellent walking opportunities as well, particularly in the Kyrenia Mountain Range, but the NCTO only produces one fairly sketchy trail guide for visitors. This describes walks from St Hilarion to Ağirdağ and from Alevkaya to Kantara, both in the Kyrenia Range. Local travel agents and tourist guides will be able to fill you in on the specifics of these and other hiking trails.

Windsurfing

Windsurfing is a widespread activity on both sides of Cyprus, though the area around Protaras in the South is particularly popular. Windsurfers can be hired out for around CY£5 per hour for solo surfing, or for CY£5 for 30 minutes of instruction.

Boating

Boats of all kinds can be hired at the major beaches in both Northern Cyprus and the Republic. Popular spots for boating include Coral Bay near Pafos, Polis/Latsi north of Pafos, Kyr-enia, Geroskipou Beach near Pafos, Dasoudi Beach near Lemesos and Larnaka Public Beach. Costs range from CY£10 for 30 minutes in a 49 HP speedboat to CY£30 for 30 minutes in a 150 HP speedboat. Prices for hiring a craft in the North are somewhat cheaper.

Diving

Diving is very popular in Cyprus since the island is free from seriously dangerous currents or other underwater perils. Organised sub-aqua clubs can be found at major tourist centres in both the North and the South and most of them run one- to three-day training courses for novices. The only restrictions are on the removal of antiquities or sponges from the sea bottom.

For further information contact the Cyprus Federation of Underwater Activities (CFUA; ☎ 02-454 647), PO Box 21503, CY-21503 Lefkosia.

Horse Riding

There is a surprisingly well-developed and organised network of horse riding facilities, in the South at least, with at least nine major centres catering for equestrian travellers, or for people who want an alternative experience. Rates run from CY£10 to 12 for either an hour's unsupervised riding or an hour's instruction. The CTO puts out a detailed flyer called *Horse Riding in Cyprus*, but for further details contact the Cyprus Equestrian Federation (☎ 02-772 515), PO Box 3381, CY-1682 Lefkosia.

Snorkelling

Snorkelling is as popular as organised diving in Cyprus and costs a lot less. Masks, snorkels and flippers can all be bought or hired if you haven't brought along your own and no special permission is required. The best area for snorkelling is probably in the less exposed coves of eastern Cyprus – especially around Protaras. In the North the beaches to the west of Kyrenia are probably the best bet.

WORK

In the Republic, work permits can only be obtained through a prospective employer applying on your behalf. The best place to look for jobs is in the *Cyprus Weekly*. During the tourist season you can sometimes pick up bar or cafe work in return for bed and board, payment is rare (if you don't have a permit).

If you want to work in Northern Cyprus, apply to the Immigration Department of the Turkish Republic of Northern Cyprus (TRNC) authorities for a work permit. Your application will be considered on its merits.

English Tutoring

It is in theory possible to find private work tutoring English in Cyprus, but the demand – such as exists in neighbouring Greece – is not as high. Cypriots are better versed in English than their Turkish or Greek mainland counterparts and the school system places high priority on teaching English. Check the local English-language papers for any possible openings.

Bar Work

This is probably the best opening for casual summer work. A leisurely stroll around the bars of Agia Napa, Pafos, Kyrenia, Larnaka or Lemesos should provide you with possible opportunities. Check also the local papers and keep your ears tuned to the local grapevine. Bar work runs from early April to late October.

Other Work

If you have skills in instructing water skiers, windsurfers, divers or even in lifesaving you should easily be able to pick up summer work. If you can drive a boat and have experience in towing parasailers, banana riders or water-skiers there is plenty of work around. Doing it officially is another thing. Most summer casual work is unofficial, though if you plan to make a career out of it you would be better off seeking a work permit.

ACCOMMODATION

Camping

There are seven licensed camping grounds in the Republic, mostly with limited opening times. They are all equipped with hot showers, a minimarket and a snack bar, and charge around CY£1.50 a day for a tent space and CY£1 per person per day. In the North there are six camping grounds, but the facilities are not as good or well developed as in the South.

Hostels

There are four HI hostels in the Republic; these are slightly cheaper if you are a member. The Cyprus Youth Hostel Association (☎ 02-442 027) can be contacted at PO Box 1328, 1506 Lefkosia. There are no HI hostels in Northern Cyprus.

Guesthouses

The *domatia* rooms, *camere, zimmer* system of Greece is not common in Cyprus, in fact it is officially discouraged. However, in Agia Napa you will see signs advertising rooms and occasionally come across them in some of the more popular mountain resorts such as the Troödos Mountains in the South.

B&Bs & Pensions

In the Republic the B&B system is generally known as agrotourism. This is genuinely a superb and often very economical way for independent travellers to see the country. Guests stay in renovated village houses or purpose-built pensions. Most of them are self-contained and fully equipped. Rates run from CY£9 for a single room to CY£35 for a luxury studio.

With few exceptions, however, agrotourism houses and pensions are all away from major centres so you will either need your own transport to get around, or will have to rely on sometimes sketchy public transport.

For the excellent colour brochure listing all places to stay contact Cyprus Agrotourism Company (☎ 02-337 715, fax 339 723), PO Box 4535, CY-1390, Lefkosia.

The North has not yet developed such a system, but a network of agrotourist houses is currently being planned.

Hotels

Hotels in the Republic are classified from one to five stars and prices for a double room range from CY£18 to CY£120. While most hotels deal primarily with package-tour groups who pay cheaper bulk rates, individual travellers can usually find a room even in ostensibly marketed 'resort' hotels.

Quality varies markedly, though prices are strictly controlled by the CTO. The rates listed in the *Cyprus Hotel Guide* (available free from the CTO) are *maximum* allowable prices and will only normally be applicable in high season (July-August). Outside that time discounts of up to 50% may apply. Many hotels have email addresses so prospective guests can do some planning before arrival in Cyprus.

The quality of hotels in the North is generally good to excellent at the top end of the scale, though the supply is necessarily smaller. Package-tour visitors constitute the bulk of guests. The same principle applies to individual travellers as in the South. There will usually be a room available for walk-ins. Room rates are normally quoted in UK pounds or US dollars. In this book we give US dollars in line with the NCTO's policy of listing room rates in greenbacks in its *North Cyprus Hotel Guide*. This is available from the NCTO, if you ask specifically for it).

Other Accommodation

In the Republic you can sometimes stay overnight in a monastery, ostensibly for free, but a donation is expected.

Sleeping rough, while theoretically possible, is not recommended and will be frowned upon. However, you might get away with it at a deserted beach as a one-off solution.

FOOD

Cypriot food is a combination of Greek and Turkish cuisine, based primarily on meat, salad and fruit. The local cheese is *haloumi*. The barbecue is a very popular way of cooking meat and fish, and a *mezes* is a traditional meal consisting of around 20 different small dishes. Dishes in both the North and South are very similar with a few local variants to make things interesting.

Local Food

Given half a chance and at least a couple of friends or family members at hand, a Cypriot will unflinchingly order *mezedes* for the main meal of the day if they are eating out. Preferably taken in the evening after a day of relative abstinence from food, a mezes meal can be a banquet for some and an enormous headache for others – *where is it all going to go?*

A mezes meal consists of three or even four rounds of dishes: dips and salads, vegetarian and other mixed dishes, meat dishes and fruit. The trick is to pace yourself and not overdo it on the bread and dips. By the time the meat arrives you may be too full. Expect to pay around CY£6 a head for a mezes meal, not including drinks.

You can still order main dishes like *mousakas* (shepherd's pie), *kleftiko* (oven-baked lamb), *ofto* (similar to kleftiko but individually packed in foil), as well as steaks, chops and fish dishes.

Fast Food

Like anywhere else in the world fast food is finding its niche in Cyprus. Hamburgers, chicken, pizzas and sandwiches all play their role in keeping fast-moving Cypriots and travellers alike fuelled and ready.

Desserts

Cypriots don't make a big thing out of prepared deserts, preferring instead fresh fruit of the season. Make a point of asking for prickly pears *(papoutsosyka)* in August. They are a pain to pick, but devilishly delicious to eat. Watermelons, rock melons (cantaloupes), peaches and nectarines are all big summer favourites.

Vegetarian

Food for vegetarians is rarely packed or marketed as such. Instead you can choose dishes made from vegetables or pulses which will more often than not appear on restaurant menus anyway. Restaurants catering primarily for tourists may not make traditional (vegetarian) dishes, unless they have cottoned on to the idea of catering to this growing and lucrative market.

Self-Catering

Dining out every day can be expensive especially if you are in Cyprus for the long run or are accommodated in a big hotel. In self-catering apartments or agrotourist houses you can usually cook for yourself very cheaply and easily. Supermarkets will have most of what you are familiar with back home and local fruit and vegetable markets will provide you with fresh produce. Even the smallest village will have a minimarket and grocery.

DRINKS
Nonalcoholic Drinks

Tea and coffee are popular, though the Greek/Turkish variety of coffee – thick and strong – is more commonly consumed. Iced instant coffee (frappe) is gaining popularity among young Cypriots. Water is drunk extensively – at least judging by the number of bottled waters on sale.

Any soft drinks you will find back home you will find in Cyprus, including designer energy drinks, uniquely British Vimto and various permutations of Coke. Fruit juices are also very popular.

Alcoholic Drinks

Drinking alcohol in the dedicated pub sense – as in the UK or Australia, for example – is generally unknown in Cyprus. Alcohol is normally taken with food or at least small snacks (mezedes). Beer comes in two brands: Cypriot-made KEO and Danish inspired but Cypriot-brewed Carlsberg. Other beers, while available, are normally more expensive. In the North you will commonly find Efes or Gold Fassl beer.

Raki (Turkish) or *zivania* (Greek) is the local firewater made from distilling the leftovers of the grape crushings. It is strong, so beware. Wine is popular on both sides of Cyprus and Commandaria from Kolossi, near Lemesos, is Cyprus' most famous export fortified wine. It dates back in popularity to the time of the Crusades.

While nominally Muslims, many Turkish Cypriots either partake of alcohol or are quite happy to let others enjoy it freely.

ENTERTAINMENT

Restaurants sometimes have live music and there are cinemas, clubs and Internet cafes open until 2 am or later in most major towns and tourist areas. Bars abound in major tourist resorts – Agia Napa having perhaps the greatest concentration of watering holes in the whole of the island.

Pubs & Bars

Pubs in the true British sense almost make the grade in some of the tourist enclaves in Protaras, Agia Napa and Pafos. At least one pub – Irish at that – makes a good showing in Lefkosia. Many do have decent British or Irish beer on tap and serve pub grub, but by and large they are just overgrown bars.

There are bars aplenty and they make no pretence of being otherwise. Drinks tend to be on the pricey side – especially if the establishments are mainly Cypriot patronised – and in tourist centres they tend to be loud, cold and busy. This applies equally to both the North and the South.

Discos

There are abundant discos in both the North and the South, with the greatest concentration being in Kyrenia and Agia Napa. There is usually a cover charge and drinks tend to be more expensive than at regular bars. They normally wind down around 1 am.

Nightclubs

Nightclubs can be found in major towns and often in resort hotels. They take over where discos leave off, tend to be somewhat more formal and fairly expensive. Floorshows are very common. As with discos the greatest concentration is in Kyrenia and Agia Napia, with a fair few in Lefkosia.

Jazz

Lovers of jazz will have to keep their ears tuned to the grapevine for possible jazz venues or festivals. The Kourion Jazz Festival near Lemesos usually kicks in during

July, but you will be hard-pressed to find anything similar in the North.

Greek Music

Summer is the best time to catch all the top-name performing musical artists from Greece. Music on offer runs the gamut from traditional demotic music to Greek rock and the quality of the artists performing is the best. You will see posters all over Cyprus each week announcing the latest act to appear. The tickets are often available from record stores or, in Lefkosia, at the Municipal Theatre box office. Do try and catch at least one concert.

The North is not so well served, though performing artists from the Turkish mainland do appear from time to time.

Classical Music

In the South classical music concerts are held at various locations throughout the year. Some are held outdoors – like at the stunning Ancient Kourion amphitheatre – while others are held in Lefkosia. Most classical concerts and other cultural events are listed in the CTO publication *Diary of Events* which usually covers a six-month period. This is available free from the CTO.

Nicosia This Month also lists any concerts that may be happening and is available by subscription from Nicocles Publishing House, (☎ 02-672 949), PO Box 23697, Lefkosia, for CY£8 for 24 issues, or sometimes free from your hotel.

Cinemas

Cinemas abound and are equally popular in both the North and the South. Recent releases are usually shown in the original language with subtitling in Greek or Turkish. A movie theatre ticket costs around TL1.5 million in the North and CY£3 in the South.

Theatre

Theatre is certainly popular among Cypriots though, unless you speak Greek or Turkish,

the entertainment value is likely to be extremely limited. Check in the local newspapers or look out for street posters advertising performances that may have some appeal for you.

SPECTATOR SPORTS

Football (soccer) is the most popular spectator sport across the whole of Cyprus with teams from a variety of leagues playing somewhere each weekend during the season (September to May). In the North there are two leagues with around 20 teams in each. Currently the top team is OCAK from Kyrenia. Entry to a match costs TL1 million, though entry to many of the lower league games is free.

SHOPPING

Cyprus is well equipped with stores catering for all tastes and requirements. Lefkosia in particular has smart fashionable boutiques as well as chain stores such as Marks & Spencer and Woolworths. The North is not as well provided for when it comes to major department stores, but there is nonetheless a wide range of goods on display. Hypermarket-style shopping malls are beginning to take off in the South and the major cities will have at least one of these shopping centres in the suburbs somewhere.

While there are not all that many hi-tech consumer items that are specifically cheap in Cyprus, many people purchase high-grade optics such as spectacles which are probably considerably cheaper than back home. Other good buys include leather goods, woven goods, ceramics, copperware, silverware, baskets and Lefkara lace. Local spirits such as *zivania*, brandy, Commandaria liqueur wine and other better quality Cypriot wines are also good purchases.

Shoes and shirts and imported textiles are of high quality and most likely much cheaper than back home.

Getting There & Away

Most travellers to Cyprus arrive by air and the great majority of them are on charter flights. Individual tickets to Cyprus tend to be expensive, though Europe-based travellers may be able to pick up cheap last minute tickets with the charter companies back home if they shop around. This applies equally to travellers to Northern Cyprus as it does to the Republic of Cyprus (Southern Cyprus), though choices and options for the travel to the South are greater.

Sea travel to Cyprus has never been overly popular among individual travellers, though it is potentially the most romantic way to do it. Unfortunately the two shipping companies that hold the monopoly on travel to the Republic of Cyprus have not made much effort to increase the romance factor and still use outdated vessels with rather nondescript on-board services to match. Ticket prices for at least a modicum of comfort on the lengthy legs from Greece or Israel are not so cheap and on top of that you must add the cost of food for – in the case of Piraeus to Lemesos at least – a full two and a half day voyage.

Sea travel to the North, while shorter than the Israel or Greece sectors, may still require an overnight on board and, while prices are naturally lower, comfort levels are not luxury cruise quality yet. Fast ferries to and from Kyrenia, however, now make the trip a little easier. Travellers to the North must also exit the way they came – via Turkey – so there is no onward travel possible to Greece or Israel, until local politics mend.

AIR

There are scheduled and charter flights from most European cities and the Middle East (around UK£230 return from London, including tax), with discounts for students. However, they are heavily booked in the high season. From Cyprus there are daily flights to Greece (CY£95), and frequent services to Israel (CY£82), Egypt (CY£94),

Jordan (CY£80), Lebanon (CY£64) and Syria (CY£69) – prices include taxes.

Ercan airport (formerly Tymvou airport) in Northern Cyprus is not recognised by the international airline authorities, so you can't fly there direct. Airlines must touch down first in Turkey and then continue on to Northern Cyprus (around UK£315 from London, including tax) and other airlines can fly you to Turkey, where you change planes.

Airports & Airlines

The Republic's airports are at Larnaka and Pafos. Larnaka airport was built hurriedly after the 1974 invasion and it shows. Facilities for passengers at this busy air terminal are basic and crowded and the airport is not user-friendly. Departing passengers at least get breathing space in a reasonably comfortable departure lounge. However, arriving passengers are shunted out the door with nary a chance to catch their breath or bearings, while the selection of car hire outlets in the small arrivals area is somewhat oversubscribed.

There are public bus services to Lefkosia and Lemesos leaving the airport forecourt between five and eight times daily. Otherwise taxis are the only other way of moving on to your destination.

Pafos airport is naturally smaller and not so frequently used by international travellers, however, it is much more convenient for those heading for the Pafos coast resorts. Some Cyprus Airways flights also stop at Pafos to and from its Western European destinations.

Ercan airport in the North is smaller still and not particularly well-equipped with arrival facilities such as baggage carts and other conveniences. Car hire must be arranged beforehand. There is no public transport to or from the airport so taxis are your only choice.

The national carrier of the Republic of Cyprus' is Cyprus Airways. It is a small but well-appointed airline and levels of service are very good. It has destinations throughout the Middle East and Europe. View its current schedules on its Web site www .cyprusair.com.cy. The South is also served by a large number of scheduled and charter airlines.

The North is served by scheduled services by Cyprus Turkish Airlines, İstanbul Airlines and Turkish Airlines. Flights to Northern Cyprus by foreign airlines must all touch down – usually just for refuelling – in Turkey before flying on to Northern Cyprus.

Buying Tickets

If you are flying to Cyprus from outside Europe, the plane ticket will probably be the single most expensive item in your budget, and buying it can be an intimidating business. There is likely to be a multitude of airlines and travel agents hoping to separate you from your money, and it is always worthwhile putting aside a few hours to research the current state of the market. Start early; some of the cheapest tickets have to be bought months in advance, and some popular flights sell out early. Talk to other recent travellers – they may be able to stop you making some of the same old mistakes. Look at the ads in newspapers and magazines (not forgetting the press of the ethnic group of the country you plan to visit), consult reference books and watch for special offers. Then phone around travel agents for bargains. (Airlines can supply information on routes and timetables; however, except at times of inter-airline war, they do not supply the cheapest tickets.) Find out the fare, the route, the duration of the journey and any restrictions on the ticket. Then sit back and decide which is best for you.

You may discover that those impossibly cheap flights are 'fully booked, but we have another one that costs a bit more...' Or the flight is on an airline notorious for its poor safety standards and leaves you in the world's least favourite airport mid-journey for 14 hours. Or they claim only to have the last two seats available for that country for the whole of July, which they will hold for you for a maximum of two hours. Don't panic – keep ringing around.

Use the fares quoted in this book as a guide only. They are approximate and based on the rates advertised by travel agents at the time of going to press. Quoted airfares do not necessarily constitute a recommendation for the carrier.

If you are travelling from the UK or the USA, you will probably find that the cheapest flights are being advertised by obscure bucket shops whose names haven't yet reached the telephone directory. Many such firms are honest and solvent, but there are a few rogues who will take your money and disappear, to reopen elsewhere a month or two later under a new name. If you feel suspicious about a firm, don't provide all the money at once – leave a deposit of 20% or so and pay the balance when you get the ticket. If they insist on cash in advance, go somewhere else. And once you have the ticket, ring the airline to confirm that you are actually booked on the flight.

You may decide to pay more than the rock-bottom fare by opting for the safety of

PAUL HELLANDER

Looking out on Lefkosia

CHRIS CHRISTO

Famagusta Gate, Lefkosia

STELLA HELLANDER

Family bread-making

PAUL HELLANDER

Makarios III looms over the Archbishop's Palace, Lefkosia.

Pafos harbour shelters a large fishing fleet.

A colourful fishing boat at Agios Georgios in the Pafos region.

Air Travel Glossary

Cancellation Penalties If you have to cancel or change a discounted ticket, there are often heavy penalties involved; insurance can sometimes be taken out against these penalties. Some airlines impose penalties on regular tickets as well, particularly against 'no-show' passengers.

Courier Fares Businesses often need to send urgent documents or freight securely and quickly. Courier companies hire people to accompany the package through customs and, in return, offer a discount ticket which is sometimes a phenomenal bargain. However, you may have to surrender all your baggage allowance and take only carry-on luggage.

Full Fares Airlines traditionally offer 1st class (coded F), business class (coded J) and economy class (coded Y) tickets. These days there are so many promotional and discounted fares available that few passengers pay full economy fare.

Lost Tickets If you lose your airline ticket an airline will usually treat it like a travellers cheque and, after inquiries, issue you with another one. Legally, however, an airline is entitled to treat it like cash and if you lose it then it's gone forever. Take good care of your tickets.

Onward Tickets An entry requirement for many countries is that you have a ticket out of the country. If you're unsure of your next move, the easiest solution is to buy the cheapest onward ticket to a neighbouring country or a ticket from a reliable airline which can later be refunded if you do not use it.

Open-Jaw Tickets These are return tickets where you fly out to one place but return from another. If available, this can save you backtracking to your arrival point.

Overbooking Since every flight has some passengers who fail to show up, airlines often book more passengers than they have seats. Usually excess passengers make up for the no-shows, but occasionally somebody gets 'bumped' onto the next available flight. Guess who it is most likely to be? The passengers who check in late.

Promotional Fares These are officially discounted fares, available from travel agencies or direct from the airline.

Reconfirmation If you don't reconfirm your flight at least 72 hours prior to departure, the airline may delete your name from the passenger list. Ring to find out if your airline requires reconfirmation.

Restrictions Discounted tickets often have various restrictions on them – such as needing to be paid for in advance and incurring a penalty to be altered. Others are restrictions on the minimum and maximum period you must be away.

Round-the-World Tickets RTW tickets give you a limited period (usually a year) in which to circumnavigate the globe. You can go anywhere the carrying airlines go, as long as you don't backtrack. The number of stopovers or total number of separate flights is decided before you set off and they usually cost a bit more than a basic return flight.

Transferred Tickets Airline tickets cannot be transferred from one person to another. Travellers sometimes try to sell the return half of their ticket, but officials can ask you to prove that you are the person named on the ticket. On an international flight tickets are compared with passports.

Travel Periods Ticket prices vary with the time of year. There is a low (off-peak) season and a high (peak) season, and often a low-shoulder season and a high-shoulder season as well. Usually the fare depends on your outward flight – if you depart in the high season and return in the low season, you pay the high-season fare.

a better-known travel agent. Firms such as STA Travel, which has offices worldwide, Council Travel in the USA or Travel CUTS in Canada are not going to disappear overnight, leaving you clutching a receipt for a nonexistent ticket, but they do offer good prices to most destinations.

Once you have your ticket, write down its number, together with the flight number and other details, and keep the information somewhere separate. If the ticket is lost or stolen, this will help you get a replacement. It's sensible to buy travel insurance as early as possible. If you buy it the week before you fly, you may find, for example, that you're not covered for delays to your flight caused by industrial action.

Round-the-World Tickets Cyprus Airways and Olympic Airways are not signatory to any RTW ticket agreement, so the best you can hope for is a discounted add-on return fare from Athens or İstanbul in addition to your main ticket. Check with your local travel agent (see suggestions following) for quotes.

Travellers with Special Needs

If you have broken a leg, you're a vegetarian or require a special diet, you're travelling in a wheelchair, taking a baby or whatever, let the airline staff know as soon as possible – preferably when booking your ticket. Check that your request has been registered when you reconfirm your booking (at least 72 hours before departure) and again when you check in at the airport.

Children under two travel for 10% of the standard fare (or free on some airlines), as long as they don't occupy a seat. They don't get a baggage allowance either. 'Skycots' should be provided by the airline if requested in advance; these will take a child weighing up to about 10kg. Children between two and 12 can usually occupy a seat for half to two-thirds of the full fare.

Departure Tax

Departure taxes in Cyprus are normally included in the cost of your air fare, so you don't need to worry about keeping extra cash at the airport. For the record you are paying CY£19.50 for the privilege in the Republic, but this figure is normally listed separately when you request airline ticket quotes. From the North the equivalent fee is UK£3.50.

The USA

While the North Atlantic air corridor is one of the world's busiest with a bewildering number of flights into Europe, direct flights into Cyprus from the USA are limited. The *New York Times*, the *LA Times*, the *Chicago Tribune* and the *San Francisco Examiner* all produce weekly travel sections in which you'll find any number of travel agents' ads.

Council Travel (www.counciltravel.com) and STA Travel (www.sta-travel.com) have offices in major cities nationwide. The magazine *Travel Unlimited* (PO Box 1058, Allston, MA 02134) publishes details of the cheapest air fares and courier possibilities for destinations all over the world from the USA. Check out TRAVEL.com (www.travel.com) for some good buy-it-yourself ticket deals. Other sites worth checking out are ITN (www.itn.net) and Travelocity (www.travelocity.com).

You can fly to Cyprus from the USA with a number of airlines, but all involve a stop and perhaps a change of airline in Europe. Among the cheaper fares are return tickets with United Airlines and American Airlines connecting with Cyprus Airways flights. Tickets start at US$1515. Other permutations with British Airways, Continental Airlines, Olympic Airways or KLM are a little more expensive at US$1580. Cyprus Airways in the US is represented by Kinisis Travel & Tours (☎ 718-267 6880) at 34-09 Broadway, Astoria, New York.

From Cyprus to the USA ADA Travelscope (☎ 05-343 111, fax 345 834, @ evie@ travelscope.com.cy) of Lemesos quoted one-way/return discounted tickets from Larnaka to New York at CY£261/400 and Los Angeles or San Francisco at CY£354/ 553, all with KLM.

Canada

Travel CUTS has offices in all major cities. The *Vancouver Sun* and *Toronto Globe & Mail* carry ads from travel agents. The magazine *Great Expeditions* (PO Box 8000-411, Abbotsford BC V2S 6H1) is useful.

Olympic Airways has two flights a week from Toronto to Athens via Montreal. From Athens you can connect with either an Olympic Airways or Cyprus Airways flight to Larnaka, both of which fly daily to Cyprus.

Voyages Campus Travel CUTS in Montreal (☎ 514-341 1649) is a good place to ask about cheap deals. You should be able to get to Larnaka and back from Toronto or Montreal for about C$1152, or from Vancouver for C$1500. Lufthansa offers one-way tickets to Larnaka from Montreal for C$709.

From Cyprus to Canada ADA Travelscope (☎ 05-343 111, fax 345 834, @ evie@ travelscope.com.cy) of Lemesos quoted one-way/return discounted tickets from Larnaka to Toronto or Montreal at around CY£312/490 with British Airways.

Australia

STA Travel and Flight Centres International are major dealers in cheap air fares. Check the travel agents' ads in the Yellow Pages and ring around.

Axis Travel Centre of Adelaide in South Australia (☎ 08-8331 3222, fax 8364 2922, @ axistravel@msn.com.au) specialises in travel to and from the Middle East, Greece and Cyprus. Contact Max Najar for any special deals going.

There are no direct services to Cyprus from Australia but a couple of airlines, Gulf and Emirates, allow you to fly more or less directly with only a stop in the Gulf States. Olympic Airways flies to Athens from Melbourne and Sydney and can usually offer good value add-on Cyprus legs. Singapore Airlines flies into Athens three times a week and there are daily connections with Cyprus Airways and Olympic Airways.

Sample return ticket prices from Australia to Cyprus range from AU$2489 to AU$2879 in low/high season. Special discounted fares of AU$1799 can also be found, but have restricted conditions.

From Cyprus to Australia ADA Travelscope (☎ 05-343 111, fax 345 834, @ evie@travelscope.com.cy) of Lemesos quoted one-way/return discounted tickets from Larnaka to Melbourne or Sydney at CY£365/645 one-way/return with Singapore Airlines via Athens.

New Zealand

As in Australia, STA Travel and Flight Centres International are popular travel agents. Connections to Cyprus are as for Australia with the additional cost of flying to and from Australia. Cyprus Airways in Australia is represented by Cyprus Tourist Agency (☎ 03-9663 3711) at 237 Lonsdale St, Melbourne.

The UK

Trailfinders in west London produces a lavishly illustrated brochure that includes airfare details. STA Travel also has branches in the UK. Look in the Sunday papers and *Exchange & Mart* for ads. Also look out for the free magazines and newspapers widely available in London. Those that are especially useful include *Footloose*, *Supertravel Magazine*, *TNT* and *Trailfinder* – you can pick them up outside the main train and tube stations.

Most British travel agents are registered with the Association of British Travel Agents (ABTA). If you have paid for your flight at an ABTA-registered agent which then goes out of business, ABTA will guarantee a refund or an alternative. Unregistered bucket shops are riskier but also sometimes cheaper.

The Globetrotters Club (BCM Roving, London WC1N 3XX) publishes a newsletter called *Globe*, which covers obscure destinations and can help in finding travelling companions.

Package holidays to the Republic of Cyprus come in all shapes and sizes but range in price from UK£340 to UK£660 for one week's accommodation with breakfast in a decent sized hotel in Pafos. Sunvil Travel (☎ 020-8568 4499) is one of the specialist tour operators covering Cyprus and can offer a wide range of packages to suit most budgets.

Regent Holidays (UK) Ltd (☎ 01983-866 670, fax 864 197, ✉ regentholidays.iow@ btinternet.com) specialises in package tours to Northern Cyprus with prices ranging from UK£295 to UK£490 for one week, depending on season and number of persons sharing.

Cyprus Airways in the UK is based in London (☎ 020-8359 1333) at 5 The Exchange, Brent Cross Gardens, NW4 3RJ.

Following are the addresses of some of the most reputable agencies selling discount tickets:

usit CAMPUS (☎ 0870-240 1010,
fax 020-7730 6893) 52 Grosvenor
Gardens, SW1 0AG
www.campustravel.co.uk
STA Travel (☎ 020-7361 6161) 86 Old
Brompton Rd, SW7 3LQ
www.statravel.co.uk
Trailfinders (☎ 020-7937 5400) 215
Kensington High St, W8 6BD
www.trailfinder.co.uk

The best deals are with British Airways who fly to Larnaka direct daily. A return ticket will cost UK£215/150 high/low season. Olympic Airways fly twice daily (via Athens) for UK£250/200 high/low season. Lufthansa flies two to four times a week (via Frankfurt) for UK£300/200 high/low season. There are some flights to Pafos but they cost around UK£300 return.

From Cyprus to the UK ADA Travelscope (☎ 05-343 111, fax 345 834, ✉ evie@travelscope.com.cy) of Lemesos quoted one-way/return fares from Larnaka to London at CY£162/190 with Cyprus Airways and British Airways.

Continental Europe
A considerable number of major European carriers fly into Larnaka airport and some also stop in Pafos, though the bulk of the traffic is made up of charter flights.

France France is linked to Cyprus with daily flights by Air France (☎ 0802 802 802; 4221FF return) and Cyprus Airways (☎ 01-45 01 93 38; 1992FF return). Olympic Airways (☎ 01-42 65 92 42; 2420FF return) also has daily flights to Athens from Paris with onward connections to Larnaka. Reliable travel agents include:

Héliades (☎ 01 53 27 28 21) 25–27 rue Basfroi,
F-75011 Paris
Paris Air Sud (☎ 01 40 41 66 66) 18 rue du
Pont-Neuf, F-75001 Paris
Atsaro (☎ 01 42 60 98 98) 9 rue de l'Echelle,
F-75001 Paris
Bleu Blanc (☎ 01 40 21 31 31) 53 avenue de la
République, F-75011 Paris
Nouvelles Frontières (☎ 08 03 33 33)
87 boulevard de Grenelle, F-75015 Paris
Planète Havas (☎ 01 53 29 40 00) 26 Avenue
de l'Opéra, F-75001 Paris

Germany Atlas Reisewelt has offices all around the country and is a good place to start checking prices. In Berlin, Alternativ Tours (☎ 030-8 81 20 89), Wilmersdorfer Strasse 94 (U-Bahn: Adenauerplatz), has discounted fares to just about anywhere in the world. STA Travel, SRS Studenten Reise Service (☎ 030-28 59 82 64), at Marienstrasse 23 near Friedrichstrasse station, offers special student (aged 34 or less) and youth (aged 25 or less) fares. Travel agents offering unpublished cheap flights advertise in *Zitty*, Berlin's fortnightly entertainment magazine.

In Frankfurt, try SRID Reisen (☎ 069-43 01 91), Berger Strasse 118. Cyprus Airways is in Frankfurt and can be contacted on ☎ 069-695 8930.

The Netherlands The cheapest deal from the Netherlands to Cyprus is with Tarom (via Bucharest) four times a week, f457/472 one-way/return. Next cheapest option is with Malev (via Budapest), four times a week for f519/599 one-way/return. With KLM or Cyprus Airways (daily) the price is f749 return. Reliable travel agents in Amsterdam include:

Budget Air (☎ 020-627 12 51) Rokin 34
NBBS Reizen (☎ 020-620 50 71) Rokin 66

Malibu Travel (☎ 020-638 32 20, fax 638 48 80, ✆ postbus@pointopoint.demon.nl) Damrak 30

From Cyprus to Europe ADA Travelscope (☎ 05-343 111, fax 345 834, ✆ evie@ travelscope.com.cy) of Lemesos quoted one-way/return fares from Larnaka to Paris at CY£162/230 and Frankfurt at CY£162/230 with Cyprus Airways.

Middle East
With Cyprus being so close to the Middle East, transport between there and Larnaka is good but tickets are rarely discounted. Possibly the best place in Israel to buy discounted tickets is at Mona Tours (☎ 02-621 1433, fax 528 3125, ✆ dave13@internet-za hav.net) at 25 Bograshov St, Tel Aviv. Ask for Dave Cohen. A one-way/return ticket to Larnaka at the time of research was selling for US$110/150 with Cyprus Airways.

From Cyprus to the Middle East ADA Travelscope (☎ 05-343 111, fax 345 834, ✆ evie@travelscope.com.cy) of Lemesos quoted one-way/return fares from Larnaka to Tel Aviv at CY£69/115, Beirut at CY£59/118, Amman at CY£61/101 and Damascus at CY£48/80, all with Cyprus Airways.

Africa
Travellers in Africa can get to Cyprus most easily via Johannesburg and Nairobi, on one of Olympic Airways regular flights through Athens. An alternative route into Cyprus is from Cairo to Larnaka direct with either Egypt Air or Cyprus Airways. Cyprus Airways and Egypt Air both fly twice a week, $US235/276 one-way/return. Tickets are available from Egypt Panorama Tours in Cairo (☎ 350 5880), 4 Rd 79 Maadi. Cash payment is advisable in preference to credit cards which may incur a hidden 10% surcharge.

From Cyprus to Africa ADA Travelscope (☎ 05-343 111, fax 345 834, ✆ evie@ travelscope.com.cy) of Lemesos quoted one-way/return discounted tickets from Larnaka to Cairo at CY£78/129 with Cyprus Airways and to Johannesburg at CY£316/429 with Emirates or CY£330/549 with Olympic Airways.

Asia
Hong Kong is the discount air fare capital of the region. Its bucket shops are at least as unreliable as those of other cities. Ask for some advice from other travellers before buying a ticket.

STA Travel, which is reliable, has branches in Hong Kong, Tokyo, Singapore, Bangkok and Kuala Lumpur. The Singapore office of STA (☎ 737 7188, fax 737 2591, ✆ sales@statravel.com.sg) is at 33a Cuppage Rd, Cuppage Terrace. Flights from Singapore to Larnaka cost S$700/950 one-way/return on a three-month ticket with Gulf Air, or S$1000/1400 one-way/return for a 12-month ticket with Emirates; quoted by STA.

From Cyprus to Asia ADA Travelscope (☎ 05-343 111, fax 345 834, ✆ evie@trav elscope.com.cy) of Lemesos quoted one-way/return discounted tickets from Larnaka to Singapore at CY£242/466 and to Hong Kong at CY£281/537. Both fares are with Singapore Airlines via Athens.

SEA
Cyprus is connected to mainland Europe by a regular car ferry service between Lemesos and Piraeus, near Athens in Greece. The Piraeus to Lemesos run may involve a stop in Patmos and Rhodes, or sometimes in Crete instead. Cyprus is connected to the Middle East by a service to Haifa in Israel.

While these services are reasonably well patronised – many of the passengers are Greek pilgrims heading for the Holy Land – the quality and level of service lags considerably behind the equivalent ferry services that link Greece and Italy where competition is stronger.

Nonetheless, getting to Cyprus by sea is a novel way of travelling and the stops at up to four different Greek Island locations make Cyprus a logical value add-on to any Greek Island-hopping trip. Budget travellers should take sufficient food and drink for the voyage since on-board prices can be expensive.

Travellers to Northern Cyprus will need to make their way to the Turkish ports of Taşucu or Mersin on the Mediterranean coast before taking the ferry to Kyrenia (Girne) or Famagusta (Gazimağusa). It is difficult to make reservations beforehand since the Turkish shipping companies do not maintain overseas booking agencies.

Ports & Shipping Companies

Lemesos is the main arrival port in the Republic and is 3km south of the town centre. The port is reasonably well-equipped for sea travellers since many mini-cruise ships use the facilities. The terminal building has banks and tourist information facilities and passport controls are swift and efficient.

However, if you are thinking of bringing your car or motorcycle to Cyprus, you will need the vehicle's registration papers, liability insurance and your domestic licence. International Driving Permits are not normally required, but it is always a good idea to have one especially if you plan to move on from Cyprus to the Middle East where it may be required.

Cyprus does not require a *Carnet de passage en douane*, but check to see if you need it for other Middle East countries such as Jordan or Egypt if you are planning to move on. This is effectively a passport for the vehicle and acts as a temporary waiver of import duty. The carnet may also need to have listed any expensive spare parts that you're planning to carry with you, such as a gearbox. This is necessary when travelling in many countries in Asia, Africa and Central and South America and is designed to prevent car import rackets. Contact your local Automobile Association for details about all documentation.

Anyone who is planning to take their own vehicle needs to check in advance what spare parts and petrol are likely to be available. However, most major vehicle makes are represented in Cyprus. Unleaded petrol is widely available, but LPG gas is not used.

There are two major ferry companies, Poseidon Lines and Salamis Lines. The

Bringing Your Car to Cyprus

If you are thinking of bringing your own vehicle to Cyprus and are expecting the European Union treatment, then read on. Customs procedures in Lemesos Port are somewhat tedious and a bit of a shock after Europe's easy come-easy go attitude. As a result of a series of scams involving the import of 'hot' (ie, stolen) vehicles from the UK and other European countries, Cypriot customs authorities have tightened regulations, so that temporarily importing a car as a tourist now requires more stringent paperwork.

After you disembark, you will be directed to the customs area. Here you will need to pay port taxes of CY£20 and fill out a longish vehicle declaration form listing all extras such as power steering, air-conditioning, CD player etc that your vehicle may have. Your insurance and driver's licence will be carefully scrutinised. Make sure your Green Card is valid for Cyprus. You can tell this if the international identification letters for Cyprus 'CY' appear on it. You will have to buy extra on-the-spot insurance if it is not endorsed.

The vehicle will then be physically inspected and particular attention will be given to the vehicle and chassis numbers. Make sure you declare them correctly on the form. If all is in order, you will be given a copy of the import declaration – don't lose it! – and you are free to drive off. You will normally get an import permit for as long as you declare your intention to stay, up to three months. After that you will need to renew the permit in Lefkosia.

Procedures in the North are not as stringent. If you are coming from Turkey you will have done most of the hard paperwork before entering the country. Make sure that your Green Card covers Asiatic Turkey and Northern Cyprus. On-the-spot insurance is normally available both at Kyrenia (Girne) and Famagusta (Gazimağusa) Ports.

Poseidon is Greek-owned and run and the latter is Cypriot-owned and run. Salamis Lines currently operates one ship on the route, the *F/B Nissos Kypros*, and while the ship is getting rather long in the tooth and there is rumour of its replacement soon, it is functional and does the job of getting passengers from A to B. Poseidon Lines runs two ships, the *F/B Sea Symphony* and *F/B Sea Harmony*, and while we cannot vouch for the quality of the service, these boats seem to have the edge. Reports from recent travellers' tales about the comfort level of both lines vary, so keep your ear to the ground for current opinions.

Routes and Fares

The cheapest tickets from Piraeus in Greece to Lemesos are US$63 for deck, US$72 for a pullman seat and from US$92 per person in a four-berth cabin. Students and those under 26 get a discount of about 20%. These prices are for one-way voyages in the low season; in the high season, prices go up by between 11% and 15%. It varies slightly between the different shipping companies, but the high season is roughly from mid-June to mid-September. A port fee of CY£20 is charged for cars. For return voyages, 20% reductions are made on the tickets (although not with the student and under 26 prices). Travellers with campervans can sleep in the van on deck and avoid expensive cabin costs when travelling on Poseidon Line's *F/B Sea Symphony*.

The Piraeus to Lemesos run is about 21 hours, so take plenty of food and drink, or money, for the voyage. From Haifa the trip takes 11 hours – usually overnight. The cheapest ticket costs CY£40.

From Northern Cyprus there are three routes to mainland Turkey: Famagusta to Mersin (UK£16), Kyrenia to Taşucu (from UK£15.60) and, during peak season, to Alanya.

Buying Tickets

Tickets can be bought at all ports of call in Greece as well as directly from the shipping line agents. Here are the main contact details for both lines.

Poseidon Lines
Cyprus: (☎ 05-745 666, fax 745 666) Poseidon Lines (Cyprus) Ltd, 124 Franklin Roosevelt St, Lemesos
Greece: (☎ 01-965 8300, fax 965 8310, @ poseidon.lines@ath.forthnet.gr) Poseidon Lines Shipping Co, Alkyonidon 32, 166 73 Voula, Athens
Israel: (☎ 04-867 4444, fax 866 1958) Caspi Travel, 76 Ha'Atzmaut St, Haifa
UK: (☎ 020-7431 4560, fax 431 5456, @ ferries@viamare.com) Viamare Travel Ltd, 2 Sumatra Rd, London NW6 1PU
Salamis Lines
Cyprus: (☎ 05-355 555, fax 364 410) Salamis Tours, PO Box 351, Lemesos
Greece: (☎ 01-429 4325, fax 452 8384) Salamis Lines (Hellas), Fillelinon 12, GR-185 36 Piraeus
Israel: (☎ 04-861 3670, fax 853 3264) A Rosenfeld Shipping Ltd, 104 Ha'Atzmaut St, Haifa
UK: (☎ 020-7431 4560, fax 431 5456, @ ferries@viamare.com) Viamare Travel Ltd, 2 Sumatra Rd, London NW6 1PU

Sailing details and ticket prices for both companies are available on the Internet at the following addresses: www.Ferries.gr/Poseidon (Poseidon Lines) and www.viamare.com (Salamis Lines).

Departure Tax

In the Republic, departure tax is CY£15 to CY£18 when leaving by sea. In Northern Cyprus it is UK£3.60. In both areas it's normally included in the cost of your ferry ticket.

ORGANISED TOURS

If you want to come on a package tour to Cyprus, you have chosen the right country, especially if you come from the UK, Scandinavia or Germany which constitute the largest source regions for organised tourism to Cyprus. Package tours can't be beaten for prices and convenience, but they do restrict you to your chosen time frame. You usually only stay in resort hotels far from the 'real' Cyprus and there is little incentive to drag yourself away from the pool and a cold beer to explore further than the hotel perimeter.

Some of the more established companies in the UK offering packaged vacations in Cyprus are:

Airtours Holidays Ltd (☎ 0870-608 1940) Wavell House, Holcombe Rd, Helmshore, Lancs BB4 4NB

Cyprair Holidays (☎ 020-8359 1234, fax 8359 1251, ✆ reservations@cyprair-holidays.co.uk)

5 The Exchange, Brent Cross Gardens, London NW4 3RJ

First Choice (☎ 0161-745 4533, fax 745 4533) Peel Cross Rd, Salford, Manchester, M4 2AN

Sunvil Tours (☎ 020-8568 4499, fax 8568 8330, ✆ cyprus@sunvil.co.uk) Sunvil House, 7-8 Upper Square, Old Isleworth, Middlesex TW7 7BJ

Getting Around

Cyprus is small enough for you to get around easily. Roads are good and well signposted – a legacy of the British colonial system – and traffic moves smoothly and without the excesses and unpredictability sometimes found in other countries in the Middle East or Mediterranean Europe.

Public transport is limited to buses and service taxis – stretch taxis that run on pre-determined routes. There is no internal train network and no domestic air services in either the North or the South. Four-lane motorways link Lefkosia with Lemesos and Larnaka and the network is being gradually expanded in the west to link Pafos. In the east the motorway now extends as far as Ormidia, 15km west of Larnaka.

It is feasible to ride around Cyprus by bicycle along ordinary highways, which parallel the motorways, where cycling is allowed but it is not such an attractive option because of the heavy traffic. However, you will need a bicycle with good gears to negotiate the long hauls up and around the Troödos Mountains and Kyrenia Range. It is probably better to limit long distance cycling trips to winter, spring or autumn since high summer temperatures can make the going tough.

The main obstacle to obtaining a full view of Cyprus is the restriction on visits between the Republic of Cyprus and Northern Cyprus. You *cannot* visit the South if you have entered Cyprus from the North. You can enter the North from the South for up to nine hours a day which, if done over a few days, will give you an idea of daily life in that part of the country. See the Lefkosia chapter for further details on crossing procedures.

Distances overall are generally short, with the longest conceivable leg (Polis to Paralimni) no more than 220km. The North, covering 37% of the island, is equally compact, but out to Apostolos Andreas at the tip of the Karpas panhandle is a considerable drive.

BUS

Buses are frequent but look like relics from England of the 1950s. However, they are comfortable, cheap and, other than services to rural areas, offer reasonably well-timed services. Some buses, usually on the main intercity routes, can transport bicycles.

Urban and long distance buses are operated by a host of private companies and run Monday to Saturday. There are no services on Sunday. Buses charge around CY£1.50 for most journeys. Major bus companies in the South are:

Lefkosia to Lemesos Kemek Transport Ltd (☎ 02-473 414, 05-747 532)
Lefkosia to Pafos Nea Amoroza Transport Co Ltd (☎ 02-236 822, 06-236 740)
Lefkosia to Larnaka Kallenos Buses (☎ 02-473 414, 04-654 890)
Lemesos to Larnaka Kallenos Buses (☎ 04-654 890)

Reservations

Bus reservations are not normally required; the one exception being the service to some of the Troödos Mountain resorts, where phone reservations are required if you want to be picked up from either Platres or Troödos in order to return to Lefkosia.

Costs

Bus ticket prices are regulated by the government and range in price between CY£0.40 and CY£4. The following table will give you an idea of the ticket prices between major towns, current at the time of research. Where direct services are not available, the intermediate cities or towns are indicated. See the individual city and town entries for frequency and times of departures.

CAR & MOTORCYCLE

Driving or riding your way around Cyprus is the only really effective way to get to know the country properly. It is essential if you want to see some of the out-of-the-way places in the Troödos Mountains or

Bus Fares between Major Centres in the Republic of Cyprus

	Lefkosia	Lemesos	Pafos	Larnaka	Troödos	Agia Napa	Paralimni	Polis
Lefkosia	-	1.5	3	1.50	1.10	2	2.50	4
Lemesos	1.50	-	1.50	1.70	2(Platres)	via Larnaka	via Larnaka	via Pafos
Pafos	3	1.50	-	via Lemesos	via Lemesos	via Larnaka & Lemesos	via Lemesos	1
Larnaka	1.50	1.70	via Lemesos	-	via Lemesos	1	1	via Lemesos & Pafos
Troödos	1.10	2(Platres)	via Lemesos	via Lemesos	-	via Larnaka & Lemesos	via Lemesos & Larnaka	via Lemesos & Pafos
Agia Napa	2	via Larnaka	via Larnaka & Lemesos	1	via Lemesos & Larnaka	-	0.40	via Larnaka, Lemesos & Pafos
Paralimni	2.50	via Larnaka & Larnaka	via Lemesos	1	Via Larnaka & Lemesos	0.40	-	via Larnaka, Lemesos & Pafos
Polis	4	4	1	via Lemesos & Pafos	via Lemesos	via Larnaka, Lemesos & Pafos	via Larnaka, Lemesos & Pafos	-

the Tyllirian wilderness, where bus transport is more or less nonexistent. The scenery throughout the country is varied, petrol stations are everywhere and facilities for bikers and motorists are very good. Picnic areas in the Troödos are usually only accessible if you have your own transport.

It is fairly expensive to bring your own vehicle and your only options are either from Israel (Haifa), Greece (Piraeus) or from Taşucu, Antalya or Mersin (Turkey). Customs procedures can be tedious (see the Getting There & Away chapter) but, for a stay of over three weeks, the cost of bringing your own vehicle will be outweighed by the cost of hiring a vehicle locally. Traffic is lighter in the North but roads are not as good as in the South where in contrast they carry much more traffic.

Parking is surprisingly cheap, with CY£0.25 getting you two hours parking in central Lefkosia. Super and unleaded petrol cost CY£0.38 for 1L, regular also costs CY£0.38 and diesel just CY£0.13. In the North all petrol costs around TL330,000 for a litre. Diesel costs TL210,000. Both leaded and unleaded petrol are widely available.

Cyprus Automobile Association (☎ 313 233) is at Hristou Mylona 12, Lefkosia. There is no Touring & Automobile Association in Northern Cyprus.

Road Rules

Traffic drives on the left in Cyprus – in both the North and the South – and locally registered cars are right-hand drive. Left-hand drive cars circulating in Northern Cyprus have usually been brought over from Turkey. The speed limit on motorways in the South is 100km/h and is often rigidly enforced by speed camera-wielding police officers. The speed limit on ordinary roads is 80km/h and in built-up areas 50km/h unless otherwise indicated. There is just one short stretch of motorway in the North linking Ercan airport with North Nicosia. Speed limits in the North are 100km/h on open roads and 50km/h in towns.

Front seat belts are compulsory and children under five years of age must not sit in the front seat. Driving a vehicle, motorcycle or even a bicycle with more than .009 milligrams of alcohol per 100 millilitres of blood is an offence.

In the Republic, motor car drivers must be over 21 years and over 18 to drive a motorcycle with an engine capacity over 50cc, or over 17 to drive a motorcycle under 50cc. In the North you must be over 18 to drive a car and the same regulations apply to motorcycles as in the South.

Road distances are posted in kilometres only and road signs are in Greek and Latin script (in the South). In the North destinations are given in their Turkish version only. Signs are large and well positioned to give drivers ample warning. International style road signs are used. American and Canadian drivers need to be alerted to the differences between their own domestic road signs and those used outside of the USA and Canada. When entering the often large roundabouts (traffic circles) give way to traffic already on the roundabout and signal your intention to turn off the roundabout. Signs in the North are white on blue and are often indistinct or small.

It is advisable to avoid rush hours in main cities, ie, 7 to 8.30 am and 1 to 1.30 pm and also 6 to 7 pm in summer (one hour earlier in winter). When driving west in the late afternoon, be aware of sun glare which can be very strong. Use sunglasses whenever driving to compensate for the normally strong reflected glare.

Rental

Cars and 4WD vehicles are widely available for hire and cost between CY£12 and CY£50 a day. In some towns you can also rent motorcycles (from CY£9) or mopeds (CY£5). Rentals cars are usually in good condition, but do inspect your vehicle before you set off. Open-top jeeps are very popular options – the Troödos Mountains literally swarm with them on hot weekends and they offer the option of dirt track driving, that adventure 'look' and natural air-conditioning. If you hire a saloon car, make sure it has air-conditioning and enough power to carry you around if there are more than two of you.

Rental cars in both the North and the South carry black on red 'Z' plates – so called because of the initial letter. Other road users normally accord a fraction more respect to 'Z' car drivers and the police are more likely to turn a blind eye for minor infractions, but don't count on it.

Purchase

Despite the finicky regulations for privately imported vehicles, cars are not prohibitively expensive and there is a fairly well-organised used-car market scene. Do bear in mind that cars are all right-hand drive and are only likely to be of any long-term use in the UK where they are probably cheaper anyway. However, if you are planning on staying any length of time in Cyprus, the purchase and resale of a car might be cheaper than the cost of bringing your own vehicle from outside Cyprus; you will have less paperwork hassles with customs.

A typical buy will cost around CY£5000 for a three to four-year-old Toyota saloon,

Road Distances (km)

	Agia Napa	Larnaka	Larnaka Airport	Lefkosia	Lemesos	Pafos	Pafos Airport	Paralimni	Polis	Troödos
Agia Napa	---									
Larnaka	41	---								
Larnaka Airport	46	5	---							
Lefkosia	80	44	49	---						
Lemesos	107	66	70	82	---					
Pafos	175	134	139	150	68	---				
Pafos Airport	170	129	104	146	63	15	---			
Paralimni	5	44	48	85	111	178	178	---		
Polis	219	169	174	185	103	35	50	219	---	
Troödos	153	112	116	78	46	114	109	158	149	---

or about CY£4500 for a Ford Fiesta of a similar age.

BICYCLE

Cycling is a cheap, convenient, healthy, environmentally sound and above all a fun way of travelling. One note of caution; before you leave home, go over your bike with a fine-toothed comb and fill your repair kit with every imaginable spare part. As with cars and motorcycles, you won't necessarily be able to buy that crucial gismo for your machine when it breaks down somewhere in the back of beyond as the sun sets.

Bicycles can travel by air. You can take them to pieces and put them in a bike bag or box, but it's much easier simply to wheel your bike to the check-in desk, where it should be treated as a piece of baggage. You may have to remove the pedals and turn the handlebars sideways so that it takes up less space in the aircraft's hold; check all this with the airline well in advance, preferably before you pay for your ticket.

The CTO in the South produces a very helpful brochure called *Cyprus for Cycling* that lists 19 recommended mountain bike rides around the south of Cyprus. These range in distance from 2.5km to 19km from the Akamas Peninsula in the west to Cape Greco in the east.

The best time for cycling in Cyprus is in winter and spring when temperatures are lower. Towns and cities in general are much more cyclist-friendly than their counterparts in other parts of the Mediterranean. In some tourist centres such as Protaras there are urban bicycle paths.

Rental

Bicycles can be hired in most areas but particularly in the Troödos where they are usually flashy, multi-geared mountain bike types. Rates start from around CY£2.50 a day. Bike hire is also very popular in the Agia Napa resort area.

Purchase

You can purchase a decent bike in the Republic if you are that keen, though you would be better looking at one of the specialist shops in Lefkosia, if you really want to invest in pedal-powered wheels. Try Zanettos Bicycles in Lefkosia. Northern Cyprus will offer less of a choice when it comes to purchasing a bicycle. Better not count on it.

HITCHING

Hitching is never entirely safe in any country in the world, and we don't recommend it. Travellers who decide to hitch should understand that they are taking a small but potentially serious risk. People who do choose to hitch will be safer if they travel in pairs and let someone know where they are planning to go.

Hitching in Cyprus is easy but not very common. In rural areas where bus transport is poor, many locals hitch to and from their businesses in the city. If you do decide to hitch, either due to enforced circumstances or just for fun, take the obvious measures to make your task easier. Stand in a prominent position with an obvious space for a ride-giver to pull in. Keep your luggage to a minimum, display your national flag if you have one, look clean and smart and above all happy. A smile goes a long way.

Hitching in the North is more likely to be hampered by a lack of long distance traffic than anything else and, in any case, public transport costs are low enough to essentially obviate the need to hitch as a regular form of transport.

LOCAL TRANSPORT
Bus

While local bus services exist in Lefkosia, Lemesos, Larnaka and Famagusta, about the only place where they are going to be of any practical use is in Lemesos, where buses to and from the port may be of some help to travellers. Buses also run to and from Kourion from Lemesos Fort, though these are tourist buses designed to get travellers from Lemesos out to the sights around Kourion rather than to move locals around. Distances between sights in most towns and cities are fairly short, so obviate the need to depend on the bus service to any great degree.

Taxi

Taxis in the South are available on a 24-hour basis and can be hailed from the street or booked ahead by phone. All taxis are equipped with meters and drivers are obliged to use them. There are two tariff periods: 6 am to 8.30 pm (Tariff 1) and 8.30 pm to 6 am (Tariff 2). Tariff 1 charges are CY£0.65 flag fall and CY£0.22 per kilometre. Tariff 2 charges are CY£0.88 flag fall and CY£0.26 per kilometre. Luggage is charged at the rate of CY£0.22 for every piece weighing more than 12kg. Extra charges of CY£0.55 per fare apply during most public holidays.

In the North taxis do not sport meters so agree on the fare with the driver beforehand. As a rough guide expect to pay around TL1 million for a ride around any of the towns.

Service Taxi

Service taxis, which take up to eight people, are run by a number of private firms and you'll usually find at least one of them operating on Sunday. You can get to most places in the Republic, but often not direct. The fixed fares are still competitive with bus travel. Either go to the taxi office or telephone to be picked up at your hotel.

Some of the major companies in each town are:

A Makris Tourist Taxi
Lefkosia: (☎ 02-766 201) Leoforos Stasinou 11
Lemesos: (☎ 05-362 555) Hellas 166
Larnaka: (☎ 04-652 929) Vasileos Pavlou 13
Pafos: (☎ 06-232 538) Grammou 2
Acropolis Vasos Taxi Co Ltd
Lefkosia: (☎ 02-760 111) Leoforos Stasinou 11
Larnaka: (☎ 04-655 555) Leoforos Makariou III 1
Lemesos: (☎ 05-366 766) Spyrou Araouzou 49
Karydas Taxi
Lefkosia: (☎ 02-755 353) Leoforos Omirou 8
Lemesos: (☎ 05-362 061) Thessalonikis 21
Pafos: (☎ 06-233 181) Leoforos E Pallikaridi 8
Kypros Taxi Co Ltd
Lefkosia: (☎ 02-751 811) Leoforos Stasinou 9c

Lemesos: (☎ 05-363 979) Hristou Hatzipavlou 193
Kyriakos Taxi Co Ltd
Lefkosia: (☎ 02-754 141) Leoforos Stasinou 27
Lemesos: (☎ 05-364 114) Thessalonikis 21
Pafos: (☎ 06-233 181) Leoforos E Pallikaridi 9
Panikos Taxi Office
Lefkosia: (☎ 02-464 720) Nikokleous 21
Pafos: (☎ 06-232 533) Leoforos Makariou III 157

Northern Cyprus only has service taxis between Kyrenia and North Nicosia (TL6 million). Normal (more expensive) taxis are also everywhere. As a rough guide, a taxi ride from Kyrenia to Famagusta will cost around TL20 million, from North Nicosia to Famagusta TL16 million.

'Tourist' taxis that await you near the Turkish Cypriot checkpoint at the Ledra Palace Hotel will take you anywhere you want to go. A round day tour to Kyrenia, Famagusta, Bellapais, Buffavento and St Hilarion will cost around CY£30.

ORGANISED TOURS

Travel agencies around the country offer a wide variety of prepackaged excursions. One of the better known operators is National Tours (☎ 02-678 000, fax 671 175, @ tourism@louisgroup.com), based in Lefkosia. Tours normally run out of the main tourist centres and range from full day tours out of Pafos to Troödos and the Kykkos Monastery for CY£13.50, day trips to Lefkosia from Agia Napa or Larnaka for CY£13, boat trips to Protoras from Agia Napa for CY£10 and half day tours of Lemesos city, a winery and Ancient Kourion for CY£9.

Further information and bookings can be obtained and made at Louis Cruise Centre offices in the following towns:

Lemesos (☎ 05-340 000)
Larnaka (☎ 04-652 2320)
Agia Napa (☎ 03-721 560)
Pafos (☎ 06-246 245)

THE REPUBLIC
OF CYPRUS

Lefkosia Λευκωσία

☎ 02 • postcode 2000 • pop 193,000

Lefkosia (formerly Nicosia and known as Lefkoşa in Turkish) is the capital of Cyprus, and is often underrated and inappropriately described. It admittedly bears the ignominy of being the world's last divided city – split more or less evenly between the Turkish-occupied North and the Republican South. Berlin too was once divided, but eventually saw better days – a wish still fervently held by both Greek and Turkish residents.

It can be searingly hot in summer and relief by the sea is as far away as you can get, but it is a lively, livable city with fine restaurants, bars and cafes. Southern Lefkosia is sophisticated and worldly, with fine, tree-lined boulevards and an engaging mix of modern and old buildings. North Nicosia still retains its old-world charm and has changed very little since the city was forcibly divided in 1974. Either way its residents are not jaded by the excesses of packaged tourism and they bestow a warm welcome to visitors, whichever side of the line they live. Cyprus' capital deserves a few days of your time.

HISTORY

Lefkosia has always been the capital of Cyprus. It was established in the middle of the wide Mesaoria plain on the Pedieos River primarily for defence purposes. The city was originally known as Ledra and grew extensively during the Byzantine period. The Venetians built the defensive walls around the city, however these did little to keep the Ottomans out in 1570. Life in Lefkosia under the Ottomans saw little growth and only when the British took control in 1878 did the city begin to spread beyond the walls.

Violence inspired by the National Organisation for the Cypriot Struggle (EOKA) against the British in the '50s and '60s saw considerable carnage on the streets of Lefkosia. Intercommunal disturbances between Greek and Turkish Cypriots in 1963

HIGHLIGHTS

- Explore the Venetian Ramparts that surround the city.
- Delve into Cyprus' ancient past at the Cyprus Museum.
- Take a day trip to the Mesaoria villages where living is at a relaxed pace.

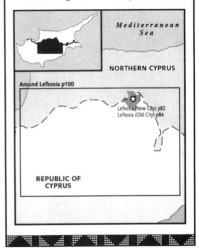

brought a de facto partition of the city. The so-called 'Green Line' came into being at this time when the British military defined the Greek and Turkish areas using a green pen on a military map. The name has stuck to this day. The Turkish invasion of 1974 finally divided the city and it has remained so ever since, chaperoned by the watchful but increasingly weary eyes of the UN peacekeeping forces.

ORIENTATION

The Old City is inside the 16th-century Venetian wall and is the most interesting area for visitors; the New City sprawls outwards south of the wall. Reduced in height and dissected by wide thoroughfares, the

81

LEFKOSIA

LEFKOSIA (NEW CITY)

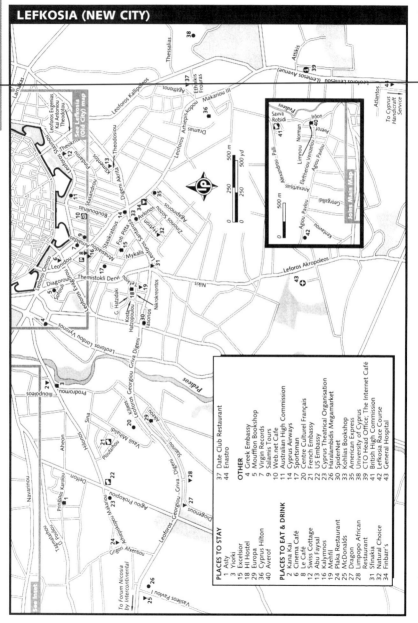

PLACES TO STAY
1 Asty
3 Yiorki
15 Excelsior
18 HI Hostel
29 Europa
36 Cyprus Hilton
40 Averof

PLACES TO EAT & DRINK
6 Kana Kai
7 Cinema Café
8 Le Café
12 Swiss Cottage
16 Abu Faysal
19 Mehfil
24 Plaka Restaurant
25 McDonalds
27 Dragon
28 Limpopo African
   Restaurant
31 Sfinakia
32 Natural Choice
34 Finbarr's
37 Date Club Restaurant
44 Enastro

OTHER
4 Greek Embassy
5 Mouflon Bookshop
9 Virgin Records
10 Web.net Café
11 Australian High Commission
14 Cyprus Airways
17 Sportsman
20 Centre Culturel Français
21 French Embassy
22 US Embassy
23 Cyprus Theatrical Organisation
26 Haralambidis Megamarket
30 SpiderNet
33 Kohlias Bookshop
35 American Express
38 University of Cyprus
39 CTO Head Office; The Internet Café
41 British High Commission
42 Lefkosia Race Course
43 General Hospital

wall is hardly visible in places. The town centre is Plateia Eleftherias on the south-western edge of the wall. The UN crossover point (Ledra Palace Hotel checkpoint) is at the far west and Famagusta Gate is to the east. At the base of the wall there are car parks and municipal gardens. See the North Nicosia chapter for orientation tips on that half of the city.

Maps

The Cyprus Tourist Organisation (CTO) has a fairly reasonable map of *Lefkosia City Centre* and, on the reverse side, *Major Lefkosia*. This is available free from all CTO offices. The *Street & Tourist Map of Nicosia* has a much better coverage of the outer suburbs and also has a street index. This map is available from most bookshops or stationery shops in Lefkosia or from SELAS Ltd, PO Box 8619, Lefkosia.

Some bookshops do stock a street directory of sorts but it is fairly poorly produced and not of much practical value. Public street map displays of the 'You Are Here' kind are found around central Lefkosia.

INFORMATION
Tourist Offices

The CTO (☎ 444 264) in the Old City is in Laïki Yitonia, a fairly touristy, restored area. It is open 8.30 am to 4 pm Monday to Friday and 8.30 am to 2 pm on Saturday. The CTO head office (☎ 337 715, fax 331 644) is in the New City at Leoforos Lemesou 19, though it is not really geared to handling over-the-counter queries from the public.

Money

The Hellenic Bank (Solonos 1a), near the CTO, provides an afternoon tourist service from 2.30 to 6.30 pm Monday to Friday in winter, and until 8 pm in June, July and August.

There are a couple of ATMs at the northern end of Lidras that accept most cards, though most banks in the New City will equally accept your plastic and dispense ready cash.

The American Express office (☎ 765 607) is at Agapinoros 2d in the New City

and it is open 8.30 am to 5 pm Monday to Friday and 9 am to 1.30 pm on Saturday.

Post

The central post office is on Leoforos Konstantinou Paleologou, close to Plateia Eleftherias. Opening hours are 7.30 am to 1.30 pm and 3 to 6 pm weekdays (closed Wednesday afternoon) and 8.30 to 10.30 am on Saturday. There is also a smaller post office close to the northern end of Lidras near the Green Line lookout and a branch on Digeni Akrita in the New City (off map). Poste restante mail is held at the Plateia Eleftherias office.

Telephone

The main telephone centre in Lefkosia is the Cyprus Telecommunications Authority (CYTA) close to Pafos Gate. You have no real cause to go there since public phones are widely available around the city, with a large concentration on Plateia Eleftherias. There are basically two types: the coin-operated British Telecom style phones and the phonecard-only CYTA phones. There are no street kiosks (*periptera*) for making phone calls as in Greece and credit card phones are nonexistent. The CYTA office does have some phone booths both inside and outside the building.

Fax

It is not easy to send a fax from a public service in Lefkosia or anywhere in Cyprus for that matter. CYTA does not provide such a service nor does the post office. Your best bet is your hotel. Otherwise check if any bookshops or stationers offer a fax service. Failing that, consider using an Internet cafe and one of the Web fax service providers like Faxaway (see www.faxaway .com) which is great for text files, but not much use for paper documents unless you can get them scanned.

Email & Internet Access

In the Old City, Cyber Cafe (❷ theatro@ Cyber-cafe.spidernet.com.cy) is at Vasiliou Voulgaroktonou 15a, open from 3 pm daily; and in the New City there's Web.net Cafe

LEFKOSIA (OLD CITY)

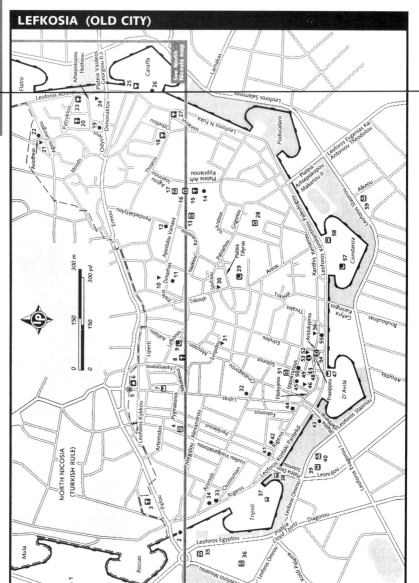

LEFKOSIA (OLD CITY)

PLACES TO STAY
33 Holiday Inn
34 Best Western Classic Hotel
44 Regina Palace
50 Tony's Bed & Breakfast

PLACES TO EAT & DRINK
10 Agios Georgios Taverna
18 Odos Othellou
21 Taverna Axiothea
23 Orpheas
24 To Steki tis Chrysaliniotissas
25 Bastione
27 Ithaki
30 Zanettos Taverna
31 Estiatorio Savvas
46 To Pyrofani
52 Xefoto
56 Arhondiko

OTHER
1 Checkpoint (Ledra Palace Hotel)
2 Pafos Gate
3 Holy Cross Catholic Church

4 Cyber Cafe
5 Lidras St Lookout
6 Police Station
7 Post Office
8 Faneromeni Church
9 Arablar Mosque
11 Municipal Market
12 Lefkosia Municipal Arts Centre
13 Makarios Cultural Foundation
14 Archbishop's Palace
15 Agios Ioannis Church
16 Folk Art Museum
17 National Struggle Museum
19 Chrysaliniotissa Crafts Centre
20 Panagia Hrysaliniotissa Church
22 University of Cyprus Workshop Theatre (THEPAK)
26 Famagusta Gate
28 Dragoman Hatzigeorgakis Museum
29 Omeriye Mosque
32 Woolworths; Ledra Museum-Observatory
35 CYTA Telephone Office
36 Cyprus Museum

37 Bus to Polis
38 City & Kallenos (to Larnaka & Agros) Bus Stations
39 Kemek Bus Station (to Pafos, Platres & Lemesos)
40 Kyriakos Service Taxi
41 Andreas Papaeracleous Photo Store
42 Cyprus Handicraft and Souvenirs
43 Foreign-language Newspaper Kiosks
45 Express Dry Cleaners
47 Central Post Office
48 Hellenic Bank
49 Laïki Yitonia
51 Leventis Municipal Museum
53 CTO
54 Cyprus Jewellers Museum
55 Cyprus Handicrafts Centre
57 Bayraktar Mosque
58 Klarios & EMAN Bus Station (to Troödos & Agia Napa)
59 Service Taxis to Lemesos & Larnaka

(✉ webnet1@dial.cylink.com.cy) at Stasandrou 10c, open from 10.30 am Monday to Saturday and 5.30 pm on Sunday.

In the New City is the inconveniently situated Internet Cafe (☎ 339 936, ✉ info@internetcafe.com.cy) at Leoforos Lemesou 17a. It is open noon to 2 am on weekdays and 2 pm to 2 am on weekends.

Travel Agencies

While there is a large number of travel agencies throughout Lefkosia, none of them is likely to offer significant price advantages over the others. Salamis Tours Ltd (☎ 762 3232, fax 758 337) at Arnaldas 7c in the New City handles ferry tickets for Salamis Lines and arranges airline tickets and other travel-related bookings.

Bookshops

There are only a few bookshops in Lefkosia that may be of interest to the foreign visitor. Foremost among these is the Moufflon Bookshop (☎ 665 155, fax 668 703, ✉ moufflon@spidernet.com.cy) at Sofouli 1. This shop deals primarily in English-

language titles – both new and second-hand – and stocks a sprinkling of the more popular regional LP guides. It has a good section of books on Cyprus – both in English and in Greek.

Kohlias Bookshop (☎ 461 766, fax 446 258) at Avlonos 9 specialises in art books and Cypriot publications, while the Soloneio Book Centre, a little way out of the centre at Vyzantiou 24 in Strovolos, might also serve your needs.

Foreign-language newspapers and magazines can be found at either of the Periptero Hellas or Miltis & Evgenis kiosks on the west side of Plateia Eleftherias.

Libraries

At least five public or semi-public libraries in Lefkosia are open for only research and reading – you cannot borrow and take home books.

Ahilleios Library (☎ 473 033) Konstantinou Paleologou 30
Makarios Cultural Centre Library (☎ 430 008)

Lefkosia Municipal Arts Centre Library
(☎ 432 577) Apostolou Varnava 19
Ministry of Education Library (☎ 303 180)
Konstantinou Paleologou
Severios Library (☎ 344 888) Plateia
Arhiepiskopou Kyprianou

Universities

The only university in Cyprus is on the south-eastern side of the New City. The University of Cyprus was established in 1989 and admitted its first students in 1992. There are four faculties, twelve departments and one archaeology research unit. It currently trains around 2300 undergraduate students. It has a Web page (www.ucy.ac .cy) where you can check out undergraduate and postgraduate courses offered by the University. For information on courses, contact External Affairs and Projects (☎ 488 529, fax 488 980, ☻ admin@ucy.ac.cy) at PO Box 200537, CY-1678 or Kallipoleos, Lefkosia, or check out the university's Web site at www.ucy.ac.cy.

Cultural Centres

A number of cultural centres offer a wide range of periodicals and books for reference. These are:

American Center (☎ 473 145) Leoforos
Omirou 33b
British Council (☎ 442 152) Mouseiou 3
Centre Culturel Français (☎ 317 771)
Z Kitieos 5
Göthe Institut – German Cultural Centre
(☎ 462 608) Markou Drakou 21
Russian Cultural Centre (☎ 441 607) Alasias 16

Laundry

Express Dry Cleaners at Ippokratous 49 in the Old City will do a service wash for you.

Toilets

Public toilets are scattered along the walls of the Venetian Ramparts; the nearest ones to the centre are by Plateia Eleftherias. There are also toilets in the Laïki Yitonia, near the CTO office. Public toilets are generally clean and well maintained. If really stuck, slip into the toilets in a bar or restaurant. No-one will really mind.

Left Luggage

There are no organised left-luggage facilities in Lefkosia. If you need to dump your bags for a few hours, try your hotel, an accommodating restaurant or even a travel agency.

Medical Services

Emergency medical treatment and assistance is provided free of charge at government hospitals or medical institutions. However, payment of the prescribed fees is required for out-patient and in-patient treatment. Make sure your medical insurance covers any emergency. Lefkosia's General Hospital (☎ 801 400) is on Leoforos Akropoleos, about 2km south of the Old City. The hospital's ambulance service can be reached on ☎ 810 475.

If you need a private doctor ring ☎ 1422. Private doctors' visiting hours are normally 9 am to 1 pm and 4 to 7 pm. Local newspapers list pharmacies which are open during the night and on weekends and holidays as well as the names of private doctors who are on call out of normal hours.

Emergency

The police station (☎ 477 434) in the Old City is at the northern end of Lidras, by the barrier. The emergency number for the police, fire service or an ambulance is ☎ 199. The number for the Narcotics Emergency Service is ☎ 1410 and the AIDS Advisory Centre is ☎ 305 515.

Dangers & Annoyances

Lefkosia is a remarkably safe city to walk around. The Old City streets, particularly near the Green Line, can appear dingy and threatening at night and solo women may be best advised to avoid them for fear of minor verbal harassment that may occur. Steer clear of edgy soldiers at UN and Greek Cypriot checkpoints and keep your camera well hidden. While it is next to impossible to inadvertently stray across the Green Line in the Old City, there are still the occasional reports of foreigners unwittingly (or perhaps even wittingly) crossing the line at less well-guarded points in the western and eastern sectors of the New City.

WALKING TOUR

Lefkosia has a number of activities to keep the visitor occupied for a few days. The New City is modern, clean and well-suited for shopping sprees or taking in a meal at a fine restaurant. Most of the sights are within the Old City and are listed here in more or less west to east order. Allow yourself at least two days to see most of the major sights, three days for the full treatment. To better orient yourself with the Old City, take one of the CTO guided walking tours, or pick up the CTO Walking Tours brochures and do it yourself (see boxed text 'Walking Tour of Old Lefkosia').

THE VENETIAN RAMPARTS

This circular defence wall which surrounds all of Old Lefkosia – North and South – while impressive looking, failed in the purpose for which it was originally built. The Venetian rulers erected the wall between 1567 and 1570 with the express aim of keeping the feared Ottoman Turk invaders out of Lefkosia. The appointed engineer Ascanio Savorgnano designed the ramparts and Francesco Barbaro built the walls to specifications, while adding 11 fortifying bastions spaced equally around the ramparts for added protection. A moat was also dug, though it was never apparently intended to contain water. In July 1570 the Ottomans landed in Larnaka and three months later attacked Lefkosia, storming the fortifications.

They have remained in place more or less unchanged ever since. Five of the bastions – the **Tripoli**, the **D'Avila**, the **Constanza**, the **Podocataro** and the **Caraffa** bastions – are still in the southern sector of Lefkosia. The **Flatro** bastion on the east side of the Old City is occupied by both Turkish, Greek Cypriot and UN military forces, while the remaining bastions – the **Loredano** (Cevizli), the **Barbaro** (Musalla), the **Quirini** (Cephane), the **Mula** (Zahra) and Roccas (Kaytazağa) bastions (see the Roccas Bastion section later in this chapter) – are in North Nicosia.

The ramparts and moat in Lefkosia are in excellent condition and are used variously to provide car parking space, venues for

Walking Tour of Old Lefkosia

Perhaps the best way to get to know the layout of the Old City is to take one of the free walking tours that depart from the CTO at 10 am every Monday, Tuesday and Thursday. The three routes are also listed in the CTO's *Walking Tours* brochure and can easily be done on your own. Otherwise, the following will take you along some of the main streets of the Old City and past many of its museums. (See individual item entries for full details.)

From Plateia Eleftherias follow Lidras and turn right onto Ippokratous. At No 17 is the **Leventis Municipal Museum**, which traces the city's development from prehistoric times to the present.

Continue to the end of Ippokratous, turn left onto Thrakis and take the dogleg onto Trikoupi. Soon you'll see the **Omeriye Mosque** on your right. Turn right onto Plateia Tyllirias and shortly after you will meet Patriarhou Grigoriou. About 125m along this street on the right is the 18th-century house of **Dragoman Hatzigeorgakis**, which is now a museum.

The next left leads to Plateia Arhiepiskopou Kyprianou, dominated by the Archbishop's Palace and a colossal statue of Makarios III. Here you'll find the Makarios Cultural Foundation, comprising the **European Art Gallery**, the **Greek Independence War Gallery** and the **Byzantine Art Museum**. In the grounds of the Foundation is Agios Ioannis Church, which was built in 1662 and has the most wonderful frescoes dating from 1736. Next door is the **Folk Art Museum**, and still nearby is the **National Struggle Museum**.

Continue north along Agiou Ioannou and turn right onto Thiseos, which leads onto Leoforos N Foka. Turn left and you'll see the imposing **Famagusta Gate**, which was once the main entrance to the city. The most direct way back to Laïki Yitonia is to take Leoforos N Foka, following the signposts to the CTO.

outdoor concerts, strolling and relaxing. In the North the walls are in poorer shape and have become overgrown and dilapidated in parts. Three gates originally punctured the walls: the Famagusta Gate in the east, the Pafos Gate in the west (see sections later in this chapter) and the **Kyrenia (Girne) Gate** in the north. Vehicle access roads at various points around the ramparts now allow regular traffic access to the Old City.

CYPRUS MUSEUM

This museum (☎ 865 888) houses the best collection of archaeological finds in Cyprus. The original building, erected in 1883, is looking tired but the collection is exemplary.

Highlights include a remarkable display of **terracotta figures** found in 1929 at Agia Irini, north of Morfou in Northern Cyprus. These figures are displayed as found and are presumed to have come from a warrior caste perhaps practising a fertility cult in the 7th to 6th centuries BC. All the figures are male and most have helmets. Another highlight is a collection of three limestone lions and two sphinxes found in the **Tamassos necropolis** in the central Mesaoria district. The statues show a definite Egyptian influence and were only discovered in 1997. They date from the Cypro-Archaic II period (475–400 BC).

Look out also for the famous **Aphrodite of Soli** statue marketed widely as the 'face of Cyprus' on tourist posters and also on the CY£5 banknote. An enormous bronze statue of the **Emperor Septimus Severus**, found at Kytherea in 1928, is the main exhibit in room 6 and can hardly be overlooked. Don't miss the fascinating display of **Cypriot mining and metallurgy** history tucked away in room 13. It makes a refreshing diversion from the abundant but often dry exhibits of bowls, craters and statuettes from Cyprus' more distant archaeological past.

The museum's opening hours are 9 am to 5 pm Monday to Saturday and 10 am to 1 pm on Sunday. Entry is CY£1.50. It's on Leoforos Mouseiou, a 10-minute walk west of Plateia Eleftherias.

THE LEDRA PALACE HOTEL CROSSING

People come here in droves to gawk at the only spot on the whole of the island where you may cross into the North. To the right and just before the Greek Cypriot police checkpoints are the remains of a ruined building, ostensibly once the **Karpasia Restaurant** which occasionally is reincarnated and used as a summer *mezes* joint. Its roofless interior is now filled with abundant graffiti and a cement wall at the rear of the outside courtyard, covered with more graffiti, sports a couple of viewing holes where you may observe life on the other side of the line across what used to be a sports field.

The crossing itself is partially blocked by a blue and white painted wall with graphic posters depicting the murder of three Greek Cypriots by Turkish counter-demonstrators near Deryneia in the eastern part of the island in 1996. On Sunday mornings Cypriot women gather to remember the 1974 invasion and hand out literature to the accompaniment of suitable songs of lamentation and protest.

While crossing to the North is legal and practised by many visitors (see the boxed text 'Crossing the Thin Green Line'), it is tacitly not encouraged and the Greek Cypriot police who register your departure do so with a resigned look of disapproval. The crossing itself is about 300m long and is bordered by barbed and razor wire for the entire length. To the left as you head north is the bullet-ridden former Ledra Palace Hotel, now occupied more or less permanently by the UN. Abandoned shops lie to the right. A white iron gate marks the entry to Turkish Cypriot-controlled territory after which lies the fairly innocuous Turkish Cypriot checkpoint building itself. A prominent sign welcomes you to the 'Turkish Republic of Northern Cyprus' while another equally prominent sign reminds you that the 'TRNC is here to stay'.

ROCCAS BASTION

The Roccas Bastion is unique throughout the whole of Cyprus in that it is the only place where Greek and Turkish Cypriots may eyeball each other at close quarters. It is situated about 200m south of the Ledra Palace Hotel crossing point and is easily

Crossing the Thin Green Line

Crossing to the North on a day trip is legal and is a fairly uncomplicated exercise. Visitors may cross between 8 am and 1 pm but must be back on the south side of the Line before 5 pm. If you are late coming home you will most likely be allowed in, but your name will be placed on the 'black list' and you will not be allowed to cross to the North again.

There is a set procedure. Present yourself at the second police office by the Ledra Palace Hotel crossing. Show your passport. If you hold two passports show the one that you used to enter Cyprus. Your name will be entered in a log. If you have a local contact phone number (your hotel number will do) it is good to be able to supply it. If you are travelling with your own vehicle – not Cyprus-registered or a hire car – there are no formalities at this end. You are now free to cross.

The UN personnel, while maintaining a checkpoint, rarely if ever check crossing travellers. Your next stop is the Turkish Cypriot police control. Present your passport and details will be entered into a computer. You will be directed to the day pass office (to the right and upstairs on the 1st floor, office on the left). Fill in a brief form, return to the police control and surrender your pass. Keep the larger white day pass receipt. You will need it when exiting. If you have your own vehicle you will be required to pay day insurance for C£2 (C£4 for a week). If there are no queues, the whole procedure should take no more than 15 minutes. You are now free to enter the North.

This is all well and good if you are a neutral foreigner. If you are Greek, have a Greek surname or the Turkish authorities suspect that you have Greek heritage, you will have problems and you will be turned back, unless you have previously applied for a visa. If your non-Greek passport shows your place of birth as being possibly in Greece or Cyprus, it will be scrutinised.

One Greek-born visitor on an Australian passport was asked where she was from. 'Greece' she replied, 'Macedonia'. She was born in Kozani in northern Greece and it showed on her passport. 'Greece or Macedonia?' queried the now suspicious police officer. 'Macedonia' she replied not un-truthfully. 'In that case' replied the seemingly assuaged officer with a smug, wry smile, 'it is OK. If it was Greece, there would be a *big* problem'. At least one Greek-born Australian managed to slip behind the Green Line for a furtive visit.

identifiable by signs prohibiting parking adjacent to the bastion walls. Look up and you will see barbed wire fencing and more often than not a clutch of curious Turkish Cypriot faces looking down into what for them is forbidden territory. The UN buffer zone separating the two sides by a normally comfortable margin virtually disappears here for a stretch of about 200m, while the border of Turkish-controlled Northern Cyprus ends at the very edge of this bastion.

Most passers-by studiously avoid making eye contact with the curious onlookers on the Turkish Cypriot side, though a waved greeting will more often than not attract a smile and friendly wave in return. If you are heading for North Nicosia on foot you can easily reach the Roccas Bastion (Kaytazağa Burcu) from the Turkish Cypriot side. Turn right after the Turkish Cypriot checkpoint

and 100m further on turn right again inside the Old City onto Zahra Sokak. The entrance to the public park built on the bastion is on your right. Do not be tempted to take photographs. Vigilant Turkish soldiers hidden away in the corner of the park will soon be on to you if you try to take a surreptitious picture. There is a little snack and newspaper stand in the park.

THE PAFOS GATE

This gate, known by the Venetians as the Porta Domenica, is the third of the traditional entrances to Old Lefkosia. The other two are the Famagusta Gate and the **Kyrenia (Girne) Gate** in North Nicosia. The gate as such, left firmly open, guards a narrow pedestrian passage under the wall. The adjoining breach in the wall that allows traffic into the Old City is a much later addition.

HOLY CROSS CATHOLIC CHURCH

Across the road from the Pafos Gate on Pafou, this church carries the unfortunate status of having its rear end stuck smack bang up against the Turkish sector and lies within the UN buffer zone. Despite these inauspicious conditions, the church still functions as a place of worship on the proviso that the back door leading onto the Turkish-controlled sector remains firmly closed. Mass times are posted inside the front door vestibule.

FANEROMENI CHURCH

This impressive structure was built in 1872 on the site of an ancient orthodox nunnery and is the largest church within the city walls. The **Marble Mausoleum** on the eastern side of the church was built in memory of martyrs of the newly declared Greek War of Independence and who were executed by the Turks in 1821.

THE GREEN LINE

While you can hardly miss the Green Line if you walk anywhere north in Lefkosia, in practice there is not a lot to see. UN and Greek Cypriot **bunkers** punctuate the Line across the city and you are not supposed to approach them too closely. The CTO signposted walking tour takes you hard up to the Line at the far eastern side of the city close to the military-controlled **Flatro Bastion**. Take the last turn left off Leoforos Athinas along Agiou Georgiou and look for the little street on the right with Taverna Axiothea (see the Places to Eat section later in this chapter). Walk to the end of Axiothea and squeeze through the gap into the next street, following the walking tour sign. You won't see a soul on the other side, but you may hear the call of the muezzin from the mosque. An area of particular desolation and destruction is towards the end of **Pendadaktylou** where it meets **Ermou**, the street that originally bisected the old city more or less equally into two. You will only meet an edgy soldier or two so keep your camera well hidden.

Most visitors head for the **Lidras St lookout**. From here you can peer over a wall at a streetscape left as it was on 20 July 1974. Look for the many bullet holes and observe the Turkish and Turkish Cypriot flags fluttering no more than 100m distant. No photographs are allowed here and you are most certainly not allowed to proceed any further. Apart from possibly provoking an international incident, it is thought that many of the streets and ruined buildings are booby-trapped with mines.

THE BAYRAKTAR MOSQUE

This prominent mosque, situated on the Constanza Bastion, marks the spot where the Venetian Walls were successfully breached by the Ottomans in 1570. The Ottoman standard bearer (for whom the mosque is named in Turkish) was immediately cut down by the defending forces but his body was subsequently recovered and buried on this spot. The mosque has been the target for terrorist activity. In the early 1960s EOKA-inspired attacks damaged the mosque and nearby tomb of the standard bearer, but it was eventually repaired and the mosque closed to the general public. As late as 1999 a plot was uncovered to bomb the mosque, though it is alleged that the would-be perpetrators were in fact Muslims who presumably had ulterior motives to stir up Greek-Turkish tensions.

ARABLAR MOSQUE

You could almost miss this diminutive mosque, squirreled away as it is on Lefkosia's backstreets. In Lusignan times it was the church of the Stavros tou Misirikou. The building, which is on Lefkonos, no longer open to the public so visits are not possible.

LEVENTIS MUNICIPAL MUSEUM

This is a small historical museum (☎ 451 474) at Ippokratous 17 with exhibits dating from before 2000 BC to the present day. Opening times used to be 10 am to 4.30 pm Tuesday to Sunday and entry was free, but the museum was undergoing a massive renovation at the time of research, so future operating hours are unknown. There is a gift shop in the museum.

THE LAÏKI YITONIA

It's twee, fairly expensive, touristy and busy, but it looks prettier than most of old Lefkosia. The Laïki Yitonia (Popular Neighbourhood) is a refurbished part of the Old City designed to catch the tourist trade with shops and restaurants. It's a bit like the Plaka district of Athens but smaller and without the backdrop of the Acropolis. You can traverse the whole area in no more than 10 minutes during which time restaurant touts will attempt to lure you into their establishments to eat. There is a wide choice of eating places, but a surprising dearth of outdoor cafeterias or bars where you can sit down and have a cold beer or an iced coffee. The CTO has an office here and you can stock up on most maps and other tourist brochures free of charge.

CYPRUS JEWELLERS MUSEUM

This small display centre in the Laïki Yitonia (Praxippou 7–9) presents the history of jewellery from the end of the 19th century to today. The exhibits include ornaments, religious items, silver utensils and old tools. It is open 10 am to 4 pm Monday to Friday and admission is free.

THE LEDRA
MUSEUM-OBSERVATORY

This unusual museum (☎ 679 396) is on the 11th floor of the Shakolas Tower, which houses the Woolworths department store, on the corner of Lidras and Arsinoi. You can use telescopes and gaze at the whole of Lefkosia from a particularly good vantage point. It is the only point where you can see over into North Nicosia to any degree. It is open 10 am to 8.30 pm daily and costs CY£0.20.

THE OMERIYE MOSQUE

This structure, dating from the 14th century, was originally the Augustinian Church of St Mary but was destroyed by the Ottomans as they entered Nicosia in 1570. The church was subsequently restored as a mosque based on a belief that this was the spot where the Muslim prophet Omer rested in the 7th century. Its rather tall minaret can be easily spotted some distance away and

entrance to the mosque is from about halfway along Trikoupi. Today the mosque is used primarily as a place of worship by visiting Muslims from neighbouring Arab countries. Non-Muslims may of course visit as long you observe the general etiquette required when visiting mosques – dress conservatively, ie, no surplus flesh showing, leave your shoes at the door and avoid official prayer times. The mosque is open 10 am to 12.30 pm and 1.30 to 3.30 pm Monday to Saturday

DRAGOMAN HATZIGEORGAKIS MUSEUM

This well-preserved and richly restored mansion at Patriarhou Grigoriou belonged to Kornesios, the Great Dragoman of Cyprus from 1779 to 1809. A *dragoman* was an 'interpreter' (Turkish *tercüman*), or liaison officer between the Ottoman and Orthodox authorities. Kornesios was a particularly wealthy and influential dragoman – said to be the most powerful man in Cyprus at the time. His lavish excess was his undoing. A peasant revolt in 1804 forced him out of Cyprus. Returning from exile five years later he was accused of treason, beheaded and his property was confiscated. Today only really one room is set up as mock living quarters and it is spread with rich floor coverings and decorations. The rest of the mansion is given over to displays of antiques and other Ottoman memorabilia.

The museum is open from 8 am to 2 pm Monday to Friday and 9 am to 1 pm on Saturday. Admission costs CY£0.50.

THE ARCHBISHOP'S PALACE

This mock Venetian building on Plateia Arhiespikopou Kyprianou was the scene of much fighting during the 1956 disturbances and latterly during the 1974 military coup and subsequent Turkish invasion of the North. While not generally open to the public, the building is the official residence of the Archbishop of Cyprus. The present building dates from 1974 when the original palace was badly damaged by the fighting. The Palace is overshadowed by an alarmingly massive and looming black **statue of**

Archbishop Makarios which stares out impassively over the square.

MAKARIOS CULTURAL FOUNDATION

This complex (☎ 430 008) on Plateia Arhiespikopou Kyprianou consists of three main exhibit areas. The **European Art Gallery** presents 120 oil paintings of various European schools of art from the 16th to the 19th centuries. The themes are mainly religious with works by Van Dyck, Rubens, Tintoretto, Lorraine and Delacroix. It is open 9 am to 4.30 pm Monday to Friday and 9 am to 1 pm on Saturday.

Nearby is the **Greek Independence War Gallery** which contains maps, copper engravings and paintings featuring persons and events from the Greek War of Independence in 1821. The **Byzantine Art Museum** has the largest collection of icons related to Cyprus. There are some 220 pieces on exhibition, covering several periods from the 5th to the 19th centuries. Among the more interesting items on display are the icons of **Christ & the Virgin Mary** (12th century) from the Church of the Virgin Mary of Arakas at Lagoudera and the **Resurrection** (13th century) from the Church of St John Lambadistis Monastery at Kalopanayiotis. In addition, there are six examples of the Kanakaria Mosaics.

FOLK ART MUSEUM

Close to the Makarios Cultural Foundation, this small museum is the main folk art and ethnographic museum in the country. The building dates back to the 15th century though some later additions have been made. Here you will see fine examples of embroidery, lace, costumes, pottery, metalwork, basketry, folk painting, leatherwork and woodcarving. The museum is open 9 am to 5 pm Monday to Friday and 10 am to 1 pm on Saturday.

NATIONAL STRUGGLE MUSEUM

This display is really for die-hard history buffs. The museum (☎ 304 550) displays documents, photos and other memorabilia from the often bloody 1955–59 National Liberation Struggle against the British. The museum is open 8 am to 2 pm and 3 to 6 pm Monday to Friday. It is at Kinyras 7.

LEFKOSIA MUNICIPAL ARTS CENTRE

For something a little less cerebral than the museums, duck into the little arcade to the right of the National Struggle Museum and head along Apostolou Varnava for one block to this hip little arts centre. Its air-conditioned interior contains an occasionally bizarre but mostly fascinating collection of art. At the time of inspection there were displays of modern clothes and furniture, packaging, cameras and cars. The centre also has a coffee shop and art library for visitors.

Opening times are 10 am to 3 pm and 5 to 11 pm Tuesday to Saturday and 10 am to 4 pm Sunday. Entry is free but donations are welcomed.

PANAGIA HRYSALINIOTISSA

This church is dedicated to the Virgin Mary and means 'Our Lady of the Golden Flax' in Greek. It is considered to be the oldest Byzantine church in Lefkosia and was built in 1450 by Queen Helena Paleologos. It is renowned for its rich collection of old and rare icons.

THE FAMAGUSTA GATE

The much-photographed Famagusta Gate (Pyli Ammohostou) is the best preserved of the three original gates that led into the old city of Lefkosia. It's in the **Caraffa Bastion** on Leoforos Athinas. Its impressive wooden door and sloping facade opens out onto a tunnel that leads through the rampart wall. The whole structure was revamped and renovated in 1981 and now serves as a concert venue and exhibition hall. Outside the tunnel and to the right is a small open-air arena where concerts by visiting artists are held, usually during the summer months. The area surrounding the gate has become a rather hip dining and eating place for fashionable Lefkosian youth (see the Places to Eat and Entertainment sections later in this chapter).

CHRYSALINIOTISSA CRAFTS CENTRE

This small arts centre at Dimonaktos 2 is worth dropping into for its display of Cypriot arts and crafts. It's open 10 am to 1 pm and 4.30 to 7.30 pm Monday to Friday but only 10 am to 1 pm on Saturday. Afternoon opening hours in winter are an hour earlier.

CYPRUS HANDICRAFTS CENTRE

This and the Chrysaliniotissa are the main outlets for the Cyprus Handicraft Service, a government-sponsored foundation which aims to preserve Cypriot handicrafts. Here you can watch pottery, woodwork embroidery and other crafts being practised and nurtured. There is one outlet at Aristokyprou 6 in Laïki Yitonia and another at Athalassas 186 in the New City (☎ 305 024).

PLACES TO STAY – BUDGET

The *HI Hostel* (☎ 444 808, *Hatzidaki 5*) is in a quiet part of the New City about six blocks from Plateia Eleftherias. Follow the signs from Tefkrou, off Themistokli Dervi. It charges CY£4.50 a night for a dorm bed and is very pleasant.

Solonos is a good street for fairly inexpensive accommodation. The best is *Tony's Bed & Breakfast* (☎ 466 752, fax 454 225, *Solonos 13*) where the cost is CY£12/20 for singles/doubles, slightly more with a bathroom. Tony also has cheaper rooms for self-catering stays of a week or more.

The one-star B&B-style *Regina Palace* (☎ 463 051, corner of Rigenis and Fokionos 42–44) is one other inexpensive inner city option. Decent rooms go for CY£15/21.

PLACES TO STAY – MID-RANGE

Most of the more expensive hotels are found in the New City, but inside the walls is the three-star *Best Western Classic* (☎ 464 006, fax 360 072, *Rigenis 94*), which charges CY£26/36 including breakfast. This option has a lot more character than the *Holiday Inn* (☎ 475 131, fax 473 337, *Rigenis 70*), where room-only rates are CY£65/89.

Outside the walls try the two-star *Asty* (☎ 773 030, fax 773 311, *Pringipa Karolou*

12) in the western suburb of Engomi. Comfortable rooms go for CY£38/63. A little farther north, not far from the British High Commission and in a quiet part of the New City, is the *Averof* (☎ 773 447, fax 773 411, *Averof 13*). Cosy rooms cost CY£22/31. This place is closer to the Old City for walkers than the Asty.

PLACES TO STAY – TOP END

All top-end hotel options are found in the New City and with only one exception are all within a reasonable walking distance of the city centre. The three-star *Europa* (☎ 664 537, fax 474 417, *Alkeou 16*) is out on the south-west side of the city and offers good accommodation for CY£33/45 without breakfast, an extra CY£4 with breakfast.

Immediately south of the Old City is the three-star *Excelsior* (☎ 368 585, fax 476 740, *Foti Pitta 4*). The hotel is well appointed and offers rooms for CY£27/45 without breakfast, an extra CY£3 with breakfast. Off-season discounts of between 25% and 30% apply at both hotels.

The *Yiorki* (☎ 844 000, fax 779 600, ✆ res.yiorki@belcy.com.cy, Prodromou 3) is a deluxe-class apartment hotel catering to mainly longer-term visitors. Well-equipped superior suites start at a tidy CY£50/70 while an imperial suite for four people will cost a healthy CY£500 per night.

Back to regular hotels, the *Forum Nicosia By Intercontinental* (☎ 356 666, fax 351 918, ✆ nicosia@interconti.com, *Leoforos Georgiou Griva Digeni*) is the only one of the bunch that is a little way out of town, in the western suburb of Engomi. Excellent rooms go for a minimum of CY£82/124, though a 30% discount applies from 1 July to 31 August.

The *Cyprus Hilton* (☎ 377 777, fax 377 788, ✆ hiltoncy@spidernet.com.cy, *Leoforos Arhiepiskopou Makariou III*) is Lefkosia's premier hotel. Rates are CY£123/142, though unpublished discounts also apply from 1 July to 31 August.

PLACES TO EAT

Dining in Lefkosia is determined by three basic location options. Eating in the Old

City, the New City or the burgeoning suburbs to the east or west. Because Lefkosia is not a prime tourist target, it is thankfully bereft of the sometimes low-quality, high-cost tourist traps elsewhere that pander to foreign palates. Dining in Lefkosia can be a real treat.

The growing internationalism of Cyprus, coupled with the fact that many Cypriots now hanker after cuisines other than their home-grown Cypriot variety, means that there is a wide array of alternative cuisines available. Chinese and Indian cuisines are among two of the main growth areas. While we stick mainly to recommendations in the New and Old Cities, suburbs like Engomi to the west or Strovolos to the south have their own culinary enclaves and a drive to either of these two areas may turn up some surprise finds. Major fast-food chains are also here, though not as obvious as in other European cities.

A word of warning. Many restaurants in Lefkosia close down for a couple of weeks in August for annual holidays. Call beforehand to be on the safe side.

Old Lefkosia

Dining here is centred on two main areas with a sprinkling of low-frills, cheap eateries scattered in between. The Laïki Yitonia is mainly popular with the lunchtime crowd of day-trippers, who then normally retreat to the coast, while the Famagusta Gate strip attracts mainly evening revellers, most of whom are local Cypriots.

Between the two main areas is the locals' dining strip. For a huge mezes meal that only costs CY£4.50, head for **Zanettos Taverna** (☎ 765 501, Trikoupi 65). Also worth checking out is **Estiatorio Savvas** (☎ 763 444, Solonos 65). It's unadorned, simple and basic but good eating, as is **Agios Georgios Taverna** (☎ 765 971, Dimarhias) on the northern side of the market.

To Pyrofani (☎ 678 282, Pasikratous 11–15) is a bit of a prize to be found in the Laïki Yitonia area It's a neat little mezedopoleio set just one block east of Plateia Eleftherias. It specialises in fish mezedes (CY£7.80 per person) and serves up about 20 different fish dishes. The haloumi-based Pyrofani is very good. Wash it all down with draught retsina, red or white wine.

For low-priced and tasty mezedes seek out **Taverna Axiothea** (☎ 430 787, Axiotheas 9), in the yuppie enclave of the Famagusta Gate area. This little unassuming joint is on the last street before the barricades begin. A few short blocks south-east is **To Steki tis Chrysaliniotissas** (☎ 430 772, Leoforos Athinas), a little restaurant that spills out onto busy Athinas. Mezedes is the best way to eat here and, unlike some other restaurants that seem to overdo it, To Steki has just about the right balance of dishes that are both tasty and imaginative.

In the Laïki Yitonia, **Xefoto** (☎ 669 208, Eshylou) gets the thumbs-up from the local community for its top-notch food usually accompanied by live music. Another Laïki Yitonia joint that stands out above the rest is **Arhondiko** (☎ 450 080, Aristokyprou 27), which specialises in Cypriot mezedes and international dishes.

New City

Cafes In the heart of the New City and by all accounts popular with the Lefkosia trendy set is the bright and modern **Le Cafe** (☎ 755 151, Leoforos Arhiepiskopou Makariou III 16). Pasta and salads are the order of the day, though many patrons just come to sip coffee and beer and be seen. In a similar vein and ostensibly catering to the movie-going crowd is **Cinema Cafe** (☎ 360 058, Leoforos Evagorou 2) where you can get an 'all you can eat' buffet for CY£3. The menus are in the little CD boxes on the tables.

For late-night coffee and cake you can do no better than **Swiss Cottage** (☎ 433 000, Leoforos Stasinou 31) on the corner of Theokritou close to the Old City. The Swiss-trained pastry chef makes some exquisite European-style tarts and flans, but prices tend to be a little steep.

Greek Cypriot Fancy rubbing your shoulders with prime ministers and presidents? Look no further than the **Date Club Restaurant** (☎ 376 843, Agathonos 2) close to the

Cyprus Hilton. Its calm, air-conditioned interior is always busy with discerning diners. If you are going to eat here take a partner or two and eat mezedes; they are tops. Prices are mid-range to expensive.

Kalymnos (☎ 472 423, Zinas Kanther 11) is an unpretentious fish tavern that gets top marks from the local diner community. Fish figures prominently, though you can get most other dishes of your choice including mezedes and steaks. There's a little bar for a pre-dinner drink. Prices are mid-range and service is attentive and subtle.

Enastro (☎ 813 333, Leoforos Lemesou 76) is another neat out-of-the-city eating venue which is very popular with the Lefkosia dining set. Prices are mid-range to slightly expensive.

The *Plaka Tavern (☎ 446 498, Plateia Arhiepiskopou Makariou III 8)* over to the west of the city centre in Engomi is a superb little Greek-style taverna. During the summer months diners eat on the little square. Mezedes is the way to eat here; but be warned there are many of them and you will need a big appetite. Prices are also mid-range to expensive. The restaurant is closed on Sunday.

Vegetarian Less than 1km from the HI Hostel, is *Natural Choice (☎ 762 674, Hytron 11)*, where you can get excellent vegetarian food. It's open from 8.30 am to 5.30 pm. Restaurants specialising in mezes meals may also do vegetarian mezedes. Ask beforehand. Indian restaurants also have excellent vegetarian selections.

Other Restaurants The *Mehfil (☎ 817 317, Nikokreontos 4)* is one of Lefkosia's longer-standing Indian eateries and has moved from its old home in Makedonitissa to reach a wider dining audience in the New City. The food is excellent and the portions large. Prices are somewhat more expensive than in most Cypriot restaurants but not excessive.

There are quite a few good Chinese restaurants in Lefkosia, many offering take-away service. One you might like to seek out is *Dragon (☎ 591 711, Leoforos Geor-giou Griva Digeni)* which opened in 1999. This restaurant has a good range of dishes all cooked by a Chinese chef. If you are tired of Cypriot mezes, give your palate a work-out with some fiery Szechuan dishes or *kung-bao*. Prices are mid-range.

Closer to the Old City is the more intimate *Kana Kai (☎ 773 820, Metohiou 25)* which does a mean Peking duck. Main course dishes are around the CY£5 mark, though you can order take-away chicken dishes for around CY£3.

For a really exotic culinary evening out try *Limpopo African Restaurant (☎ 777 444, Stasinou 3, Engomi)*. If you don't mind feasting upon hapless game such as crocodile, kudu, zebra and ostrich then Limpopo is it. You can have favourites like chicken and beef. Prices are expensive; count on around CY£12.75 for grilled kudu fillet steak or CY£10.90 for zebra Kariba. The restaurant is west of the New City on the Troödos road and is open for lunch and dinner.

Lebanese food comes no better than at *Abu Faysal (☎ 760 353, Klimentos 31)* in the New City, three blocks south of the Constanza Bastion. The restaurant is an old house in a quiet backstreet and you dine in a leafy courtyard. Lebanese mezedes are the best option – ask for a bottle of Lebanese Ksara Riesling wine to wash them down.

ENTERTAINMENT
Pubs & Bars
The most popular bar strip is around the Famagusta Gate in the Old City. *Bastione (☎ 433 101, Leoforos Athinas 6)* is a neat little bar built into the wall next to Famagusta Gate, while *Orpheas (Athinas)*, on the opposite side and nearer the barbed wire of the Green Line, pulls the crowds who prefer to sit out on the pavement.

Ithaki (☎ 434 193, corner of Thiseos and Foka) is probably the hippest of the bars here and occupies a prominent corner position straddling Leoforos Athinas and Thiseos. *Odos Othellou (Othellou 1)*, one block west and just away from the main drag, is a relaxed place for a beer or a coffee. None of these places really gets going until after 10 pm.

In the New City, *Sfinakia (corner of Leoforos Santaroza and Dervi)* packs in a crowd of poseurs and people-watchers, while lovers of Irish ale and stout will do best to make for *Finbarr's (☎ 376 625, Leoforos Arhiepiskopou Makariou III 52B)*. Here a creamy pint of Caffrey's will set you back CY£3, but some drinks are cheaper during the long 'happy hour' from 4.30 to 8 pm. It also serves Irish staples such as beef and stout pie (CY£5.45) or a jazzed up basil and chicken boxty (CY£5.85).

Traditional Music

The best way to get to see and hear some traditional music performers is to head for any of the restaurants offering live music, such as Xefoto in the Laïki Yitonia. Otherwise keep your eyes peeled for street posters in the summer months advertising visiting musical artists from Greece. Choices here run the gamut from rock to folk and there is usually a procession of top quality acts visiting Cyprus. Get in touch with promoters Papadopoulos & Schinis Productions Ltd (☎ 05-372 855, ✆ schinis@cytanet.com.cy) for interesting upcoming events.

Classical Music

Lefkosia does occasionally host classical concerts and the best way to find out about them is to look at the *Diary of Events* booklet published by the CTO or *Nicosia this Month*. Other than these two avenues, watch for street posters or drop by the Municipal Theatre box office, diagonally opposite the Cyprus Museum on Mouseiou.

Cinemas

There are a number of cinemas scattered around Lefkosia that show varying permutations on the latest films and sometimes reruns of English-language movies. All foreign-language films are subtitled in Greek. Entry is normally around CY£3 per person. Following is a list of the more central movie theatres in Lefkosia.

Opera (☎ 445 375) Hristodoulou Sozou 9
Othellos (☎ 350 579) 28 Oktovriou 1
Pallas (672 584) Arsinois 1

Zina Pallas (☎ 674 128) Theofanous Theodotou 18

Theatre

Plays performed in Lefkosia are almost always in Greek – somewhat limiting if you have no knowledge of the language. Nonetheless there is a thriving local theatre scene with the Cyprus University Theatre Workshop (THEPAK; ☎ 434 801) regularly putting on good quality shows at its little theatre close to the Green Line near the Famagusta Gate.

Also try the Cyprus Theatrical Organisation (☎ 781 105) at Delfon 12 in the New City, or Theatro ENA (☎ 349 203) which is at Leoforos Athinas 4 in the Old City for any productions that may meet your linguistic needs. Opposite the Cyprus Museum is the Municipal Theatre box office (☎ 463 028) at Mouseiou 4. Here you can find flyers for all upcoming events – musical as well as theatrical – and buy your tickets.

See also the *Nicosia this Month* and the *Diary of Events* pamphlets available from the CTO, though some events may not be listed in the latter publication since this goes to print several months before the events take place.

SPECTATOR SPORTS
Football

Football (soccer) is the main spectator sport in Lefkosia with some 19 teams battling it out for supremacy over three leagues. The football season is from September to May.

Horse Racing

Lefkosia Racecourse, in the western suburb of Agios Dometios, caters for the popular pastime of horse racing. If you are a betting shop punter, try the very modern and well-organised Sportsman (☎ 472 444) in the New City on Thefanous Theodotou 15. Other than the horses you can bet on Australian Rules and European soccer matches and all betting forms are in English or Greek.

SHOPPING

The two main shopping areas are along Lidras in the Old City and Leoforos

Domed ovens are common in rural Cyprus.

Agia Napa Monastery, east of Larnaka

Drying tobacco along the Karpas Peninsula.

A goat herd tends his flock near Agia Marina, a Mesaoria village south-west of Lefkosia.

Garlic is a key ingredient of Cypriot cooking

Kontosouvli, lamb kebabs, cooking over a spit

The Troödos region produces Cyprus' best wine.

Treasures may be found in the wares of street vendors in Lemesos.

Columns of the amphitheatre, Ancient Kourion

Christian basilica, Ancient Kourion

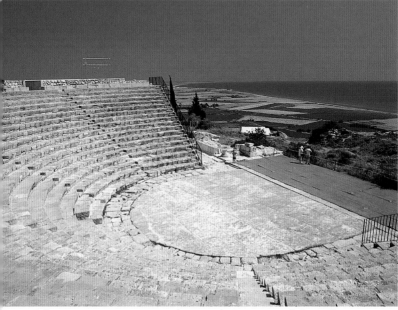

The amphitheatre at Ancient Kourion, west of Lemesos, hosts concerts and plays in the summer.

The Sanctuary of Apollon Ylatis, near Kourion, was originally established in the 8th century BC. Pictured are some of the remains of Roman buildings destroyed by an earthquake in AD 365.

Arhiepiskopou Makariou III in the New City. Tourist shops tend to be centred in the Old City. Shopping hours are 8.30 am to 1 pm and 4 to 7 pm in summer (2.30 to 5.30 pm in winter). Shops close on Wednesday and Saturday afternoons and also all day Sunday. Good buys are handicrafts, Lefkara lace, jewellery, shoes and prescription eye wear. Bargaining is not a feature of shopping in Cyprus.

Shoes and clothing can be found along Stasikratous and Leoforos Arhiepiskopou Makariou III which run parallel to each other in the New City. Cypriot-made shoes are an especially good buy, but watch out for obvious locally made clones – Timberland footwear is a prime example.

Lefkosia's local Woolworths (☎ 447 801) is nothing like the Woolworths you find back home. It's a classy department store selling good quality items at fairly upmarket prices. Woolworths occupies the Shakolas Tower on Lidras in the centre of the Old City.

Music lovers might want to head for Virgin Records (☎ 761 190) at Arnaldas 8 just off Leoforos Stasinou near the D'Avila Bastion. Here you can get all the latest Greek and non-Greek releases as well as buy tickets for the many music concerts that come to Lefkosia in the summer months.

Lefkara lace can be found at Cyprus Handicraft & Souvenirs (☎ 680 090) at Rigenis 20 and all photography needs are catered for further along the same street at the well-stocked Andreas Papaeracleous Photo Store (☎ 666 101) at Rigenis 48 in the Old City.

Out in Engomi opposite McDonald's is Haralambidis on Vasileos Pavlou I. Here you can find anything you can find back home in the very well-stocked megamarket – from coconut milk to Christmas cards.

GETTING THERE & AWAY
Air
Lefkosia's international airport is in the UN buffer zone and is no longer a functioning airport. All air passengers for Lefkosia will enter via Larnaka airport.

Most airline companies that serve Cyprus maintain offices or representatives in Lefkosia including:

Cyprus Airways (☎ 751 996, fax 755 271) Leoforos Arhiepiskopou Makariou III 50
Alitalia (☎ 674 500, fax 671 894) Leoforos Evagora 52
British Airways (☎ 761 166, fax 766 017) Leoforos Arhiepiskopou Makariou III 52A
KLM (☎ 671 616, fax 459 497) Zinonos Kanther 12
Olympic Airways (☎ 462 101, 451 329) Leoforos Omirou 17

Bus
There are a lot of private companies operating out of Lefkosia. Kemek (☎ 463 989) at Leonidou 34 has five buses a day to Lemesos (CY£1.50; fewer on Saturday) and one to Pafos (CY£3) at 6.30 am via Lemesos. Kallenos (☎ 654 850) operates from Plateia Dion Solomou and has seven buses a day (in summer) to Larnaka (CY£1.50). For Polis you can take a minibus at 11.30 am daily except Wednesday and Sunday (CY£4) or a shared taxi at 1.30 pm daily except Tuesday and Saturday (CY£5). These leave from the Tripoli Bastion next to Plateia Dion Solomou. For further information call SOLIS Shared Taxis on ☎ 466 388.

Klarios (☎ 453 234) goes to Troödos (CY£1.10) once a day at 11.30 am and much more frequently to Kakopetria – up to 13 services per day in summer (CY£1.10). EMAN (☎ 473 414) runs to Agia Napa (CY£2) on weekdays at 3 pm, departing from the Constanza Bastion car park.

Buses to Kambos via the Kykkos Monastery (CY£1.50) leave at noon on Monday to Saturday, but only return from Kambos (again via Kykkos) the following day at 6 am. Buses to Pedoulas (CY£2) go at 12.15 pm, Monday to Saturday and are run by Zingas Bus (☎ 463 989). They depart from the Kemek bus stand at Leonidou 34.

There is one bus a day (weekdays only) at 1.30 pm to Paralimni, Protaras and Agia Napa (CY£2.50) operated by the Paralimni-Deryneia Bus Co (☎ 444 141). This departs from the Kyriakos service taxi office at Stasinou 27.

LEFKOSIA

Car & Motorcycle

Traffic approaching Lefkosia tends to come from one of two directions: the Troödos Mountains to the west or Larnaka and Lemesos in the south. The Larnaka-Lemesos motorway ends fairly abruptly on the southern outskirts of Lefkosia about 6km south of the Old City. By following the extension of the motorway into the city centre, you will eventually reach Leoforos Arhiepiskopou Makariou III, the main thoroughfare in the New City. Traffic from Troödos will enter the city along Leoforos Georgiou Griva Digeni. In order to reach the Old City when coming from Troödos, turn left on Leoforos Dimosthenous Severi and follow the signs to the city centre. From Larnaka or Lemesos turn right off Leoforos Makariou III along Afroditis (signposted).

Parking is most easily found at the large car parks abutting the city bastions, to the right of Leoforos Arhiepiskopou Makariou III, or to your left if you approach from the Troödos. The most convenient one for new arrivals is the large lot between the D'Avila and Constanza bastions on Leoforos Stasinou. Cost is a minimum of 25 cents for two hours. Buy a ticket from the machine and display it by sticking it to the inside of your windscreen.

Leaving Lefkosia is made easy by the prominent signs all along Leoforos Stasinou. Be wary, however, of the many one-way streets and the numerous on-street parking restrictions. Other than that, driving or biking your way through Lefkosia is generally hassle-free and orderly. Avoid the peak period of 11 am to 1 pm when traffic can be very heavy (and slow) midweek.

Hitching

While it is, in theory, possible to hitch out of Lefkosia, you would have to get yourself some way out of the city to secure a good position. The Lefkosia-Lemesos/Larnaka motorway starts somewhat messily about 5km south-east of the New City. The short stretch of motorway leading west towards the Troödos starts a little more cleanly in the suburb of Strovolos, about 3km west of the city centre. Take a taxi to both starting points – the cost of which may, in any case, negate any gains made in hitching further afield in the first place. It's best to stick to the inexpensive bus or slightly more expensive service taxis.

Service Taxi

Just outside the city walls near Laïki Yitonia are A Makris (☎ 466 201) and Kypros (☎ 464 811) at Leoforos Stasinou 9 and 11 respectively; both taxi companies service Larnaka (CY£2.10) and Lemesos (CY£3).

To Northern Cyprus

Depending on prevailing politics, you're usually allowed into Northern Cyprus for a day visit. The border crossing at the Ledra Palace Hotel is open 8 am to 5 pm. You may cross to the North between 8 am and 1 pm but you must be back by 5 pm. You simply walk to the Turkish Cypriot checkpoint and complete a short form in return for an entry permit. Private cars can be taken over the border, but not hired ones. There is theoretically no limit to the number of times you can do this, but you will undoubtedly arouse suspicion in the Greek Cypriot guards if you attempt the crossing too frequently.

GETTING AROUND

The city bus station is at Plateia Solomou; Lefkosia Buses operates numerous routes to and from the city and suburbs.

Also at Plateia Dion Solomou is A Petsas & Sons (☎ 462 650) where you can hire cars. To hire motorcycles ring Geofil on ☎ 466 349.

There are no bicycles for rent in or around the Old City.

To/From the Airport

There is no public or airline transport between Lefkosia and Larnaka or Pafos airports. If you are in a hurry an expensive taxi is your only option. It is cheaper to take a bus or service taxi to Pafos or Larnaka and then a local urban taxi to the airport.

Local Transport

There is a network of urban buses serving Lefkosia but because most of the major sites and hotels are within walking distance of each other, urban buses are probably of limited use.

Taxi Taxis are widely available and are generally modern air-conditioned vehicles, usually comfortable Mercedes. Flag a taxi on the street or take one from a designated taxi stand. 'Taxi sharing', such as is common in Greek cities like Athens, is not permitted and taxi drivers are normally courteous and helpful. Fares are strictly controlled by the taxi board. You pay what the meter says, plus any additional surcharges for luggage and late night services.

Around Lefkosia

Few people make the effort to explore the area immediately to the south and west of Lefkosia. At first glance it doesn't seem to have a lot to offer. The sprawling plain known as the Mesaoria looks hot and uninviting in midsummer, but it is rife with greenery in winter and spring. There are a couple of ancient archaeological sites to tempt history buffs and a sprinkling of churches and monasteries to woo the spiritually minded. The ordinary villages of the Troödos foothills offer a glimpse of how Cypriot life has been for ages – essentially untouched by the excesses or needs of the tourist industry.

A car will be necessary to see some of the sites listed here.

ANCIENT TAMASSOS

Homer mentioned Ancient Tamassos in the *Odyssey* (1.184) where it is referred to as Temese. The goddess Athina says to Odysseas' son, Telemachos, 'We are bound for the foreign port of Temese with a cargo of gleaming iron, which we intend to trade for copper'. The site of this otherwise obscure and little-known city kingdom is on a small hillside about 17km south-west of Lefkosia next to the village of Politiko. Tamassos' main claim to fame was its seemingly endless supply of copper – the mineral from which the name of Cyprus

(Kypros in Greek and Kıbrıs in Turkish) is derived. A copper-producing settlement dates from at least the 7th century BC and production of copper ran well into the Hellenistic period. Excavations of the remains of the citadel commenced in 1889 and two tombs dating back to the 6th century BC were discovered. Today these two tombs constitute the major attraction of the site since the citadel itself is little more than a scattering of nondescript foundations.

The tombs probably contained the remains of the kings of the citadel and, while they no doubt once held rich burial treasures, looters have long since spirited away what may have been buried with the kings. A hole in the roof of the larger tomb shows where grave robbers once broke in. The walls are carved unusually in such a way as to imitate wood – a feature that some archaeologists have linked to a possible Anatolian influence at the time of the citadel's zenith. Some theorists suggest that Tamassos was even part of the Hittite Empire.

The site is open 9 am to 3 pm Tuesday to Friday and 10 am to 3 pm on Saturday and Sunday. It is closed on Monday. Entry is CY£0.75.

MONASTERY OF AGIOS IRAKLEIDIOS

Easily combined with an excursion to Tamassos is a visit to the nearby Monastery of Agios Irakleidios. Irakleidios was born in Tamassos and guided the saints Paul and Barnabas around Cyprus. He was later made the first bishop in Cyprus by Barnabas. Many miracles were subsequently attributed to the bishop, including demon exorcisms.

The original church was built on the present site in the 5th century AD, but the current monastic buildings date from the late 18th century. The church today boasts the usual panoply of frescoes and icons, and on a table to the east side of the church you can spot a reliquary containing one of the bones and skull of St Irakleidios.

THE MESAORIA VILLAGES

'Safari' tours often take travellers to see some of the villages of the Mesaoria as part

LEFKOSIA

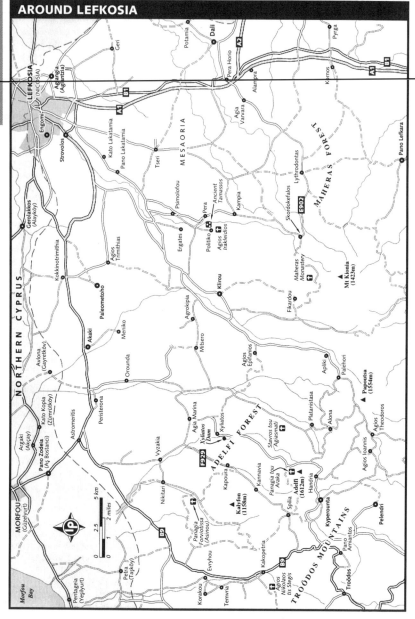

AROUND LEFKOSIA

of a wider tour round Cyprus. One of the more popular areas is the region to the southwest of Lefkosia known as the Mesaoria, meaning 'between the mountains' in Greek. In this case it refers to the plains lying between the Kyrenia Range to the north and the Troödos Massif to the south. While you could rent a vehicle and randomly drive around the Mesaoria, roads tend to fan out haphazardly along roughly defined valleys and ravines and traversing from one valley to another can be a little slow as the roads are narrow and twist and turn.

One of the more popular villages is **Pera**, a couple of kilometres from Tamassos. While there are no specific sights as such, Pera is nonetheless a pretty village and a stroll through the cobbled backstreets will lead photographers to some particularly captivating street scenes – old houses covered in bougainvillea, old stone jars as you see on the cover of this guide, pretty doors, cats on walls – the kind of stuff that postcards are made of. Visitors frequently stop at the local *kafenio* for refreshments, while the local gentry and often the village priest sip coffee and engage in gossip in a world where time means little.

This author spent two months in the small village of **Agia Marina** near Xyliatos while researching this book. The village has little going for it as a tourist sight, but its laid-back ambience and cool climate make it an ideal base away from the tourist excesses and busy city life found elsewhere in Cyprus. The villages of **Orounda** and **Peristerona** nearby both have interesting and photogenic churches. Roads from the Mesaoria area all lead in various ways to the higher reaches of the Troödos, via Pitsylia, offering a slower but more scenic route into the mountains.

This option is particularly useful to be aware of on weekends when Lefkosians in their hundreds storm the Troödos via the main B9 road (through Astromeritis and Kakopetria) for picnics and a day out in order to escape the heat of the city. On Sunday evenings in summer you would be advised to seek an alternative route from the Troödos to Lefkosia through the Mesaoria in order to avoid inevitable delays.

PLACES TO STAY & EAT

Agrotourism is the way to go in the Mesaoria, though there is really only one place serving the region. *Avli Georgallidi (☎ 02-499 922, fax 517 712, ✉ avli@cytanet .com.cy, Markou Drakou 3)* is in the village of Lythrodontas, 25km from Lefkosia. Close to the Maheras Forest, Lythrodontas is a cool, get-away-from-it-all kind of place and this agrotourist house can sleep up to 14 people in five self-contained rooms. It has a courtyard, phones, central heating and log fires. Twin rooms cost CY£20 while CY£38 will get you a suite for up to five people.

You will find a tavern or restaurant in most villages or even in out of the way places along the road. Many Lefkosians come to the country to eat on weekends and usually have their favourite haunts. Advertised widely in the area around Agia Marina is *Katoï*, in the village itself. Its lights are visible from afar at night and it commands a great view over the Troödos foothills and Mesaoria. The restaurant serves solid Cypriot staples and a pretty imaginative selection of mezedes. Prices are mid-range.

If you are organised enough you can have some pleasant picnics at picnic grounds, usually situated in cool and leafy spots. Try the **Xyliatos Dam** near the village of the same name, or **Kapoura** on a picturesque back road (the F929) linking Vyzakia with Kannavia, or even high up in the Maheras Forest at **Skordokefalos** along the E902 that leads to the Maheras Monastery. All picnic grounds have BBQ areas, tables, chairs and most importantly shade.

GETTING AROUND

While public buses – often colourful and old-fashioned – link most of the Mesaoria villages with Lefkosia, they are basically scheduled to service workers and schoolchildren not curious travellers, so will be of limited use. Here you will need your own transport, though if you have the time and patience you should be able to get around – perhaps fitfully – by hitching. Locals hitch fairly regularly and you might find it an interesting diversion to pick up someone yourself, if you have your own wheels.

Lemesos & the South Coast

The area south of the Troödos Mountains today constitutes the heartland, both physically and economically, of the Republic of Cyprus. Here lie Cyprus' largest city, its main seaport, some of its most important archaeological sites and medieval remains, as well as one of the most important military bases in the whole of the Mediterranean region. It is a land of rolling brown hills – where the Troödos Massif meets the sea in a series of languid bays and sandy beaches. This is a land of vigorous tourism, with choices for those who like it quiet – as in the far west of the region – and for those who like it raucous – as in the tourist strip of Lemesos.

Ancient Kourion, perched on a bluff overlooking azure Episkopi Bay west of Lemesos, was home to an advanced civilisation from as early as the 13th century BC and later played an important role in the spread of Christianity throughout the island. Ancient Amathous to the east of Lemesos was one of Cyprus' four original kingdoms and was founded 100 years before Christ. Richard the Lionheart first set foot in Cyprus in the 12th century – perhaps the island's first British colonist – and liked the country so much he kept it for himself. The English are still here and occupy the whole of the Akrotiri Peninsula where housing estates more reminiscent of England's home counties than the eastern Mediterranean are not uncommon.

Lemesos and the South Coast are a great base for visitors wishing to be in easy touch with all of Cyprus. Take your time to explore its many hidden facets.

Lemesos

☎ 05 • postcode 3000 • pop 151,200

Brash, bold and carrying the reputation as the city that never sleeps, Lemesos grew up quickly after the Turkish invasion of Cyprus in 1974, having been forced to replace Fam-

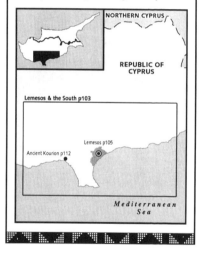

agusta as the nation's main port. It was also obliged to shoulder the mantle of the country's tourist boom. Still known to many as Limassol, Lemesos is the second-largest city in Cyprus and is the main passenger and cargo port. Originally comprising what is today known as the Old City radiating out from the Old Fishing Harbour, Lemesos has necessarily outgrown its original geographic limits to now encompass a sprawling tourist suburb some 12km in length. The haphazard and hurried development that took place in Lemesos post-1974 is all too obvious. At first sight the city has a rough workaday appearance. The tourist

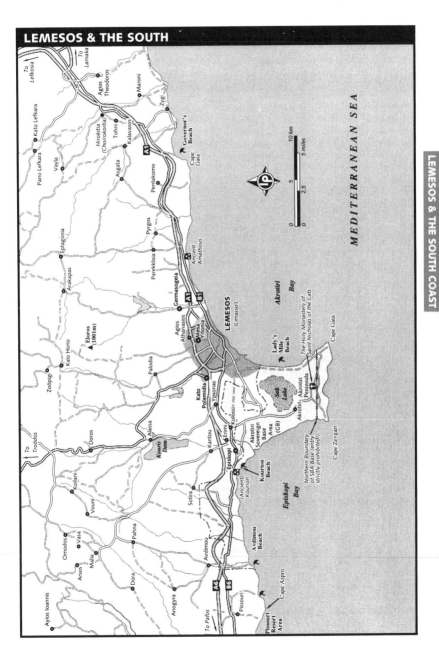

LEMESOS & THE SOUTH

MEDITERRANEAN SEA

centre is a riotous confusion of bars and restaurants and you could be excused for forgetting that the sea is there at all.

Still, Lemesos is a city with soul. Its Old City is experiencing a slow gentrification, with little bars and restaurants appearing among run-down buildings close to what once was the city's busy and thriving Turkish quarter. In this area you can still see artisans plying their trade in the backstreets, the muezzin still calls the few Muslim faithful to prayer and the medieval castle where Richard the Lionheart married Berengaria draws tourists to the city's most famous landmark.

The tourist centre, with its ubiquitous and incongruous fur shops, is as popular with Russian tourists as it is with northern Europeans who come here in droves. Bars stay open late and restaurants, while not the best in the city, serve every kind of cuisine imaginable. Lemesos is a good base for touring the attractions of the South Coast.

HISTORY

Little is known about the early history of Lemesos, its near neighbour Amathous and later Kourion, stealing whatever limelight had hitherto existed. In 1191 Crusader king, Richard the Lionheart, put Lemesos on the map, so to speak, when he arrived to rescue his sister and fiancee who had been shipwrecked and mistreated by the then ruler of Cyprus, Isaac Komninos. Richard subsequently defeated Komninos in battle and took Cyprus and Lemesos for himself. The city prospered for at least 200 years with a succession of Knights Hospitaller and Templar who established themselves in the area until earthquakes, marauding Genoese (1373) and Saracens (1426) finally reduced Lemesos' fortunes to virtually nought. Things were no better under the Ottomans and Lawrence Durrell, writing as late as 1952 in *Bitter Lemons of Cyprus,* noted upon arrival in Lemesos that 'we berthed towards sunrise in a gloomy and featureless roadstead, before a town whose desolate silhouette suggested that of a tin-mining village in the Andes'.

ORIENTATION

Lemesos' Old City is fairly compact but the New City now extends for 12km east along the seafront encompassing the main tourist centre. Buses and taxis arrive within a short distance of each other in the Old City, though the New Port where all ships and ferries dock is about 3km to the west of the Old City.

INFORMATION
Tourist offices

The Cyprus Tourism Organisation (CTO) has offices at the ferry terminal (☎ 343 868), at Spyrou Araouzou 15 (☎ 362 756, fax 746 596) and in the tourist centre (☎ 323 211, fax 313 451) at Georgiou 1, 22a. Opening times during the summer months of June to August are 8.15 am to 2.30 pm and 4 to 6.15 pm, except Tuesday and Friday, when they are closed. Times outside of summer are subject to change.

Money

You can change money on arrival at the New Port, but there are some banks around the centre of the Old City equipped with ATMs for cash withdrawals. The Bank of Cyprus on Agiou Andrea is probably the most convenient to the Old City, and there are others in the tourist centre.

Post & Communications

The main post office is quite central in the Old City, a block north of the pedestrian zone. Poste restante mail is also held here.

The city has at least four Internet cafes, though the most convenient for travellers in the Old City is CyberNet (@ cafeinfo@zenon.logos.cy.net) at Eleftherias 79, two blocks north-west of the CTO. On weekdays it doesn't open until 1 pm. Another Old City Internet cafe is Explorer on Agias Zonis. Both charge around CY£2 per hour.

Travel Agencies

ADA Travelscope (☎ 343 111, fax 345 834, @ evie@travelscope.com.cy), not far from the Archaeological Museum on Konstantinou Paleologou 25b , offers a wide variety of services and can book discounted airline tickets for most destinations.

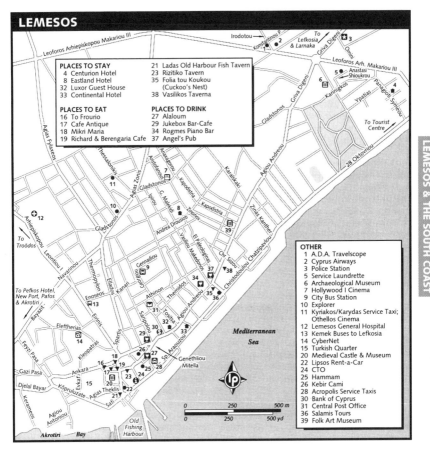

LEMESOS

PLACES TO STAY
4 Centurion Hotel
8 Eastland Hotel
32 Luxor Guest House
33 Continental Hotel

PLACES TO EAT
16 To Frourio
17 Cafe Antique
18 Mikri Maria
19 Richard & Berengaria Cafe

21 Ladas Old Harbour Fish Tavern
23 Rizitiko Tavern
35 Folia tou Koukou
    (Cuckoo's Nest)
38 Vasilikos Taverna

PLACES TO DRINK
27 Alaloum
29 Jukebox Bar-Cafe
34 Rogmes Piano Bar
37 Angel's Pub

OTHER
1 A.D.A. Travelscope
2 Cyprus Airways
3 Police Station
5 Service Laundrette
6 Archaeological Museum
7 Hollywood I Cinema
9 City Bus Station
10 Explorer
11 Kyriakos/Karydas Service Taxi;
   Othellos Cinema
12 Lemesos General Hospital
13 Kemek Buses to Lefkosia
14 CyberNet
15 Turkish Quarter
20 Medieval Castle & Museum
22 Lipsos Rent-a-Car
24 CTO
25 Hammam
26 Kebir Cami
28 Acropolis Service Taxis
30 Bank of Cyprus
31 Central Post Office
36 Salamis Tours
39 Folk Art Museum

Salamis Tours (☎ 355 555, fax 364 410) maintains its head office here at Salamis House on 28 Oktovriou, close to the CTO, and issues ferry tickets to Israel and Greece. Poseidon Lines (☎ 745 666, fax 745 577) at Leoforos Roosevelt 124 also runs ferries to Greece and Italy, but is somewhat inconveniently placed halfway between the city centre and the New Port.

Laundry

There are at least four laundrettes scattered around Lemesos. The two most central are the Service Laundrette near the Curium Palace Hotel at Anastasi Shioukrou 20 and the Quick Service Laundrette at Griva Digeni 144b.

Medical Services

Lemesos' General Hospital (☎ 330 777) is on Arhiepiskopou Leontiou I, 500m northwest of the Old Fishing Harbour.

Emergency

For an ambulance, police or the fire service, call ☎ 199. For night pharmacy assistance telephone ☎ 1415. The Narcotics Emergency Service is on ☎ 1410 and the AIDS

Advisory Centre can be reached on ☎ 02-305 515. The police station is on the corner of Griva Digeni and Omirou on the Lefkosia road.

WALKING TOUR

Most of Lemesos' central sights can be seen in an easy half-day, do-it-yourself walking tour starting from the main CTO office. The CTO does not organise guided walks. Start with the Medieval Castle & Museum, then thread your way through the narrow streets of the former **Turkish quarter** on to Agiou Andreou which is home to most of Lemesos' shops. Head along Agiou Andreou to the Folk Art Museum, which is halfway along, and eventually make for the Archaeological Museum. Stroll through Lemesos' nearby **park** and walk towards the **promenade**. Walk back along the promenade to your starting point at the CTO office perhaps for a relaxing lunch in the vicinity of the Medieval Castle.

LEMESOS MEDIEVAL CASTLE & MUSEUM

Lemesos' most famous tourist attraction is its castle and museum. In attractive gardens on the west side of the Old City on Irinis, the castle was built over the remains of an original Byzantine castle in the 14th century. In 1191 Richard the Lionheart, while on his way to the Third Crusade, stopped briefly in Lemesos and ended up defeating and exiling the then unpopular Byzantine prince of the island, Isaac Komninos. At the same time he acquired Cyprus for himself. Seizing the opportunity to cement his relationship with his fiancee Berengaria, he married her in the chapel of the original Byzantine castle, and followed that with her coronation as Queen of England. The chapel and Byzantine castle have long since gone and in its place was built the current structure.

The castle looks rather unassuming and you can wander its gardens for free. In them you will find an old **olive oil press** that dates from the 7th to 9th centuries. The press itself was found in Dounettis, while a nearby millstone was found north of Lemesos.

They were transported and reassembled here. The oil press is based on a simplified version of a Hellenistic and Roman *trapetum* which uses only one millstone. Roman historian Pliny described this kind of equipment for making oil.

In order to appreciate the castle you will have to enter the Medieval Museum (☎ 330 419) itself and browse among its varied and at times arresting collection of artefacts transferred from the original Lefkosia Medieval Museum, after the division of that city in 1974. The interior is divided into a series of rooms and chambers on varying levels. All have thematic displays of Byzantine and medieval objects of interest including Ottoman pottery, gold religious objects, tombstones, weapons and suits of armour. In the Grand Hall, to the right and on a lower level as you enter, there is a good display of black and white photos of Byzantine sites all over Cyprus.

You can climb up to a rooftop promenade, though the views are less than spectacular, given that the castle is not all that high. The museum is open 9 am to 5 pm Monday to Saturday and 10 am to 1 pm on Sunday. Admission is CY£1.

THE HAMMAM

Close by, near the mosque, is a newly restored **hammam**, where you can get a steam bath and sauna or a massage for CY£5. This is not a tourist site as such, but a working steam bath and the perfect antidote to a hard day walking around in Lemesos' often humid climate. It is off Genethliou Mitella and it is open 2 to 10 pm daily. All sessions are mixed.

KEBIR CAMI

The Grand Mosque, on Genethliou Mitella, was once home to Lemesos' large Turkish Cypriot population and now serves the few that remain and other visiting Muslims from Middle East countries. As with any mosque, visitors are requested to dress conservatively, leave shoes by the door and avoid visiting at prayer times. There are no fixed opening hours as such. If the gate is open, step inside the courtyard and take a look.

MICK WELDON

After a day of exploring Lemesos, relax with a sauna and massage at the Hammam.

ARCHAEOLOGICAL MUSEUM

Lemesos' Archaeological Museum (☎ 330 157) is on the corner of Vyronos and Kaningos. It houses a rather nondescript collection of items dating from Neolithic and Chalcolithic times, consisting primarily of shards and implements for domestic use, through to Mycenaean pottery. There is a display of Classical pottery, jewellery and oil lamps as well as curiously modern-looking glass bottles and vials. The exhibits are generally pleasing only to dedicated museum heads and if you have been to the Cyprus Museum in Lefkosia, you are unlikely to be very impressed with this tired-looking collection. Still, it's worth a browse and it is at least a refreshing alternative to Lemesos' other more worldly attractions over in the tourist centre.

The museum is open 9 am to 5 pm Monday to Saturday and 10 am to 1 pm Sunday. Entry costs CY£0.75.

FOLK ART MUSEUM

This somewhat mediocre museum (☎ 362 303) is housed in an old mansion at Agiou Andreou 253, not far from the city centre. It displays woodwork, traditional dress, jewellery and traditional household utensils.

There is a guidebook for sale at the ticket desk. The museum is open 8.30 am to 1.30 pm Monday to Friday and additionally from 3 to 5.30 pm (4 to 6.30 pm in summer) on Monday, Tuesday, Wednesday and Friday. Entry costs CY£0.50.

WET 'N WILD

If you are young, or still aspire to be, then Lemesos has a water theme park just for you. There are actually three of them but Wet 'n Wild (☎ 318 000) is the most convenient and probably the best of the three. It's in the middle of the tourist centre, set back a few hundred metres from the beach-front. Boasting such attractions as raft rides, inner tube rides, body flumes, speed slides, a lazy river, a wave pool, and activity pool, a kiddie's pool and the wet bubble, there is enough to keep you wet and weary for more than a whole day.

If you are coming to Lemesos by car, exit at the Moutagiaka exit (junction 23) on the A1 motorway. Opening times are 10 am to 6 pm. Entry costs CY£5 for children aged two to 12 years, CY£10 for children over 13 years. Children under two enter free of charge.

PLACES TO STAY

The good news is that there are plenty of hotels in Lemesos. The bad news is that they are mostly all along a 9km-long tourist centre to the north-east of the Old City. They are often crowded and overpriced and since many were built in a hurry after the 1974 Turkish invasion of Cyprus, the shoddy workmanship is beginning to show. The Old City offers few really high quality, guest-friendly establishments, but they are more used to walk-in travellers and likely to have rooms vacant. Nonetheless, a forward booking is probably a good idea if you are planning on hitting Lemesos in summer.

Places to Stay – Budget

For budget and independent-living travellers, the nearest camping ground is *Governor's Beach Camping* (*☎/fax 632 878*) – 20km east of town. Not really an option unless you have your own wheels and are

LEMESOS & THE SOUTH COAST

more attuned to caravaners rather than to campers.

The cheapest hotels are clustered in the Old City, to the east of the castle. A reasonable one with large, clean rooms is the *Luxor Guest House* (☎ 362 265, *Agiou Andreou 101), which charges CY£6 per person, no breakfast.

A decent two-star hotel near the Old City is the *Continental Hotel* (☎ 362 530, *fax 373 030, Spyrou Araouzou 137)* on the waterfront. It has quite pleasant singles/doubles with a bathroom for CY£15/25, which includes breakfast. Still within walking distance of the Old City is the two-star *Eastland Hotel* (☎ 377 000, *fax 359 600, Drousiotis 23)* that offers reasonable rooms for CY£17/28.

Places to Stay – Mid-Range

Further west but still within reasonable walking distance is the three-star *Centurion Hotel* (☎ 86 266, *fax 591 032, Pan. Symeou 6)* offering B&B-style accommodation for CY£20/27. The three-star *Best Western Pavemar* (☎ 587 000, *fax 587 711, @ pavemar@spidernet.com.cy, 28 Oktovriou; off map)* is at the beginning of the tourist centre and handy to both sides of town. Rates are CY£38/50 for singles/doubles and it offers a good range of facilities including a pool.

The two-star *Pefkos Hotel* (☎ 377 077, *fax 377 083, @ pefkotel@logos.net.cy, corner of Kavazoglou and Misiaouli 86),* on the west side of the Old City, is the nearest hotel to the port, yet still within walking distance of the Old City. Good rooms go for CY£20/27 all year round.

Places to Stay – Top-End

Lemesos' really good hotels are at the far north-eastern end of the tourist centre with the *Le Meridien Limassol* (☎ 634 000, *fax 634 222, @ meridien@zenon.logos.cy.net; off map)* leading the pack. This five-star establishment is 12km out of the Old City. While it has escaped the crush of the central tourist centre, it's perhaps a shade too close for comfort to the Moni power station looming a couple of kilometres east. Still,

for CY£101/140 you do get a luxury hotel with better distractions than a mere power station.

The five-star *Amathus Beach* (☎ 321 152, *fax 327 494, amathus@spidernet .com.cy; off map)*, 3km closer to Lemesos, is another high-flyer. With rates a shade under the Le Meridien's, it still offers every conceivable facility and a decent beach to match. Discounts of between 30% and 40% apply at both these hotels out of season.

PLACES TO EAT

Lemesos' dining and drinking arena is quite distinctly divided between the older, more traditional local Cypriot scene in the Old City and the ritzy, glitzy scene in the tourist centre, 3km north-east of the Old City. In between these areas and along the beachfront strip are a number of bars and restaurants that fall in between the two extremes.

There is little to be said in favour of the tourist centre bar and restaurant scene. It is brash, tacky, kitsch and with few exceptions, such as the various yachting club restaurants at the southern end, offers little in the way of quality, authenticity or value. Greek Cypriot restaurants invariably offer mediocre meze deals with ostensibly genuine floor shows. These usually entail a game where patrons try to light a newspaper stuck into the tail of the pantaloons of the male dancer. If you like heavy nightlife, manufactured fun, undiscerning crowds and bland food, the tourist centre is your paradise. If it's something a little mellower you are after, the following recommendations from the Old City are worth seeking out.

For a lunchtime snack and a cold beer make for the gaudily (KEO) coloured *Richard & Berengaria Cafe* on the castle square. A couple of doors to the left is the slightly less gaudy *Cafe Antique*, popular with evening coffee and brandy drinkers.

Still further along the same street is the *To Frourio* (☎ 359 332, *Tsanakali 18),* a little restaurant tavern housed in an 18th-century listed building that does excellent meat and vegetarian mezedes. It is closed on Sunday. The excellent and low-key *Rizitiko Tavern* (☎ 348 769, *Tzamiou 4–8)* is tucked

Eating in Cyprus

If there's one thing you are going to remember about a visit to Cyprus, it's the food. Cypriot food is not all that different to the cuisines of Greece, Turkey and the Levant, but there is one culinary speciality that has become almost institutionalised to the point where it may be regarded as the national culinary pastime – eating *meze*.

Meze means 'appetiser' and is the same word in Greek and Turkish. Eating meze-style means enjoying a full meal via a series of small dishes that are eaten communally and brought to the table in rounds. To really appreciate a meze meal – and most restaurants do serve them – you will need at least three fellow diners with largely empty stomachs since you will be grazing on up to 30 different dishes.

The meal usually starts with a round of dips: hummus, garlic and potato dip, fish roe salad, tahini, plus olives, bread and fresh salad to get you going. Take it easy on the bread and dips here since it is very easy to fill up prematurely. At this point you may also get octopus in wine sauce, snails in tomato sauce, pickled capers and cauliflower, rubbery *haloumi* cheese and wild greens in oil and lemon.

A range of fish dishes normally follows these starters and these in turn are quickly followed by tasty meatballs, rissoles and sausages. If all that wasn't enough, the main dishes haven't even arrived yet! These are normally succulent kebabs, tender meat baked in a sealed oven and sizzling charcoal-grilled chicken. Dessert is usually fresh fruit.

A meze meal is a challenge as much as it is a culinary experience. The trick to successful meze eating is to eat light, or not at all at lunch (or breakfast). Pace yourself carefully and eat very slowly. Don't overdose on any particular meze dish. Remember you are supposed to be sampling the dishes not dining on them. Some restaurants also serve vegetarian meze courses. Ask beforehand. Wash it all down with some fine Cypriot wine, enjoy yourselves and 'kali orexi' or 'afiyet olsun' – bon appetit!

away nearby and spills out onto the narrow street at night. The *afelia* (CY£3.90) and *kleftiko* (CY£4.50) are home-made quality and worth every cent.

Two streets back is the popular *Mikri Maria* (☎ 357 679, *Angyras 3*) run by two attentive women. Main course dishes go for around CY£3. Tables also spill out onto the street.

For a rare experience and some great atmosphere, look for the *Folia tou Koukou* (Cuckoo's Nest, ☎ 357 046, *Agiou Andreou 228*). This oddball eatery, looking more like an antique shop, is one of Lemesos' hidden treats. The gregarious owner may join you for an ouzo or two and passing musicians may call in for an impromptu *rembetika* session. This place closes down for a month in summer. Prices are reasonable.

Further along the same street is *Vasilikos Taverna* (☎ 375 972, *Agiou Andreou 252*), which does great steak dishes. Prices are a bit on the high side though. Fish is best sampled at the *Ladas Old Harbour Fish*

Tavern (☎ 365 760) right next to the Old Fishing Harbour. The menu depends on what fish has been caught on the day and runs in price from CY£9.50 for 500g of swordfish to CY£35.60 for a kilo of lobster. Look out for the two resident pelicans at the door. The restaurant is closed on Sunday.

ENTERTAINMENT
Bars

The *Jukebox Bar-Cafe* (*Agiou Andreou 43*) is a neat, hip little joint that offers snacks, drinks and over 10 different kinds of coffee concoctions ranging in price from CY£1.25 to CY£1.95. Food is served until 6.30 pm only. *Rogmes Piano Bar* (*Agiou Andreou 197*) is a quiet, relaxed little bar and a couple of blocks along you will find the friendly *Angel's Pub* (*Agiou Andreou 219*) which is a little more lively. *Alaloum* (*Loutron 1*) near the hammam is primarily a gay hang-out.

In the city that never sleeps, the tourist centre 3km north-east of the Old City offers more bars and nightclubs than you could ever work your way through during a two-week vacation.

Cinemas

There are about four cinemas scattered around Lemesos which sometimes show reruns of English-language movies. All foreign-language films are subtitled in Greek. Entry is normally around CY£3 per person. The following is a list of the more central movie theatres in town. Call about the latest celluloid offerings. If you hang on long enough, after the often pre-recorded Greek announcement, you will get an English message with details of the movies on offer.

Hollywood 1 (☎ 362 436) Gladstonos 104
Othellos (☎ 374 306) Thessalonikis 19
Pallas (☎ 362 324) Evklidou 2

SHOPPING

Most of Lemesos' clothes, shoes and appliance shops are clustered along the pedestrianised streets of Agiou Andreou in central Lemesos, but also filter out through most of the backstreets of this area. Functional hardware – like Cypriot BBQs known as *foo-koo* – can be found in the streets leading off from the Medieval Castle area. Tourist souvenir shops and fur coat boutiques are all clustered along the length of the main drag in the tourist centre, northeast of central Lemesos.

GETTING THERE & AWAY

Air

The Cyprus Airways office (☎ 373 787) is at Leoforos Arhiepiskopou Makariou III 203, a 20-minute walk north-east of the main CTO office. Lemesos is more or less equidistant from Pafos and Larnaka airports. Service or private taxis are the only way to reach either airport.

Bus

Kemek has frequent daily services to Lefkosia (CY£1.50) and Pafos (CY£1.50) from the corner of Enoseos and Irinis, north of the castle. From here there is also a

weekday bus at noon to Agros (CY£1.50) in the Troödos Mountains.

Kallenos goes to Larnaka (CY£1.70) from the Old Fishing Harbour or from outside the CTO. From Monday to Saturday, the Kyriakos/Karydas service taxi company has a minibus that goes to Platres (CY£1.50) at 11.30 am from its office on Thessalonikis.

Service Taxi

Close to the CTO at Spyrou Araouzou 65, Acropolis Service Taxis (☎ 366 766) leave every half an hour for Lefkosia (CY£3), Larnaka (CY£2.60) and Pafos (CY£2.30). Kyriakos/Karydas (☎ 364 114), at Thessalonikis 21, travels the same routes.

International Ferry

Lemesos will invariably be your first port of call if you come to Cyprus by sea. Scheduled ferry services operate to Israel and Greece only. You can buy ferry tickets from any travel agency or direct from Salamis Tours Ltd (☎ 355 555) or Poseidon Lines (☎ 745 666). The port is 5km south-west of town. (See the introductory Getting There & Away chapter for more information.) Travellers with vehicles are advised to make return bookings well in advance in summer since demand is high and vehicle places are limited.

Cruises

Two and three-day cruises depart from Lemesos all year. They go to Haifa (Israel), Port Said (Egypt), a selection of Greek islands, and sometimes (in summer) to Lebanon. You can book at any travel agency, but you cannot use these cruises to exit Cyprus, unless you decide to jump ship.

GETTING AROUND

The city bus station is on A Themistokleous, close to the municipal market. Bus No 1 goes to the port, bus No 16–17 to Kolossi and bus No 30 runs north-east along the seafront. The CTO gives out a very useful *Limassol Urban Bus Routes* timetable.

Buses also run hourly on the hour between 9 am and 1 pm from the castle to Kourion and its beach, via Episkopi. Return times are 11.50 am, 2.50 pm and 4.50 pm. A one-way ticket costs CY£0.70. From April to October there's a daily Governor's Beach bus that leaves from the Old Fishing Harbour at 9.50 am, making stops at about 23 locations along the seafront with the last one at 10.02 am at the Meridien Hotel. The bus returns at 4.30 pm. A return ticket costs CY£2.

Lipsos Rent-a-Car (☎ 365 295) is at Richard & Berengaria 6 (opposite the castle) and is the only car rental place in the Old City. There are many more rental agencies in the tourist centre.

Around Lemesos

ANCIENT KOURION
This spectacular archaeological site, 19km west of Lemesos, is perhaps Cyprus' best known tourist attraction. Kourion attracts hordes of daily visitors, so if you wish to view it with a modicum of peace and quiet come early in the morning or late in the afternoon. These are better times for photography anyway. Ancient Kourion is close to two other attractions in the immediate vicinity, the Sanctuary of Apollon Ylatis and Kolossi Castle. All three could be combined into a day trip, followed perhaps by a swim at **Kourion Beach** spread out temptingly below the ancient site of Kourion itself.

Ancient Kourion was a cliff-top settlement most likely first founded in Neolithic times, probably because of its strategic position high on a bluff overlooking the sea. It became a permanent settlement about the 13th century BC, when Mycenaean colonisers established themselves here. According to Greek historian Herodotus, Stasanor, king of the then prosperous city, turned traitor in 497 BC and sided with the Persians in their attempt to secure Salamis, just off the Greek mainland. A later king of Kourion, Pasicretes, then sided with Alexander the Great in his fight against the Persians at the siege of Tyre in 332 BC.

The settlement also prospered under the Ptolemies and Romans. A pre-Christian cult of Apollo was active among the inhabitants of Kourion in Roman times, as documented by the nearby Sanctuary of Apollon Ylatis (see the following section). Christianity eventually supplanted Apollo worship and, despite disastrous earthquakes in the region, an **early Christian Basilica** was built in the 5th century AD, testifying to the ongoing influence of Christianity on Kourion by this time. Pirate raids 200 years later severely compromised the viability of the now Christian bishopric and the Bishop of Kourion was obliged to move his base to a new settlement at nearby **Episkopi**, which means 'bishopric' in Greek. Kourion essentially declined as a settlement from that point and was not rediscovered until tentative excavations at the site began in 1876 and continued until 1933.

The site is dominated by its magnificent **amphitheatre**, which is a reconstruction of a smaller theatre that existed on the same site, high on the hill overlooking the sea. The original theatre was destroyed in earthquakes during the 3rd century. The current amphitheatre gives a good idea of how it would have been at its peak. Today it's used for cultural events such as plays, jazz festivals and music concerts by Cypriot and visiting Greek singers and bands.

Nearby is the **Annexe of Eustolios**, probably a private residence dating from the 5th century. Its colourful, Christian-influenced mosaic floors are well preserved and make minor mention of the builder Eustolios and the decidedly non-Christian patron Apollo. Look for the Christian motifs in the shape of cross-shaped ornaments and birds and fish.

The **early Christian Basilica**, perhaps built in the time of Bishop Zeno, displays all the hallmarks of an early church with foundations clearly showing the existence of a narthex, diakonikon, various rooms, baptistery and atrium. Some floor mosaics are also visible among the remains of the basilica.

North-west is the so-called **House of the Gladiators**, thus named because of two fairly well-preserved floor mosaics depicting gladiators in combat dress. Two of these gladiators, Hellenikos and Margaritis, are depicted practising with blunt weapons.

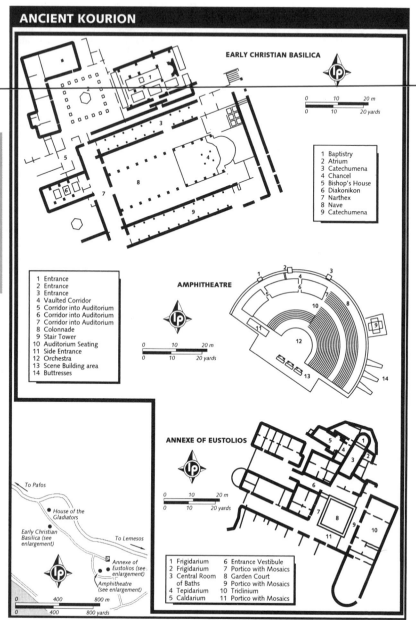

ANCIENT KOURION

EARLY CHRISTIAN BASILICA

1 Baptistry
2 Atrium
3 Catechumena
4 Chancel
5 Bishop's House
6 Diakonikon
7 Narthex
8 Nave
9 Catechumena

1 Entrance
2 Entrance
3 Entrance
4 Vaulted Corridor
5 Corridor into Auditorium
6 Corridor into Auditorium
7 Corridor into Auditorium
8 Colonnade
9 Stair Tower
10 Auditorium Seating
11 Side Entrance
12 Orchestra
13 Scene Building area
14 Buttresses

AMPHITHEATRE

ANNEXE OF EUSTOLIOS

To Pafos

● House of the Gladiators

Early Christian Basilica (see enlargement)

To Lemesos

🅿 Annexe of Eustolios (see enlargement)

Amphitheatre (see enlargement)

1 Frigidarium
2 Frigidarium
3 Central Room of Baths
4 Tepidarium
5 Caldarium
6 Entrance Vestibule
7 Portico with Mosaics
8 Garden Court
9 Portico with Mosaics
10 Triclinium
11 Portico with Mosaics

LEMESOS & THE SOUTH COAST

The site is open 7.30 am to 7.30 pm (to 5 pm in winter). Admission is CY£1.

THE SANCTUARY OF APOLLON YLATIS

This second complex of the larger site is about 2km west of Kourion. The precinct was established in the 8th century BC in honour of the god Apollo who was considered to be god of the woods; *ylatis* means 'of the woods' in Greek. The once woody site now has far less vegetation, but retains a good scattering of remains that give a reasonable idea of the layout of the original sanctuary. The remnants that you see are from buildings of the Roman era that were levelled by a large earthquake in 365 AD.

The **main sanctuary** has been partly restored and the imposing standing columns mark the extent of the restoration. Also discernible is a **palaestra** (or sports arena) and **baths** for participating athletes, the **priests' quarters** and a rather depleted **stadium** 500m to the east which once seated up to 6000 spectators.

The sanctuary is open 9 am to 7.30 pm daily (9 am to 5.30 pm from October to April). Entry costs CY£0.75.

KOURION MUSEUM

This small museum, in the village of Episkopi 14km west of Lemesos, is somewhat out of the way for visitors to the Kourion site. The village is served by bus from Lemesos (see Getting Around in the earlier Lemesos section) but it is not all that easy to visit both the museum and the ancient site. The collection mainly comprises terracotta objects from Kourion and the Sanctuary of Apollo Ylatis and is housed in what used to be the private residence of archaeologist George McFadden. The museum is signposted off the Lemesos-Kourion road as well as in Episkopi village itself. It is open 7.30 am to 2.30 pm Monday to Friday and 3 to 6 pm on Thursday from November to March. Admission is CY£0.75.

KOLOSSI CASTLE

This rather grandly labelled site is less of a castle as such and more a fortified tower house, sitting incongruously between the vineyards and houses of the village that took the same name. It is nonetheless a worthwhile detour as much for its value as a reminder of the rule of the Knights of Saint John in the 13th century.

The site was known by the name Kolossi at about the time Richard the Lionheart was marrying Berengaria at nearby Lemesos, but it is not believed that a castle actually existed at the time. Lusignan king Hugh I granted the land to the Order of St John of Jerusalem, known as the Knights Hospitaller, in 1210 and it must be assumed that the first structure was built at that time. Eight years later the Knights Hospitaller formally moved their headquarters from Acre to Lemesos after their defeat in the final Crusade and the Kolossi Castle took on the significance of being the focus for conventual life of the Order from 1301. In 1310 the Hospitallers transferred their headquarters yet again to Rhodes but maintained the Kolossi stronghold as a commandery.

This commandery became one of the richest possessions of the Knights, producing wine – from which the famous Cypriot wine, Commandaria, took its name – and sugar cane. However Mameluke raids of 1425–26 compromised the prosperity of the commandery and no doubt damaged whatever infrastructure existed at the time. The current structure dates from 1454 and was probably built over the older fortified structure by Grand Commander Louis de Magnac whose coat of arms is visible on the east wall of the castle.

The castle is accessible by a short drawbridge that was originally defended by a machicolation high above, through which defenders would pour molten lead or boiling oil on the heads of unwanted visitors. Upon entering you come across two large chambers, one with an unusually large fireplace and a spiral staircase that leads to another two chambers on the second level. The chambers are empty so it is hard to imagine what they would have been like in their heyday. The only tangible remains of occupation is a wall painting of the crucifixion in the first-level main chamber. The spiral staircase leads to the roof where the battlements, restored in 1933, lend a final castle touch.

The basement consists of three storage vaults which were originally only accessible from above but now have a door leading out into the moat. To the east of the castle is an outbuilding, now called the **sugar factory,** where cane was processed into sugar.

The castle is open 9 am to 7.30 pm (to 5.30 pm in summer). Entry is CY£0.75.

AKROTIRI PENINSULA

In 1960, when Cyprus belatedly received her independence from colonial administration, Britain managed to negotiate terms that saw the new Republic of Cyprus ceding 158 sq km (99 sq miles) of its territory to its former colonial masters. This territory, now known as the Sovereign Base Areas (SBAs), is used for military purposes by the British who have a couple of well-established and solidly entrenched garrisons on the two SBAs in Cyprus. A large chunk of these areas occupies the Akrotiri Peninsula, immediately south-west of Lemesos, while the actual border of the Akrotiri SBA territory runs as far west as Avdimou Beach (see Beaches later in this chapter).

The only indication that you are on 'foreign soil' is the odd sight of British SBA police patrolling the territory in special police vehicles. SBA (ie, British military) law applies here, so if you are booked for any traffic infringement while driving in the area you'll be booked by British military police. To the immediate west of the peninsula, along the old Lemesos-Pafos road, you will come across green playing fields, cricket pitches and housing estates more reminiscent of Aldershot than Lemesos.

The lower half of the peninsula is out of bounds since it is a closed **military base,** complete with its own large airfield. The village of Akrotiri itself is the only true settlement within the SBA (borders were set in order to exclude most settlements) and its only real claim to fame is that its inhabitants are accorded the privilege of dual citizenship. British military personnel often eat here at the several tavernas and may be seen on days off on flash mountain bikes tackling the dirt tracks surrounding the large salt lake in the middle of the peninsula.

The only real sights are the **Fassouri plantations,** a large swathe of citrus groves across the north of the peninsula, interwoven with long, straight stretches of road overhung by tall cypress trees. They create wonderfully cool and refreshing corridors after the aridity of the southern peninsula. Then there is the oddly named **Holy Monastery of Saint Nicholas of the Cats,** positioned on the edge of the salt lake with its back to the SBA base fence, and reached by a good dirt road from Akrotiri or via a not so obvious route from Lady's Mile Beach.

This monastery, and its original little church, were founded in 327 by the first Byzantine governor of Cyprus, Kalokeros, backed by Helen, mother of Constantine the Great. At the time, the Akrotiri Peninsula and indeed the whole of Cyprus was in the grip of a severe drought and was overrun with snakes, so building a monastery was fraught with practical difficulties. A large shipment of cats was subsequently brought in to combat the reptile threat and the ultimately successful felines stayed. The peninsula was in fact known for a time as 'Cat Peninsula' before reverting to plain 'Peninsula' which is what Akrotiri means in Greek. There is a little renovated church that dates from the 13th century and a sprawling monastery building. The many somnolent cats snoozing in the shade of the monastery colonnades far outnumber the four solitary sisters who now look after the monastery that received a much-needed renovation in 1983.

ANCIENT AMATHOUS

This rather nondescript archaeological site 11km east of Lemesos belies its original importance. Amathous was one of Cyprus' original four kingdoms – the others were Salamis, Pafos and Soloi. Legend has it that the city was founded by Kinyras, the son of Apollo and Pafos. It is also said that Kinyras introduced the cult of Aphrodite to Cyprus (see the boxed text 'The Cult of Aphrodite' in the Pafos chapter). Founded in about 1000 BC the city had an unbroken history of settlement until about the 14th century, despite depredation at the hands of Corsairs during the 7th and 8th centuries. In 1191, when Richard the Lionheart appeared on the scene, the city was already on the decline. With its harbour silted up, King Richard was obliged to disembark on the beach to claim the once proud and wealthy city. He promptly applied the royal *coup de grâce* by destroying it and Amathous was no more.

It is rather difficult to get an overview of the site without visual guidance since much of the stone and marble has long been looted and carted away for other building projects. Most of Amathous' best treasures were removed by the infamous American consul of Larnaka, Luigi de Cesnola (see also The Pierides Foundation Museum section in the Larnaka chapter). To the right as you enter the site is an explanatory pedestal with a schematic map of the area. This will help you to understand how the city was originally laid out. Excavations only started in earnest in 1980 and to date the two main visible features are an **early Christian basilica** in the so-called lower city and the remains of a sanctuary to Aphrodite on the **acropolis** immediately behind the lower city.

The full extent of the ancient city has yet to be discovered. Excavations are made difficult by the considerable growth of tourist hotels on both sides of the site. The remains of the **ancient harbour** have been found at sea. Occasional free summer concerts are held within the grounds of Amathous. Look for posters at the site or check with the CTO in Lemesos. The site is open 9 am to 7.30 pm (to 5 pm in winter). Admission is CY£0.75.

BEACHES

Lemesos' city beaches, while reasonable and to the casual observer popular enough, are not exactly Waikiki material. You are going to have to move out of Lemesos if you want some space and freedom from the masses that congregate along the tourist centre's crowded beach scene. The nearest and easiest option is **Lady's Mile Beach**, named after a horse owned by a former

colonial governor who took his mare to exercise on the beach. This 7km stretch of flat, shadeless sand stretches south beyond Lemesos' New Port along the eastern side of the British-controlled Akrotiri Peninsula (see the previous section). Given its current ownership, it is surprising there is a beach scene at all, but on summer weekends the citizens of Lemesos flock here in large numbers to relax on its golden sand and in its rather shallow waters. The most popular spot seems to be at the far southern end, hard up against the barbed wire fence and prohibiting signs of the British Sovereign Base Area. A couple of beach tavernas serve the crowds and provide some shade and respite from an otherwise barren beachscape. Bring your own shade if you plan to sit on the beach all day. Unfortunately getting here requires your own transport since no public transport serves the area.

Governor's Beach, some 30km east of Lemesos, is probably a better option for travellers without their own transport. A private bus commutes daily between Lemesos and this beach enclave (see Getting Around in the Lemesos section of this chapter), leaving visitors enough time to spend a relaxing day on a reasonably decent beach made up mainly of dark sand which can get very hot in the height of summer. There are a couple restaurants here and at least one place to stay, though the overall ambience is slightly marred by the sight of the large Vasilikos power station looming 3km to the west.

Kourion Beach, also reached by public transport from Lemesos, is a long stretch of mixed pebbles and sand and attracts a large number of local swimmers. Some 17km west of Lemesos and still within the Sovereign Base Area, the beach is also without shade other than that provided by the three largish beach tavernas. Locals like to drive their cars and 4WDs practically up to the water's edge. The eastern end of the beach (prominently marked) is unsafe for swimming, so head for the western end. This beach is best combined with your trip to Ancient Kourion.

Better still, but only for bathers with wheels, is **Avdimou Beach**, a further 17km

LEMESOS & THE SOUTH COAST

west of Kourion Beach. This low-key beach is wide and sandy with clean and usually less rough water than Kourion and has one beach taverna (see the following section). At Pissouri, yet another 10km beyond Avdimou, you will come to the popular but still tasteful resort of Pissouri Bay. This very pleasant relaxed beach enclave pulls in a fair slice of the package-tour crowd, but it is also a good alternative base for individual travellers. A rather large number of restaurants and tavernas ply their trade here and the beach is sandy and well supplied with handy sun loungers and umbrellas.

PLACES TO STAY & EAT

A great place to base yourself for a few days is the little village of Episkopi, 14km west of Lemesos. *To Spiti tou Andoni* (☎ 05-232 502, fax 233 113, @ katerina .travel@cytanet.com.cy) is a wonderful little agrotourism hotel built around a leafy and cool garden. There are beautiful double rooms and a self-contained studio ranging from CY£12 to CY£20 per person.

Over in Pissouri Bay, *Kotzias Hotel Apartments* (☎ 05-221 014, fax 222 449) are an ideal mid-range option for travellers wishing to base themselves by the sea for a few days. Summer season prices for a one-bedroom apartment are CY£20 per day or CY£26 for a two-bedroom apartment.

In Episkopi, the *Episkopi Village Inn* (☎ 05-232 751) is right next door to To Spiti tou Andoni and is the best place to eat in the village. It is closed on Sunday.

On Avdimou Beach is *Kyrenia Beach Restaurant* (☎ 05-211 717), the only beach eatery. It is laid back and relaxing while offering a fairly predictable range of meat and fish dishes.

At Pissouri Bay there is a wide choice of restaurants. Among the better ones is *Yialos Tavern* (☎ 05-221 747) with an upstairs balcony, but set back a bit from the sea. *Symposio* (☎ 05-221 158) is on the main road and features live music every Friday night and the *Vineleaf Tavern* (☎ 05-221 053) is situated nearby among pleasant vines. All offer similar menus with marginal differences in prices which are all mid-range. Bank on around CY£5 per person for a mezes spread.

GETTING AROUND

There's little choice here; it's your own transport or nothing at all. Other than Kourion, which is linked with Lemesos by daily public buses, and Governor's Beach, which is served by a daily private bus service (see Getting Around in the Lemesos section), reaching any of the other places described above is going to require hired transport or expensive taxis.

The Troödos Massif

The mountains of the Troödos Massif rise grandly above the scorching plains and coastal strips of Cyprus' south, culminating in Mt Olympus, the country's highest peak at 1952m. In the past the mountains have provided refuge to religious communities, colonial civil servants and the wealthy of the Levant seeking respite from the heat. More recently it attracts skiers in winter and, in summer, hikers and weekend picnickers throng the spiralling mountain roads in their 4WD jeeps and recreational vehicles.

Visitors to the Troödos should allow themselves at least a week to see most of what the region has to offer. The mountains are clad in a blanket of pine trees – Aleppo pine is the predominant species – and are crisscrossed with a network of winding but good roads that link all points of habitation. Public transport to the Troödos is sketchy at best so this is one region where having your own transport is highly recommended. However hikers, having established themselves at one of the area's main settlements, will find plenty of activities without feeling the need to move around on wheels. The Cyprus Tourism Organisation (CTO) has sponsored a number of well-marked and well-maintained hiking trails around the mountains.

Many people come to visit the beautiful frescoed monasteries that dot the valleys and foothills of the Troödos. These old churches and monasteries, many dating from the 15th century, developed as a means of self-preservation at times when Orthodoxy was feeling the pinch at the hands of its numerous colonial rulers. The often brilliant frescoes that decorate these churches are unique through the whole of Cyprus.

The regions can be roughly divided into four sections, each of which is probably better tackled as a discrete entity. However, having your own vehicle will give you ample opportunity to overlap between regions.

HIGHLIGHTS

- Contemplate the splendour of the frescoes and mosaics in Byzantine monasteries.
- Hike through forests, orchards and mountain ridges in the shadow of Mt Olympus.
- Spot the endangered white and yellow Cyprus crocus in the mountains.

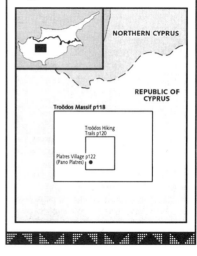

NORTHERN CYPRUS

REPUBLIC OF CYPRUS

Troödos Massif p118

Troödos Hiking Trails p120

Platres Village p122 (Pano Platres)

Troödos Central
Κεντρικό Τρόοδος

The central region is dominated by Mt Olympus, around which are scattered settlements, ski runs, hiking trails and picnic grounds. Mt Olympus is ultimately a bit of a disappointment since you can't actually get to the summit.

From the beginning of January to the beginning of March you can usually ski on the slopes of Mt Olympus – known in Greek as Hionistra. Although it is cooler up

117

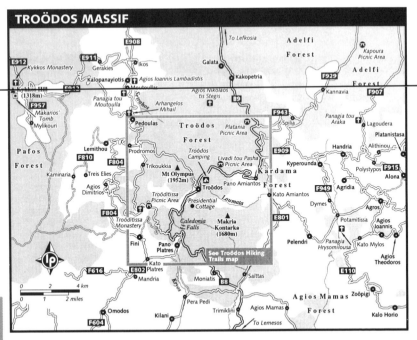

TROÖDOS MASSIF

on the Troödos than on the plains, hiking is probably best undertaken in spring or autumn when there is no summer heat haze and the superb views can be better appreciated.

ORIENTATION

This area consists primarily of two settlements: Troödos itself, just below the summit of Olympus, and the larger village of Pano Platres, 6km farther down the southern slope. The Central Troödos can be reached by way of a reasonably fast road from Lemesos (the B8) or by its continuation (the B9) up the northern flanks from Lefkosia.

The Troödos Central can also be accessed from the east (the Pitsylia district) and from the west (Pafos and the Pafos hinterland) by good but often winding and slow roads. At peak times, such as Sunday evenings, seeking out an alternative route back to the coast is advisable since traffic can be very heavy.

Public buses serve Platres and Troödos and there is a regular service taxi link between Platres and Lemesos.

TROÖDOS Τρόοδος
☎ 05

At first glance there is not much to the small village of Troödos. It consists of little more than a main street, a few restaurants and some scattered public buildings. The greatest amount of current activity comes from the building of a new military base along the Lefkosia road. Yet Troödos does draw huge crowds of people who exit their coaches and hire cars to wander up and down the one main street gawking at the few souvenir stalls. In the car park at the northern end of the main street, on any given day at least 90% of the vehicles are hire cars, identifiable by their black on red number plates.

Despite such potentially inauspicious initial impressions, Troödos is pleasant

THE TROÖDOS MASSIF

enough to base yourself for a few days and the hikes, or even the low-key horse riding available, will keep you active enough. One hotel rents out mountain bikes and if you are fit there are enough forest roads and trails to keep even the most fanatic mountain biker happy for a week. Kids are catered for with a reasonable playground adjacent to the main street. Nightlife is another matter, with none to speak of other than perhaps a drink at the bar of your hotel. Most day visitors have long since departed by the time the sun sinks below the summit of Hionistra.

Orientation

From Troödos, one road leads north and downwards towards Lefkosia while another heads west to Prodromos and further afield. The approach road from Lemesos and Platres comes in directly from the south. There is a small store with a post office agency, several prominent old UK-style phone boxes and plenty of road signs – some of them totally confusing.

The Troödos Hiking Trails

The four designated trails give you a good overall picture of the flora of the Troödos. Many of the trees and plants you pass are marked with both their Latin and Greek names. There are frequent rest stops with wooden benches conveniently positioned beneath shady trees to allow you to catch your breath or simply to admire the views.

The TCO has published a fairly useful booklet called *Nature Trails of the Troödos,* which outlines all the trails and gives a description of the flora and natural features to be found along the way. Detailed though not professional maps of the trails accompany the text.

The Artemis Trail Of the four, this is the one that you should perhaps tackle first. It is the newest of the trails and takes you round the summit of Mt Olympus in a more or less circular loop. The trailhead begins/ ends at a little car park off the Mt Olympus summit road. It's better to get there by car to avoid the 1.5km walk along the often

busy highway. The trailhead sign directs you to walk clockwise though there is no reason why you should not tackle it anticlockwise. The trail end is unmarked and on the opposite side of the Olympus summit road.

The complete walk should take you no more than 2½ to 3½ hours, allowing for stops along the way. It is 7km long with very little climbing. The track runs alternately through partly shaded and open areas and the views on the south side over the foothills are indeed spectacular. Look out for signs to the **giant pine trees** and take care not to lose the trail around the ski runs on the north side. There is no water along the route so take your own supplies.

The Atalanti Trail This trail is for people who like walking. It is long – about 9km – and involves a fair hike along the main Prodromos-Troödos road to get back to your starting point. The Atalanti trail – named in honour of the ancient forest nymph – runs at a lower altitude than the Artemis trail but follows roughly the same route. It is relatively easy going and is well marked. There is a spring with drinking water some 3km from the trailhead at Troödos.

The views are not as spectacular as those from the trail higher up but it is a most enjoyable walk, perhaps better enjoyed by hikers with time on their hands. At the end of the main trail, instead of walking back along the main road, you can head upward along a connecting track and meet up with the Artemis trail. Follow this trail clockwise until you come to the Artemis trailhead.

The Caledonia Trail The Caledonia trail begins about a kilometre down the Troödos-Platres main road, close to the **Presidential Cottage**. The trail follows the course of the **Kryos River** – in reality a gurgling stream – as it winds its way down a thickly wooded and shady valley to Platres. The trail ends at the nostalgically named **Caledonia Falls**. It's long (2km), is the shortest way to the village of Platres and is a good way to work up an appetite for lunch at one of the restaurants. You can return the way you came or

THE TROÖDOS MASSIF

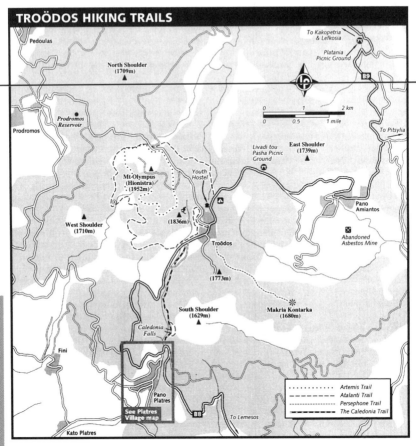

TROÖDOS HIKING TRAILS

Pedoulas

To Kakopetria
& Lefkosia

Platania
Picnic Ground

North Shoulder
(1709m)

B9

Prodromos
Reservoir

Prodromos

To Pitsylia

0   1   2 km
0   0.5   1 mile

Livadi tou
Pasha Picnic
Ground

East Shoulder
(1739m)

Youth
Hostel

Mt Olympus
(Hionistra)
(1952m)

Pano
Amiantos

West Shoulder
(1710m)

(1836m)

Troödos

Abandoned
Asbestos Mine

(1773m)

South Shoulder
(1629m)

Makria Kontarka
(1680m)

Caledonia
Falls

Fini

Pano
Platres

.... Artemis Trail
– – – – – – Atalanti Trail
--------------- Persephone Trail
-■-■-■- The Caledonia Trail

See Platres
Village map

B8

To Lemesos

Kato Platres

THE TROÖDOS MASSIF

arrange to be picked up by car in Platres. You can easily hitch back to Troödos.

The Persephone Trail This is probably the easiest trail to undertake if you are based in Troödos without transport. Known in Greek as the Makria Kontarka trail, it is a simple out-and-back hike through attractive pine forest and some open areas. The trail is 3km long and should take you about 45 minutes to reach the **lookout** – the object of the walk. From here you can gaze out over the southern foothills, or if you look to your left you will see the enormous scar caused by mining and tailings of the now closed asbestos mine at Pano Amiantos. The marked trailhead begins opposite the Troödos police station. From the main street walk south along the narrow road heading upward to the left and you will quickly find the trailhead after about 200m.

Horse Riding
It's hardly *Bonanza* stuff, but there is a small horse-riding outfit next to the public conveniences on the south side of the village. Short escorted rides around Troödos cost CY£3 for 15 to 20 minutes.

Picnic Grounds

Although it is easy enough to set up a picnic more or less anywhere in the Troödos, experienced picnickers might want to head for one of the well-organised picnic grounds on the approach roads to the Troödos summit. Bear in mind that lighting open fires anywhere is not allowed, so a picnic ground is the best solution if you wish to grill chops or spit roast some Cypriot *kontosouvli*. A particularly good picnic ground is the **Livadi tou Pasha** 3km down the Troödos-Lefkosia road on the left and thankfully before the ghastly sight of the former Pano Amiantos asbestos mine. There is a BBQ area and many fixed benches and tables scattered among the pine trees.

Farther along the Lefkosia road, and past the Karvounas crossroads heading towards Kakopetria, is the very popular **Platania** (Plane Trees) picnic ground, about 8km from Troödos. This place does get inundated with weekend revellers, but is well organised and has plenty of shaded facilities including a children's adventure park. Get there early if you want to pick a good position.

Places to Stay & Eat

A kilometre or so north along the Lefkosia road and in a pine forest, there is a reasonable *camp site (☎ 421 624)*, which is open from May to October. Charges are CY£1 per person and CY£2 for a tent. There is an on-site restaurant and minimarket.

The Troödos *HI Hostel (☎ 422 400)*, badly in need of a coat of paint, is usually open from April to October (depending on the weather) and charges CY£5 for the first night and CY£4 thereafter. Ignore the conflicting signposting in Troödos village; the hostel is set back 200m on the left as you head down the Lefkosia road. Up a notch is the laid-back *Jubilee Hotel (☎ 420 107, fax 420 119)*, some 350m from the village along the Prodromos road. It's popular with school groups so peace may be at a premium here. Singles/doubles are CY£25/35, though discounts of up to 50% are common in the off season. You can rent mountain bikes here.

Rather more luxurious is the three-star *Troödos Hotel (☎ 420 135, fax 420 160)*, where rooms cost CY£27/48, including breakfast.

Other than the restaurant at the camping ground, your eating choices are limited to two rather anglicised restaurants. *Ben Nevis* serves kebab and chips for CY£2.50 and *Fereos* next door does a Cypriot *kleftiko* meal for CY£5. The *Troödos Hotel* farther down the street has a somewhat more refined in-house restaurant where a local trout lunch will cost you CY£4.50.

Getting There & Away

There is a Clarios Bus Co (☎ 02-453 234) that leaves the Constanza Bastion in Lefkosia at 11.30 am (Monday to Friday) for Troödos via Kakopetria. It departs from Troödos for Lefkosia at 6.30 am, but only if reservations have been made in advance. A one-way ticket costs CY£1.10. Service taxis do not operate out of Troödos.

PLATRES Πλάτρες
☎ 05

In the 'good old colonial' days, Platres was *the* mountain vacation resort for the well heeled and well connected. This included such luminaries as King Farouk of Egypt and Nobel Prize-winning Greek poet, Odysseas Elytis. This was, of course, long before beach vacations had become *de rigueur* among the burgeoning classes of sun worshippers who fled en masse to the beaches of Cyprus' North and South. Platres was modelled after colonial hill stations in India and offered all the trappings of a cool mountain retreat: forest walks, gurgling streams, relief from the searing heat of the plains and gins and tonic to be taken on the balconies of old-world hotels catering for their guests' every wish.

Those days are more or less gone and today Platres caters for walkers, retirees, travellers who still prefer the hills to the beaches, and the purely curious who either make the drive up in rented cars, or as part of Troödos 'safaris' in long wheelbase Landrovers. Most easily accessible from Lemesos, Platres is still a fine place for a day or two of indolence coupled with a walk or two and perhaps followed by lingering sunset cocktails.

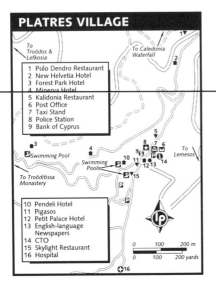

PLATRES VILLAGE

To
Troödos &
Lefkosia

To Caledonia
Waterfall

1 Psilo Dendro Restaurant
2 New Helvetia Hotel
3 Forest Park Hotel
4 Minerva Hotel
5 Kalidonia Restaurant
6 Post Office
7 Taxi Stand
8 Police Station
9 Bank of Cyprus

Swimming Pool

To Lemesos

Swimming
Pools

To Troöditissa
Monastery

10 Pendeli Hotel
11 Pigasos
12 Petit Palace Hotel
13 English-language
    Newspapers
14 CTO
15 Skylight Restaurant
16 Hospital

0   100   200 m
0   100   200 yards

Orientation

Platres is at first sight confusingly strung
out around a series of snaking roads, just
off the main Lemesos-Troödos highway.
All public transport arrives at and departs
from the area adjoining the CTO office.
The police station and post office are also
here. Platres basically consists of the upper
road that is home to a number of hotels and
the lower road that is home to its restaurants, shops, bars and three swimming
pools. The service taxi rank is next to the
CTO office.

Information

The CTO office (☎ 421 316) is well stocked
with brochures on the Troödos, as well as
the rest of Cyprus, and the staff is very willing to help with queries. The office is open
9 am to 3 pm Monday to Friday and 9 am
to 2 pm on Saturday. There is a branch of
the Bank of Cyprus on the main street, but
no ATM. Credit card advances can be obtained inside the bank. It is open 8.15 am to
12.30 pm Monday to Friday. The Platres
hospital is about 600m south of the village
centre just off the main road to Kato Platres
and Omodos.

English-language newspapers may be
purchased at the little shop opposite the
Bank of Cyprus.

Things to See & Do

Apart from succumbing to the temptation to
sip gins and tonic in the company of a good
novel around one of Platres' three **swimming
pools**, more energetic visitors might care to
take a walk along one of the 11 marked **hiking trails** in the neighbourhood. Four of the
trails have been described previously in the
Troödos section and the Caledonia Trail is
quite accessible on foot from Platres.

Other options may include hikes from
Platres to Fini (a longish 9km downhill
route perhaps requiring a taxi or lift back),
Platres to Perapedhi (slightly shorter at
7km) or a shorter but uphill option, **Platres
to Pouziaris** that is only 3km. These walks
and others are described in greater detail in
the CTO brochure *Platres,* which also contains a map of the village.

Prodromos is a small village to the west
of Troödos. It used to have a sizable hill
station clientele, but has not weathered the
changes as well as Troödos and Platres. It
might not be worth the downhill roll from
Troödos just to visit Prodromos, but if you
are heading for Kykkos or the Marathasa
Valley you pass through Prodromos anyway. The main claim to fame of this quiet
little backwater is that it is officially
Cyprus' highest village at 1400m elevation.
That said, its role as a base for touring the
region is limited by its choice of accommodation, currently limited to one rather expensive resort.

Omodos, on the south-west flank of
Troödos Central, is Cyprus' wine capital. It
is very attractively sited amid sprawling
vineyards and has traditional stone houses
punctuating its winding streets. The central
area is paved over with cobbled stones and
is accessible to pedestrians only. What is
unusual about Omodos is that it is built
around a monastery, the Byzantine **Moni
Timiou Stavrou** (Monastery of the Holy
Cross), which was originally built in
around 1150 and was extended and extensively remodelled in the 19th century. There

are restaurants and souvenir shops in Omodos, though your best souvenir is perhaps a bottle of wine and your own photos.

The 13th-century **Troöditissa Monastery**, while clearly signposted off the Troödos-Platres road, is primarily a working religious establishment and is not too inclined to receive curious onlookers. Nonetheless, the monastery is in a beautiful setting and is open for suitably pious visitors (6 am to noon and 2 to 8 pm daily). It was founded on the basis of a miraculous icon discovered in a nearby cave and which had been guarded by two hermits until their death. At this point the potential significance of the icon was recognised and the monastery was established. You can visit the nondescript cave by following a marked track signposted to the east of the monastery turn-off.

Places to Stay & Eat

Accommodation options in Platres are decidedly more favourable than uphill in Troödos. Probably the best choice for first-timers to Platres would have to be the very comfortable and tasteful one-star *Minerva Hotel (☎ 421 731, fax 421 075, ✉ minerva@cylink.com.cy)*. Spotless rooms in the older part of the hotel, or even better minisuites in the newer annexe at the rear, go for CY£15/28 for singles/doubles including breakfast. Each room has private facilities and a phone and off-street parking is available. The hotel is on the upper street.

The Swiss-looking two-star *Petit Palace Hotel (☎ 422 723, fax 421 065, ✉ gregoryg@spidernet.com.cy)* is as central as you can get and offers neat en-suite rooms with breakfast for CY£25/32. Another notch up is the three-star *Pendeli Hotel (☎ 421 736, fax 421 808, ✉ pendeli@cylink.com.cy)*, with its cool welcoming lobby and inviting swimming pool. Modern, fan-cooled rooms are available for CY£26/52. The *New Helvetia Hotel (☎ 421 348, fax 422 148, ✉ helvetia@spidernet.com.cy)* is at the north-eastern end of the village near the main through highway. Well-appointed rooms are CY£32/46.

At the top end of the scale is the four-star *Forest Park Hotel (☎ 421 751, fax 421 875, ✉ forest@cytanet.com.cy)*, set among pine trees and conspicuously apart on the west side of the main village centre. Accommodation with all creature comforts will cost you CY£46/72. Discounts apply to all these hotels out of high season.

There is a cluster of restaurants and cafeterias close to the main drag. For a quick snack like a toasted *lountza* (smoked and marinated loin of pork) and bacon sandwich with a cold KEO beer, drop by the *Pigasos* snack bar overlooking the main road junction in the village.

Kalidonia Restaurant (☎ 421 404, Olympou 41) is very popular among local Cypriot diners and can get very crowded, but the food is good and the prices right. Also well patronised and recommended for its mezes menu (CY£6 per head) is the *Skylight Restaurant (☎ 422 244)*. There is an attached swimming pool which patrons may use for free. Non-diners pay CY£2.

Probably the best place to eat is *Psilo Dendro Restaurant (☎ 421 350, Aïdonion 13)* and trout farm. Set back from a bend in the road above Platres, you could be forgiven for assuming that there was no restaurant since it is hidden behind a rather innocuous building (part of the trout farm that supplies the restaurant). Delicious trout dishes go for around CY£4.50.

Getting There & Away

Buses leave Lemesos at 11.30 am Monday to Saturday for Platres, and at 7.30 am in the other direction back to Lemesos. A one-way ticket costs CY£2.

Service taxis (☎ 421 346) regularly run between Platres and Lemesos for CY£2 per person.

The Marathasa Valley Κοιλάδα Μαραθάσα

The beautiful Marathasa Valley is best approached from the Lefkosia side of the Troödos, though it's no great hassle to enter the valley from Troödos via Prodromos.

THE TROÖDOS MASSIF

The valley extends from Pedoulas – at the southern end and famous for its spring waters – to the plains that open out onto Northern Cyprus. The Setrahos River flows through the valley and empties into Morfou Bay in the North.

The drive up the valley from the north is particularly impressive, especially the final winding climb up to the amphitheatrically displayed village of Pedoulas that lies at the head of the valley. Pilgrims heading for the Kykkos Monastery from Lefkosia used to transit the valley, but now take a newly improved side road via Gerakies. While not physically within the confines of the Marathasa Valley – it is actually out on the edge of the Tyllirian wilderness – we include the Kykkos Monastery in this section for convenience.

The valley is home to a couple of frescoed churches worth visiting and is probably best visited in springtime when the wild flowers and cherry trees are in bloom and the whole valley is imbued with riotous colour.

ORIENTATION

The main settlement is Pedoulas at the southern end of the valley and high up on the escarpment. Pedoulas is the major tourist centre for the region, has banks and a post office and is linked to Lefkosia by a daily bus that goes through to Platres. The best accommodation and eating options are also in Pedoulas.

Lower down the valley, the villages of Kalopanayiotis and Moutoulas are colourful, though less touristy. A spur road from Kalopanayiotis to Gerakies is the most direct way to the Kykkos Monastery if approaching from the north.

PEDOULAS Πέδουλας

Pedoulas, at the southern end of the valley before the rise over the Troödos ridge, is the main settlement and tourist centre in the Marathasa Valley. It is well known for its cool air, bracing climate and bottled spring water that can be found on sale all over Cyprus.

There are more than enough accommodation options to absorb most visitors

for a few days. However Pedoulas can be busy with day-trippers, either travellers in hire cars or tourists in buses that ply the often winding routes of the Troödos Valley.

The Church of Arhangelos Mihail

This gable-roofed church is in the lower part of Pedoulas village. It dates from 1474 and visitors can see restored **frescoes** depicting the Archangel Michael, the Sacrifice of Abraham, the Virgin and Christ, Pontius Pilate and the Denial of Christ. If there is no-one in the church, seek out the village priest by asking in the local cafe.

KALOPANAYIOTIS

Καλοπαναγιώτης

The village of Kalopanayiotis does not offer the same variety in the way of accommodation and eating options as Pedoulas, but is nonetheless a useful stopover point along the valley. It is home to at least one impressive Byzantine church and visitors to Kykkos can save some time and distance by taking the newly upgraded road from Kalopanayiotis to Kykkos, via Gerakies.

There are a couple of places to stay but not much choice in the way of restaurants. Still, Kalopanayiotis is typical of the mountain villages of the Troödos Valley and its more down-to-earth ambience may appeal to travellers looking for a quieter and perhaps more genuine item.

The Church of Agios Ioannis Lambadistis

The church is signposted from the long serpentine main street of Kalopanayiotis and is reached by following a road downwards and then upwards again at the opposite side of the valley. Built in the traditional Troödos church style with a large barn-like roof, it is actually three churches in one, built side-on to one another over a period of 400 years from the 11th to the 15th centuries. The original **Orthodox church** has a double nave, to which has been added a **narthex** and a **Latin chapel**.

This composite church is one of the better preserved of the Troödos churches and visitors come for its intricate and colourful frescoes. The best **frescoes** are the 13th-century works in the main domed Orthodox church, especially those dedicated to Agios Irakleidios, the Entry into Jerusalem, the Raising of Lazarus, the Crucifixion and the Ascension. The vivid colour scheme of the frescoes suggests that the artists hailed originally from Constantinople.

More frescoes can be viewed in the narthex and Latin chapel and date from the 15th to the 16th centuries. In the Latin chapel the scenes depict the **Akathistos** hymn which praises the Virgin Mary, while the **Arrival of the Magi** represents the Magi on horseback in a style less Byzantine in its execution than the earlier frescoes in the Orthodox section of the church.

The church is open 8 am to noon and 1.30 to 6 pm daily from May to September. Outside those months you will have to seek out the village priest to open up for you. Photographs are not allowed and entry is free, though donations are encouraged.

The Panagia of Kykkos Monastery

This richest and most famous of Cyprus' religious institutions had humble if rather odd beginnings. The founder of the monastery was a hermit called Isaiah, who lived in a cave near the monastery's site in the 11th century. One day while out hunting, the Byzantine administrator of Cyprus, Manouil Voutomytis, crossed paths and words with Isaiah. Because of his self-imposed ascetic lifestyle, Isaiah refused to talk to the self-important Voutomytis who promptly beat up the hermit.

Later, while suffering an incurable illness in Lefkosia, Voutomytis remembered how he had mistreated the hermit Isaiah and asked for him to be sent for in order that he might ask for forgiveness – on the off-chance that his act of charitable penance might also restore his failing health. In the meantime, God had already appeared to Isaiah and asked him to request Voutomytis to bring the icon of the Virgin Mary to Cyprus from Constantinople. This icon had been painted by Luke the Apostle (St Luke).

After much delay and soul searching by Voutomytis, the icon was brought to Cyprus with the blessing of the Byzantine emperor in Constantinople, Alexios I Komninos. The Emperor's own daughter developed the same illness that had afflicted Voutomytis and was cured after Isaiah's timely and, by extension, divine intervention. The icon now constitutes the *raison d'être* for the Kykkos Monastery and has been kept for over four centuries, sealed in a silver-encased phylactery.

The current imposing, modern-looking monastery structure dates from no later than 1831. Nearly all of the beautiful mosaics and other cosmetic features of the monastery's walls and hallways are of recent design and execution, which in no way detracts from their beauty. The monastery grounds are open to the public and attract a steady stream of visitors all year round.

The most appealing part of a visit to Kykkos is the absolutely exquisite **Byzantine Museum** (☎ 02-942 736), with its breathtaking collection of Byzantine and ecclesiastical artefacts. The museum interior is a work of art in itself and it could well take up a couple of hours of your time just to admire the rich and priceless items. There is a small **antiquities display** on the left after you enter, a large **ecclesiastical gallery** with Early Christian, Byzantine and post-Byzantine church vestments, vessels and jewels, a small circular room with manuscripts, documents and books, and a rich display of icons, wall paintings and carvings in a larger circular chamber. Visitors are treated to appropriately soothing Byzantine church music.

The Kykkos Monastery is open from dawn until dusk year-round and the Byzantine Museum is open 10 am to 6 pm daily (to 4 pm from November to May). Entry is CY£1.50. A comprehensive *Visitors Guide* in English and other languages is available from the ticket office for CY£3.

Tomb of Archbishop Makarios III

If you have already made the long trip out to Kykkos, it is worth the extra effort to visit the tomb of Archbishop Makarios III on Throni Hill, 2km beyond the monastery. It is not too obvious how to get there; follow the road past the main entrance of the monastery and the car park until it bends right and heads upwards. There is a little parking area at the ~~top with a mobile cafeteria. Take the right~~ road to reach the tomb more efficiently.

The tomb is quite sombre and non-descript – a stone sepulchre overlaid with a black marble slab and covered by a rounded stone-inlaid dome. It cannot be approached directly and is permanently guarded by a couple of bored-looking soldiers. The tomb was apparently prepared in considerable haste, since Makarios died unexpectedly.

Farther up the hill is the little **Throni Shrine** with an icon of the Virgin Mary. The views from here on a clear day are spectacular with the long serpentine road leading to Kykkos from the east clearly visible snaking over the ridge tops.

PLACES TO STAY & EAT

At Pedoulas you can try *Rooms to Rent* (☎ 02-952 321) on the south side of the village where comfortable doubles go for around CY£10. Then there's the one-star but comfortable *Jack's* (☎ 02-952 350, fax 952 817) closer to the village centre with rates ranging from CY£28 to CY£41, or the no-star but big and airy *Mountain Rose*

Archbishop Makarios – Priest and Politician

Archbishop Makarios III – ethnarch and religious leader of Cyprus for all of its brief period of independence as a united island – was born Michael Hristodoulou Mouskos on 13 August 1913 in Pano Panagia, a small village in the western foothills of the Troödos Mountains. He studied in Cyprus and at Athens University and graduated ultimately from the School of Theology at Boston University. In 1946 he was ordained the Bishop of Kition and became archbishop in 1950.

To many observers it may seem strange that a religious leader could also be the political leader of a nation, but Makarios III was only carrying on a tradition that had begun long ago during Cyprus' domination by foreign powers and cultures. In those dark times, Greek Orthodox Cypriots looked to their clergy for leadership and guidance. Makarios was the culmination of the people's aspirations for independence and identity.

Makarios was initially associated with the movement for *enosis*, or union with Greece. He opposed the idea of independence, or Commonwealth status for Cyprus, as well as Turkish demands for separation *(taksim)*. During the three-year uprising of the 1950s the British suspected him of collaboration with the terrorist pro-enosis movement EOKA (the National Organisation for the Cypriot Struggle), under the leadership of General Georgios Grivas. He was exiled in the Seychelles. However, Makarios was a politician, not a terrorist, and was brought back to Cyprus in 1959. He negotiated a compromise independence agreement with the British and was elected president of the new independent state of Cyprus on 13 December 1959.

While distancing himself from the extremes of the enosis movement, Makarios embarked on a tightrope act of trying to appease the Turkish Cypriot minority in Cyprus and attempting to forge a foreign policy of non-alignment. However he was seen by the Turkish Cypriots as being anti-Turkish and serious sectarian violence broke out in 1963, leading to the ultimate division of Cyprus 11 years later. The Americans and the West saw him as being too accommodating to communism and feared another Cuba crisis, this time in the Mediterranean.

The Greek Junta, abetted by the CIA and pro-enosis EOKA-B (post-independence) activists in Cyprus, launched a coup in 1974 with a view to assassinating him and installing a new government. The coup backfired; Makarios escaped, the Turks invaded and took 37% of northern Cyprus, the Junta fell and Makarios returned to preside over a now truncated state.

He died on 3 August 1977 and is buried on a hilltop tomb close to the Kykkos Monastery in a site of his own choosing. He is still remembered fondly as Cyprus' greatest leader and statesman.

(☎ 02-952 727, fax 952 555) at the southern end of the village with rooms for CY£18/32. If you have a car and fancy a view, the two-star *Treetops* (☎ 02-952 000, fax 952 230), on the way out of town to Gerakies and Kykkos, is good value at CY£23/34.

Pedoulas has the best choice of places to eat, with the *Mountain Rose* offering a good restaurant with dishes at around CY£3 each. For excellent outdoor dining and views down the valley, *Meteora* on the north side of the village does cheap meat dishes at CY£2 a go.

Visitors to the Kykkos Monastery might care to detour about 8km to **Kampos** (see Around Pafos section in the Pafos and the West chapter), where there are two or three centrally located outdoor tavernas that are eager to attract the monastery trade on a Sunday afternoon.

GETTING THERE & AWAY

There is a daily bus (Sunday excluded) at 12.15 pm from Lefkosia to Pedoulas (CY£2) which returns to Lefkosia the following morning at 6 am. This bus is operated by Zingas Bus in Lefkosia (☎ 02-463 989) or in Pedoulas (☎ 02-952 437) and travels via Prodromos on the south side of the Troödos ridge.

The Solea Valley
Κοιλαδα Σολέα

The route through the Solea Valley to the north of the Troödos Massif is the fastest and most direct way into the area from Lefkosia. The Solea Valley parallels its less explored neighbour to the west – the Marathasa Valley – and is home to a number of attractive traditional villages and a couple of frescoed churches. The valley served as the hide-out area for insurgents of the National Organisation for the Cypriot Struggle (EOKA) during the anti-British campaign of the 1950s. It is traversed by the Karyiotis River and is popular with weekend visitors from Lefkosia, as testified by the numerous restaurants and picnic areas dotting the sides of the valley.

ORIENTATION

The main village serving the region is Kakopetria where banks, petrol stations, restaurants and accommodation can all be found. The village is actually off the main road itself, but through buses call into the village centre. It is possible to exit the valley via alternative mountain roads to both the east and west. While these routes are slower and unpaved in parts, they're often more picturesque.

KAKOPETRIA Κακοπετριά

Kakopetria is the main village of the Solea Valley and as such attracts the lion's share of visitors, many of whom are Sunday picnickers to the Troödos from Lefkosia and who drop in to Kakopetria on the way back to the capital for a coffee and a stroll. It is a pleasant place nonetheless, strung out along both banks of the Karyiotis River with a disproportionate share of restaurants and hotels. The name derives from the words *kaki petra* which mean 'wicked stone'. Legend has it that a line of stones along the ridge above the village brought good luck to newlyweds. One day, perhaps during an earthquake, some of the stones fell onto a hapless couple and killed them. The name of the village was thus born.

People today come to relax and take in the still old-world atmosphere of Kakopetria. The village is also handily placed for visits to two more of the Troödos' Byzantine church treasures.

Agios Nikolaos tis Stegis

The Church of St Nicholas of the Roof – to give its name in English – is the most easily accessible and potentially more interesting of the two churches. This rather odd-looking place of worship is prominently signposted from the Kakopetria and lies about 3km to the west of the village on the Pedoulas mountain road. It was named because of its large and heavy roof, the erection of this tall barn-like church commenced in the 11th century. A dome and narthex came later and the characteristic Troödos pitched roof was added in the 15th century as protection against the heavy snows that sometimes fall in Kakopetria.

As in other Troödos churches, the art of icon and fresco painting flourished here in the Middle Ages when Orthodoxy was sought refuge from the then dominant Latin church administration in Cyprus. Unfettered and untouched by central Latin administration, Orthodox fresco painting saw some of its most brilliant and creative work being produced in the mountains of Cyprus. The **frescoes** at Agios Nikolaos are the usual convolution of images and styles, but among those worth seeking out is an unusual depiction of the Virgin Mary breastfeeding Jesus. Look out also for images of the Crucifixion, the Nativity and the Myrrh Carriers showing an angel on top of Christ's empty tomb.

Photos (without flash) may be allowed, but the fussy lay caretaker may subtly suggest you make a donation to the church collection box. The church is open 9 am to 4 pm Tuesday to Saturday and 11 am to 4 pm on Sunday. Entry is free, but donations (to the church) are welcomed.

Panagia Forviotissa (Asinou) Church

This beautiful Unesco-listed church is not technically in the Solea Valley, but is easily accessible from Kakopetria or Lefkosia. On the perimeter of the Adelfi Forest, 10km north-east – as the crow flies at least – from Kakopetria, the Panagia Forviotissa is reached by a circuitous route over the mountain ridge east of Kakopetria, or via a well-signposted fast route from the B9 road from Lefkosia, via Vyzakia.

The church arguably boasts the finest set of Byzantine frescoes in the Troödos and if you feel that you have overdosed elsewhere, the calm rural setting of the Panagia Forviotissa makes for a delightful day out and can be combined with a picnic in the adjoining forest. The styles and motifs of the frescoed interior cross several artistic generations and are quite arresting.

Most of the interior images date from the 14th and 15th centuries and portray many themes found elsewhere in the Troödos Byzantine churches. However it is the sheer vibrancy of the colours that make the Asinou frescoes so appealing and it is definitely worth the detour to see them.

Father Kyriakos of nearby Nikitari village is the priest and caretaker of the church and, if he is not already tending to groups of Cypriot pilgrims at the church, he can be summoned on his (mobile) phone (☎ 09-689 327) or found in the village itself – ask at the kafenio. There is no entry fee but donations are welcomed. Official opening times are 9.30 am to 12.30 pm and 2 to 4 pm Monday to Saturday and 10 am to 1 pm and 2 to 4 pm on Sunday.

PLACES TO STAY & EAT

Kakopetria offers about the only real eating and sleeping options in the Solea Valley and the choices are good. There are six hotels and about 10 places to dine. The two-star *Hekali* (☎ 02-922 501, fax 922 503, ✉ hekalihotel@cytanet.com.cy, Grigoriou Digeni 22) is central and has singles/doubles for CY£20/36, with 30% discounts out of season. The three-star *Hellas* (☎ 02-922 450, fax 922 227, A Mammantou 4) is reasonably priced at CY£24/43. Unofficial rooms to rent can be located by checking out the streets on the western side of the river.

Eating out is best on the west bank of the Karyiotis in the restored, folksy streets of the old village. The restaurants in the village centre are fine, but the area can get crowded with tourists and the restaurant service is subsequently mediocre. The *Old Mill* is a pleasant spot to dine as is the *Village Pub*. Prices are reasonable and menus offer no real surprises with predictable but well-prepared Cypriot dishes on offer.

GETTING THERE & AWAY

Kakopetria is served by Clarios Company buses (☎ 02-453 234) that run up to 13 times daily in summer (CY£1.10), the first one departing from Lefkosia at 6.10 am and the last one at 7 pm. There are only two buses on Sunday in July and August (CY£1.90), leaving at 8 am and 6 pm. Seven buses leave Kakopetria for Lefkosia

THE TROÖDOS MASSIF

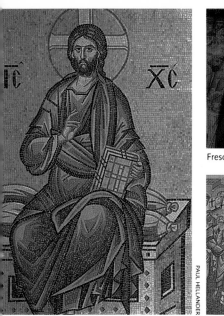

Mosaic, Kykkos Monastery

Fresco, Agios Nikolaos tis Stegis, Kakopetria

Mosaic, Kykkos Monastery

The interior of the Kykkos Monastery, in the Troödos Mountains, is richly frescoed.

STELLA HELLANDER

The present Kykkos Monastery in the Troödos Mountains was built in 1837.

JON DAVISON

The village of Pedoulas is well known for its cool air, bracing climate and spring water.

between 4.30 and 8 am on weekdays, with two later services at 1.30 and 2.30 pm. In July and August, there are departures on Sunday at 6 am and 4.30 pm only.

Pitsylia Πιτσυλιά

The widespread region of Pitsylia is the least well-known and visited segment of the Troödos Mountains. It stretches from the Karvounas crossroads north of Troödos village to the Maheras Monastery in the east. Pitsylia is home to another clutch of frescoed Byzantine churches, an important Orthodox monastery, some pretty mountain villages and some challenging walks for longer-distance hikers.

ORIENTATION
There is no real centre to Pitsylia. Instead, the region encompasses a number of small north-south valleys leading to the west-east ridge of the Troödos Massif and a number of smaller valleys on the southern side of the ridge. Main villages in the area are **Kyperounda**, **Agros**, **Platanistasa**, **Alona** and **Palehori**.

HIKING
The CTO has created about eight marked hiking trails in the Pitsylia region. With the exception of two short circular trails they generally require an out-and-back approach, unless you are prepared to keep on hiking to the next village or transport link. Most are about 5km (or less), so will require a good half-day's trekking to complete. The walks take hikers through a combination of forests, orchards, mountain ridges, villages and mountain peaks and offer some of the best recreational hiking in Cyprus. A short description of the eight trails follows:

Trail 1: Doxasi o Theos to Madari Fire Station (3.75km, 2 hours) A panoramic ridgetop hike with excellent views

Trail 2: Teisia tis Madaris (3km, 1½ hours) A circular cliff-top hike around Mt Madari (1613m) with excellent views

Trail 3: Lagoudera to Agros (6km, 2½ hours) A longish hike through vineyards and orchards with spectacular views from the Madari-Papoutsas ridge

Trail 4: Panagia tou Araka (Lagoudera) to Stavros tou Agiasmati (7km, 3 hours) The longest hike, linking two of the most important Troödos Byzantine churches through a forest, vineyards and stone terraces

Trail 5: Agros to Kato Mylos (5km, 2 hours, circular) An easy hike through cherry and pear orchards, vineyards and rose gardens

Trail 6: Petros Vanezis to Alona (1.5km, 30 minutes, circular) A short hike around the village of Alona, passing through hazelnut plantations

Trail 7: Agia Irini to Spilies tou Digeni (Caves of Digenis) (3.2km, 1½ hours) An easy out-and-back hike to the secret hide-out of the EOKA resistance fighters during the 1955–59 insurgency

Trail 8: Asinou – Agios Theodoros (4km, 2 hours) A forest hike from the Unesco-listed church of Panagia Forviotissa (Asinou) to the village of Agios Theodoros

The CTO pamphlet *Cyprus – Nature Trails* describes all the hikes in some detail and provides basic maps, but hikers would be advised to take along a more detailed map of the region.

STAVROS TOU AGIASMATI CHURCH
This Unesco-listed Byzantine church is famous for its frescoes that decorate its gable roof and were painted by Filippos Goul in 1494. Access to the church requires some forethought (you must obtain the key from the priest at Platanistasa village 5km away and, of course, return it).

The church is somewhat remote, hidden along a sealed side road off the Platanistasa-Orounda highway (E906), though it can be approached by a signposted but unsealed road from the next valley to the west through which the E907 Polystypos-Xyliatos road runs.

PANAGIA TOU ARAKA CHURCH
This more accessible and more frequently visited church looks, from the outside, more like a Swiss cattle byre than a place of worship. Its enormous all-encompassing snowproof roof and surrounding wooden

trellis all but conceal the church within. The **paintings** inside the church are a wide selection of neoclassical works by artists from Constantinople. The vivid images on display run the usual thematic range, with the impressive Pantokrator in the domed tholos taking pride of place. Look out also for the Annunciation, the Four Evangelists, Matthew, Mark, Luke and John, the Archangel Michael and the Panagia Arakiotissa, the patron of the church. The unusual name of the church – *arakiotissa* means 'of the wild pea' – owes it origin to the vegetable that grows in profusion in the district.

The church is open 9 am to 6 pm daily and entry is free, though donations are always welcomed. Photography is theoretically not allowed, though non-flash shots may be permitted by the watchful priest caretaker if things are quiet.

THE MAHERAS MONASTERY

It is a fair hike out to this sprawling monastery, perched in the foothills of the eastern Troödos Massif and under the all-seeing, enormous radar installation on Mt Kionia (1423m) to the south-west. The Maheras Monastery was founded in a similar way to the Kykkos Monastery (see the Marathasa Valley section earlier in this chapter). About 1148 a hermit by the name of Neophytos found an icon guarded by a sword (*maheras* means knife or sword in Greek) in a cave near the site of the present monastery. The monastery developed around the icon and flourished over the years. Nothing remains of the original monastery structures; the current building dates from around 1900.

The monastery is a popular outing for Cypriots who come as much for the cooler climate as for spiritual enlightenment. There is a small cafeteria in the grounds and some pilgrims may also stay overnight. One less spiritually inspired visitor was Grigoris Afxentios, during the EOKA uprising of 1955–59. This fearsome EOKA leader hid out in a cave just below the monastery, but was eventually tracked down and killed by British soldiers in 1957. A huge black statue of the hero now looms over a commemorative shrine.

The monastery is open for group visits only from 9 am to noon on Monday, Tuesday and Thursday. These should be conducted with reverence and solemnity. Individual visitors may be able to attach themselves to visiting groups, though most will consist of Cypriot pilgrims. The approach to the monastery is best undertaken via Klirou and Fikardou (see the next section) since the alternate route via Pera and the E902, while very pretty, is winding and tortuously slow.

FIKARDOU VILLAGE Φικάρδου

This postcard-pretty village is close to the Maheras Monastery and visits to both are easily combined. Fikardou is the 'official' village in a clutch of preserved villages in the eastern Troödos Massif. Its Ottoman-period houses with wooden balconies are quite a visual relief after the cement structures of many modern Troödos mountain villages. That said, there is not a lot to Fikardou. The central strip is no more than a couple of hundred metres and photo opportunities are frustratingly elusive. Most visitors – many on Troödos 'safaris' – content themselves to idly sit at the village's cafe-cum-restaurant while awaiting the next move. Still, if you are in the region a visit is recommended since there are few places left in Cyprus that retain at least a tenuous architectural link with the past like Fikardou.

Wineries

The south flank of the Troödos Massif is home to a number of excellent vineyards and wineries. One worth considering a visit is the **Pitsylia Winery,** between the villages of Platres and Pelendri on the southern side of the Troödos. This small winery welcomes visitors for a tour and tasting. Wines produced here are made from the local varietal grapes Mavro Ambelissimo, Xynisteri, Ofthalmo and Pambatzies and are pretty palatable red, whites and rosés. Visiting times are fairly loose, but it's probably a good idea to ring beforehand.

To reach the Pitsylia Winery (☎ 05-372 928, ✉ tsiakkas@swaypage.com), turn west just before Trimiklini village if you are

LPP

Troödos wineries welcome visitors for tasting, touring and sampling.

coming up from Lemesos. Turn left before the village if you are coming from Platres.

PLACES TO STAY & EAT

Sleeping and dining choices are limited in the Pitsylia region with only the village of

Agros providing accommodation with some comfort. The three-star ***Rodon*** (*☎ 521 201, fax 521 235, @ rodon@spidernet .com.cy)* in Agros has decent singles/doubles for CY£29/44, though 20% discounts may be had out of season.

All villages have small tavernas or restaurants but many may only open during summer or on weekends. None merits any particular mention though in fairness you will not go hungry and the quality is fairly uniform. There are many picnic areas in the region with the Skordokefalos picnic area east of the Maheras Monastery particularly worth mentioning.

GETTING THERE & AWAY

Transport into and out of the region is strictly functional and designed to get people to and from Lefkosia for work or business. Local buses link most major Pitsylia villages with Lefkosia, but usually leave early in the morning and return to the villages in the early afternoon. Potential visitors should not rely on them for planned day trips to the region. This is an area where you need time and energy; hiking from one village to another and perhaps hitching to a better-served transport artery is probably your best bet.

THE TROÖDOS MASSIF

Larnaka & the East

The majority of visitors to Cyprus arrive at Larnaka international airport in Cyprus' south-east and their first impressions of the island are invariably formed by the drive from the airport to their hotel. Larnaka is the largest town in the region and it has played its part in Cypriot history. The streets of the present day town are built over the ancient city of Kition. Lazarus who was raised from the dead by Jesus came to live in Larnaka and brought Christianity to Cyprus.

An important Islamic shrine in honour of the aunt of Mohammed sits forlornly at the edge of a shimmering salt lake close to Larnaka airport. The island's first documented settlers lived in round stone houses in the remarkable Neolithic settlement of Hirokitia, west of Larnaka. Along the sweeping expanses of Larnaka Bay and clustered around the sandy coves of Cape Greco is the heart of Cyprus' blooming tourist industry.

At Agia Napa, on the far eastern edge of Cyprus, travellers can witness a party that continues from April to November, yet within a few kilometres is a secluded beach where few visitors venture. Inland and away from the high life and occasional excesses of the coast you will find small, timeless villages more reminiscent of the Australian outback than Mediterranean Europe where the potato is king, not the tourist dollar. It is here in eastern Cyprus that the poignant and painful division of the island is only too obvious. Travellers curious enough to learn about the country's troubled recent past can stare across barbed wire fencing – the Attila Line – into the ghost town of Varosha, abandoned by fleeing Greek Cypriots in 1974 and never resettled. Yet, against the odds, the east is home to one village where Greeks and Turks still manage to live together in harmony – a reminder of how things used to be. The east offers its visitors both cerebral and corporal pleasures and a stay here will not easily be forgotten.

HIGHLIGHTS

• Peak over barbed wire into the ghost town of Varosha which was abandoned in 1974.

• Bargain for an exquisite piece of hand-made Lefkara lacework.

• Wind down on the beaches of Agia Napa after a night out in the clubs.

Larnaka

☎ 04 • pop 67,300

Larnaka is the first port of call for most visitors to Cyprus. However, unless you are booked to stay in Larnaka itself you will more than likely be whisked off from the nearby airport to your hotel with nary a glimpse of this most attractive of Cypriot cities.

Both a commercial port and yacht marina, Larnaka is also home to Cyprus' largest community of foreigners. Many Lebanese Christians took refuge here during that country's troubles in the '80s.

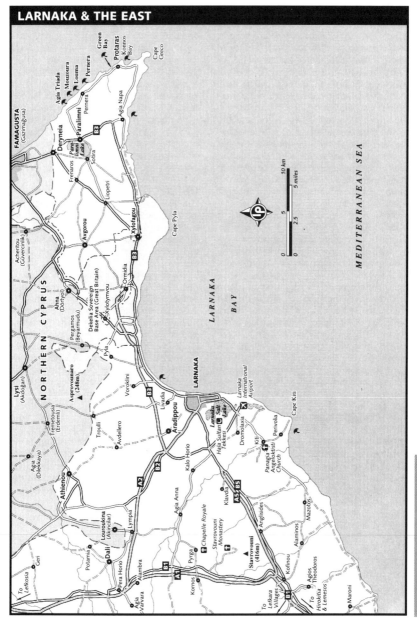

LARNAKA & THE EAST

Many never went home. Foreign governments in the past tended to use Larnaka as a base for their consulates in preference to inland and less easily accessible Lefkosia. The city was also home to a large Turkish Cypriot population prior to 1974 who, following the division of the island by their mainland compatriots, were obliged to ruefully flee to the North.

Larnaka is a resort destination and the town centre and the tourist strip to the northeast are equally popular choices for foreign visitors. There are not many gripping sites to tempt the amateur archaeologist or historian and the city is best enjoyed for its relaxed dining, easy ambience and warm though occasionally torrid climate.

HISTORY

Larnaka was originally established as a Mycenaean colony sometime between the 14th and the 11th centuries BC. It prospered as the port for export of copper and other metals mined in the Troödos Mountains and at Tamassos to the west. The city flourished well into Hellenistic times despite siding with the Persians in the Greek-Persian wars. Kimon of Athens arrived in 450 BC to subdue Kition, but died prematurely outside the city walls. His statue now graces the long Larnaka promenade. Zenon of Kition, the Stoic philosopher and darling of the Athens intelligentsia, was born in Larnaka in 335 BC. His radical philosophies seem not to have pleased Zenon himself in the final analysis. He died by his own hand at the age of 98.

Lazarus, raised from the dead by Jesus Christ, brought Christianity to Larnaka and became its first bishop. When he finally died, he was buried in the vault of the church that now carries his name. Little more is known about Kition until at least the 14th century when it took the name of Salina because of the nearby salt lake. Larnaka in Greek means 'funerary chest' and it is likely that the city received this name as a result of ancient tombs discovered in the early days of its development in the 16th century.

Under the Ottomans the city was an important port and became home to a grow-

ing number of dignitaries. Many of them were emissaries from foreign countries and a disquieting number of them engaged in amateur archaeology. Much of Larnaka's archaeological wealth was secretly sequestered and spirited away during this time.

Over the period of British rule of 88 years, the Larnaka gradually fell behind Ammohostos (Famagusta) and Lemesos in importance. It only really received a demographic jolt following the influx of refugees from the North in 1974 and the development of its hitherto backwater airfield as the country's prime international airport.

ORIENTATION

Larnaka is a reasonably compact city and most major sites and facilities are within walking distance of transport terminals and central hotels. The city centre is surrounded by Leoforos Grigori Afxentiou to the north, Leoforos Artemidos to the west, Leoforos Faneromenis to the south and in the east by Leoforos Athinon. Leoforos Athinon is a landscaped, paved street lined with palm trees and is known commonly as the Finikoundes (Palm Trees) Promenade. Within the rectangle formed by these major avenues is the main business and central tourist district. Immediately south of this area and adjoining the seafront is the former Turkish district, the beginning of which is marked by the Grand Mosque and Larnaka Fort.

Buses to/from Deryneia and Paralimni arrive at and depart from the bus stop opposite the police station. All other buses arrive at and depart from the bus stop on the Finikoundes Promenade opposite the Four Lanterns Sunotel. Service taxi terminals are all close to the town centre and Larnaka airport is a mere 6km south of the central business district.

INFORMATION
Tourist Offices

The CTO (☎ 654 322) is on Plateia Vasileos Pavlou, two short blocks west of the Sun Hall hotel. It's open 8.15 am to 2.30 pm and 3 to 6.30 pm Monday to Saturday, but is closed on Wednesday and Saturday afternoons. There is also a CTO at the airport.

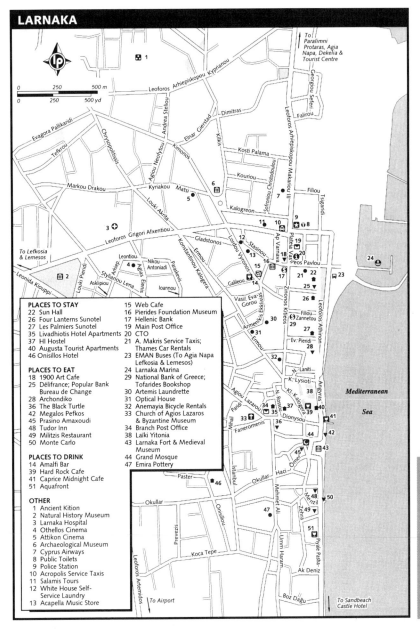

LARNAKA

PLACES TO STAY
22 Sun Hall
26 Four Lanterns Sunotel
27 Les Palmiers Sunotel
35 Livadhiotis Hotel Apartments
37 HI Hostel
40 Augusta Tourist Apartments
46 Onisillos Hotel

PLACES TO EAT
18 1900 Art Cafe
25 Délifrance; Popular Bank
   Bureau de Change
28 Archondiko
36 The Black Turtle
42 Megalos Pefkos
45 Prasino Amaxoudi
48 Tudor Inn
49 Militzis Restaurant
50 Monte Carlo

PLACES TO DRINK
14 Amalfi Bar
39 Hard Rock Cafe
41 Caprice Midnight Cafe
51 Aquafront

OTHER
1 Ancient Kition
2 Natural History Museum
3 Larnaka Hospital
4 Othellos Cinema
5 Attikon Cinema
6 Archaeological Museum
7 Cyprus Airways
8 Public Toilets
9 Police Station
10 Acropolis Service Taxis
11 Salamis Tours
12 White House Self-
   Service Laundry
13 Acapella Music Store

15 Web Cafe
16 Pierides Foundation Museum
17 Hellenic Bank
19 Main Post Office
20 CTO
21 A. Makris Service Taxis;
   Thames Car Rentals
23 EMAN Buses (To Agia Napa
   Lefkosia & Lemesos)
24 Larnaka Marina
29 National Bank of Greece;
   Tofarides Bookshop
30 Artemis Laundrette
31 Optical House
32 Anemayia Bicycle Rentals
33 Church of Agios Lazaros
   & Byzantine Museum
34 Branch Post Office
38 Laïki Yitonia
43 Larnaka Fort & Medieval
   Museum
44 Grand Mosque
47 Emira Pottery

Mediterranean
Sea

Airport flight information can be obtained on ☎ 643 300.

Money

There are facilities to exchange money at Larnaka airport; they're open for all flights. ~~Within the precinct of the city centre there~~ are a number of banks for changing money and some of them maintain afternoon tourist hours. There is a National Bank of Greece ATM on Zinonos Kitieos and a Hellenic Bank ATM in the same street, 200m farther north on the opposite side. There is a Popular Bank bureau de change at the northern end of the Finikoundes, which is open 8.15 am to 12.30 pm daily.

Post & Communications

The main post office is close to the CTO office on the Plateia Dimokratias (Plateia Vasileos Pavlou) and poste restante mail is held here. There is also a smaller branch close to the church of Agios Lazaros.

There are at least four Internet cafes in town. An easy one to find is Web Cafe (☎ 654 954, ✉ webcafe@webcafe.com.cy) at Lordou Vyronos 54, 300m west of the CTO on the corner of Viktoros Hugo. It is open 10 am to 3 am daily and charges CY£4 per hour.

Travel Agencies

The Larnaka branch of Salamis Tours (☎ 656 464, fax 650 698) is at Leoforos Grigoriou Afxentiou 7 in central Larnaka. As well as Israel or Greece boat tickets, you can get a wide range of other travel-related services here.

Bookshops

The Tofarides Bookshop (☎ 654 912) at Zinonos Kitieos 45–47 in the city centre is the best place to go for English-language books, stationery and maps. It also stocks a large selection of oil paints and acrylics for the benefit of budding or committed artists. Academic & General, on Ermou 41, is another possibility.

Laundry

You can get your clothes washed and pressed at Artemis Laundrette on Armenikis

Ekklisias 12 or at the White House Self-Service Laundry, Shop 5, Helen Court. A full-service wash costs around CY£4, while a self-service wash and dry will cost around CY£2.

Toilets

There are signposted public toilets 100m east of the CTO office at the northern end of the city centre. Ducking into a cafe or large restaurant, at a moment of need, probably will not raise too many eyebrows if the walk to the toilets is just too far.

Medical Services

Larnaka's main public hospital (☎ 630 311) is north-west of the city centre on Leoforos Grigoriou Afxentiou.

Emergency

For an ambulance, police or the fire service, call ☎ 199. For night pharmacy assistance ring ☎ 1414. The Narcotics Emergency Service is ☎ 1410 and AIDS Advisory Centre is ☎ 02-305 515. The police station is easy to find on the corner of Leoforos Grigoriou Afxentiou and Leoforos Arhiepiskopou Makariou III, near the yacht marina.

WALKING TOUR

The CTO runs a couple of free, chaperoned walks from its office starting at 10 am on Wednesday and Friday. This is a painless way to get an introduction to the layout and attractions of Larnaka.

ANCIENT KITION

Much of present-day Larnaka is built over the original site of Ancient Kition so no excavations are expected to be carried out unless Larnaka is demolished – an unlikely prospect. What is left of the ancient city is a small site known as **Area II**, a rather nondescript and essentially uninteresting site about 1km north-west of the city centre. A raised walkway takes you over what is left of the remains of Ancient Kition, where excavations sporadically continue. Labels or explanations are sparse, so unless you are an amateur archaeologist, the layout may not mean much to you.

The site is open 9 am to 2.30 pm Monday to Friday and entry costs CY£0.75.

ARCHAEOLOGICAL MUSEUM

Larnaka's Archaeological Museum is second best to its more illustrious partner, the Pierides Foundation Museum. There is of course a wide collection of predictable pottery, much of it Mycenaean pottery found at Kition. There is a reconstructed Neolithic tomb from Hirokitia, terracotta votive figures, Roman glassware and even folk art. Spread out over five rooms the collection is worth a browse, though you may get a sense of *déjà vu*, if you have already visited the Cyprus Museum in Lefkosia.

The museum (☎ 630 169) on Kalogreon is open 9 am to 2.30 pm Monday to Friday and additionally from 3 to 5 pm on Thursday from October to April. Admission is CY£0.75.

CHURCH OF AGIOS LAZAROS & BYZANTINE MUSEUM

This hard-to-miss church at the southern end of Larnaka owes its existence to a rather interesting story. Tradition says that Jesus raised Lazarus, the brother of Mary and Martha, from the dead. Immediately after he was expelled by the Jews and came to Larnaka, and was subsequently ordained as a bishop by St Barnabas. He reportedly remained a bishop for 30 years. After he died (a second time) he was buried where the current church stands. His relics did not stay entombed for very long after their discovery in 890, as they were transported to Constantinople and subsequently removed to Marseille in 1204.

The church structure itself is a mix of Latinate and Orthodox influences, the most obvious example being the prominent bell tower that is visible for some distance around. The church was in fact used by both Catholic and Orthodox worshippers for some 200 years; this is affirmed by inscriptions in Latin, French and Greek that can be seen in the portico.

The **Tomb of Lazarus** is under the altar, accessible by stairs to the right, but in fact comprises just one of several sarcophagi in the catacomb. This demonstrates that the area was used as a general burial place rather than as a specifically designated tomb for Lazarus. The church is open 8 am to 12.30 pm and 3.30 to 6.30 pm daily (afternoon hours are one hour earlier in winter). Admission is free.

In the courtyard of the church is the **Byzantine Museum** (☎ 652 489), which houses a collection that supplants a previous ecclesiastical collection lost over the period 1964–74. During that time the original collection containing priceless relics and artefacts was housed in Larnaka Fort, which had come under Turkish administration following the insurgencies of the early '60s. In 1974 the administration of the fort reverted once more to the Greeks, but the priceless treasures had apparently disappeared. All that is left of the original collection is the catalogue and the missing items are still being sought. The present collection was assembled in their place and it is still a fairly extensive and impressive display of Byzantine ecclesiastical artefacts, icons and church utensils. Many of the items on display have been donated by Russian clerics.

The museum is open 8.30 am to 1 pm and 4 to 6 pm daily (2.30 to 5 pm in winter). Entry costs CY£1.

GRAND MOSQUE

The Cami Kebir, or Grand Mosque, stands alone on the periphery of both the former Greek and Turkish quarters of Larnaka. Somewhat underused since 1974, the mosque is nonetheless the spiritual home to Larnaka's Muslim community. Originally built in the 16th century and once the Latin Holy Cross Church, the current building is the result of a 19th-century restoration. The mosque reluctantly accepts visitors, though not during prayer times and you may also be able to climb the **minaret** for a small fee. The views are quite impressive.

LARNAKA FORT & MEDIEVAL MUSEUM

The fort stands prominently at the water's edge dividing Larnaka's former Greek and Turkish sectors. Originally a Lusignan-era castle, the present structure is a result of re-modelling by the Ottoman from around 1605, but is otherwise fairly unimpressive. There is little to see in the castle itself, but the upper floor contains a small Medieval Museum with various displays from Hala Sultan Tekkesi and Ancient Kition. The open area inside the fort is occasionally used for concerts and other cultural events.

The fort and museum are both open 9 am to 7.30 pm Monday to Friday only (9 am to 5 pm in winter). Admission is CY£0.75.

NATURAL HISTORY MUSEUM

This small but varied and interesting collection of exhibits is dedicated primarily to the fauna, flora, geology, insect and marine life of Cyprus. Displayed in a series of seven rooms (with an eighth one under construction), the museum is very popular with school groups and is an excellent introduction to the natural history of the island, which would otherwise be very hard to witness.

The museum (☎ 652 569) isoff Leoforos Grigoriou Afxentiou in the Municipal Gardens and is open 10 am to 1 pm and 4 to 6 pm (to 5pm in winter) from Tuesday to Sunday. Entry is CY£0.20.

THE PIERIDES FOUNDATION MUSEUM

This former private residence of the Pierides family houses an admirable collection of artefacts in the grandly named Pierides Foundation Museum (☎ 652 495). Founder Dimitrios Pierides commenced this private collection in 1839 as a way to stave off the depletion of Cyprus' archaeological inheritance by amateur archaeologists/diplomats, such as the infamous Luigi Palma di Cesnola. This US consul in Larnaka spirited away an enormous number of artefacts, which are now in New York's Metropolitan Museum. The Pierides Museum competes vigorously with the state-operated Archaeological Museum and features artefacts and finds from all over Cyprus. The exhbition includes a fairly comprehensive chronological represent-ation of Cypriot history from prehistoric times (7000–1500 BC), the Mycenaean/Achaean period (1400–1100 BC), the Iron

Age (1050–54 BC), the Roman occupation, through to the later Byzantine, Crusader, Frankish, Venetian and Ottoman periods of rule.

There are five rooms in the museum, each arranged chronologically. Items to look out for are a terracotta of a nude man sitting on a stool in room 1. Water or wine that is poured into his head exits from his penis. What use this statuette originally served can only be surmised. Room 4 is devoted to a fascinating collection of **Roman glassware** and room 5 is given over to a display of **Cypriot folk art**, with weaving and embroidery, woodcarvings and traditional costumes.

The museum is on Zinonos Kitieos 4 and is open from 9 am to 1 pm and 4 to 7 pm (3 to 6 pm in winter) Monday to Friday and 9 am to 1 pm on Saturday. Admission costs CY£1.

PLACES TO STAY

Larnaka offers a reasonable range of accommodation options spread out quite evenly across its downtown area as well as in the hotel stretch east of the town centre. Popular options are self-contained apartments, which are excellent value if there are at least two of you and you prefer to self-cater. There are over a dozen two-star hotels (too many to list here) all offering high- season accommodation ranging from CY£17.50 to CY£40 per person. All up, there are close to 100 accommodation options. The free CTO *Hotel Guide* gives all the details.

Places to Stay – Budget

There are two budget options in Larnaka, since the accommodation scene is pitched firmly at the middle of the range (family) apartment group and the top-end resort hotel scene. The first is *Forest Beach Camping* (☎ 644 514), 8km towards Agia Napa. The site is somewhat run down but it is passable. The *HI Hostel* (☎ 621 188, Nikolaou Rossou 27) is just east of St Lazaros church and charges CY£3.50 a night for bed in a mixed or single-sex dorm. It's a small place and facilities are minimal, but there is a little kitchen and communal toilets and showers. HI cards are not required and there is no discount for holders.

Places to Stay – Mid-Range

The best options here are hotel apartments where you can be self-contained and cook for yourself, but they are usually only for a minimum stay of two days. Forward bookings are always a good idea.

The two-star *Les Palmiers Sunotel* (☎ *627 200, fax 627 204, Athinon 12*) is central, reasonable and has singles/doubles from CY£16 to CY£27, with 20% discounts in the off season. *Augusta Tourist Apartments* (☎ *651 802, fax 627 080, Athinon 102*) is a smallish, modern block of holiday apartments right on the Finikoundes Promenade. They are very clean and neat and have a kitchen and TV. The cost is CY£24 for two people; air-conditioning is CY£2.50 extra per day.

In a similar vein but operating more like a hotel is *Livadhiotis Hotel Apartments* (☎ *626 222, fax 626 406, ✆ livadhio@cytanet .com.cy, N Rossou 50*). It is somewhat cheaper charging CY£17 for a two-person studio. These neat apartments are fully self-contained with kitchenette, phone and TV and are also very centrally located.

About 500m west of the fort, in a very quiet part of town, is the friendly two-star *Onisillos Hotel* (☎ *651 100, fax 654 468, Onisillou 17*). Rooms with a bathroom cost CY£25/33, including breakfast. The *Sandbeach Castle* (☎ *655 437, fax 659 804, Piyale Pasha; off map*) is as close to the sea as you will get in this price range. Its neat rooms go for CY£18/24.

Places to Stay – Top-End

You'll find the only two hotels above two stars within the city centre. The first is the three-star *Four Lanterns Sunotel* (☎ *652 011, fax 626 012, ✆ crown@cytanet .com.cy, Athinon 19–24*) at the northern end of the Finikoundes Promenade. Comfortable accommodation ranges from CY£40 to CY£70 (no off-season discounts).

A block further north is the four-star *Sun Hall* (☎ *653 341, fax 652 717, Athinon 6*), which is equally well-equipped, offers good

rooms from CY£40 to CY£62, with a 25% off-season discount.

There is a cluster of four-star hotels on the Larnaka-Dekelia road 8km north-east of Larnaka along the tourist strip.

PLACES TO EAT

Like the hotel scene, eating areas are split between Larnaka town and the tourist strip heading out towards Deryneia. While you will find some excellent dining choices out on the tourist strip, recommendations here are limited primarily to establishments within the town centre itself.

For a quick snack or promenade breakfast, look no further than the French international-chain delicatessen/patisserie *Délifrance* at the northern end of the Finikoundes. Croissants, cakes, decent coffee – you name it, it's all here. For a quick lunch or evening snack, seek out the *Prasino Amaxoudi* sitting cheek-by-jowl with the Grand Mosque in the old Turkish quarter. Here you'll get good-value, freshly prepared *souvlaki, döner kebab* or *haloumi* pitta sandwiches for around CY£1.

Good company, coffee and good-value snacks (CY£3.50) can be had at the *1900 Art Cafe* (☎ *623 730, Stasinou 6*). It's open 9 am to 2 pm and 6 pm to midnight every day and is closed on Tuesday. Gutted by fire in 1996 but refurbished by sheer determination and help from the mayor of Larnaka is *Black Turtle* (☎ *650 661, Mehmet Ali 11*), a great little mezes taverna that features live music four nights a week (Wednesday to Saturday) when only mezedes are served that cost CY£6.50 per person. Don't be put off by the turtle shells on the wall; the owner is really a turtle lover.

The stretch of beachfront south of the castle is less touristy and home to at least three places worth seeking out. *Monte Carlo* (☎ *653 815, Piyale Pasha 42*) sits right on the water's edge and is a great place to dine in peace. Meat mezedes cost CY£5.95 and fish mezedes are CY£6.95 per person. Across the road and a little further south is *Militzis Restaurant* (☎ *655 867, Piyale Pasha 28*), which is best at providing traditional oven-cooked dishes at around CY£3.50. Try the delicious oven-baked lamb *ofto lysiotiko*. Lovers of Guinness stout can hardly miss the sign outside the *Tudor Inn (Lala Mustapha Pasha 11),* just off Piyale Pasha. Apart from serving up pints of the famous Irish brew, the Tudor Inn is also a decent steak restaurant with a variety of offerings being served at CY£8.90 a pop.

Back nearer the centre and at the southern end of the Finikoundes is the *Megalos Pefkos (☎ 628 566, Angyras 7),* perhaps marginally the best of a clutch of fish taverns on this small street. Swordfish at a reasonable CY£4 a serve is often the best buy, but there are plenty of other dishes on offer also. You dine in a pleasant waterside setting.

On the Finikoundes proper is the well-known *Archondiko (☎ 655 905, Athinon 24)* housed in an old heritage Larnaka mansion. This is a great place to watch the parade of skateboarders and hair-braiders while mezedes (CY£6.50 per person) are probably the best choice for dining.

ENTERTAINMENT

Larnaka is a very pleasant place to hang out for a while or watch people over a beer or a coffee. Tourists make their own fun in the long tourist strip 8km north-east of the city, while locals and city-oriented travellers hang out along the Finikoundes Promenade and the little streets just inland from the sea. You will not find the rowdy, packed element of the tourist centres of Agia Napa or Lemesos, and fun in Larnaka is pursued at a more sedate pace.

Pubs & Bars

The small Laïki Yitonia holds a swathe of bars and discos, including a predictably dark, cold and noisy *Hard Rock Cafe*. While this strip is popular with visitors, the locals tend to avoid the Laïki Yitonia. The *Amalfi Bar*, on the corner of Galileou and Lordou Vyronos, attracts the young and hip of Larnaka to its upstairs verandah. On Piyale Pasha in the Turkish quarter, sea lovers can sip cocktails and spirits at *Aquafront*, while still on the sea at the southern end of the Finikoundes, the *Caprice Midnight Cafe* is a great spot for an evening pint or vodka and coke while taking in the water views.

Cinemas

There are a number of cinemas scattered around Larnaka, with all foreign-language films subtitled into Greek. Entry normally costs around CY£3 per person. The Attikon (☎ 652 873) at Kyriakou Matsi 5 and the Othellos (☎ 657 970) at Agias Elenis 13 are two of the more central movie theatres in the town.

SHOPPING

Pottery is a good buy in Larnaka and a good place to see it being made and to buy an item to take home is Emira Pottery (☎ 623 952) on Mehmet Ali 13 in the old Turkish quarter. The best place for music purchases is Acapella (☎ 664 165) at Lordou Vyronos 50. Discount optical items are a good buy at the Optical House (☎ 655 436) in the town centre at Ermou 95–97, where your sight is tested for free.

GETTING THERE & AWAY
Air

Larnaka international airport is only 6km from the centre of the city. Most flights to Cyprus arrive and depart from here. Cyprus Airways (☎ 654 294) is at Leoforos Arhiepiskopou Makariou III 21 and there is another office (☎ 692 700) at Larnaka airport.

Bus

The stop for EMAN buses to Lefkosia, Lemesos and Agia Napa is almost opposite the Dolphin Cafe restaurant on the waterfront. On Sunday there is only a service to Agia Napa. See the introductory Getting Around chapter for ticket prices.

Service Taxi

Acropolis (☎ 655 555), opposite the police station on Leoforos Arhiepiskopou Makariou III, and A Makris (☎ 652 929), on the north side of the Sun Hall hotel, operate services to Lefkosia (CY£2.10) and also to Lemesos (CY£2.60).

Yacht

Yachties might be interested to know that Larnaka has an excellent private marina (☎ 653 110, fax 653 113, ✉ larnaka.marina@ cytanet.com.cy) offering a wide range of berthing facilities for up to 450 yachts. These include telephone, fax and telex services, repair facilities, laundry, showers, lockers, post office boxes and a minimarket and provisions store. The marina is an official port of entry into Cyprus.

GETTING AROUND
To/From the Airport

Bus No 19 from St Lazaros church goes near the airport, which is 6km from Larnaka city centre. The first bus is at 6.20 am and the last at 7 pm in summer, 5.45 pm in winter. A private taxi costs around CY£4.

Bus

A Makris buses run every 30 minutes from the north side of the Sun Hall hotel to the tourist hotel area, 8km along the coast on the road to Agia Napa (CY£0.80 return).

Car & Motorcycle

Thames Car Rentals (☎ 656 333) is next door to A Makris and rents cars. There are also several car rental booths at the airport. You can hire motorcycles or mopeds from Anemayia (☎ 645 619) on the Larnaka-Dekelia road; ring for free delivery.

Bicycle

Bicycles can be hired at Anemayia (☎ 658 333, mobile 09-624 726), which has its office in the middle of the city at Zinonos Kitieos 120. Call for free delivery, which is promised within 10 minutes. Prices range from CY£3 to CY£5 for daily rental.

Around Larnaka

The sights around Larnaka overlap to some degree with those of Lemesos. Those in the west of the Larnaka region can easily be visited as day trips from Lemesos or even from Lefkosia. Limited public transport does not make it easy to get to the sights, so

you are once again going to have to rely on your own wheels or inventiveness to get around the area.

BEACHES

Swimming is definitely not one of the highlights of the Larnaka coastline. While Cypriots and foreigners alike swim quite contentedly at either of Larnaka's artificially constructed city beaches or at the less congested beaches off the hotel strip to the north-east, none is particularly enticing. The water is by and large clean and the sand shelves gently, but serious beach lovers should consider moving further east to Agia Napa or Protaras for a more enjoyable swim. To the south-west, the struggling resorts of **Cape Kiti** and **Perivolia** offer scrappy, narrow beaches, but compensate for less than idyllic strips with some decent tavernas which could make for a pleasant lunchtime excursion.

HIROKITIA

Archaeology buffs and early-history lovers should make the trip out to the fascinating Neolithic site of Hirokitia, which is 32km from Larnaka. It is perhaps best combined with a day trip to either Lemesos or Lefkara (see the following section). Dating from around 6800 BC, this Unesco World Heritage site is perhaps one of the earliest permanent human settlements in Cyprus. The original Hirokitians lived in round mud huts and practised a relatively sophisticated lifestyle for the time. It is thought that they came from Anatolia or the coast of present-day Lebanon. The original settlement was built on an easily defendable hillside, surrounded by a large perimeter wall. Inside the wall around 60 individual houses have been found – the better-preserved can be identified by the remains of their circular walls. Reconstructions of the houses have been built at the foot of the hill and, although they look a bit out of place, it is worth seeing them since it is difficult to imagine the buildings from their scant remains.

Visitors view the various sections of the site via steps and a series of walkways that overlook the key points of the settlement.

LARNAKA & THE EAST

Signs give a clear description of the main features of each area and the walkway finishes at the top of the hill where the best remains are to be found.

Hirokitia is open 9 am to 7.30 pm daily (until 5 pm from October to April) and costs CY£0.75. There is ample parking and a snack bar with refreshments.

LEFKARA

One of Cyprus' most famous exports is its exquisite lace and most of it comes from the pretty mountain villages of **Pano Lefkara** and **Kato Lefkara**. Reached by a fast road from the Lefkosia-Lemesos motorway (A1), or by a winding but more picturesque road from Hirokitia via Vavla, Lefkara – to give the two settlements their more common name – is an excellent day's outing for visitors from Lefkosia, Larnaka or Lemesos. The story goes that in the Middle Ages the women of Lefkara took up lace-making to supplement family incomes while the men were away working at sea or on the plains. More enterprising stay-at-home husbands took up making silverware. Leonardo da Vinci is said to have taken some lace home to Italy and ever since then travellers and lace lovers the world over have being doing much the same.

The village is pretty enough even if you are not keen on frilly patterns or intricately designed tablecloths. A wander around its picturesque streets is almost certain to guarantee an invitation to 'see my lace' from the many women who sit at doorways, seemingly whiling away their hours in a relaxing hobby. In reality they are fuelling a lucrative business, and competition to sell their lace can be intense. The lace is undoubtedly of high quality and exquisite, but not necessarily dirt cheap. Bargain hard if you want a particular piece or try in the nearby villages, some of which also sell Lefkara lace.

For visitors interested in the history of the craft, there is the **Traditional Museum of Embroidery & Silver-Smithing** (☎ 04-342 326) where you can get a better insight into these two flourishing trades. The museum is open 9.30 am to 4 pm Monday to Thursday and 10 am to 4 pm on Friday and Saturday.

It is closed on Sunday and admission is CY£0.75.

CHAPELLE ROYALE

Just off the Lefkosia-Lemesos motorway (A1) and close to the village of Pyrga is Chapelle Royale or Royal Chapel, a small Lusignan shrine dedicated to Agia Ekaterini (St Catherine). Established by the Latin king Janus in 1421 (the last of Cyprus' Crusader kings), the church is quite unassuming, but inside you can see an interesting French-influenced set of **wall frescoes**, not all of which are in good condition. You should be able to make out paintings of the Last Supper, the Raising of Lazarus, the Washing of Christ's Feet and the Ascension. Note the inscriptions in French – not Greek – bearing in mind that this was the official language of Lusignan Cyprus.

The church is open daily from dawn to dusk (CY£0.75) and is best combined with a visit to Stavrovouni and Lefkara.

STAVROVOUNI MONASTERY

High up in the hills (668m) above the Lefkosia-Lemesos motorway (A1) is the impressive Stavrovouni Monastery, the oldest monastery in Cyprus. Reached by a steep winding road, it is only worth making the trip up here if you are male. Women are not allowed to enter the monastery, though the superb views from the monastery grounds over the Mesaoria and the Troödos Mountains may be enough reason to make the trek. Colin Thubron documented his stay in the monastery during his walking trek around Cyprus in 1972 in the book *Journey into Cyprus,* where he describes the monastery as a 'lodestar for pilgrims in the wake of the Crusades'.

The origins of the monastery – the name means 'mountain of the cross' – date back to 327 when it was allegedly founded by the Empress Helena, mother of Constantine the Great, while on her way to Jerusalem. She is said to have erected a wooden cross containing a nail from the cross of Jesus. A small piece of Empress Helena's cross is now preserved in a silver cross in the church.

The monastery is a working religious community consisting of a few young monks who live to follow their ascetic principles, not to entertain visitors. If you come to visit (and are male) arrive before 11 am or after 2 pm as the monastery is closed to outsiders in the middle of the day. Leave your camera behind as photos are not allowed. If you are a genuine or professed pilgrim you may be invited to stay.

PANAGIA ANGELOKTISTI CHURCH

At Kiti village, 7km south-west of Larnaka, you will find the domed cruciform 11th-century church of Panagia Angeloktisti. Literally meaning 'built by angels', this church is a reincarnation of an earlier structure from the 5th century (of which only the apse remains) and has now been incorporated into the current building. Visitors come for the 6th-century **mosaics** which have survived from the original apse, but were only discovered in 1952. In a striking depiction, you can see the Virgin Mary, with baby Jesus in her arms and the angels Gabriel and Michael standing next to her.

The church is a place of worship so time your visit to avoid a service – unless you choose to participate which you are at liberty to do. Otherwise it is open 8 am to noon and 2 to 4 pm Monday to Saturday (summer only). On Sunday it is open for regular services. Entry is free, but a donation is always welcomed. Bus No 6 from Larnaka runs a number of times daily to and from Kiti.

LARNAKA SALT LAKE

Arriving at Larnaka's international airport in summer, you can hardly miss the vast expanse of white salt bordering the airport perimeter less than a few hundred metres from the runway. This is Larnaka's salt lake where, in winter, you can see colonies of flamingos and other migratory birds. In summer the lake slwly dries up leaving a thin film of salt. In the Middle Ages salt mining was carried on here, but pollution from aircraft exhaust in modern times has rendered the salt commercially useless. Signs warn potential adventure-drivers in

MARTIN HARRIS

The spectacular Hoopoe passes through Cyprus on it annual migratory path.

4WDs to keep off and walkers are not particularly encouraged – not that there is any reason to encourage them as the temperatures here in midsummer become extreme.

HALA SULTAN TEKKESI

On the western side of the Larnaka salt lake is one of Cyprus' most important Islamic pilgrimage sites. It is a **mosque** surrounded by date palms, cypress and olive trees and looking very much the part of a desert oasis, in stark juxtaposition to the arid salinity of the adjoining salt lake. It was founded in 674 when Umm Haram, the reputed aunt of

Mohammed, fell from a mule, broke her neck and died. She was buried on the site of the current Tekke (meaning Muslim shrine) and her tomb and subsequent mosque have become important places of worship for Muslims. Hala Sultan means 'Great Mother' in Turkish and refers to Umm Haram.

The Tekke stands empty for most of the year, except during visits by curious tourists and Muslim visitors from the Middle East. However, as part of a limited cross-Line access agreement, Turkish Cypriots from the North may visit the Tekke twice a year on goodwill pilgrimages. In reciprocation, Greek Cypriots may twice a year visit the monastery of Apostolos Andreas at the tip of the Karpas Peninsula in the North.

The Tekke is open 9 am to 7.30 pm every day (to 5 pm from October to April) and entry is nominally free, though a donation is normally expected. A rather bored-looking curator will give visitors a quick tour and historical spiel and take them over to the tomb and sarcophagus of Hala Sultan herself. The interior is maintained as a working mosque with a layer of prayer mats covering the floor, so remove your shoes before entering. Local bus No 6 will drop you off at the approach road to the Tekke from where you will have a 1km walk.

PLACES TO STAY & EAT

The village of Lefkara provides about the only satisfactory accommodation solution for travellers in the area. In any case most sights are easily reachable on a day trip from Larnaka. In Pano Lefkara there is the one-star *Lefkarama* (*☎/fax 342 000*) with basic singles/doubles for CY£14/20, or the two-star *Agora* (*☎ 04-342 901, fax 342 905*) that is OK for CY£22/32 and offers a 20% off-season discount.

Lefkarama also has a restaurant offering a wide selection of dishes. The *Lemonies* has a pleasant outdoor garden and serves up good meat dishes such as kebabs and steaks.

GETTING AROUND

Other than bus No 6, which will take you to both the Hala Sultan Tekkesi and the Panagia Angeloktisti church from Larnaka, transport

pickings for the other sights are thin on the ground. Hired transport is the only way to get around. Even hitching – always a touch-and-go option – is tricky because much of the travelling involves using the motorways and the need to get off at different exits.

AGIA NAPA Αγία Νάπα
☎ 03 ● pop 2500

From its humble beginnings as a small, insignificant fishing village, Agia Napa now shoulders the mantle of Cyprus' prime sun-and-fun tourist resort. Famagusta's Varosha beach strip and former prime resort was locked behind barbed wire and oil barrels following the North's takeover in 1974. Agia Napa is not everyone's cup of tea and 90% of people visiting here are overseas tourists on packages intent on specific and limited pleasures – drinking, eating and sunning themselves. That said, it is unquestionably popular. Restaurants, hotels and bars are still sprouting up like mushrooms in a dark cave and the unfettered growth of the town has hardly abated in more recent years.

The beach, while crowded, is good and the nightlife never stops. If you are under 30 years of age, you may want to think twice about coming here for a holiday. If you turn up in the high season (from mid-July to mid-August), accommodation will be hard to find. While hoteliers are more used to package-tour visitors, most places will cater for individuals if room is available. If you are not staying here, at least visit the place once to see what all the fuss is about.

Orientation

Agia Napa is strung out, rather like washing to dry, from east to west along the shoreline. Leoforos Nissi is the main west-east street, and arrivals from Larnaka commonly enter Agia Napa along here. Running north-south at the eastern end of Nissi is the other main artery, Leoforos Arhiepiskopou Makariou III. Heading east is Leoforos Kryou Nerou. Agia Napa's main point of focus is Plateia Seferi, known universally as 'the Square'. Several of the streets leading off the Square are pedestrianised. Buses arrive at the

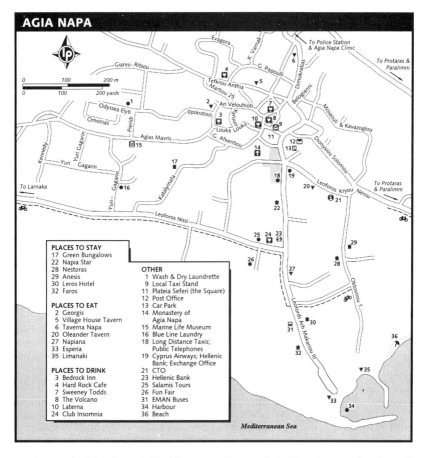

AGIA NAPA

0   100   200 m

0   100   200 yards

Evagora

To Police Station
& Agia Napa Clinic

To Protaras &
Paralimni

Gianni–Ritsou

K. Varnali

G. Papoulli

Dimokratias

Tefkrou Anthia
Martiou 25

Ari Velouhioti

Ippokratous

Odyssea Elyti

Omonias

Pieridi

Agias Mavris

Kennedy

Yuri Gagarin

Yuri Gagarin

Yuri Gagarin

To Larnaka

Katalymata

Louka Louka

G. Afxentiou

Belogianni

Misaouli

& Kavazoglou

Dionysiou Solomou

Leoforos Kryou Nerou

To Protaras &
Paralimni

Leoforos Nissi

Leoforos Arhi Makariou III

Oktovriou 1

Mediterranean Sea

PLACES TO STAY
17 Green Bungalows
22 Napia Star
28 Nestoras
29 Anesis
30 Leros Hotel
32 Faros

PLACES TO EAT
2 Georgis
5 Village House Tavern
6 Taverna Napa
20 Oleander Tavern
27 Napiana
33 Esperia
35 Limanaki

PLACES TO DRINK
3 Bedrock Inn
4 Hard Rock Cafe
7 Sweeney Todds
8 The Volcano
10 Laterna
24 Club Insomnia

OTHER
1 Wash & Dry Laundrette
9 Local Taxi Stand
11 Plateia Seferi (the Square)
12 Post Office
13 Car Park
14 Monastery of
   Agia Napa
15 Marine Life Museum
16 Blue Line Laundry
18 Long Distance Taxis;
   Public Telephones
19 Cyprus Airways; Hellenic
   Bank; Exchange Office
21 CTO
23 Hellenic Bank
25 Salamis Tours
26 Fun Fair
31 EMAN Buses
34 Harbour
36 Beach

southern end of Leoforos Arhiepiskopou Makariou III near the harbour. Long distance taxis arrive and depart from a stand close to the Square. The police station is north of the Square at the junction of Dimokratias and the Larnaka-Protaras ring road.

Information
Tourist Offices The CTO (☎ 721 796) is at Leoforos Kryou Nerou, about 200m south-east of the main Square. It's open 8.15 am to 2.30 pm and 3 to 6.30 pm Monday to Friday, but is closed on Wednesday and Saturday afternoons.

Money Agia Napa is exceptionally well stocked with banks, ATMs and exchange offices that are open at all hours of the day. Convenient ATMs are provided by the Hellenic Bank on Leoforos Arhiepiskopou Makariou III and just north of the Square on Tefkrou Anthia. An exchange office is combined with the ATM machine on the corner of Leoforos Arhiepiskopou Makariou III and Leoforos Kryou Nerou, next to Cyprus Airways.

Post & Communications The post office is on D Liperti, about 100m east of the main

Square. Convenient public phones are next to the long distance taxi stand 100m south of the Square on Leoforos Arhiepiskopou Makariou III.

Travel Agencies Salamis Tours (☎ 721 911), at Leoforos Nissi 4c, is not only the agent for the Nissos Kypros ferry boat for Israel and Greece but is a general travel agency as well, offering a wide range of travel related services. The office is diagonally opposite the Fun Fair.

Laundry There are a couple of laundries that can be used by travellers. The Wash & Dry Laundrette at Odyssea Elyti 23, 500m west of the Square, is a do-it-yourself place where a half-hour wash and half-hour dry will cost you CY£2 all up. The Blue Line Laundry on Yuri Gagarin, 600m south-west of the Square, is a service laundry shop where you drop your gear off and pick it up 24 hours later. Both are open 8 am to 7 pm daily except Sunday.

Toilets The best bet for a toilet break is to duck into one of the many bars near the Square. No-one will really mind.

Medical Services The nearest hospital is at Paralimni (☎ 03-821 211), about a 15-minute taxi ride away. The Agia Napa Clinic (☎ 723 222), also known as the Olympic Napa, is another option for medical care. For information on pharmacies open out of hours ring ☎ 192.

Emergency For an ambulance, the fire service or the police call ☎ 199. The Narcotics Emergency Service is ☎ 1410 and the AIDS advisory centre is ☎ 02-305 515.

Beaches

Once all the throngs of sun revellers have moved on, Agia Napa's beach is predictably good. The beach is usually very crowded and strewn from end to end with umbrellas and beach loungers, but everyone seems to be able to find a spot for themselves somewhere.

If you're looking for a bit of solitude, hire a scooter and move on to Cape Greco,

Konnos or Green Bay beaches south of Protaras (see Beaches in the Protaras section later in this chapter). If you just want the water and not the sand, head 3km west out of Agia Napa for **Water World** (☎ 724 444), supposedly Cyprus' best water theme park. Here you can tube, twirl, splash and slide to your heart's content. Queues can be long at peak times, so choose your time carefully. Entry costs CY£8 for a day session (children pay CY£5) and the park is open 10 am to 7 pm daily (April to October).

Boat Cruises

A large number of boat cruises operate out of Agia Napa's crowded little harbour. Most head out for trips around Cape Greco to the beaches of Protaras and Pernera, advertising their destination as 'Famagusta'. All must turn back before reaching Famagusta of course, since this city is under the control of the Turkish military.

Cruises typically cost CY£3 per person and are nominally advertised as 'party cruises'. These include music and drinks (extra cost) on board and stops for swimming. One such operation is Party Cruise 99 (☎ 09-637 233). Ask for Nikos. Cruises depart at 11.30 am and return at 4 pm daily.

Fun Fair

What Agia Napa lacks in culture it sure makes up for in sheer exhilarating, gut-wrenching thrills and spills. The smallish fun fair is dominated by three expensive super rides. You have to try one of them at least once. At around CY£12 for a few minutes of adrenalin-pumping excitement, these rides may not cure your hangover, but they'll give you an experience to remember.

First up and the oldest is the **Skycoaster** (☎ 09-609 535). For CY£12, and an extra CY£8 for an on-board video of your ride, you will fly through the sky on an enormous swing strapped into a horizontal harness. It's open 4 pm to 1 am daily. Yet flying in the Skycoaster is peanuts compared to the thrills of the two other rides.

The **Rocket Bungee** (☎ 09-414 770) is an Australian-designed super ride in which you are strapped, two at a time, into an open orb that is attached to two huge bungee cords. The cords are tightened and your orb (the Rocket) is hurled skywards at 4Gs as you shoot 45m (150 feet) upwards in 1.5 seconds. You bounce up and down, upside down and right way up, totally disoriented until the energy in the cords is expended. For CY£8 you can have a video of your onboard terror or exhilaration – whichever applies to you. The Rocket Bungee is open 3 pm to 3 am daily and costs CY£12 a shot.

The **Slingshot** (☎ 09-640 608) is similar to the Rocket Bungee, but uses metal cables instead of bungee cords, so it goes higher and faster, according to the owners. You are slung 100m high in 1.3 seconds at 6Gs and the Slingshot is touted as the 'highest, fastest ride in the world'. However the action is over somewhat faster than the Bungee Rocket, which may be just as well for some nervous riders. Videos and T-shirts are also available and the ride also costs CY£12.

Have a go on at least one of the rides – preferably before you have dinner and certainly not as a means to mix your cocktails.

Marine Life Museum

This little private museum (☎ 723 409) is hidden away in the lower ground floor of the modern Agia Napa town hall. While not earth-shatteringly arresting, it does provide some relief from the hype and hedonism of most of Agia Napa's nightlife. If you are into marine biology, fossilised shells, stuffed fish, sharks, turtles and sea birds then drop in for a quick visit. The display is fairly limited, but well laid out and documented. The museum is open 9 am to 2 pm Monday to Saturday and 3 to 6 pm on Thursday Entry is CY£1/0.50 for adults/children; those under six enter free.

Monastery of Agia Napa

The beautifully cloistered monastery is incongruously sited next to the pub and club scene of the Square next door. Best visited in the early morning after the revellers have gone to bed, the monastery is an oasis of calm amid the crass commercialism of Agia Napa's entertainment scene.

Built in around 1570 by the Venetians, the monastery is named after the 'holy handkerchief' that was used by St Veronica to wipe the face of Jesus as he carried his cross to Calvary. It is a remarkably well-preserved monastery and was indeed used as such up until 1790. Visitors enter from either the north or south side. Outside the south gate is a prominently labelled enormous sycamore fig tree which is said to be over 600 years old. A cool marble fountain is the centrepiece of the courtyard and dates from 1530. It is covered by a large dome mounted on four pillars.

The church itself, on the west side of the courtyard, is sunken somewhat lower than the courtyard level and is rather dark and gloomy inside. The whole monastery is ringed by a stout protective wall designed initially to keep marauding pirates at bay, but now ostensibly serving a better purpose in keeping inebriated foreign visitors at a respectable distance from its hallowed ground.

Places to Stay

At least 90% of visitors come to Agia Napa with booked accommodation and if you turn up between mid-July and mid-August without a booking you may have trouble finding a spot to stay. Accommodation ranges from unlicensed rooms (normally a rarity in Cyprus) to five-star hotels. Most hotels will welcome independent travellers as long as there is space available. Prices are cheaper in the off season, though quite a large number of hotels only operate from March to October. The following hotels are all cheaper to mid-range establishments and are all fairly centrally located.

At the bottom of the scale, in price at least, is **Leros Hotel** (☎ 721 126, fax 721 127, Leoforos Arhiepiskopou Makariou III). It's a small, homey place and decent singles/doubles with breakfast will cost you CY£17.50/28. Next is the two-star **Anesis** (☎ 721 104, fax 722 204, 1 Oktovriou 7) with good rooms for CY£28/CY£32 including breakfast.

The **Nestoras** (☎ 722 880, fax 722 881, ✆ nestor@logos.net.cy, Oktovriou 1 no 8) is diagonally opposite the Anesis and offers

LARNAKA & THE EAST

even better accommodation for CY£29.50/ 42, which also includes breakfast. The three-star *Napia Star (☎ 721 540, fax 721 671, ✉ alasland@cytanet.com.cy, Leoforos Arhiepiskopou Makariou III 12)* is closer to the action and offers comfortable rooms for CY£34/48, while nearer to the harbour is *Faros (☎ 723 838, fax 723 839, ✉ vavlitis@ spidernet.com.cy, Leoforos Arhiepiskopou Makariou III)* with superior rooms at CY£42/56 including breakfast.

Finally, you can always try the *Green Bungalows (☎ 721 511, fax 722 184, ✉ anas tassiadesa@cytanet.com.cy, Katalymata 19)*, a superior B-class apartment hotel. This place is only open from April to October but does offer cosy double apartments for CY£30. Breakfast is an extra CY£2.

Places to Eat

Without guidance, eating in Agia Napa can be a bit of a hit-and-miss affair. The big fast-food chains are all close to each other and there is an eating place almost every 50m or so. Many pander only to tourists, but others pull in a knowledgable local clientele as well. There is Indian, Chinese and Mexican cuisine on offer, so you are not short on choices. In general, prices are somewhat higher than elsewhere on Cyprus though not outrageously so. Try those described for starters, but follow your nose and gut instinct if you see something that takes your fancy.

Down by the harbour, where the surrounding area is gradually being repaved and upgraded, are a few waterside eateries. On the east side of town is *Limanaki (☎ 721 600)*, specialising in fish, with dishes from CY£4.50 to CY£7.50. Closer to the water is *Esperia (☎ 721 635)*, boasting slightly more upmarket decor and a marginally better location. Enormous fish and meat dishes sell for similar prices as at the Limanaki.

Closer to Agia Napa central is the *Napiana (☎ 722 891, Leoforos Arhiepiskopou Makariou III 29)*, a busy establishment with exceptionally attentive service. Steaks are the big seller here with the rich chateaubriand for two at CY£8.50 per person. Soups and *stifados* (rich beef stew) are on the menu

and are a cheaper option. Napiana is open for lunch and dinner.

Oleander Tavern (☎ 721 951, Kryou Nerou) does the best kebabs in town. The owner was coy about giving away the recipe, but it entails wine, herbs and spices and you can see the kebabs cooking on the spit inside the restaurant. Other than kebabs, you can have mousakas for CY£3.95 and vegetarian spaghetti for £3.50. It's open for lunch and dinner.

Somewhat folksy and perhaps a bit too close to the bar scene, but still a decent choice, is *Village House Taverna (☎ 724 135, Tefkrou Anthia 11)*. If you can't decide what you want to eat, go for the daily set menu (see the board) for which you'll pay around CY£6.95. It's open all day.

A couple of places that rate well according to the CTO are *Taverna Napa (☎ 721 280, Dimokratias 15)*, a little way north of the main action, and *Georgis (☎ 721 838, Ippokratous 9)*. The former is a cosy little taverna with a broad range of dishes at mid-range prices; the latter specialises in flambé dishes and generally gets good reviews from the local dining community. These two places operate evenings only.

Entertainment

If you have come to Agia Napa, you are probably here for one purpose – to drink – and this is the place to do it. Bars and music rock on until around 2 am then it's time to hit the clubs. The central area within 200m of the Square is a riotous confusion of noise, karaoke, disco beats and clinking glasses. There are almost 20 bars and 15 clubs to choose from and nightlife never stops.

There's the *Hard Rock Cafe* on Tefkrou Anthia with cold beer and live music. Just a two-minute walk further towards the beach is the *Bedrock Inn*, a grotesque Fred Flintstone and Barney Rubble-style karaoke palace on the corner of Louka Louka and Agias Mavris that really pulls in the crowds. For people-watching choose the balconies of the pubs on the Square. *The Volcano* has probably got the best location with its all-seeing upstairs balcony, though if you fancy a sit-down on the Square, then

Laterna is the place to go. *Sweeney Todds* on the north side of the Square is the newest kid on the block and has reputedly the best sound system in town.

Nightaholics can always seek pre-dawn solace and more drinks at *Club Insomnia* on Leoforos Nissi 4. Advertising 'quality chill-out time' and 'happy sunshine music' this club is for serious all-nighters. Conveniently opposite McDonald's, it's open 4 to 7 am, and fills an obvious gap in Agia Napa's now fully all-night party scene.

Getting There & Away
The bus is the best and only budget way to get to Agia Napa. There are nine direct buses to/from Larnaka (CY£1) in summer and one daily bus to Lefkosia (CY£2) at 8 am (returning at 3 pm). There are more or less hourly (on the hour) buses to Paralimni and Protaras (CY£0.40). All buses leave from the bus stop between the Square and the harbour.

Private taxis (from the taxi stand close to the Square) vary, with rates from CY£13 to Larnaka airport, CY£18 to Lefkosia, and CY£40 to the Troödos Mountains. There are no service taxis.

Cyprus Airways (☎ 721 265) has an office at Leoforos Arhiepiskopou Makariou 17. The nearest airport is at Larnaka.

AROUND AGIA NAPA
Agia Napa is a convenient starting point for a number of pleasant half-day or one-day trips around the western quadrant of Cyprus. Indeed, on most summer days, squadrons of bare-backed scooter riders throng the coastal roads leading out of Agia Napa. You can choose to seek out another beach, visit the villages of the hinterland, see what the Brits are up to on one of their Sovereign Base Areas, or peer over into the ghost town of Varosha from vantage points right on the Attila Line.

Protaras
Protaras is a slightly watered-down version of Agia Napa. It is another beach resort area, but is more spread out, has a better range of beaches and tends to give visitors more breathing space. That said, Protaras is geared almost exclusively to the resort crowd with sprawling hotels, lawns and swimming pools. While day visitors are more than welcome they tend to feel a little left out. There seem to be enough restaurants and bars to compensate, though finding one that is beyond simply adequate can take some doing – most offer unimaginative meals served by uninspired non-Cypriot waiting staff.

Beaches Protaras is best known for its beaches. While they do not compare to the postcard-pretty beaches of Greece they are the best the Republic has to offer. Starting from the northern end you will find diminutive **Agia Triada Beach**. Used mainly as a boat launching area, the water is shallow, the sand a little coarse and cars tend to be parked along its 200m curving length. Ice cream sellers are the only source of nourishment, so bring a lunch if you want food.

Next along is **Mouzoura Beach** (blink and you'll miss it). It's fairly small and compact and popular with Cypriot sunbathers. Its 100m length sports a good but narrow sand strip and some shade under the trees at the southern end of the beach. Get in early if you want a spot. The sand does drop away quickly so it might not be suitable for non-swimmers or young children. There are ample parking facilities and at least one good restaurant and a large hotel for people who choose to base themselves here.

Farther south and moving into the busy beach zone is **Louma Beach** in the northern extension of Protaras called Pernera. Its 450m curving strand is protected by an artificial bay. The sand is fine and has space for all visitors. The water is clean and shelves gently. There is shade under the trees at the northern end. Water sports are catered for by Baywater Water Sports who offer banana tube rides (CY£3), paragliding (CY£12 a flight), water-skiing lessons (CY£10) or 30 minutes on a jet ski (CY£20). Sun loungers and umbrellas rent for CY£1 each.

Skipping a fairly lengthy section of coast with few swimming options, the next busy beach is **Protaras Beach** which is a smaller version of Louma Beach. It is 200m long, is curving and has good soft sand but little shade. However, the water is also shallow and shelves suddenly. Sun loungers and umbrellas are for rent at CY£1 each. Five restaurants surround the beach and compete for trade, but parking is not so brilliant. Your best bet is to select your restaurant first and park in its lot, or park away from the beach and walk. The TABA Diving centre (☎ 03-832 680) here offers certified three-day PADI scuba diving courses for CY£120 or four-day open water courses for CY£190.

Finally, if you want to avoid the crowds and sort of get away from it all in Protaras, head for **Green Bay Beach** at the far southern end of the beach strip. It is the first obvious beach you will come to if approaching Green Bay from Agia Napa. There are two parts to the beach: a sandy strip with umbrellas and loungers to rent on the north side and some little sandstone platforms 100m farther south where, if you get in early enough, you can claim a very pleasant spot. Refreshments are a bit of a walk away. The nearest minimarket with ice creams and beer is back on the approach road.

Cape Greco

Die-hard lovers of lands' ends will no doubt head for Cape Greco, about 7km from Agia Napa or 4km from Protaras. It's hardly a safari though. A good road, narrow in parts, leads in and out of the area thus obviating the need to backtrack any length. Unfortunately you can't get to the end of the Cape itself. As on Mt Olympus in the Troödos the Brits have requisitioned the last piece of ground to install a radar ground station that is firmly fenced off from the public. However all is not lost. Some of the best swimming can be had here if the weather is not too windy. From the scruffy car park, walk north towards the little bay and clamber down onto the rocks. A few rock platforms support swimmers who really don't want to be part of the Protaras beach scene. The water is absolutely idyllic here.

Paralimni

Paralimni has reluctantly taken over from Ammohostos (Famagusta) as the capital of the eastern section of Cyprus. While you will have little reason to come here other than out of curiosity, or if you are touring the area by scooter, it is a pleasant little town seemingly a universe away from the hustle and bustle of the tourist scene only a few kilometres away on the coast. There is a pleasantly paved central square with two versions of the church of Agios Georgios (new and old), a sprinkling of restaurants and shops and perhaps a gaggle of curious tourists.

Deryneia

People usually come to Deryneia for one reason alone – to peer into no-man's land and stare at the firmly closed 'border' that separates Northern Cyprus from the South. During the belated second invasion by the Turks of the North in August 1974, the Turkish army encircled and occupied the deserted holiday resort centre of Varosha (Maraş in Turkish). Troops moved towards Deryneia and halted abruptly just below the rise on which the town is located and which now gives it its unparalleled but politically charged view into Northern Cyprus.

There are at least two viewing platforms from which you can see into the North. **Annitas** (☎ 03-823 003) is the better of the two, and is essentially a private apartment block which had the luck/misfortune to be the last building in the South that was not occupied. From the top floor viewing platform (entry CY£0.50) you can see the Greek Cypriot barracks, the blue and white UN building and, further still, the cream-coloured Turkish Cypriot post with the Turkish and Turkish Cypriot flags flying defiantly. Both flags are now safely protected by barbed wire after two violent and fatal incidents in 1996 (see the boxed text 'The Deryneia Martyrs').

Graphic videos and wall posters in the little viewing platform cafeteria will describe events that shocked and still linger in the collective memory of Greek Cypriots. Binoculars are handed out to visitors as part of the entrance ticket. The stark cityscape to the right and north of Deryneia is Varosha; it is to all intents and purposes dead and

The Deryneia Martyrs

On 11 August 1996 a Berlin-to-Cyprus peace ride by motorcyclists from around Europe ended at the Greek Cypriot village of Deryneia adjoining the Green Line that divides Northern Cyprus from the Republic of Cyprus. Among the riders that day was a young Greek Cypriot from Protaras by the name of Tasos Isaak. Newly married, his young wife was pregnant and carrying their first child.

At the protest that marked the end of the ride and in memory of the continuing occupation of the North by Turkish forces a melee developed, with clashes between Greek Cypriots and Turkish Cypriots in the UN buffer zone that separated the two communities. During the running clashes with Turks from the North – many of whom it is widely believed belonged to the paramilitary organisation the Grey Wolves from the Turkish mainland – Tasos Isaak was inexplicably cut off from his fellow demonstrators. He was set upon by thugs carrying wooden clubs and iron bars.

Before the astonished eyes of the demonstrators and at least one photographer present, Isaak was beaten deliberately and viciously to death. He was unarmed and dressed only in jeans and a shirt. Turkish police stood by and watched. Isaak's lifeless body was later recovered by UN personnel.

Three days later, after Isaak's funeral, a crowd once more gathered at the Deryneia checkpoint to protest against this unprovoked and unwarranted death. Among the protesters this time was Solomos Solomou, a 26-year-old friend of Isaak, who was enraged at the death of his friend. Despite repeated attempts to hold him back, Solomos eluded the UN peacekeepers and slipped across the no-man's land to one of the flagpoles carrying the Turkish Cypriot flag. Cigarette in mouth, he managed to climb halfway up the flagpole before being struck by five bullets that came from the Turkish Cypriot checkpoint building and possibly from bushes sheltering armed soldiers. Solomos' bloody slide to death down the flagpole was captured dramatically on video, and is replayed endlessly at viewing points that today overlook the tragic site of the Deryneia murders.

The memories live on vividly in the minds of Greek Cypriots. The graphic photos of Isaak and Solomos, as well as that of an old man caught picking mushrooms in the buffer zone and then subsequently shot, are displayed on the Greek side of the Ledra Palace Hotel crossing in Lefkosia. Security is tight at Deryneia now, but tensions run ever high. Life and death can be as fragile as a Damoclean thread in Cyprus.

abandoned and has been left in the way it was occupied in 1974. Only rats and a few Turkish military details now inhabit its overgrown streets.

The Dekelia Base

As part of the hard-won deal between the nascent Republic of Cyprus and Great Britain in 1960, the British were granted rights to two major Sovereign Base Areas (SBAs) as well as access to a series of retained sites scattered around the country where satellite ground stations and radio listening stations were located. The Dekelia SBA is the second of the two major base areas taken over 'in perpetuity' by the canny Brits. (See the Lemesos and South Coast chapter for details about Akrotiri.)

The area comprises a sizable chunk of eastern Cyprus and runs from Larnaka Bay to the current Attila Line border with the North. In reality, the Dekelia SBA cuts off the Paralimni district from the rest of the Republic of Cyprus since the SBAs are deemed to be foreign territory. In practice there are no 'border' controls, although formidable grey iron gates on the road at the SBA entrances prove that British territorial integrity could be invoked at any time should circumstances prove necessary.

You are not supposed to 'tour' the SBA and photographs are a no-no. You can't actually enter the base installations themselves without passes and permits, but you can freely drive around the territory itself. Although the British military play it very low-key and rarely make themselves visible to casual travellers, the installations at Dekelia are a crucial intelligence-gathering apparatus. They continue to play a role in monitoring radio traffic in the Middle East and keeping a watch on regional military activity with sophisticated over-the-horizon (OTH-B) radar units.

The Attila Line is less rigorously monitored here since there is no UN buffer zone as such. Turkish Cypriots from the North may come and go freely and move around within the SBA; many do so in order to visit the sole Turkish-Greek village left in Cyprus at Pyla (see the following section). The informal Line crossing points at Pergamos and Agios Nikolaos, while not open to casual visitors, are in total contrast to the tense atmosphere perceptible at the Ledra Palace Hotel crossing point in Lefkosia. Visitors should be extra vigilant about inadvertently wandering into the North as there have been documented cases of southerners or foreigners being arrested and held by Northern authorities after accidentally straying across the sometimes indistinct Line.

These days, travellers heading to Agia Napa and Protaras from Larnaka are neatly diverted around (though still through) the SBA by an extension of the motorway which, by the end of 1999, had reached as far as Ormidia, safely on the east side of Dekelia.

The Kokkinohoria

The Kokkinohoria villages are to Cyprus what Idaho is to the USA. They both produce famous potatoes. Kokkinohoria means 'Red Villages' and are so-called not because of their political allegiances, but for the colour of the rich earth over which these once backwater but now prospering villages are built. The red soil of the Agia Napa hinterland is striking and appears almost suddenly, soon after the village of Ormidia. Coupled with a rash of wind-powered water pumps that litter the rolling landscape, this part of Cyprus is in many ways geographically akin to the outback of Australia.

Potatoes and also *kolokasi* (a kind of root vegetable similar to the Pacific Islands' taro) grows profusely in the mineral-rich soil. Up to three crops of potatoes are cultivated annually here – no doubt contributing significantly to Cypriots' predilection for chips with everything. The main villages are **Xylofagou**, **Avgorou**, **Frenaros**, **Liopetri** and **Sotira** and, while they offer little to the tourist per se other than a glimpse of rural Cyprus or the occasional excellent country taverna, they are great to tool around on a scooter and are in total contrast to the coastal resorts to the east and south.

Drivers might note that there is a useful alternate route from Agia Napa to Larnaka via the Kokkinohoria – especially on Sunday evenings in summer when everyone is heading home from a day at the beach. The direct Agia Napa-Larnaka highway up to where the motorway starts at Ormidia can get hopelessly jammed. Drivers are advised to loop north via Frenaros and join the Famagusta-Dekelia road. Head directly and swiftly for the motorway north of Xylotymvou. This way you will also enter the Dekelia SBA, passing the abandoned villages of **Achna** to your right and in the UN buffer zone. Signposting in the Kokkinohoria is pretty poor at times so make sure you have a decent map to avoid going round in circles.

Pyla

The unlikely village of Pyla (Pile in Turkish) is the only place on the whole of Cyprus where Greek Cypriots and Turkish Cypriots still live together in harmony. Admittedly that harmony is reinforced by the presence of the UN peace-keeping contingent and a watchful Turkish military lookout post on the ridge high above the village, but it works. Pyla is in the UN buffer zone and, unlike elsewhere in Cyprus, this buffer zone area is open to all and sundry. That means Cypriots from both the North and the South.

The main feature of the village, illustrating the continuing peaceful coexistence of Turk and Greek, is the village square where on one side a red and white coloured Turkish Cypriot coffee shop eyes up a blue and white coloured Greek Cypriot kafenio on the other side. Overlooking the middle of the square is the 'referee's' chair positioned prominently outside the UN watchtower and occasionally occupied by an Irish or Argentinian soldier in a blue beret.

Greeks and Turks live in mixed neighbourhoods and by all accounts mind their own business and get on with living normally. Cross-cultural mixing is low-key and not obvious to casual observers. The Greeks are somewhat peeved that they carry the burden of local taxes and the utility costs of their neighbours while the Turks pay nothing and get the benefit of access to both the North and the South. This is the only place in the South – other than on the Dekelia SBA – that you will see Northern Cyprus-registered cars. Look for the thin red band around the otherwise identical licence plates, or the giveaway Turkish script on the plate frame. Many Turkish Cypriot residents of Pyla run two cars – one North-registered and the other South-registered, thereby getting the best of both worlds. Photography is not allowed.

If you don't want to backtrack to the Larnaka motorway, take the winding road out of Pyla signposted to Pergamos, entering the SBA about 1km outside the village. From here you can cut across the SBA to the motorway to Ormidia.

Places to Stay & Eat

Without exception, all hotel options are clustered along the Pernera-Protaras strip in this part of Cyprus. Most are resolutely geared to package-tour visitors and the choice is enormous, with over 90 places on offer. These range from two-star to five-star hotels and A-class and B-class hotel apartments. Budget accommodation is thin on the ground, with virtually no backpacker scene to speak of. Bookings are recommended in the high season and would-be travellers are advised to get hold of the free CTO *Hotel Guide* that gives a full listing.

One place that you might look at is the newish A-class hotel apartment *Aeolos* (☎ *03-832 810, fax 722 809, Louma Beach),* which is not listed in the CTO guide. This spotless establishment is right on the beach and offers well-equipped rooms from CY£20 to CY£42 for up to four people.

This author took pot luck and found a very decent room for three people at the three-star resort hotel of *Cavo Maris (☎ 03-832 043, fax 832 051, ✉ cavo@cytanet.com.cy).* There are a couple of pools, a rocky but pleasant beach, restaurants, bars and nighttime activities. Posted room rates start from CY£39 and CY£74 for singles/doubles but a 30% discount often applies even in season.

Eating options are as broad as the accommodation possibilities. While hotels all tend to be of a predictable and uniform quality, some restaurants can be downright bad. Choose prudently. In central Pernera there is a cheap and excellent pub-restaurant called *Nautilus Inn (☎ 03-831 042)*. It's on the main road away from the beach and so can pass on its rental saving to its food and drink. Jacket potatoes with chilli cost only CY£1.20, top-class draught Guinness or Kilkenny is CY£2 a pint and there are 11 varieties of bottled Belgian lager ranging from CY£1.40 to CY£2.50. For guests of the Aeolos hotel at Louma Beach, *Kalamies* restaurant is handy and does *afelia* for CY£3 or a cheeseburger and chips for CY£2.30.

At Protaras try *Anemos (☎ 03-831 488)* at Fig Tree Bay. It's a busy and popular spot and prices are mid-range. At Mouzoura Beach is *Mouzoura Beach Restaurant (☎ 823 333)*. It's another large scale eatery, but it tends to draw a predominantly Cypriot crowd, thus ensuring that the food quality is better than average. Good pork chops (CY£4.50) and tender kalamari (CY£5) are recommended.

Getting Around

No public transport other than the Protaras-Paralimni to Larnaka bus is going to help you much here. The cheapest option is to hire a scooter in either Protaras or Agia Napa. Rates vary, but are usually very reasonable. Make sure you choose a scooter with some power in its engine; it is a fair haul across the backblocks of the Paralimni region on underpowered transport. A scooter is the best option for beach hopping along the Pernera-Protaras coastal strip.

A car is the best way to see the region in comfort. Rates from smaller private companies in Protaras or Agia Napa are usually better than those offered by big-name hire car companies. A group of four should be able to hire a small 4WD open-top jeep fairly cheaply.

As the whole area is reasonably flat, cycling is an ideal way of getting around the Kokkinohoria.

Pafos & the West

For a long time the far western quadrant of Cyprus was considered to be the island's Wild West. Isolated both physically and culturally from the heartland of the country, the region gained a reputation for backwardness and introspection. Its people were considered canny, yet undereducated, and the Greek and Turkish dialects of the west were among the most difficult for an outsider to understand.

Nowadays only Greeks live in this area, their Turkish Cypriot compatriots having reluctantly moved to the North in 1974. The region is no longer considered a backwater and indeed it attracts an increasing share of the burgeoning tourist influx, as witnessed by the ranks of sumptuous resort hotels that stretch north and south from Pafos, the region's capital.

Pafos is a delightfully breezy town. Here you can combine both culture and entertainment in a conveniently sized package. You will find some of Cyprus' most stunning archaeological gems, such as its Roman mosaics and Tombs of the Kings cheek-by-jowl with the resort hotels and golden beaches. Cultivated bananas grow in profusion along the south-western littoral, yet the Akamas Peninsula is one of the island's last unspoilt wildernesses and is home to flora and fauna spedies found only on Cyprus.

Pretty villages, untouched by time, litter the valleys of the hinterland and the vast Pafos Forest melts almost imperceptibly into the sombre tracts of the Tyllirian wilderness in the North. Small beach resorts that have not yet succumbed entirely to commercialisation await discerning travellers and there are abundant land and sea-based activities to suit every taste. What is more, the west has its own international airport and visitors to Cyprus may fly into the country directly from many European destinations. An investment of some time in the western region of Cyprus will be well rewarded.

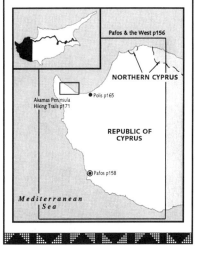

Pafos

☎ 06 • postcode 8000 • pop 37,300

While Lemesos is brash and Larnaka is demure, Pafos is quite user-friendly and is one of Cyprus' most livable cities. The tourism boom has seen the capital of the west receiving considerably more of the tourist dollar than its sisters further east. Kato Pafos (Lower Pafos) is the port annex of Ano Pafos (Upper Pafos) and is home to the greatest number of archaeological sites in the area. It provides a lively and friendly ambience in its renovated port area where

PAFOS & THE WEST

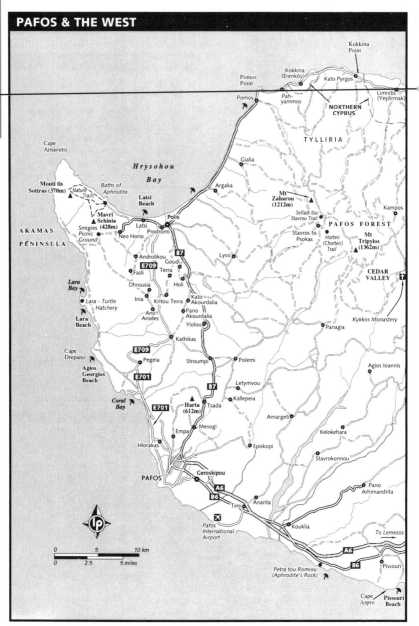

Kokkina Point

Pomos Point

Kokkina (Erenköy)

Kato Pyrgos

Limnitis (Yeşilirmak)

Pomos

Pah-yammos

NORTHERN CYPRUS

Cape Arnaoutis

Gialia

Hrysohou Bay

Argaka

TYLLIRIA

Mt Zaharou (1212m)

Mouti tis Sotiras (370m)

Nature Trails

Baths of Aphrodite

Latsi Beach

Selladi tou Stavrou Trail

Kampos

PAFOS FOREST

Mavri Schinia (428m)

Smigies Picnic Ground

Latsi

Polis

Prodromi

Stavros tis Psokas

Horteri (Chorteri) Trail

Mt Tripylos (1362m)

AKAMAS PENINSULA

Neo Horio

Androlikou

Goudi

B7

Lyso

CEDAR VALLEY

Fasli

Terra

Holi

Lara Bay

Dhrousia

Inia

Kritou Terra

Kato Akourdalia

Kykkos Monastery

Lara - Turtle Hatchery

Ano Arodes

Pano Akourdalia

Panagia

Lara Beach

E709

Yiolou

Kathikas

Cape Drepano

E709

Pegeia

Stroumpi

Polemi

Agios Ioannis

Agios Georgios Beach

E701

Coral Bay

E701

Harta (612m)

Tsada

Letymvou

Kallepeia

Amargeti

Kelokehara

Empa

Mesogi

Episkopi

Hlorakas

Stavrokonnou

PAFOS

Geroskipou

A6

Pano Arhimandrita

B6

Timi

Anarita

Pafos International Airport

Kouklia

To Lemesos

0   5   10 km

0   2.5   5 miles

Petra tou Romiou (Aphrodite's Rock)

A6

B6

Pissouri

Cape Aspro

Pissouri Beach

visitors, unlike elsewhere in Cyprus' ports, can actually swim. With its palm tree lined boulevards, tasteful public and private buildings, Pafos is a downright pleasant place to spend a holiday. There are ample restaurants and watering holes and if you tire of the beach annex you can always retire to Ano Pafos (known also as Ktima) for an afternoon's stroll or evening meal.

ORIENTATION

The two distinct sections of Pafos are 2km apart. Public buses and service taxis arrive at Ano Pafos and to get to Kato Pafos you can take local bus No 11, walk or take a taxi. Leoforos Apostolou Pavlou links the two parts of Pafos and Leoforos Georgiou Griva Digeni (named after the leader of the guerilla independence movement, National Organisation for the Cypriot Struggle or EOKA) leads east out of Ano Pafos towards Lemesos. Leoforos Evagora Pallikaridi heads north out of Ano Pafos to Polis.

INFORMATION
Tourist Offices

The CTO office (☎ 253 341) is at Gladstonos 3, just down from the main square in Ano Pafos. It is open 8.15 am to 2.30 pm and 3 to 6.30 pm Monday to Saturday, but is closed on Wednesday and Saturday afternoons. There's another tourist office at the airport.

Money

There are plenty of banks and accompanying ATMs in both Ano and Kato Pafos and between the two along Leoforos Apostolou Pavlou. The Popular Bank and National Bank both have easy-to-find ATMs in Ano Pafos. The Hellenic Bank in Kato Pafos, in addition to an ATM, has an exchange service that keeps long hours. There are other private exchange services in both centres. You can also change money at Pafos International airport.

Post & Communications

The main post office is in Ano Pafos, on Nikodimou Mylona, just west of the main square. Poste restante mail is held here. There is another branch in Kato Pafos on Agiou Antoniou, which is open afternoons

only. The CYTA office is on Leoforos Georgiou Griva Digeni in Ano Pafos, but public phones are everywhere. The most convenient phones are on the waterfront close to the harbour in Kato Pafos. The most central Internet cafe is Surf Cafe (✉ surfcafe@cytanet.com.cy) at Gladstonos 1, very close to the CTO. The charge is CY£3 an hour.

Travel Agencies

The Pafos branch of Salamis Tours (☎ 235 504, fax 235 505) is at Leoforos Georgiou Griva Digeni 44. It can issue you with your ferry tickets for Greece and Israel as well as air tickets to most destinations outside of Cyprus.

Bookshops

The Moufflon Bookshop (☎ 234 850) is an offshoot of the bookshop of the same name in Lefkosia. Opened in September 1999 it has a good selection of foreign-language books, newspapers and magazines. It is at Kinyras 30 in Ano Pafos and is open 8.30 am to 1 pm and 4 to 7 pm. It closes at 2 pm on Wednesday and Saturday.

Foreign-language newspapers can also be bought at Stazo Trading on the waterfront in Kato Pafos and at the Ano Pafos Foreign Press kiosk on the main square.

Medical Services

The Pafos General Hospital can be phoned on ☎ 240 111 and information on private doctors on call can be obtained by ringing ☎ 1426.

Emergency

For an ambulance, the police or the fire service call ☎ 199. For information on night pharmacies operating out of hours call ☎ 1416. The AIDS Advisory Service can be reached on ☎ 02-305 515 and the Narcotics Emergency Service can be contacted on ☎ 1410. The police station is on the main square in Ano Pafos.

WALKING TOUR

A do-it-yourself walking tour of Pafos most conveniently combines the sites of Nea

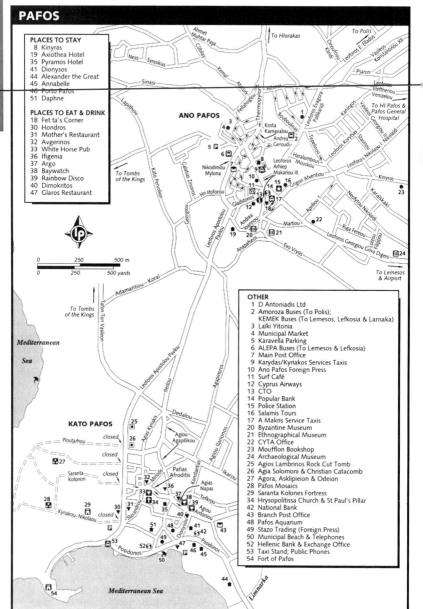

PAFOS

PLACES TO STAY
8 Kinyras
19 Axiothea Hotel
35 Pyramos Hotel
41 Dionysos
44 Alexander the Great
45 Annabelle
46 Porto Pafos
51 Daphne

PLACES TO EAT & DRINK
18 Fet ta's Corner
30 Hondros
31 Mother's Restaurant
32 Avgerinos
33 White Horse Pub
36 Ifigenia
37 Argo
38 Baywatch
39 Rainbow Disco
40 Dimokritos
47 Glaros Restaurant

OTHER
1 D Antoniadis Ltd
2 Amoroza Buses (To Polis);
  KEMEK Buses (To Lemesos, Lefkosia & Larnaka)
3 Laïki Yitonia
4 Municipal Market
5 Karavella Parking
6 ALEPA Buses (To Lemesos & Lefkosia)
7 Main Post Office
9 Karydas/Kyriakos Services Taxis
10 Ano Pafos Foreign Press
11 Surf Café
12 Cyprus Airways
13 CTO
14 Popular Bank
15 Police Station
16 Salamis Tours
17 A Makris Service Taxis
20 Byzantine Museum
21 Ethnographical Museum
22 CYTA Office
23 Moufflon Bookshop
24 Archaeological Museum
25 Agios Lambrinos Rock Cut Tomb
26 Agia Solomoni & Christian Catacomb
27 Agora, Asklipieion & Odeion
28 Pafos Mosaics
29 Saranta Kolones Fortress
34 Hrysopolitissa Church & St Paul's Pillar
42 National Bank
43 Branch Post Office
48 Pafos Aquarium
49 Stazo Trading (Foreign Press)
50 Municipal Beach & Telephones
52 Hellenic Bank & Exchange Office
53 Taxi Stand; Public Phones
54 Fort of Pafos

ANO PAFOS

KATO PAFOS

Mediterranean Sea

Mediterranean Sea

To Tombs of the Kings

To Tombs of the Kings

To Hlorakas

To Polis

To HI Pafos & Pafos General Hospital

To Lemesos & Airport

0   250   500 m
0   250   500 yards

Pafos with the early Christian sites of Kato Pafos. Follow that with a brisk 2km walk (or take bus No 11) up to Ano Pafos for lunch and then an afternoon tour of the upper city's three museums.

NEA PAFOS

Nea Pafos (New Pafos) is the name given to the sprawling archaeological site that occupies the western segment of Kato Pafos, north of the harbour and west of Leoforos Apostolou Pavlou. Nea Pafos refers to the Ancient City of Pafos which was founded in the late 4th century BC. Palea Pafos (Old Pafos) was in fact Kouklia, south-east of today's Pafos and the site of the Sanctuary of Aphrodite. Cyprus at that time was part of the kingdom of the Ptolemies, the Graeco-Macedonian rulers of Egypt whose capital was in Alexandria. Nea Pafos became an important strategic outpost for the Ptolemies and the settlement grew considerably over the next seven centuries.

The city was originally encircled by massive walls and occupied an area of approximately 950,000 sq m, reaching several hundred metres east of today's Leoforos Apostolou Pavlou. The streets were laid out in a rectangular grid pattern and archaeological excavations have shown evidence of commercial and cultural activity over the life of the city. Nea Pafos was ceded to the Romans in 58 BC, but remained the centre of all political and administrative life of the whole of Cyprus while reaching its zenith during the 2nd or 3rd centuries AD. It was during this time that Nea Pafos' most opulent public buildings were constructed, including those that house the now famous Pafos Mosaics.

Nea Pafos went into decline following an earthquake in the 4th century that badly damaged the city, and indeed many cities in Cyprus. Subsequently, and for prevailing political and strategic reasons, Salamis in the east became the new capital of Cyprus and Nea Pafos was delegated to the status of a mere bishopric. It was at this time that the fine Basilica of Hrysopolitissa was built (see later in this chapter). Arab raids of the 7th century set the seal on the city's demise and

neither Lusignan settlement (1192–1489), when the Saranta Kolones Fort and Pafos Fort were built (see section later in this chapter), nor Venetian and Ottoman colonisation revived Nea Pafos' fortunes.

The current archaeological sites are being slowly excavated since it is widely believed that there are as many treasures still to be discovered as have already been revealed. Visitors can spend a busy half day exploring the sites. With the exception of the Pafos Mosaics complex, access is free. The following comprise the major sites in the open archaeological area to the immediate west of Kato Pafos.

Agora, Asklipieion & Odeion

The Agora or forum and Asklipieion date back to the 2nd century AD and constitute the heart of the original Nea Pafos city complex. The Agora consists mainly of the Odeion, a semicircular theatre that that was restored in 1970 but does not look particularly ancient. The Agora is discernible by the remains of marble columns which form a rectangle in the largely empty open space and what is left of the Asklipieion, the healing centre and altar of Asklepios – the god of medicine – runs east to west immediately on the south side of the Odeion. Entrance to all three is free and the site is permanently open.

Pafos Mosaics

Pafos' second most popular attraction is an impressive collection of intricate and colourful mosaics in the southern sector of the archaeological park immediately to the south of the Agora. Discovered by accident during levelling operations in 1962, excavations carried out by the Department of Antiquities brought to light remains of a large and wealthy residence from the Roman period with exquisite coloured mosaics decorating its extensive floor area. Subsequently named the **House of Dionysos** (because of the large number of mosaics featuring the god of wine, Dionysos) this complex is the largest and most well known of the mosaic houses.

Look out for striking **mosaics** depicting Pyramos and Thisbe (room 16) The Triumph of Dionysos (room 4) and a series of panels depicting the Four Seasons (room 4). Altogether there are 34 rooms displaying a striking variety of themes. The mosaics are best viewed for their colours when given a sprinkling of water, but this treat is seldom afforded mere tourists. Thus the colours are not as bright as they appear in the excellent official *Guide to the Pafos Mosaics* on sale for CY£3 at the ticket kiosk – recommended reading if you want a blow-by-blow account of the mosaics on view.

A short walk away are the smaller **Villa of Theseus** and **House of Aion**. The latter is a purpose-built structure made from recycled stones found on the site and housing a panel of 4th-century mosaics. The house was named after the pagan god Aion who is depicted in the mosaic display, which itself is made up of five separate panels. Although the image of Aion has been damaged somewhat, the name Aion and the face of the god can be clearly seen.

The Villa of Theseus is most likely a 2nd century private residence and is named after a mosaic representation of the hero Theseus fighting the Minotaur. The building occupies an area of 9600 sq m and 1400 sq m of mosaics have so far been uncovered. The round mosaic of Theseus and the Minotaur is remarkably well preserved and can be seen in room 36. Other mosaics to look out for are those of Poseidon in room 76 and Achilles in rooms 39 to 40.

Entrance to the entire mosaics complex (☎ 240 217) costs CY£1.50 and the site is open 8 am to 7.30 pm daily. Allow at least two hours to see the three houses properly.

Saranta Kolones Fortress

Not far from the mosaics complex you will come across the remains of the medieval Saranta Kolones Fortress. *Saranta kolones* in Greek means 'forty columns' which once was a feature of the now almost levelled structure. Little is known about the precise nature or history of the original fortress other than that the structure was built by the Lusignans in the 12th century and was subsequently destroyed by an earthquake in 1222. What you see today dates from that time. The structure had four huge corner towers and another four intermediary towers along the joining walls. A few desultory arches are the only real visual evidence of its original grandeur. Entry is free.

AGIA SOLOMONI & CHRISTIAN CATACOMB

This fairly nondescript tomb complex just off Leoforos Apostolou Pavlou was the burial site of the Seven Machabee Brothers who were martyred during the time of Antiochus IV Epiphanes. The entrance to the catacomb is marked by a collection of votive rags tied to a large tree outside the tomb. This ostensibly pagan practice is still carried out by Christian visitors today. The tomb was used as a church in the 12th century as can be witnessed by the still-visible frescoes.

AGIOS LAMBRINOS ROCK CUT TOMB

A little farther north on the side of **Fabrica Hill** are a couple of enormous underground caverns dating most likely from the early Hellenistic period. These are also burial chambers associated with the two saints Lambrianos and Misitikos. The interior of the tombs show frescoes which indicate their use as a Christian place of worship.

HRYSOPOLITISSA CHURCH & ST PAUL'S PILLAR

This fairly extensive site – still being excavated – was home to one of Pafos' largest religious structures. What's left are the foundations of a **Christian basilica** (built in the 4th century) and they aptly demonstrate the size and magnificence of the original church. This was ultimately destroyed during Arab raids in 653. Green marble columns from the original church lie scattered around the site and **mosaics** from the church floor are still visible. Further reincarnations of the basilica were built over the years leading to the present small **Agia Kyriaki** church. The overall area is loosely roped off and signs request visitors to keep off, so you can't get a total picture of the remains.

PAUL HELLANDER

Interior of Hala Sultan Tekkesi, Larnaka

CHRIS CHRISTO

Adonis Falls, near Kamares village, Pafos region

JON DAVISON

Pano Lefkara, 50km west of Larnaka, is famous for its exquisite handmade lace work.

Hrysopolitissa Church, Kato Pafos

Tombs of the Kings, Nea Pafos

Aphrodite's Rock, near Latsi, Pafos region

Tombs of the Kings, underground tombs and chambers used as a necropolis in ancient Nea Pafos.

What is visible on the western side of the basilica is the so-called **St Paul's Pillar** where St Paul was allegedly tied and scourged 39 times before he finally converted his tormentor, the Roman governor Sergius Paulus, to Christianity.

On the north-west side of the site is a tiny **early Christian basilica**, the entrance to which has almost been completely taken over by the gnarled root of an overgrowing tree. Entry to the church site is free.

FORT OF PAFOS

Unlike the interesting fort and medieval museum at Lemesos, Pafos' fort is rather dull, musty smelling and bereft of any arresting exhibits that may shed some light on its role in the city's earlier history. It boasts an attractive site – perched out on the edge of the new harbour – but its only real attraction is the view from the roof. The fort is in fact all that remains of an earlier Lusignan fort built in 1391. The rest of it was destroyed by the Venetians less than a hundred years later. Entry is via a drawbridge over a moat and costs CY£0.75. It is open 9 am to 7.30 pm daily (to 5 pm from October to April).

PAFOS AQUARIUM

The Pafos Aquarium (☎ 253 920) at Artemidos 1 has fishy specimens of all kinds on display and a fun family hour or two can easily be spent here. Entry is a pricey CY£3.75 for adults and CY£2 for children, though a family pass can be had for CY£10. The Aquarium is open 10 am to 10 pm daily year-round.

TOMBS OF THE KINGS

Pafos' most popular – and certainly most impressive – attraction is the sprawling site of the Tombs of the Kings. This World Heritage site is 2km north of Kato Pafos on a rocky, convoluted ledge overlooking the sea. It contains a set of well-preserved underground tombs and chambers used as a necropolis by residents of Nea Pafos during the Hellenistic and Roman periods from the 3rd century BC to the 3rd century AD. The name of 'Tombs of the Kings' was coined to reflect the impressive appearance of the uncovered tombs and the heavy Doric style of the column pediments rather than any royal pedigree of the people buried in the necropolis.

The seven discovered tombs are scattered over a wide area and all are accessible to the public. The most recently restored tomb is No 3 and is perhaps the most impressive, with a below-ground atrium surrounded by impressive Doric columns. Other tombs, accessible by stone stairways, have niches built into the walls where bodies were stored. Most of the treasures of the tombs have long since been spirited away by grave robbers – notably the American consul of Larnaka, Luigi Palma de Cesnola, in the late 19th century.

The tombs are unique in Cyprus and owe their *peristyle* court structure to Egyptian influences. The ancient Egyptians believed that tombs for the dead should resemble houses for the living and this tradition is demonstrated amply here. A recently excavated Ptolemaic tomb bears all the hallmarks of this influence.

Allow at least two hours to visit the site and time your visit during the early morning as it can get very hot walking around the sprawling necropolis. The tombs are open 8.30 am to 7.30 pm (to 5 pm from October to April). Admission is CY£0.75. To get there jump on bus No 15 heading for Coral Bay from Kato Pafos or take a 30-minute walk – less if you make the downhill walk from Ano Pafos.

ARCHAEOLOGICAL MUSEUM

This small museum (☎ 240 215), a bit out of the way in Ano Pafos, houses a varied and extensive collection of artefacts from the Neolithic period to the 18th century. Displayed in four rooms, the collection includes jars, pottery and glassware, tools, coins and coin moulds. Hellenistic and Roman artefacts include a limestone grave stele, marble statuettes, votive objects, pottery from the House of Dionysos (see the earlier section in this chapter on the Pafos Mosaics) and terracotta figures of dogs and stags. All in all, a collection for the admirer of archaeological minutiae without any outstanding items on display. It is worthy of a browse before visiting Ano Pafos' other two museums.

The Archaeological Museum is on Leoforos Georgiou Griva Digeni, about 1.5km from the centre of Ano Pafos. It is open 9 am to 5 pm Monday to Friday and 10 am to 1 pm on weekends. Entry costs CY£0.75.

BYZANTINE MUSEUM

This noteworthy museum (☎ 231 392) is at Andrea Ioannou 5 and adjoins the Pafos Bishopric. It is worth visiting for its collection of icons from the 13th and 14th centuries, ecclesiastical vestments, church vessels, documents and copies of scriptures. The museum is open 9 am to 7 pm Monday to Friday (9 am to 5 pm from October to May) and from 9 am to 2 pm on Saturday. Admission is CY£1.

ETHNOGRAPHICAL MUSEUM

Also in Ano Pafos, the privately owned and maintained Ethnographical Museum (☎ 232 010) at Exo Vrysis 1 houses a varied collection of coins, traditional costumes, kitchen utensils, Chalcolithic axe heads, amphorae and other assorted items. There is more of the same in the garden, including a Hellenistic rock cut tomb.

Opening hours are 9 am to 1 pm and 2 to 7 pm Monday to Friday (to 5 pm from October to April) and 9 am to 2 pm on Saturday. Entry costs CY£0.50.

PLACES TO STAY

Accommodation in Pafos is plentiful with a huge array of hotels to soak up the large tourist/traveller presence. The majority is designed for package-tour groups, though all hotels will invariably fit you in if there is a vacancy. Many of the hotels not listed here are along the 'hotel strip' to the north of Kato Pafos and, apart from having a handy beach nearby, are normally totally self-contained with pools, restaurants and bars.

The cheapest accommodation choice is *Geroskipou Zenon Gardens* camp site (☎ 242 277), 5km south of Kato Pafos and behind the summer cinema. It is close to the beach and you camp in the shade of trees.

A tent or caravan costs CY£1.50 plus CY£1.50 per person. There is another camp site at Coral Bay, 11km north of Pafos. *Feggari* (☎ 621 534) has 47 sites and charges the same as Geroskipou.

The *HI Hostel* (☎ 232 588) is quite a way north of Ano Pafos at Leoforos Eleftheriou Venizelou 37 (off map). To get there, walk up Leoforos Evagora Pallikaridi, turn right into Leoforos Eleftheriou Venizelou and the hostel is 750m along here on the left. It is rather run down and costs CY£4.50 per person for a dorm bed.

At the northern end of Gladstonos, the renovated, traditional pension *Kinyras* (☎ 241 604, fax 242 176, ✉ info@ kiniras.cy.net, Leoforos Arhiepiskopou Makariou III 91) provides bed and breakfast for CY£30/47 for singles/doubles (up to 35% cheaper if you book via the Internet). All rooms have private facilities and there's a very pleasant garden at the back with a rather good restaurant. Also in Ano Pafos is the friendly two-star *Axiothea Hotel* (☎ 232 866, fax 245 790, Ivis Mallioti 2), where accommodation with breakfast is CY£23/31.50. On the high ground to the south of the CTO, it has a glass-fronted bar and reception with wonderful views of the sea – perfect for sunset watching.

Moving down to Kato Pafos the selection can become bewildering. Cheapest is the one-star *Pyramos Hotel* (☎ 235 161, fax 242 939, Agias Anastasias 4). It's central, basic and reasonable. Rates are CY£22/34 (20% discount in the off season). Also very central is the better three-star *Dionysos* (☎ 233 414, fax 233 908, Dionysou 1). For CY£37/57 you get well-appointed rooms, with a 50% off-season discount. Closer to the sea is the three-star *Porto Pafos* (☎ 242 333, fax 241 341, ✉ vavlitis@ spidernet.com.cy), a well-established hotel with many facilities. Rates are CY£36.50/ 53, but the hotel offers no off-season discounts.

A pretty decent three-star hotel at the far northern end of the hotel strip heading out to Coral Bay is the *Queen's Bay* (☎ 246 600, fax 246 777; off map). This is a hotel for package-tour travellers, but you will often find a spare room if you ring ahead.

You'll need a car to get here as it is 9km north of Pafos at Kisonerga. Published rates are CY£36.50/53 with breakfast, but up to 50% discounts apply out of season, or if you can pass yourself off as a 'local'.

Back in Kato Pafos, *Daphne* (☎ 233 599, fax 233 110, Alkminis 3) is an A-class apartment hotel. For between CY£36 and CY£59 you get a fully equipped, neat, self-catering studio or apartment for two to four people. The location is also very central. If you want extra luxury then the four-star *Alexander the Great* (☎ 265 000, fax 265 100, @ alexander@kanika-group.com, Leoforos Posidonos) has most of the facilities you probably need and is right on the beach. Its spacious rooms go for CY£54.50/75, including breakfast. Discounts of 35% apply out of season.

Finally, the five-star *Annabelle* (☎ 238 333, fax 245 402, @ thanos.hotels@spidernet.com .cy, Leoforos Posidonos) is Pafos' best and most expensive hotel. Luxurious single rooms start at CY£98 and doubles reach a maximum of CY£190. Breakfast is included. Discounts of 20% apply out of season.

PLACES TO EAT

Pafos has a wide selection of eateries spread far and wide across both Ano and Kato Pafos, though the greater concentration is to be found in Kato Pafos and out along the hotel strip heading north. These establishments run the gamut from raucous British style pubs to swish bars; fast-food fish and chip joints to ethnic restaurants offering Mexican, Chinese and Indian food in addition to Cypriot staples. The following cover a cross section of some of the better Cypriot dining spots.

Starting in Ano Pafos, a quick cheap meal can be had at the ever-popular *Fetta's Corner* (☎ 237 822, Ioanni Agroti 33). Locals tend to eat here and you can get a large meal for two with wine for around CY£13. You can always shop for yourself and stock up on picnic items at the *Municipal Market* near the covered bazaar area not far from Kinyras.

Moving down to Kato Pafos you will first come across two establishments fairly close

to each other. The first is *Hondros* (☎ 234 256, Apostolou Pavlou 96), advertising itself as the oldest restaurant in Pafos. The food is reliable, solidly Cypriot and good quality. Prices are mid-range. Across the road and set back from the street in the Basilica Centre is *Mother's Restaurant* (☎ 263 474, Apostolou Pavlou), a popular and medium-priced restaurant offering a wide selection of Cypriot dishes. Children have their own menu – a rarity in Cyprus.

In the backstreets of Kato Pafos you will find a few good places. *Avgerinos* (☎ 232 990, Minoös 4) is popular with Cypriots – and for good reason. The food is genuine, not over-priced and excellently cooked. Try the draught local wine. Fish dishes are a speciality. *Argo* (☎ 233 327, Pafias Afroditis 21) nearby is a quaint restaurant and is also favoured by locals. The service is friendly and the oven-baked dishes are recommended.

Dimokritos (☎ 233 371, Dionysou 1) has been around for a while and if you want enter tainment with your meal this is the place to come. Music and dancing are on most evenings and one dancer can manage to balance 34 glasses on his head and still keep going. Food is meat- and fish-based and prices are mid-range. *Ifigenia* (☎ 243 504, Agamemnonos 2), is tcked asay a block or two to the west, and is a cosy family-run establishment with modestly priced home-cooked food as well as mezedes, meat and fish dishes.

The seafront *Glaros Restaurant* (☎ 250 489, Leoforos Posidonos 7), usually known as the Seagull Restaurant, is the nearest you will get to a 'Greek Island' setting. It is a bit on the expensive side – because of its waterside setting no doubt – but it is a very pleasant place for an evening meal. An excellent *stifado* goes for around CY£4.80, while an equally excellent Cypriot *afelia* costs CY£3.80 – both are recommended if you fancy a change from fish. Draught wine is available.

ENTERTAINMENT

As far as drinking is concerned, you can choose from raucous British-style pubs to swish bars. Avoid the noisy 'pubs' dominated by tourists along the seafront and move inland to the backstreets. *Baywatch* is a busy bar on the junction of Konstantias and Agias Napas and is in a prime position for people-watching. Directly opposite is the *Rainbow Disco* that cranks up each night to offer drinkers a place to sweat it all off. If you are after some decent beer from the UK, the *White Horse Pub* is about 250m west along the same street and is probably the best of the bunch – at least it has been around the longest. Draught UK beers are on tap and the place pulls a sizable expat crowd.

GETTING THERE & AWAY
Air
Pafos' international airport is 8km southeast of Pafos. Many charter flights and some scheduled flights arrive at and depart from here. Cyprus Airways (☎ 233 556) has its main office in Pafos at Gladstonos 37–39 and another office at the airport (☎ 422 641).

Bus
The Nea Amoroza/Kemek (☎ 236 822) bus companies operate to Polis, Lemesos and Lefkosia. The office is at Leoforos Evagora Pallikaridi 79, north-east of Ano Pafos' main square; there are around 10 buses a day to Polis (CY£1) and two per day to Lemesos (CY£2) and Lefkosia (CY£3). There are also three buses daily (except Sunday) to and from Pomos village (CY£1.10), north of Polis.

ALEPA Bus Co (☎ 234 455) also has daily buses to Lefkosia and Lemesos. If you book in advance you can be collected from your hotel; otherwise the buses leave from the central bus station near Karavella Parking.

Service Taxi
Kyriakos/Karydas (☎ 232 459) at Leoforos Evagora Pallikaridi 9 and A Makris (☎ 232 538) at Grammou 2, opposite the police station, have service taxis to Lemesos (CY£2.30) every half hour. Travellers heading for Lefkosia (CY£5.30) or Larnaka (CY£4.90) will travel via Lemesos.

GETTING AROUND
The urban bus station in Ano Pafos is at Karavella Parking, behind the Nea Amaroza bus company office. From here buses leave for various local destinations. Bus No 10 runs every 20 to 30 minutes from here for Coral Bay and its associated beach (CY£0.45). Bus No 11 leaves every 10 to 15 minutes for Kato Pafos (CY£0.40).

Another bus service (No 15) runs via Kato Pafos linking Geroskipou Beach, 3km to the south-east of Kato Pafos, and Coral Bay, 12km to the north. This service is every 15 to 20 minutes and follows the coastal route and major hotel strip. The cost is CY£0.45.

For Pafos international airport, ALEPA Bus Co runs bus No 12 every day from Coral Bay at 9 and 11 am and 1, 3 and 5 pm. This bus goes via the coastal hotel strip, Kato Pafos and Geroskipou Beach. The cost is CY£0.50 plus an extra CY£0.50 for luggage. Call ☎ 234 410 in advance if you want to be picked up.

A regular taxi to the airport from Pafos will cost between CY£5 and CY£7, depending on where you are picked up.

D Antoniades Ltd (☎ 233 301), at Leoforos Evagora Pallikaridi 111–13, rents mountain bikes, motorcycles and mopeds.

Around Pafos

With a hire car at your disposal some of the time and a sense of curiosity you can spend a few pleasant days exploring the western Troödos foothills and villages, the wild and desolate Akamas Peninsula or the seldom visited and sparsely populated Tyllirian wilderness of north-west Cyprus. While a conventional vehicle will take you to most destinations described in the following sections, you might be more satisfied hiring a small off-road vehicle to get to the out-of-the-way places. A scooter is great for pottering around beach resorts, but you will be severely short-changed if you attempt to tour the region on one. Many private tour companies run jeep safaris out of Pafos and Polis, should you prefer to let others do all the hard work.

POLIS Πόλις
☎ 06

There are not too many places left in Cyprus that haven't totally succumbed to the lure of the fast buck and, in some cases, overdevelopment, but Polis (or Polis Hrysochous) is one of those places. Polis is on the wide Hrysohou Bay that runs along the north-west sweep of Cyprus from the tip of the Akamas Peninsula at Cape Arnaoutis to Pomos Point at the start of Cyprus' Tylliria wilderness. This small town is ideally situated for holidays that actually leave you time to relax.

Polis is an ideal base for trekking in the Akamas, swimming at a number of nearby beaches, touring the wine-making villages of the Akamas Heights or exploring the often wild and under-visited north-west of Cyprus. Once the haunt of adventurous travellers from Germany, Britain and Scandinavia seeking an alternative holiday, Polis has gentrified somewhat these days. While it still caters primarily to the independent visitor, low-key development has crept in and provides, in turn, better accommodation possibilities and some of the best and most affordable dining to be had in the whole of Cyprus.

Orientation

The town is set back about 2km from the sea on a gradual rise and is fairly compact. The centre of the town is a pedestrianised zone from which most important streets radiate. Buses from Pafos arrive at the Nea Amoroza bus office on Kyproleonto on the south side of town, one of the two approach roads from Pafos. Restaurants and central accommodation are all within easy walking distance, though the camping ground is a fairly lengthy 2km trek out to the beach area.

Information

The CTO office (☎ 322 468, 321 327) at Agiou Nikolaou 2 is very central and open 9 am to 1 pm and 2.30 to 5.30 pm Monday

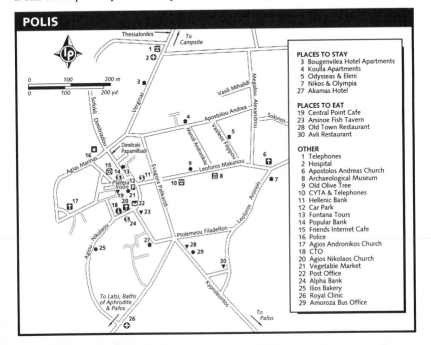

POLIS

Thessalonikis
To Campsite

0 100 200 m
0 100 200 yd

PLACES TO STAY
3 Bougenvilea Hotel Apartments
4 Koulla Apartments
5 Odysseas & Eleni
7 Nikos & Olympia
27 Akamas Hotel

PLACES TO EAT
19 Central Point Cafe
23 Arsinoe Fish Tavern
28 Old Town Restaurant
30 Avli Restaurant

OTHER
1 Telephones
2 Hospital
6 Apostolos Andreas Church
8 Archaeological Museum
9 Old Olive Tree
10 CYTA & Telephones
11 Hellenic Bank
12 Car Park
13 Fontana Tours
14 Popular Bank
15 Friends Internet Cafe
16 Police
17 Agios Andronikos Church
18 CTO
20 Agios Nikolaos Church
21 Vegetable Market
22 Post Office
24 Alpha Bank
25 Ilios Bakery
26 Royal Clinic
29 Amoroza Bus Office

to Saturday, but is closed Wednesday and Saturday afternoons. There are plenty of mountain bike, motorcycle and car rental companies.

You can check your email at the Friends Internet Cafe (☎ 321 679, @ friends.internet .cafe@cylink.com.cy) just north of the pedestrianised zone for CY£3 an hour. Friends is open daily from 10 am until 2 am.

Fontana Tours (☎ 321 555, @ louis.papas@ cytanet.com.cy), at Apostolou Pavlou 147, books air and other transport tickets and organises safari tours and boat trips to the Akamas Peninsula. You can also organise hire cars here for between CY£14 and CY£46 per day, and accommodation from CY£17 for a basic room to CY£45 for an apartment for two to three people.

There are several ATMs scattered around town, as well as banks to exchange travellers cheques. The Popular Bank on Plateia Iroön (the main square) and the Hellenic Bank on Leoforos Makariou are the most central. Dr Dimitris Polydorou (☎ 09-622 331) of the Royal Clinic at Efessou 13 is on call most hours to assist travellers in need of medical assistance. The town's hospital (☎ 321 431) is on Verginasis between the camp site and the town centre.

The Cyprus Telecommunications Authority (CYTA) office and a clutch of phones are on Leoforos Makariou, while there are more phones handy for campers near the hospital.

Things to See & Do

Polis is the kind of town where visitors prefer to stroll and unwind rather than actively seek out entertainment or cultural stimuli. Nonetheless there is a new and pretty reasonable **Archaeological Museum** (☎ 322 955) on Leoforos Makariou that can offer you some cerebral distractions from strolling and dining. It is open 8 am to 2 pm on Monday, Tuesday, Wednesday and Friday, 8 am to 6 pm on Thursday and 9 am to 5 pm on Saturday. Admission costs CY£0.75.

There is an extremely old **olive tree** close to the museum, for those interested in such floral phenomena. The trunk of the tree is almost split in two but it is still producing olives after 600 years. The church of **Agios Andronikos** has recently revealed some of its Byzantine frescoes. Ask for the key from the CTO office.

In summer various free concerts take place in the Town Hall Square under the banner of 'Summer Evenings in Polis'. These run the gamut from traditional dancing, music and folkloric events to classical and jazz music concerts. Call the CTO office for details. Other ticketed concerts, often given by top-name artists from Greece (Nikos Papazoglou was here in the summer of 1999), take place in the Eucalypt Grove (Evkalyptonas) at the Polis camp site. These outdoor events can be magic on a hot summer night. Tickets cost between CY£6 and CY£10.

However, Polis' greatest drawcard is the proximity of the Akamas Peninsula with its hiking trails, fabled baths of the island's patron goddess and fine swimming at Latsi, 3km to the west (see the following sections for details of these features).

Places to Stay

About 1km north of Polis towards the sea is a *camp site (☎ 321 526)* surrounded by eucalyptus trees and right next to the beach. It's signposted from the town centre, is a fairly large site and is well shaded with good facilities. The cost is CY£1.50 for a tent and CY£1 per person.

The next cheapest is the *Akamas Hotel (☎ 321 521, fax 321 561, Grigori Digeni 14)* with singles/doubles for CY£6/10. The rooms are small but adequate and some have good views. The hotel also sports a good restaurant.

The *Koulla Apartments (☎ 321 542, Apostolou Andrea 15)* offer clean and well-appointed self-contained units that cost around CY£22 for two people. One block to the east are the fine apartments of *Odysseas & Eleni (☎ 321 172, fax 322 279, Vasileos Filippou)*, which cost CY£20 and CY£25 for a two-person unit. There is also a swimming pool for guests.

Still further out is another small hotel apartment complex called *Nikos &*

(☎ *321 274, fax 321 607, Arsinois 1)* that also has a pool and air-conditioned apartments for approximately CY£23 for two people.

Finally, the ***Bougenvilea Hotel Apartments*** *(☎ 322 201, fax 322 203, Verginas 13)* is a lovely flower-covered complex with pleasant and airy two-person studios for between CY£30 and CY£32. This price drops by up to 50% out of season. Breakfast is CY£2 extra.

Places to Eat

Polis leaves most other tourist resorts for dead when it comes to the quality and value for money of its eating establishments. Great bread and snacks can be had at the ***Ilios Bakery*** along Agiou Nikolaou. For a quick snack and beer and a spot of people-watching, ***Central Point Cafe*** probably has the edge over the other pedestrian-zone eateries in the main square. Sandwiches and pizzas are on offer at reasonable prices.

The atmospheric ***Arsinoe Fish Tavern*** *(☎ 321 590, Grigori Digeni)* on the south side of the pedestrian zone is housed in an old stone building and dining is alfresco. Fish is the speciality and costs around CY£3.50 per dish. Try the exquisite octopus. A fish mezes meal will be around CY£5.50 per person.

Nearby the Arsinoe in the discreet and relaxing ***Old Town Restaurant*** *(☎ 322 758, Kyproleontos)* dining is in a leafy, secluded garden with running water. Its specialities include chicken broccoli (CY£5.50), *stifado lefkaritiko* (stewed veal in red sauce – CY£5) and duck cacciatore (CY£7.50).

Round the corner is the welcoming ***Avli Restaurant*** *(☎ 321 418, Arsinois)* that tempts passers-by with its outside spit and oven. Spit-roasted meat dishes and oven-cooked Cypriot specialities are the prime choice here. Prices are cheap to mid-range.

Getting There & Away

The Nea Amaroza bus company office is on Kyproleontos, beside the Old City Restaurant. It runs more or less hourly buses to Pafos (CY£1, 40 minutes) and in summer also has services to Latsi (CY£0.40) and the Baths of Aphrodite (CY£0.50) at 10 am, noon and 3 pm. At 9.30 am there's also a daily bus from the main square to Lefkosia (CY£4).

Beaches

Starting at Polis, the nearest stretch of sand is the one in front of the Polis camp site – fine if you don't want to move far from Polis or are already camping there. Otherwise, the best beaches accessible from Polis are those

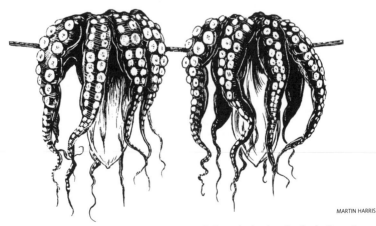

MARTIN HARRIS

Octopus hung up to await the creative attention of the chef. Try the local seafood selections at any of the restaurants specialising in local delicacies.

on the eastern side of **Latsi,** a small fishing village 5km to the west of Polis. They tend to be mixed sand and pebble and somewhat exposed to the vagaries of the weather, but they are popular enough and well serviced with restaurants. East of Polis, Hrysohou Bay stretches seemingly endlessly northwards, and while on the map the potential for finding a good, quiet beach looks promising, disappointment is in store. What beaches there are tend to be scruffy and isolated, somewhat more exposed to the elements and interspersed with unwelcoming sandstone outcrops. Other than a well-organised picnic ground close to the beach and about 6km north of Polis, facilities for beachcombers are fairly sparse until you reach Pomos another 11km further north.

On the western side of the Akamas Peninsula things get better as you move southwards. **Lara Beach,** with its accompanying **turtle hatchery,** is really only accessible by 4WD vehicles from the south, ie, from Pafos. The beach is wild, exposed and totally undeveloped other than for a small beach taverna. More easily accessible is **Agios Georgios Beach,** which can be reached by conventional vehicle easily from Polis (via Pegeia) or Pafos (via Coral Bay). It is a 100m stretch of shadeless sand and rock sharing the water with a little boat harbour, but beach umbrellas and loungers are for hire. There is a small beach cantina and a couple of restaurants up on the bluff overlooking the beach to feed hungry bathers. It's not a flashy beach, but it's quiet and clean and some people prefer it that way.

Coral Beach on the other hand, barely 12km from Pafos, is a well-developed and busy stretch of very attractive sand. If you like regimented loungers and symmetrical lines of umbrellas and large crowds, all of whom somehow seem to find a decent spot of sand to lie on, then Coral Beach is for you. There are several different stretches of the beach all accessible from different parts of the approach road. The cafeterias on the beach are indifferent and serve mainly hamburgers and chips or varieties thereof.

While it is unlikely that you would make a trip just for a swim, there is a fairly decent beach at the **Petra tou Romiou** (Aphrodite's Rock) in the far south of the region. Take your swimming gear if you're heading off to see the rock anyway, it's a great place to cool off. The beach is pebbled for the most part and sits on both sides of the rock. As long as there is not a sea swell running the water is calm and clean. However, the beach does shelve fairly quickly and there are a few tricky currents farther out to be aware of. This is a swimmer's rather than a paddler's beach. An underground tunnel leads to the car park and cafeteria on the other side of the main road.

Baths of Aphrodite

The grandly titled Baths of Aphrodite (Loutra tis Afroditis) sound more appealing than they actually look. Aphrodite, patron goddess of Cyprus, came to the island in a shower of foam and nakedness (according to Botticelli's painting of the event, at least) to launch a cult on the island that has remained to this day. Legend has it that Aphrodite came to this secluded spot 11km west of Polis to bathe after entertaining her lovers.

The baths are nothing more than a cool water pool in an open rock cave, fed by trickling water from rocks above. Cocooned in creepers, vines and assorted vegetation the baths look very tempting – especially after a hard day's hiking around the Akamas. However neither bathing in nor drinking of Aphrodite's fabled bath water is allowed and you will no doubt be jostling for elbow room with the many tourists who make the trip to see the baths and who perhaps leave nonplussed at all the fuss.

To get to the baths follow the well-marked paved trail from the car park at the end of the sealed Polis road and you'll come across them after about 200m. If you're suitably inspired, you can continue up the path to start the Aphrodite Nature Trail, which conveniently starts and ends here (see the following section on the Akamas Peninsula).

THE AKAMAS HEIGHTS VILLAGES

Travellers between Pafos and Polis have a choice of two routes: the faster inland (B7)

The Cult of Aphrodite

Cyprus is indelibly linked to the ancient worship and reverence of the goddess Aphrodite. She (Venus in Roman mythology) is known primarily as the Ancient Greek goddess of sexual love and beauty, though she was also worshipped as a goddess of war – particularly in Sparta and Thebes. While prostitutes often considered her their patron, her public cult was usually solemn and even austere.

The name is thought to derive from the Greek word *afros* meaning 'foam'. Cypriot legend has it that Aphrodite arose out of the sea off the south coast of Cyprus. She was enveloped in white foam produced by the severed genitals of Ouranos (Heaven), after his son Chronos threw them into the sea. The people of Kythira in Greece hold a similar view, and an enormous rock off the south coast port of Kapsali is believed by Kytherians to be the place where Aphrodite really emerged.

Despite being a goddess, Aphrodite was nonetheless prone to taking on a few mere mortal lovers, among whom the better-known were Anchises (by whom she became mother to Aeneas) and Adonis (who was killed by a boar while hunting). His death was later lamented by women at the festival of Adonia. It is said that Aphrodite retired to the Baths of Aphrodite to refresh herself after consorting with her mortal males.

MARTIN HARRIS

Statue of Aphrodite – ancient patron goddess of Cyprus.

The main centres of worship on Cyprus for the cult of Aphrodite were at Pafos and Amathous. Among her symbols were the dove, pomegranate, swan and myrtle. Greek art represented her either as an Oriental nude-goddess type, or as a standing or seated figure similar to all other goddesses. Ancient Greek sculptor Praxiteles carved a famous statue of Aphrodite and it later became the model for the Hellenistic statue of the goddess now known as the *Venus de Milo*.

road or the slower but more picturesque western road (E701/709) via the villages of the Akamas Heights. If you take the latter route from Pafos, the climb to the heights only starts at the largish escarpment settlement of **Pegeia** from where you can branch north-west towards the southern approach to the Akamas Peninsula. Once you are up on the heights, you will

come across a series of villages that enjoy a cooler climate, grow fine wine grapes and are prettier than most Cypriot villages. They also make a useful alternate base for travellers wishing to avoid the busy beach scene of the coast further south.

The most easily accessible vilage is **Kathikas**, famous for its vineyards and wine and home to a couple of good restaurants.

From Kathikas you can detour back onto the B7 via the picturesque **Pano** and **Kato Akourdalia** where you have the option of staying overnight, or for a few days. If you proceed from Kathikas without detouring to Pano and Kato Akourdalia you will be able to detour off the main road west towards the popular and much-visited villages of **Dhrousia** and **Inia**, or east to **Kritou Terra** and **Goudi**, both of which offer accommodation options.

What the villages offer is peace and quiet, great views, respite from the heat of the plains and valleys, picturesque streetscapes, good wining and dining and relaxed enjoyable touring. If you prefer to be based in either Pafos or Polis the villages are easily accessible and visited, even for an evening meal in the country.

THE AKAMAS PENINSULA

This anvil-shaped chunk of western Cyprus, jutting almost defiantly out into the eastern Mediterranean, is one of Cyprus' last remaining wilderness regions. The other is the Karpas Peninsula in the far east of Northern Cyprus. There is at least one good reason why the Akamas has remained relatively untouched for so long. The British army has used the interior of the peninsula as a firing range for a long time now and has never been too happy about adventure travellers spoiling their games. While not strictly part of the Sovereign Base Area agreements of 1960, the Cypriot government has tacitly allowed the Akamas to be used for military purposes. This state of play has not sat well with environmentalists and conservationists whose lobbying and occasional outspokenness has brought about the controversial status of the Akamas into wider public consciousness.

It could be argued that by isolating the peninsula for dubiously self-serving purposes – such as giving the British army room to play commandos – the wilderness aspect is being preserved de facto. However, the spent and perhaps even unspent ordnance littering the land doesn't look too politically or environmentally sound in today's green-tinged world of politics and agrotourism.

Despite the odds, visitors can still traverse the Akamas as long as they are prepared to walk, ride a trail bike or bump along in suitably sturdy 4WD vehicles. Visitors with less stamina can do it the easy way on board tour boats that sail the Akamas coastline from Latsi. The peninsula can be approached from two sides: from the east via Polis, or from the south via the little village of Agios Georgios (see the earlier Beaches section). Tracks linking the two entry points are very rough – perhaps deliberately left rough so as to discourage too much traffic – and care should be taken if riding or driving, as much to avoid live firing ranges as to avoid becoming stuck in a big rut.

The peninsula's big attraction is the abundant flora and fauna that is a result of the Akamas being the easternmost point of the three major flora zones of Europe. Around 600 plant species are found here and 35 of them are endemic to Cyprus. There are also 68 bird species, 12 types of mammals, 20 species of reptiles and many butterflies, of which the native *Glaucopsyche Pafos* butterfly is the symbol of the region.

The Akamas Hiking Trails

Easily the most popular way to get a taste of the Akamas is to spend a few hours trekking one of the four listed trails that run through the north-eastern sector of the peninsula. All can start and end at one of two points – the Baths of Aphrodite or the **Smigies** picnic ground, reached via an unsealed road 2.5km east of **Neo Horio**.

The most popular two trails are those that start and end at the Baths of Aphrodite. They are both longer than the Smigies trails and offer better views. The first of the trails is the aptly named **Aphrodite Trail**. This is a three-hour circular loop, 7.5km in length. It heads inland and upwards to begin and this can be tiring on a hot day, so make an early start if you can. Halfway along the trail at the so-called **Castle of Rigena** you can see the ruins of a Byzantine monastery before heading up to the summit at the **Mouti tis Sotiras** (370m). At this point you head eastwards and down towards the coastal track, which will eventually lead you back to the car park.

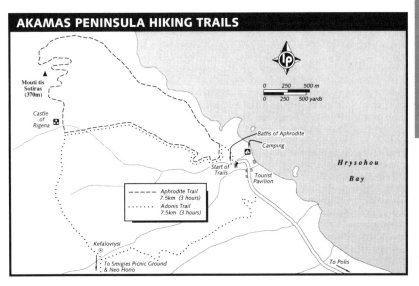

AKAMAS PENINSULA HIKING TRAILS

Mouti tis
Sotiras
(370m)

Castle
of
Rigena

Baths of Aphrodite

Camping

Start of
Trails

Tourist
Pavilion

Hrysohou

Bay

0   250   500 m
0   250   500 yards

Aphrodite Trail
7.5km (3 hours)

Adonis Trail
7.5km (3 hours)

Kefalovrysi

To Smigies Picnic Ground
& Neo Horio

To Polis

The second hike, the **Adonis Trail**, shares the same initial path as Aphrodite as far as the Castle of Rigena, but then turns left and southwards before looping back to the car park. Allow at least three hours for this trail which is also about 7.5km in length. Alternatively you can continue on to the Smigies picnic ground and end your hike there. However, you will then have the problem of getting back to civilisation, if you have not arranged a pick-up beforehand.

Water is usually available at two points along the above trails: at Kefalovrysi and the Castle of Rigena. However don't count on it in high summer. These trails in any case are best attempted in spring or autumn or if you must do it in summer – when it can get extremely hot – just before sunrise.

The CTO produces a step-by-step, plant-by-plant description of these two trails in a booklet entitled *Nature Trails of the Akamas,* available from the main CTO offices. Numbers in the text refer to locations on the maps found on the last page and there is a detailed botanical glossary that describes the plants you are likely to spot. There is as yet no similar brochure for the two trails that commence from the Smigies picnic ground; the circular

5km, two-hour **Smigies Trail** and the circular 3km, 1½-hour **Pissouromouttis Trail**, both of which afford splendid views of Hrysohou Bay, Latsi and Lara Bay to the west.

The Avgas Gorge

Also known as the Avakas Gorge, this narrow split in the Akamas Heights escarpment is a popular hiking excursion. The gorge is reached by vehicle from the western side, via Agios Georgios (see Beaches in the earlier Polis section). You can drive more or less up to the gorge entrance, though low-slung conventional vehicles will have to take care. The hike up the gorge, which becomes a narrow defile with cliffs towering overhead, is easy and enjoyable. There is usually water in the gorge until at least June. The walk will take no longer than 30 to 40 minutes after which you must turn back, although some groups do press on upwards – with some difficulty – emerging on the escarpment ridge and then finding their way to the nearest village of Ano Arodes (not much use if you have left your vehicle at the gorge entrance).

If you have not taken a picnic with you, excellent food is available at a lunchtime taverna on a hill overlooking both the gorge and the beach (see Places to Eat later in this section).

TYLLIRIA

If the Akamas is Cyprus' last wilderness then the vast Tylliria region comes close to being Cyprus' last forgotten land. Comprising a swathe of sparsely populated forested territory and a few desultory beach resorts nestled between Hrysohou and Morfou bays, the Tyllirian wilderness is worth a day or two of exploring.

Tylliria really felt the pinch when it was effectively isolated from the rest of Cyprus following the Turkish invasion of 1974. The main access road from Morfou into the region was closed and is only occasionally opened to allow passage by civilians from both the North and South on humanitarian visits. Paradoxically, a small parcel of territory known in Greek as **Kokkina** and in Turkish as **Erenköy** remains isolated in the same way – but in this case from the rest of Turkish-occupied Northern Cyprus, surrounded as it is by Greek Cypriot territory.

Prior to 1974, the villages of Tylliria contained a sizable Turkish Cypriot population. During the EOKA-led anti-Turkish aggression of the early 1960s Turkish Cypriots were gradually forced to leave their villages and eventually seek umbrage in the Turkish Cypriot port of Kokkina/Erenköy. This strategic piece of land had hitherto been used to ship in arms and supplies from Turkey for Turkish Cypriots. The village remained a Turkish Cypriot stronghold even after the 1974 invasion and despite being some 9km away from the cease-fire line (the Attila Line). However, the villagers have long since been shipped out of Kokkina/Erenköy to be resettled in the former Greek village of **Yiallousa**, now renamed by the Northern Cyprus authorities **Yeni Erenköy** (New Erenköy).

Kokkina/Erenköy presents an effective obstacle to easy passage between the coastal village of Pahyammos in west Tylliria and Kato Pyrgos in east Tylliria. Travellers must now traverse a sealed but narrow and bumpy inland road that bypasses the jealously guarded Kokkina/Erenköy enclave. Even though it is possible to stop at one point and peer into what is now a Turkish military base, UN observers who maintain the peace between edgy Greek and Turkish soldiers perched opposite each other on the heights may signal you to move along lest you unwittingly cause an 'incident'.

The remote beach resort of **Kato Pyrgos** is as far out of the way as you can get in the Republic, yet it attracts a regular summer clientele of Cypriots who come for its isolation, cheap accommodation and food and totally uncommercialised, laid-back ambience. The village is strung out along a wide bay that runs from Kokkina Point to where the Attila Line meets the sea. You can bathe at a number of locations along the bay, though the most popular spot seems to be the far eastern end close to the Line. There are a number of restaurants and low-key hotels, but Kato Pyrgos is accessible purely under your own steam since no public transport other than private taxis reach this far.

Pahyammos means 'broad sand' in Greek and in theory counterbalances Kato Pyrgos on the western side of Kokkina/Erenköy. Despite such a promising name, the village doesn't actually sport such a glorious beach and the settlement is considerably smaller and more strung out than Kato Pyrgos.

Although technically part of the Kykkos Monastery sector of the Troödos, the pretty village of **Kampos** is literally stuck out on the southern edge of the Tyllirian wilderness with these days only one road in and out. The road that leads north from the village now comes to an ignominious end after 12km at the Attila Line and curious drivers must turn back to Kampos. Still you could do worse; Kampos is an ideal spot for lunch, especially if you have been visiting the Kykkos Monastery (see the Marathasa Valley in the Troödos Massif chapter). There is even one hotel should you decide to stay put for the night.

Tylliria is now less isolated than it was, thanks to the completion of a good sealed road that leads across the Tyllirian hinterland and northern extent of the vast **x** linking the Kykkos Monastery with Kato Pyrgos and

Pahyammos. Take it slow though. The road while good is *very* winding and tiring to drive. Most maps still show it as unsealed, but it was completed in mid-1999 and is a much shorter, if more challenging, route into the Tyllirian wilderness than the traditional road from the south-east via Polis.

If taking this route make sure to detour slightly to the popular forest resort of **Stavros tis Psokas**, accessible also from Pafos (51km) via a picturesque road, but still unsealed for a considerable distance. This vast picnic site is a forest station responsible for fire control in the Pafos Forest. There is a restaurant that offers hostel-style accommodation available here and it is surprisingly popular among day-trippers and Cypriots wanting to 'get back to the woods'. In a small enclosure signposted from the main parking area you can try to get a glimpse of the rare and endangered native Cypriot **moufflon**, once hunted extensively as a pest, but now limited to scant patches of forest and a moufflon reserve the Stavros tis Psokas. Move quietly and slowly if you want to see the herd of moufflons – a sort of cross between a sheep and a mountain goat – they are very shy and move away if they see too many people approaching. The moufflon is the stylised symbol portrayed in the Cyprus Airways' logo.

Hiking

You can also partake of some forest trekking from the Stavros tis Psokas forest station. There are two trails. The **Horteri Trail**, a 5km, two-hour circular hike, loops round the eastern flank of the Stavros Valley. The trail starts at the **Platanoudkia Fountain** about halfway along the approach road to the forest station from the Stavros Saddle (Selladi tou Stavrou) on the main through road. The hike involves a fair bit of upward climbing and can get tiring in the heat of summer so tackle the walk early in the day if you can.

The second trail is the **Selladi tou Stavrou**, a 2.6km circular loop of the northern flank of the Stavros Valley. The start is prominently marked from the junction of the forest station approach road and the main through road (the Saddle). A longer alternative route (7km, 2½ hours) is to tackle the trail anticlockwise and then branch south (right) to the **heliport**. From there you can walk along a forest road to the forest station proper. The CTO foldout brochure *Cyprus – Nature Trails* describes these two trails in greater detail.

Cedar Valley

If you are touring the western Troödos hinterland, you may wish to detour onto an unsealed road to visit the lovely Cedar Valley. This cool valley of indigenous Cypriot cedars *(Cedrus brevifolia)* is home to a large number of these unusual trees – close cousins to the better known Lebanese cedar. The valley is approached via a winding forest road from the Pafos side of the Troödos Mountains, or along a signposted road from the Kykkos (eastern) side of the Troödos along the Kykkos-Stavros tis Psokas road. There is a picnic ground here and the opportunity to do some hiking (2.5km) to the summit of **Mt Tripylos** (1362m).

Panagia & Makarios' Birthplace

Fans of Cypriot political history may wish to make an excursion to the birthplace of Cyprus' famous son and once archbishop-president of Cyprus, **Makarios III**. Set in the western foothills of the Troödos Mountains, the village can only be approached from Pafos. There is the **Makarios Cultural Centre** (open 9 am to 1 pm and 2 to 5 pm; free entry), which is less grandiose than the title would suggest. It contains some memorabilia from Makarios' life as politician and priest and plenty of photos. The **childhood house** of Makarios is perhaps of more interest. It is well signposted from the village centre and is normally open 10 am to 1 pm and 2 to 6 pm daily (free entry also). The quite large house contains photos and more memorabilia from the life of the younger Makarios.

Aphrodite's Rock

This grandly titled rock perched off the otherwise craggy southern coast of Pafos district is known in Greek as *Petra tou*

Romiou (Rock of Romios) a name that has nothing to do with Aphrodite, but alludes to the Greek folk hero Digenis Akritas. He apparently used to hurl large rocks – like this one – at his enemies. 'Romios' is another word meaning 'Greek'. However, legend has it that Aphrodite, ancient patron goddess of Cyprus, emerged from the sea at this point in a surge of sea foam. This claim is also upheld by the residents of the island of Kythira in Greece.

Irrespective of who is right, most visitors either come for the usually spectacular **sunset**, best viewed from either the signposted **Tourist Pavilion**, or from a roadside car park about 1.5km further east. Note that the actual rock is the most westerly of the sea rocks visible here. Some visitors confuse the larger fan-shaped rocks with the actual Petra tou Romiou. There is a decent beach here (see the earlier Beaches section), a passable cafeteria and a restaurant and gift shop at the Tourist Pavilion which is signposted off the main road.

Places to Stay

If you are looking to stay somewhere other than Polis or Pafos, yet still require the convenience of being in a central location, the Akamas Heights villages are a good bet. In the villages are a series of agrotourist houses and pensions. At Kato Akourdalia you might opt for *To Exohiko tis Olgas* (☎ 02-761 438, fax 474 988, ✉ lakes@spidernet.com.cy), run by American Garry Lakes. This lovely 200-year-old stone residence offers relaxed, self-contained accommodation at CY£40 per day for two people, with an additional CY£5 a day for each extra person.

In Kathikas try *Helidona* (☎ 06-233 358, fax 244 467, ✉ iolarch@spidernet.net.cy), where a small self-contained apartment for two to three people goes for CY£20. In Goudi look out for the beautiful wood and stone houses of *Kostaris* (☎ 09-626 672, fax 06-212 339, ✉ kostaris@cytanet.com.cy). This complex of three houses has a swimming pool and rates are CY£45 a night for two people. For more on this complex and other agrotourism houses look at the Web

site www.windowoncyprus.com/agrotourism_in_cyprus.htm.

In the Pafos Forest the Stavros tis Psokas forest station has a *Hostel* (☎ 06-332 144) with cool rooms for around CY£10 a night per person. At Kato Pyrgos the *Ifigeneia Hotel* (☎ 06-522 218) is fairly new and central and has singles/doubles for CY£22/29 while the rates at the nearby *Pyrgiana Beach* (☎ 06-522 322, fax 522 306) are CY£18/25.

Places to Eat

Close to the entrance of the Avgas Gorge in the southern Akamas area is a great little eating oasis called the *Viklari* (☎ 06-996 088) which provides lunch (only) for hungry hikers. For CY£4 you get a delicious *kleftiko* BBQ and can relax at heavy stone tables while enjoying great views. Look for signs to the 'Last Castle' from the coast road and seek out jovial owner Savvas Symeou. His two enormous Great Danes are very guest-friendly dogs, despite their intimidating size.

In Kathikas village two eateries pull in evening crowds from both Pafos and Polis. The *Araouzos Taverna* (☎ 06-632 076) serves hearty traditional Cypriot dishes. Identify the owner from his portrait hanging over the door. Closer to the main square but on the same street, *Taverna Imogeni* (☎ 06-633 269) offers similar home-cooked food and when visited by LP was hosting an impromptu late-night *rembetika* session in the narrow courtyard. Prices at both restaurants are mid-range with mezes costing CY£6 per head.

Kato Pyrgos has a fair sprinkling of restaurants and tavernas. *Klimataria*, at the far eastern end, is right on the beach and has the cosiest feel and the food is pretty reasonable. More easily spotted and also on the beach in the centre of the resort strip is the laid-back *Periklis Fish Tavern*.

Getting There & Away

Public transport in the region is primarily geared to getting travellers to and from Pafos and Polis, where buses provide the main link. Nea Amoroza bus company of

Pafos (see Getting There & Away in the Pafos section) runs three buses daily (except Sunday) to and from Pomos village north of Polis (CY£1.10). ALEPA Bus Co runs local bus No 15 to Coral Bay from Pafos every 15 to 20 minutes daily except Sunday (CY£0.45). Outside of these options, travellers in the region must use their own form of transport or take taxis. Hire car firms operate in both Pafos and Polis.

Pafos is linked to Lemesos and further afield by bus and service taxi and by hourly buses to and from Polis. Pafos is linked to the outside world by scheduled and charter flights from its international airport, 13km to the south-east of the city.

NORTHERN CYPRUS

North Nicosia (Lefkoşa)

pop 39,973

Overshadowed by its busier and better known half to the south, North Nicosia (known as Lefkoşa in Turkish) is the quieter half of the world's last divided capital. North Nicosia is seen by some as a backwater and by others, living south of the Green Line that divides the troubled city, as a poignant reminder of the bitter division that has kept Turkish Nicosians apart from Greek Lefkosians, even before the events of 1974. Despite the odds and the continuing sense of ignominy, North Nicosia carries on with life the best way it can and bestows a warm welcome upon the gradual trickle of travellers that make the effort to visit.

Easily visited on a day trip across the Green Line from Greek Lefkosia (South Nicosia), or from the northern resort of Kyrenia (Girne), North Nicosia offers a glimpse into the past of an old city that has changed little since 1974. Visitors can see *hammams* and ancient markets, visit dusty backstreets where timeworn artisans still ply their traditional crafts and trades, as well as explore a slowly developing modern city that is seeking to create its own identity while still being shunned by the international community.

International visitors to North Nicosia will receive a warm welcome. The streets are safe and uncrowded, though busy traffic can occasionally make navigating the narrow streets of the Old City a little unnerving. The Old City can be seen easily in half a day and while most visitors come and depart on the same day, there is pleasant accommodation and fine dining for the adventurous few who wish to sample nightlife on the 'other' side of the infamous Green Line.

HISTORY

North Nicosia, not surprisingly, shares much of the same history as its dismembered southern sector. The city has always been the capital of Cyprus, built on the wide Mesaoria (Mesarya) Plain as defence

- Wander through the narrow streets of the Old City and watch traditional artisans at work.

- Enjoy a refreshing steam bath and massage at the Büyük Hammam Turkish bath house.

- Visit the ancient sites of Vouni and Soloi, west of the city.

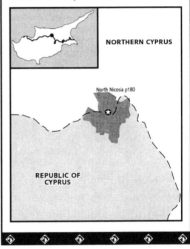

NORTHERN CYPRUS

North Nicosia p180

REPUBLIC OF CYPRUS

against marauding seafarers. The Venetians, who briefly held Nicosia between 1489 and 1571, built the extensive stone defensive walls around the capital to keep out the invading Ottomans. These impressive-looking fortifications did not ultimately keep the attackerss at bay and in 1570 the Turkish presence in the city was felt for the first time. Nicosia saw little development until the British assumed control of the whole of Cyprus in 1878. Hereafter, Nicosia extended beyond its walls and new suburbs spread out in all directions.

Nicosia was effectively divided into Greek and Turkish sectors in 1963 when

NORTH NICOSIA

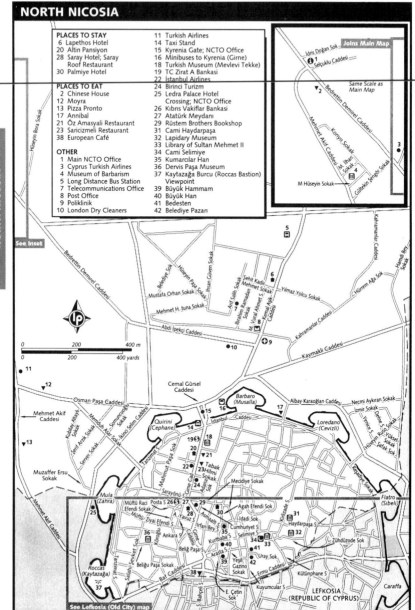

PLACES TO STAY
6 Lapethos Hotel
20 Altin Pansiyon
28 Saray Hotel; Saray
    Roof Restaurant
30 Palmiye Hotel

PLACES TO EAT
2 Chinese House
12 Moyra
13 Pizza Pronto
17 Annibal
21 Öz Amasyali Restaurant
23 Saricizmeli Restaurant
38 European Café

OTHER
1 Main NCTO Office
3 Cyprus Turkish Airlines
4 Museum of Barbarism
5 Long Distance Bus Station
7 Telecommunications Office
8 Post Office
9 Poliklinik
10 London Dry Cleaners

11 Turkish Airlines
14 Taxi Stand
15 Kyrenia Gate; NCTO Office
16 Minibuses to Kyrenia (Girne)
18 Turkish Museum (Mevlevi Tekke)
19 TC Zirat A Bankasi
22 Istanbul Airlines
24 Birinci Turizm
25 Ledra Palace Hotel
    Crossing; NCTO Office
26 Kibris Vakiflar Bankasi
27 Atatürk Meydanı
29 Rüstem Brothers Bookshop
31 Cami Haydarpaşa
32 Lapidary Museum
33 Library of Sultan Mehmet II
34 Cami Selimiye
35 Kumarcılar Han
36 Dervis Paşa Museum
37 Kaytazağa Burcu (Roccas Bastion)
    Viewpoint
39 Büyük Hammam
40 Büyük Han
41 Bedesten
42 Belediye Pazarı

violence against Turkish Cypriots by EOKA (National Organisation for the Cypriot Struggle) insurgents forced them to retreat into safe enclaves or ghettos. The Green Line, as it has become known, was established when a British military commander divided up the city on a map with a green pen. The name Green Line has remained ever since. The Turkish military invasion – many Turkish Cypriots saw it as a rescue operation – of 1974 formalised the division between the two halves of the city. A wary truce was brokered by the blue-bereted members of the UN peacekeeping forces, who had been guarding the Green Line since the sectarian troubles of 1964. Despite sporadic negotiations between both sides and the occasional offers of intervention by foreign would-be guarantor powers, the reunification of the city looks as far off as it did when it was formally split.

ORIENTATION
The Old City of North Nicosia is easy to navigate. If you get lost, you will eventually arrive at the Venetian Walls which you can easily follow in order to reach the main point of reference, the Kyrenia Gate (Girne Kapısı). Running south from the Kyrenia Gate is Girne Caddesi that leads onto Atatürk Meydanı, the main square, identifiable by a large portrait of Kemal Atatürk. Here you will find all the banks, shops and hotels of North Nicosia. To the east of the square are the Korkut Effendi and Selimiye districts where most of North Nicosia's sights are found. To the immediate south close to the Green Line is a small pedestrianised area with shops and restaurants. Other than the two districts in the Old City just mentioned, there are also the Karamanzade, Arabahmet, Kafesli Yenicami, Ayyıldız and Akkavuk districts.

Day visitors to North Nicosia will arrive to the west of the Old City via the Ledra Palace Hotel, at the UN-controlled checkpoint between Northern Cyprus and the Republic. From here it is a 10-minute walk to the Kyrenia Gate. Arrivals by service taxi or minibus will alight close to Kyrenia Gate itself, while long distance bus arrivees will find themselves about 1km north of Kyrenia Gate. The New City spreads some distance north from Kyrenia Gate with Bedrettin Demirel Caddesi leading north-west to Kyrenia and Kemal Aşik Caddesi leading north-east to Famagusta (Gazimağusa).

Maps
The North Cyprus Tourist Organisation (NCTO) produces a reasonably useful *City Plan of Lefkoşa* in both English and Turkish. These should be available at the Ledra Palace Hotel NCTO office. Otherwise you will have to ask at one of the NCTO offices in North Nicosia. Commercially produced maps of Cyprus available in your local bookshop at home sometimes have city maps that include North Nicosia. Maps of Nicosia (Lefkosia) published by the CTO in the South do not show street details of North Nicosia.

INFORMATION
Tourist Offices
Built into Kyrenia Gate is a NCTO office with maps and brochures on Northern Cyprus. It is open 9 am to 5 pm Monday to Friday and 9 am to 2 pm on Saturday, closed on Sunday. An NCTO branch office opened at the Ledra Palace Hotel crossing in late 1999 and is open 9 am to 5 pm Monday to Saturday and 9 am to 2 pm on Sunday.

If you don't find the information you want at these two offices, you can always make the 2km trek out to Bedrettin Demirel Caddesi to the main NCTO Office (☎ 227 9112, fax 228 5625, ✆ turizm@dbby.trnc .net). It's a long walk, so take a cab from Kyrenia Gate (TL1 million).

Money
You can change your money into Turkish lira (TL) at any of the money changing facilities just past the Ledra Palace Hotel passport control booth. ATMs for credit cards can be found at the TC Zirat A Bankasi at the northern end of Girne Caddesi, or at the Kıbrıs Vakiflar Bankasi on Atatürk Meydanı. You can change your currency at these two banks or at private exchange offices nearby.

Post

The main post office is on Sarayönü Sokak, just west of Atatürk Square. The telecommunications office is on Arif Salih Sokak in the New Town, west of the Telecom tower; it's open 8 am to midnight daily.

Telephone

There are public telephone booths scattered throughout old North Nicosia, all of which use prepaid phone cards. You may purchase phone cards from post offices. Your mobile phone, if configured for global roaming will work on either of the North's two GSM mobile network services.

Fax

There is no public fax service as such. However, private bookshops may offer user-pays fax services.

Email & Internet Access

The easiest outlet to find is the Internet Cafe (☎ 227 9701, 🖂 megabir@cypronet.net) at Gültekin Sengör Sokak.

Travel Agencies

Birinci Turizm (☎ 228 3200, fax 228 3358) at Girne Caddesi 158A issues ferry tickets to Turkey and airline tickets, as well as offering a range of other travel-related services.

Bookshops

Visitors to North Nicosia should not miss the Rüstem Brothers bookshop on Girne Caddesi opposite the Saray Hotel. Owner Kemal Rüstem presides over organised chaos with books, old and new, piled ceiling high. In among the chaos you will find some English titles to take your fancy.

Laundry

The London Dry Cleaners (☎ 227 8232) on Abdi İpekçi Caddesi in the New City will do you a service wash as well as dry clean your clothes.

Medical Services

North Nicosia's main hospital is the Burhan Nalbatanoğlu Devlet Hastahanesi (☎ 228 5441; off map). There is also the Poliklinik (☎ 227 3996) where foreigners can seek medical treatment.

Emergency

In an emergency ring ☎ 112 for the hospital, ☎ 155 for the police or ☎ 199 for the fire station. The nearest police station is on Atatürk Meydanı.

Dangers & Annoyances

North Nicosia is a safe city at any time of the day and visitors should feel no concern about walking the streets. At night the Old City can become rather quiet and visitors may feel intimidated walking alone along dimly lit and sometimes narrow streets. Avoid them if you feel uncomfortable. The areas abutting the Green Line look threatening with large black and red signs that clearly forbid photography or trespassing in the buffer zone. Heed the warnings.

On the Roccas Bastion (Kaytazağa Burcu) at the western end of the Old City limits, where you can look over into Lefkosia, do not take photographs. Watchful soldiers stationed – not so obviously – on the bastion may accost you and even confiscate your camera.

WALKING TOUR

A self-paced walking tour is most conveniently started and finished at the Ledra Palace Hotel crossing, especially if you are visiting North Nicosia on a day trip from the South. From the checkpoint walk 100m and turn right onto Memduh Asar Sokak and you will almost immediately cross into the **Old City**. Turn right along Zahra Sokak and walk past the line of mostly empty houses that can be seen by visitors observing North Nicosia from the Greek Cypriot side of the Ledra Palace Hotel crossing. Note the rusting oil barrels and gun placements to your right. Enter the small park further along to your right that sits atop the Roccas Bastion (Kaytazağa Burcu) and stare out through the fence down into Greek Cypriot Lefkosia. This is the only point along the whole of the Attila and Green Lines that Turkish and Greek Cypriots can eyeball each other at such close quarters.

From the Roccas Bastion head eastwards towards the centre of Old Nicosia along narrow streets with tastefully restored houses. Make a left turn along Salahi Şevket Sokak and then right into Beliğ Paşa Sokak to visit the Derviş Paşa Museum, a small ethnographical collection housed in an old Turkish mansion. Follow Beliğ Paşa Sokak until it leads you into the **pedestrianised zone** in the centre of the city. Note the restaurants and cafes for lunch later. Follow Araşta Sokak past the Büyük Hammam steam baths until you arrive at the locked Ottoman bazaar, the Bedesten, across the street from which is the local market, the Belediye Pazarı. Hard to miss is the uncompleted former Lusignan cathedral of Agia Sofia, now the Cami Selimiye, incongruous with its soaring minarets attached after the Ottoman conquest. Drop by the two Turkish caravanserais, the Büyük Han and the Kumarcılar Han, which are both nearby.

If you have time seek out the Library of Sultan Mahmut II close by Two blocks farther east are the Lapidary Museum and the Cami Haydarpaşa, which was originally the 14th-century church of St Catherine. Retrace your steps westwards along Idadi and Mecidiye Sokak and make for Atatürk Meydanı from which it is a short stroll north along Girne Caddesi to the Mevlevi Tekke, originally home of the Whirling Dervishes (the mystic Islamic sect), but now the Turkish Museum. At the northern end of Girne Caddesi you will see Kyrenia Gate, cut off from its protective walls when the British created a throughway for vehicular traffic.

From the Kyrenia Gate it is a brisk 10-minute stroll inside the **Venetian Walls** back to the Ledra Palace Hotel crossing, or the pedestrian zone for lunch. If you still have time, you can hop on a minibus, or take a service taxi to Kyrenia for lunch instead. This walk can just as easily be started and commenced at Kyrenia Gate. Allow a leisurely two hours.

DERVIŞ PAŞA MUSEUM

This small ethnographical collection is North Nicosia's equivalent of Lefkosia's Dragoman Hatzigeorgakis Museum. The building is an old mansion built in 1807 and belonged to a wealthy Turkish Cypriot, Derviş Paşa, who published Cyprus' first Turkish-language newspaper. The house was turned into an ethnographic museum in 1988. Household goods, including an old loom, glassware and ceramics, are displayed in former servants' quarters on the ground floor. Upstairs is a rich display of embroidered Turkish costumes and, in the far corner, a sumptuous *selamlık* – a retiring room for the owner of the mansion and his guests, replete with sofas and hookah.

The museum is on Beliğ Paşa Sokak and is open 9 am to 7 pm daily, but closed from 1 to 2 pm in winter when it also closes at 4.45 pm. Entry costs TL750,000.

BÜYÜK HAMMAM

The Büyük Hammam is a world-famous working Turkish bath frequented by male and female locals and tourists. The entrance is via an ornate low door, sunk six feet below street level. The door was originally part of the 14th-century Church of St George of the Latins. Inside you may be able to see a nail that marks the point where in 1330 the waters of the Pedieos River (Kanlı Dere) rose and drowned 3000 Nicosians. The hammam is open 7.30 am to 10 pm daily. A refreshing steam bath and a massage (male masseurs only) cost UK£8.

BELEDIYE PAZARI

Unlike the former Ottoman Bazaar of the Bedesten across the road, the Belediye Pazarı is a working and functioning produce market. It opens at 6 am and closes down at around 3 pm Monday to Saturday. While there is nothing architecturally or historically noteworthy about the building, it is a great place to stock up on picnic items and take photographs of wonderfully coloured displays of fruit and vegetables.

CAMI SELIMIYE

North Nicosia's most prominent landmark – clearly visible from the South also – is the Cami Selimiye, or Selimiye Mosque. This strange-looking building, a sort of cross between a Gothic church and mosque has an interesting history. Work first started on the church in 1209 and progressed slowly. Louis IX of France, on his way to the Crusades, stopped by in 1248 and gave the building process a much needed shot in the arm by offering the services of his retinue of artisans and builders. However, the church required another 78 years before it was completed and finally consecrated in 1326 as the **Church of Agia Sofia**.

Between 1326 and 1570 when the Ottomans arrived, the church suffered subsequent depredation at the hands of the Genoese and the Mamelukes and severe shaking from two earthquakes in 1491 and 1547. The Ottomans stripped the building of its Christian contents and added two minarets between which the Turkish Cypriot and Turkish flags now flutter.

Today the Cami Selimiye is a working mosque – albeit an odd-looking one with strong French Gothic style – and you can go inside. Observe the usual etiquette when visiting a mosque. Dress conservatively, take your shoes off and observe silence if prayers are in progress. The Gothic structure of the interior is still apparent despite Islamic overlays such as the whitewashed walls and columns and the reorientation of the layout to align it with Mecca. Note the ornate west front with the three decorated doorways, each of a different style. Look out also for four **marble columns** relocated from Ancient Salamis and now placed in the apse off the main aisles.

The mosque is open daily following no set times. If it's closed try to time your visit to one of the five Muslim prayer sessions. Entry is free.

BEDESTEN

The ruined and usually locked Bedesten was originally a small Byzantine church built in the 6th century and augmented in the 14th century by a Catholic church. During the 82-year rule of the Venetians in Cyprus (1489–1571) it became the church of the Orthodox Metropolitan. After the Ottomans took Nicosia in 1570 the church was used variously as a grain store and general market,

but was basically left to disintegrate. Today you can peer through the fencing and still make out the layout of the original churches. The complex, on Selemiye Meydanı, is earmarked for eventual restoration, so access to the site can be erratic at times. The north doorway has some splendid-looking **coats of arms** originally belonging to noble Venetian families who may have been supporters of the Orthodox Church which, despite the Catholic dominance of religious life in Cyprus, was nonetheless allowed to continue about its business.

Medieval tombstones from various parts of Cyprus are currently kept in a section of the Bedesten and may be viewable, depending on the level of restoration of the overall complex and on whether the authorities have opened this section.

Access to the Bedesten is courtesy of the attendant at the Library of Sultan Mahmut II. If you ask, the attendant will show you the Bedesten and the Lapidary Museum. There is no entry charge for the Bedesten. The fee for the library applies to the Lapidary Museum and the Bedesten. It is open 8 am to 1.45 pm and 2 to 4.45 pm in summer, 8 am to 12.45 pm in winter, from Monday to Saturday.

LIBRARY OF SULTAN MAHMUT II

The Library of Sultan Mahmut II is housed in an octagonal building erected in 1829. The library contains some 1700 books and the interior is decorated with a calligraphic frieze in blue and gold. Some of the books are up to 700 years old and the more historic ally valuable tomes are displayed in special display cases.

The library is on Haydarpaşa Sokak and is open 9 am to 2 pm in summer and 9 am to 1 pm and 2 to 4.45 pm in winter. Entry costs TL750,000. The same ticket also gives you access to the Bedesten and the Lapidary Museum.

LAPIDARY MUSEUM

A visit to the Lapidary Museum is usually included in a visit to the Library of Sultan Mahmut II. This is a 15th-century building containing a varied collection of sarcophagi, shields, steles, columns and a Gothic window rescued from a Lusignan palace that once stood near Atatürk Meydanı. Opening hours are the same as for the library.

CAMI HAYDARPAŞA
The Cami Haydarpaşa on Kirlizade Sokak was originally built as the 14th-century Church of St Catherine but now functions as an art gallery. It is the second most important Gothic structure in Nicosia after the Selimiye Mosque. The outside and inside of the structure are quite ornate, sporting gargoyles, dragons, shields and human heads. The gallery is open 9 am to 1 pm and 2.30 to 5 pm, Monday to Friday and 9 am to 1 pm on Saturday. Entry is free.

BÜYÜK HAN & KUMARCILAR HAN
The Büyük Han (Great Inn) is a rare surviving example of a Middle Age Turkish equivalent of a hotel, known also as a caravanserai. In the Middle Ages travellers and traders could find accommodation at these hans, as well as a place to stable their horses, trade their goods and socialise with fellow travellers. The Büyük Han was built in 1572 and is built around a central courtyard. Some 67 rooms look out onto the courtyard from two storeys. Today the structure is slowly being converted to a museum and may still be closed when you visit. You can peer through a gap in the wooden gates and see the courtyard and the accompanying restoration work.

Not far away on Agah Efendi Sokak is the better-preserved and now functioning Kumarcılar Han (Gambler's Inn), a late 17th-century caravanserai. Shops occupy the outer perimeter now and the Department of Antiquities has offices inside. There is a quiet courtyard and access to both hans is normally allowed between 9 am to 2 pm every day in summer and 9 am to 1 pm and 2 pm to 4.45 pm in winter. Admission costs TL200,000.

TURKISH MUSEUM
The Turkish Museum, once known as the Mevlevi Tekke Museum, is a former 17th-

MICK WELDON

The dance of the Whirling Dervish is rarely seen in modern-day Cyprus or Turkey.

century monastery of the mystic Islamic sect known as the Whirling Dervishes. The basis of their spiritual philosophy is Sufism and the Dervishes were followers of a 13th-century poet known as Jelaluddin Mevlana Rumi. They flourished for 700 years in Turkish life until they were banned by Atatürk in 1925. Their public persona is most commonly exemplified by their strange, slow whirling trance-like dance. In this they slowly whirl in a circular fashion, one palm held upwards and the other downwards to symbolise man's position as a bridge between Heaven and Earth.

The Dervishes have long since left the Tekke and this fine old building is now a museum displaying Dervish artefacts as well as photographs, embroidery, calligraphy, illuminated Qurans and other Turkish Cypriot memorabilia. The museum is on Girne Caddesi and is open 7.30 am to 2 pm, Monday to Friday and additionally on Monday from 3.30 pm to 6 pm. Entry costs TL750,000.

MUSEUM OF BARBARISM
While the Turkish Cypriots may have taken down the gruesome posters and photographs to greet arrivals at the Ledra Palace Hotel crossing, they have not forgotten the atrocities committed by Greek Cypriots and

NORTH NICOSIA

in particular EOKA thugs against the Turkish Cypriot community. The museum is in a quiet suburb to the west of the Old City and takes a bit of seeking out. On 24 December 1963 a mother and her children, along with a neighbour, were shot dead in their bath by EOKA gunmen. The bloodstained bath is retained as one of the exhibits in this rather macabre museum. There are other photodocumentary displays, particularly of Turkish Cypriots murdered in the villages of Agios Sozomenos and Agios Vasilios.

The museum is at M İrhan Sokak and is open 9 am to 2 pm daily. Admission to the museum is TL750,000.

PLACES TO STAY

Most of the budget hotels are around the Selimiye Mosque area and in the streets east of Girne Caddesi. They all have dormitory-style rooms where a bed costs around US$6, but they are pretty dire places.

Better is **Palmiye Hotel** (☎ *228 7733, Mecidiye Sokak)* where singles/doubles cost US$10/15. Also passable is **Altin Pansiyon** (☎ *228 5049, Girne Caddesi 63)*, which costs US$12/16 without breakfast. The best hotel in the Old Town is the three-star **Saray** (☎ *228 3115, fax 228 4808, Atatürk Meydanı)* charging US$36/60 with breakfast.

In the New City the three-star **Lapethos Hotel** (☎ *228 7611, fax 228 750, Kemal Aşik Caddesi)* is the city's best accommodation choice. Rooms go for US$60/85.

PLACES TO EAT

Eating in North Nicosia doesn't offer too many choices, unlike Kyrenia which is positively overflowing with many high-quality eateries. Lunchtime diners are better off with a couple of places on Girne Caddesi, or sticking to a clutch of eateries in the centre of the Old City near the Green Line. Evening dining is more of a problem since the Old City is fairly subdued after dark and not many people entertain themselves here. There is a scattering of restaurants in the northern suburbs of North Nicosia, usually hard to find and best reached by taxi.

In Araşta Sokak opposite the Bedesten is a shop which makes delicious halva on the premises. Nearby is the **Belediye Pazarı**, a large covered market selling fresh produce, clothes and knick-knacks. **Pizza Pronto** (☎ *228 6542),* on Mehmet Akif Caddesi next to the British High Commission, does great pizzas as well as other Tex-Mex dishes. A large pizza will cost around UK£4.

On Girne Caddesi two friendly restaurants are situated competitively next to each other, **Saricizmeli** and **Öz Amasyali**, which are open all day. A substantial Turkish hot buffet will cost around UK£3 in either establishment. If you head for the pedestrianised zone close to the Green Line you will invariably be accosted by the affable Hussein, a Bulgarian Turk, who will steer you towards the **European Cafe** (☎ *227 715, S Bahçeli Sokak).* An excellent meal of kebabs and salad with ice cold beer will not cost you more than UK£6.

Guests at the Saray Hotel may dine at the top-floor **Saray Roof** (☎ *227 3115)* restaurant where you can enjoy a fine evening view with your meal. The cuisine is Turkish and European and a meal with wine will cost around UK£10. **Annibal** (☎ *227 1835, Saraçoğlu Meydanı)* is a long-established kebab house close to the Green Line at the eastern end of the Old City and is probably worth a try.

On the road out to Kyrenia is the **Chinese House** (☎ *227 7924, Bedrettin Demirel Caddesi),* a pleasant oasis along one of North Nicosia's busiest arteries. Cantonese Chinese fare is on offer here and will cost you around UK£12 a head for a set course meal. **Moyra** (☎ *228 6800, Osman Paşa Caddesi 32)* is a pleasant restaurant offering traditional Cypriot steaks and kebabs. Count on around UK£15 a head for a very filling meal.

ENTERTAINMENT

Turkish Cypriots themselves admit that nightlife in their capital is not all that hot – at least in the Old City. If it's noise and fun you are looking for, forget it or go to Kyrenia. Entertainment North Nicosia-style is mainly taken in restaurants or at home – no real use for travellers. Resign

sign yourself to a pleasant meal and a drink back at your hotel bar rather than pin your hopes on the high life.

SHOPPING
North Nicosia does not have the wide range of shops and goods that Kyrenia does but you can find inexpensive jewellery and optical items such as spectacles that can even be ordered and made for you in 24 hours. Be wary of fake Rolexes and other designer gear that is sold openly – often as 'genuine imitations' – and don't expect too many bargains on imported goods. Local or Turkish-made items are always good value, but don't expect to bargain – it is not part of the shopping scene. If you are on a day trip from the South, forget about shopping – you cannot take it back across the Line with you and the Greek Cypriot police will tell you as much before you cross over.

GETTING THERE & AWAY
Air
Ercan airport (known to Greek Cypriots as Tymvou airport) is about 14km east of North Nicosia and is linked by a fast expressway. There are scheduled flights to London and several destinations in Turkey. All charter flights operate from Ercan (☎ 231 4703), though occasionally some flights are diverted to a military airport at Geçitkale (Lefkoniko; ☎ 227 9420), nearer Famagusta when Ercan is being serviced.

The three offices of the airlines serving Northern Cyprus are all based in North Nicosia. Their addresses are as follows:

Cyprus Turkish Airlines (Kıbrıs Hava Yolları) (☎ 227 3820) Bedrettin Demirel Caddesi
Istanbul Airlines (İstanbul Hava Yolları) (☎ 228 3140) Girne Caddesi 144
Turkish Airlines (Türk Hava Yolları) (☎ 227 1061) Mehmet Akif Caddesi 32

Bus
The long distance bus station is on the corner of Atatürk Caddesi and Kemal Aşik Caddesi in the New Town. Buses to major towns leave from here. You may prefer the bus to the sometimes hair-raising rides in service taxis or *dolmuşes*.

Car & Motorcycle
Drivers and riders will enter North Nicosia via one of two main roads that lead directly to the Old City. If you come from Famagusta or Ercan airport you will enter North Nicosia via Mustafa Ahmet Ruso Caddesi. This road leads directly to Kyrenia Gate. Arriving from Kyrenia you will first negotiate a large roundabout near the satellite suburb of Gönyeli and enter North Nicosia via Tekin Yurdabay Caddesi and eventually Bedrettin Demirel Caddesi, which also leads to Kyrenia Gate.

Parking is usually not a problem in North Nicosia, though finding a place in the Old City may get tricky if you arrive late in the morning on a working day. If you arrive early you can easily park on Girne Caddesi. Note, however, that the road running past Kyrenia Gate along the Venetian Walls in the New City is one-way, running east-west. If you are heading for Kyrenia Gate from the Ledra Palace Hotel crossing, you will have to take a roundabout, clockwise circular route along Bedrettin Demirel Caddesi, Abdi İpekçi Caddesi and Cemal Gürsel Caddesi to position yourself to enter Kyrenia Gate by car or motorcycle. A better solution is to turn immediately right after passing the Ledra Palace Hotel crossing and enter the Old City via Memdah Asar Sokak. Turn left onto Tanzimat Sokak as soon as you cross the moat and you will reach the Kyrenia Gate after about 200m.

Drivers returning to the Ledra Palace Hotel crossing from Kyrenia are advised to take the last turn right immediately before the roundabout with the Honda showroom and make for the crossing via a more or less direct backstreet route along Hasane İlgaz Sokak. This way you will avoid being caught up in the traffic merry-go-round of the one-way system.

Hitching
The cheap cost of public transport essentially obviates the need to hitch around the North. However, if you are a confirmed hitch-head or you are trying to break a hitching record then you are advised to

position yourself at the large roundabout 3km north-west of the city centre from where roads lead in three major directions: to Morfou, Kyrenia and Famagusta, signposted as Güzelyurt, Girne and Gazimağusa in Turkish.

Service Taxi & Minibus

Minibuses (known as *dolmuş*) to local destinations and further afield start from various termini outside the Venetian Walls and also from İtimat bus station just outside Kyrenia Gate. Destinations include Kyrenia (TL500,000) and Famagusta (TL750,000). Service taxis also leave from the same bus station.

To the Republic of Cyprus

If you have entered the North from outside Cyprus, you cannot under any circumstances enter the South directly. Many travellers are unaware of this prohibition by the Republic of Cyprus authorities and do attempt to cross from North to South. You can theoretically be arrested by the South's immigration police for entering Cyprus illegally. In all likelihood you will be sent back to the North with just a stern warning, but your name will be taken and it is unlikely that you will be allowed into the South even via an indirect route.

The only indirect way you can get into the Republic of Cyprus from Northern Cyprus is to return to Turkey and to then exit Turkey to Greece. Marmaris to Rhodes is the nearest exit point and requires a ferry crossing. From here you can take a ferry to Lemesos. Alternatively, you could make your way to Haifa in Israel via Syria and Jordan and take a ferry on to Lemesos. If you have the money, you can fly to İstanbul, from there to Athens and from Athens to Larnaka!

GETTING AROUND
To/From the Airport

Buses to Ercan airport go from the Cyprus Turkish Airlines office (☎ 227 1240) on Bedrettin Demirel Caddesi. They depart two hours before any flight and cost UK£1. A taxi will cost UK£7.80.

Public Transport

While there are public buses in North Nicosia they tend to mainly service the suburbs outside of the Old City and are only really useful if you need to get to a hitching spot, or to the NCTO office on Bedrettin Demirel Caddesi on a traveller's budget. Buses leave from near Kyrenia Gate.

Car

You can hire a car in North Nicosia. Try Budget Car Rental (☎ 228 2711, fax 228 6125) at M İrfan Bey Sokak or Sun Rent-A-Car (☎ 227 8787, fax 228 3700). If you are coming from the South, call ahead (see Telephones in the Facts for the Visitor chapter for tips on how to do it) and see if they will meet you at the Ledra Palace Hotel crossing. Rates start at around UK£25 but are usually negotiable.

Taxi

There are plenty of taxi ranks though the most convenient and easy to find is at Kyrenia Gate. A ride to anywhere in town should cost no more than TL1 million, though as a tourist you may be asked for more – say, TL1.5 million. Above that and you are probably being ripped off. Ask the driver the rate before getting into the taxi.

Among the more reliable taxi companies in North Nicosia are Ankarar Taxi (☎ 227 1788), Ozner Taxi (☎ 227 4012), Terminal Taxi (☎ 228 490) and Yilmaz Taxi (☎ 227 3036). Call ahead if you wish to be picked up at your hotel or from a restaurant.

When you cross into North Nicosia from the South you will almost certainly be approached by tourist cab drivers offering to take you on tours of the North. They would prefer to give you the full treatment for around CY£30, but in practice you can ask to be taken to wherever you like – like Kyrenia for the day and you will pay less accordingly. These drivers are not rapacious – though they are keen for your custom – and they will often act as unofficial and at times informative guides. This is the best solution if you want a taste of the North without the hassles of organising it yourself.

Around North Nicosia (Lefkoşa)

The landscape stretching east and west of North Nicosia is a vast, flat brown region called the Mesarya – the name is derived from the Greek 'Mesaoria', which means 'between the mountains'. In summer it looks desolate and uninviting, in winter it comes alive with greenery and wild flowers. It's easy to drive around as for the most part it's flat. In the east, where the Mesarya is at its most flat, the countryside offers few specific tourist sights and is unlikely to tempt you to linger. The western Mesarya holds more promise and the following sights make for an alternative tour of the North away from the beach scenes of the north and east coasts.

You will need a car to make any headway with getting around the western quadrant of Northern Cyprus which loosely covers the territory south of the Kyrenia Range and westwards to the agricultural city of Morfou (Güzelyurt), Morfou Bay, the one-time mining port of Karavostasi (Gemikonaği), the pretty hill village of Lefka (Lefke) and two obscure but worthwhile **archaeological sites** in the far west.

Distances are relatively small and the whole excursion can be made into a loop, returning to North Nicosia via the **Kormakitis Peninsula** (Koruçam Burnu) and Kyrenia. If Kyrenia is your base, you can easily do the loop anticlockwise.

MORFOU (Güzelyurt)

The once busy city of Morfou – signposted as Güzelyurt in the North – was home to Cyprus' lucrative citrus industry at one time. Sunzest, the company owned by renegade and runaway Cypriot businessman Asil Nadir, used to produce vast quantities of orange juice for the export market. The factory now languishes in receivership and the potentially lucrative citrus industry has taken a severe downturn.

This is bittersweet news to the Greek Cypriots who were particularly aggrieved when the Morfou **citrus groves** were lost to

Once Upon a Train

Few people today would realise that Cyprus once boasted a rail system. It was not extensive, but for over 50 years trains ran the length of the island traversing the vast Mesaoria/Mesarya Plain and linking the western port of Karavostasi (Gemikonaği) with the main port of Famagusta in the east.

The Cyprus Government Railway (as it was known) was 60km in length and there were stations every 3 to 4km. Between Famagusta and Lefkosia (Lefkoşa) there were two passenger trains a day in each direction and the trip took two hours travelling at a speed of between 32 and 48km an hour – hardly an express service. To travel the extra 38km to Morfou (Güzelyurt) took another two hours. The branch line to Karavostasi was used mainly for freight.

Standard gauge steam engines were fuelled by coal imported from England, or even the Admiralty Yards in Port Said in Egypt. The water used in the engines had to be softened chemically so as not to damage the boilers and all lighting was with acetylene lamps. While the engines ran like clockwork, the main problem was the maintenance of bridges which could be washed away by sudden and unusual winter torrents.

Freight ultimately came to be more important than passenger traffic, but even the trains could not compete with the emergence of diesel-powered trucks that came onto the scene in the mid-1940s. The last train left Lefkosia for Famagusta on 31 December 1951 and the Cyprus steam era came to a sad end. There are few signs of the old railway line today, the most visible ones being a stretch of line and an old steam engine near Morfou and a railway tunnel near the Land Gate in Famagusta.

Turkish forces in 1974. Most were proudly owned by Greek Cypriots and when meeting someone who has been to the North they invariably ask after the health of their beloved citrus groves.

You can hardly miss the citrus groves; they start shortly before the village of

Masari (Sahinler) and stretch all the way to the sea. Watered by a series of underground aquifers, they are beginning to feel the pinch. This is a result of a drop in the level of the aquifer reserves and of a rise in the salinity of the underground water, as well as from a sometimes less than loving approach to their cultivation and maintenance. In fairness though, this visible degradation to the casual observer is no doubt due, to some degree, to the disruption of the citrus industry brought about by Sunzest's demise.

In better days, in the earlier half of the 20th century, oranges were shipped by train from Morfou to Famagusta from where they were exported overseas. Why facilities were never developed for their export at the nearer port of Karavostasi is rather odd. Incidentally, the train route was never used by passengers and has long since fallen into disrepair. What's left of the track, plus an old steam engine is *supposed* to be visible off the Morfou-Kyrenia road, not far from Morfou itself. After a concerted scouting of the area in question, we could not find the site, despite assurances that it does exist.

Morfou today offers scant interest for the tourist. Travellers may content themselves with wandering around a low-key, rather tatty-looking agricultural town with a few narrow winding streets, small shops and life totally unfazed or dependent upon tourism. The Orthodox church of **Agios Mamas**, once visited by the Greek Cypriot faithful for the reputed miraculous qualities of a strange liquid that emanated from the tomb of the patron saint at irregular intervals, is usually firmly closed, but is supposed to open. It competes for attention with a splendid-looking new mosque that has been built, in seeming defiant juxtaposition, across the square.

KARAVOSTASI (Gemikonaği)
From Morfou the good highway barrels westwards towards **Morfou Bay**, passing even more citrus groves. Bathing at Morfou Bay is no real treat. The beaches are exposed, pebbly and rather thin, though you can take a dip at one or two obvious spots along the way as long as the sea is not too choppy. Prior to 1974 inhabitants of the Troödos foothills in the South would make the short trip to Morfou Bay to swim. Now the nearest beach for them is over 100km away at Larnaka.

The bay is dominated by the once flourishing port of Karavostasi (signposted in Turkish as Gemikonaği) and you will spot the long-abandoned and slowly disintegrating jetty before you actually catch sight of the port itself. The town was once home to a large American-run mining enterprise that for many years mined the now scarred hinterland immediately south and east of Karavostasi. That industry ceased after 1974 and the town has taken on a backwater appearance, not unlike the town of Kato Pyrgos farther along the coast at Tylliria but in the Republic.

Nonetheless, it still supports a small local tourist industry and restaurants. Small beaches to the west of Karavostasi testify to the area's pull on the few visitors who prefer alternative dining and bathing options to the often crowded and more expensive spots elsewhere in the North. There is at least one decent hotel in town and Karavostasi is one place you might wish to base yourself for a day or two.

Swimming is best undertaken at a couple of sheltered beaches to the west of the town of Karavostasi, or in front of the Mardin Restaurant, a little closer but still on the west side of the town.

LEFKA (Lefke)
From the centre of Karavostasi a road runs off at right angles to the hillside village of Lefka. The turn-off is not well signposted, but it is hard to miss. The village is an easy 10-minute drive along a fast straight road and is the unlikely home for a hardy bunch of British expats. The village derives its name from the Greek word *lefka* meaning 'poplar'. There are seemingly more palm trees than poplars these days, but Lefka's position amid riotous greenery and rolling hills does give the village a pleasant feel and it is not surprising that its foreign residents stay here despite its de facto status of isolation. The practical tragedy is that access

to the vast hinterland of Tylliria and the Pafos Forest is no more than 2km apart, but is as firmly closed to Lefkans as lovely Lefka and its access to the sea is to Cypriots on the other side of the Attila Line. The only way out is back the way you came.

ANCIENT SOLOI

A good reason for venturing out west is to visit two archaeological sites. The first of these is Ancient Soloi, one of the 10 ancient city kingdoms of Cyprus. Soloi traces its origin back to an Assyrian tribute list (700 BC) where the original city was referred to as Si-il-lu. In 580 BC King Philokyprios moved his capital from Aepia to Si-il-lu on the advice of his mentor and Athenian philosopher Solon. Philokyprios promptly renamed the citadel Soloi in honour of Solon. In 498 BC Soloi, along with most of the other city kingdoms of Cyprus (Amathous being the exception), rose up against the Persians but was ultimately captured and languished until Roman times when it flourished once again, thanks to the rich copper mines nearby. As happened in other parts of Cyprus, Soloi suffered looting and sacking at the hands of Arab raiders in the 7th century.

The site consists of two main parts: the basilica nearest the entrance to the site and the theatre along a short path up a hill south of the basilica. The remains of a royal palace can also be found on the acropolis next to the theatre, though it is believed that this dates from a later period.

The **basilica** is now covered with a large open-walled, tin-roofed structure that protects the remains and the archaeologists who are still working sporadically on excavations. St Mark received baptism here from St Auxibius and the first church is thought to have been built in the second half of the 4th century. As is the case with most archaeological remains, it is difficult to imagine the size and extent of the church, which by all accounts was an impressive structure. What is immediately obvious are the remains of the **decorated floors**. Notable among those visible is a **mosaic of a swan** surrounded by floral patterns and four

small dolphins nearby. The heavy roof over the sanctuary has spoiled the view as the light to view the mosaics is reduced as a result of the protective roof.

The **Roman theatre** has been restored considerably since much of the original stonework was carted away by the British to rebuild the dockside of Port Said in the late 19th century. As such, it does little for the imagination, but in its time the theatre could accommodate up to 4000 spectators. Nearby the now famous Roman statuette of **Aphrodite of Soloi** was discovered. This is now in the Cyprus Museum in Lefkosia. The site is open 9 am to 5 pm daily and entry costs TL1.5 million. It is easily spotted from the Karavostasi-Vouni road but the road to the site is easily missed. As you approach Soloi from Karavostasi look out for the small black and yellow sign *Soli Harabeleri* on the right-hand side of the road – it may be obscured by vegetation – turn sharp left inland at this point along a narrow road to the site itself (300m).

ANCIENT VOUNI

Viewed in the early morning or late afternoon light, this rather surreal and 'what's it doing here?' site is a bit of a mystery. Its hilltop location is simply superb and is reached along a narrow road off the main highway. Look for the black and yellow *Vouni Sarayı* sign pointing north and up the hill. The final approach road is normally blocked by a barrier, so leave your vehicle and walk the rest of the way up. There is no entry fee and no apparent guardian so you can wander at will.

The site, ostensibly supporting a **palace** or large complex of buildings, dates back to the 5th century BC. The palace was built by the leaders of the pro-Persian city of Marion (today's Polis) following the failed revolt of the Ionian Greeks against the Persians – the details of this incident were described by Herodotus in Book V of his *Histories*. Built to keep watch over the activities of nearby pro-Greek Soloi, the palace consisted of a discernible megaron, private rooms and steps leading down to a courtyard under which is a cistern. A curious guitar-shaped stone still stands and seemingly supported a windlass. The palace was burned down in 380 BC and never re-established. Today the site stands forlornly on its magnificent hilltop commanding some of the best views of the region.

On your walk up to the palace look out for the **charcoal ovens** by the roadside. This unusual small industry fuels Cypriots' insatiable appetite for barbecuing meat in the traditional *kontosouvli* style – chunks of lamb on a spit and grilled over a charcoal barbecue.

PLACES TO STAY & EAT

Your only real viable option to stay anywhere west of the North Nicosia district is at Karavostasi or, at a pinch, at Morfou. In Morfou you could elect to stay at the basic *Güzelyurt Otel* (☎ 714 3412). It's not flash but at US$10/15 for a single/double you can't complain.

In Karavostasi you can stay at the comfortable *Soli Inn* (☎ 727 7575, fax 727 8210, Gemikonaği), situated by the sea on the west side of the town. Rates are US$45/60 per night including breakfast, but it also has longer-term self-catering rates of US$90 for a two-bedroom apartment for four persons.

If you have had the forethought to assemble picnic items like bread, cheese, tomatoes, fruit and a bottle or two of wine from Nicosia's Belediye Pazarı or from a supermarket in Kyrenia, you might want to take a picnic break at the shaded *Piknik Alanı*, an organised picnic ground between Morfou and Karavostasi. You will come across the site on your right a kilometre before the road meets the sea at Morfou Bay.

At Karavostasi you could take lunch at *Mardin Restaurant* on the beach at the western end of the town. The place is prominently signposted and there is plenty of parking. The food is good and not too expensive. Fish and steaks feature prominently. *Soli Inn Restaurant* in the hotel of the same name also caters to the hungry traveller and food is well-prepared and reasonably priced. One traveller suggested *Şah* (☎ 714 3064) near the bright bus station on the south side of town. *Meze* here is supposed to be excellent.

GETTING AROUND

There are regular daily buses to Morfou from North Nicosia (every 30 minutes) and onward bus transport to Karavostasi and Lefka (every 30 minutes) from Morfou. Overall though, getting around is better conducted under your own steam, especially if you want to see Soloi and Vouni. You may be able to charter a taxi from Nicosia for a two to three-hour trip and this may work out more economical if there are at least two of you.

Only the arches remain after an earthquake destroyed Saranta Kolones Fortress, Pafos, in 1222.

Muslims are called to prayer in North Nicosia from minarets like this one (background).

The 13th-century Othello's Tower, Famagusta

Remains of the Venetian Palace, Famagusta

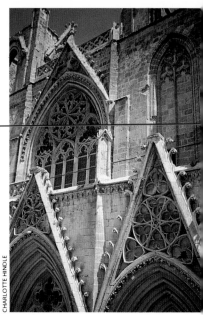
Lala Mustafa Paşa Mosque, Famagusta

The site of the ancient kingdom of Salamis, north of Famagusta, has a fully restored amphitheatre, a gymnasium surrounded by the majority of its marble columns and adjacent baths and mosaics.

Kyrenia & the North Coast

The sight of the diminutive and picturesque harbour of Kyrenia is unforgettable to most first time visitors. There are not many (if any) places like it in Cyprus. Kyrenia is a visual gem, backed by tall Gothic mountains and overlooking an azure sea leading across to the coast of Turkey, some 90km distant. Retired British civil servants long ago discovered the beauty of the North and many settled here after years of service in scattered lands throughout the former British Empire, preferring the milder clime of Kyrenia to the cold and rain of the UK. Kyrenia's most famous colonial son Lawrence Durrell lived near Kyrenia, his idyllic life documented in his slow-paced nostalgic novel *Bitter Lemons of Cyprus.*

Augustinian monks settled here in the 12th century and built a monastery, the incongruous ruins of which still dominate the surrounding landscape. Fairytale castles were built by a displaced French dynasty on the lofty crags of the Kyrenia Range and their stark remains can still be explored to this day. The king of cartoons, Walt Disney is said to have been so inspired by one of the castles that he modelled Disneyland Castle on what he saw. Life for visitors to the North is still slow-paced and relaxed yet accommodation is plentiful and reasonably priced, restaurants abound and offer high-quality varied dining. Picnicking and hiking in the Kyrenia Range is another ideal way to spend a week or so in this timeless sun-drenched sector of Cyprus. The north coast can be fast yet subtle – it requires your time and attention and it won't disappoint.

Kyrenia (Girne)

pop 12,543

Kyrenia is the North's jewel and many Greek Cypriots still remember the town wistfully in their songs and poems as many of them lived here prior to 1974. Politics aside, Kyrenia (spelled also Kyrenia in

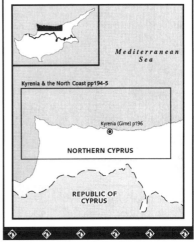

Mediterranean Sea

Kyrenia & the North Coast pp194-5

Kyrenia (Girne) p196

NORTHERN CYPRUS

REPUBLIC OF CYPRUS

Greek and known as Girne in Turkish) is a beautiful little town on the north coast of Northern Cyprus, no more than a 30-minute drive from the centre of North Nicosia. It constitutes the nucleus of the North's tourist industry and it is here and along the surrounding coastline that you will find more hotels, restaurants and bars per square kilometre than anywhere else on the north side of the island.

Kyrenia is identified inextricably with its pretty, horseshoe-shaped harbour around which nestle restaurants, hotels, bars and shops. The harbour has long since ceded its role as the main port of Kyrenia, now it is far too small to service any craft other than tourist boats and small yachts that crowd its cluttered quays. Two kilometres to the east, a large purpose-built harbour now receives commercial and passenger shipping, mainly from Turkey.

Apart from its harbour, Kyrenia is known for its immense Byzantine castle that was once used as a prison by the British. It's now home to the Kyrenia Shipwreck Museum that preserves one of the oldest shipwrecks ever recovered from the sea.

Writer Lawrence Durrell appreciated the beauty of Kyrenia in the early 1950s when he bought a house in the village of Bellapais (Beylerbeyi) nearby in the Kyrenia Range foothills. Many British visitors followed suit and today Kyrenia is home to a thriving expatriate community of British residents who boast their own church, and cultural and social club.

HISTORY

Kyrenia's history is inexorably linked to the fortunes of its castle. Before the building of the castle little is known about the town. It is thought that the town was settled by mainland Greeks 10 centuries before Christ. Kyrenia was certainly one of the 10 city

kingdoms of Ancient Cyprus, but there is little left to document the town's earlier history. Arab raids of the 7th and 8th centuries levelled what there was of the settlement. It was only in the late 12th century when the Byzantines built the castle, possibly over the remains of an earlier existing Roman fort, that Kyrenia's fortunes took an upward turn.

The Lusignans had a hand in the development of the castle and it was used variously by them as a residence and as a prison. Over the period of their 82 years of tenure, the Venetians extended the castle and built the bulbous seaward bulwark that we can see today. During the Ottoman rule Kyrenia functioned primarily as a port – effectively the only port on the north coast. During British rule the town became a favourite place for retiring ex-colonial British civil servants.

Almost all Greeks and many British retirees fled in 1974 following the Turkish invasion when the beaches to the west of Kyrenia were used as the prime beachhead for the landing of Turkish forces. More than 25 years later, Kyrenia has recovered from the turbulence and supports a modest but

KYRENIA & THE NORTH COAST

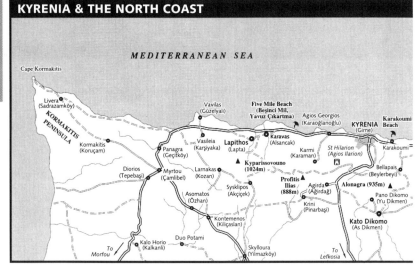

growing tourist influx mainly from Britain, Germany and Turkey.

ORIENTATION
The town of Kyrenia is spread out over a wide area, but the central section – the Old Town, where most travellers hang out – is small and compact enough, making it difficult to get lost. Taxis and minibuses arrive in Kyrenia along Ecevit Caddesi and stop at or near the main square (Belediye Meydanı), which is about 200m immediately south of the Old Harbour. To the west of Belediye Meydanı runs Hürriyet Caddesi along which you will find shops and money exchange offices. To the east runs Mustafa Çağatay Caddesi which takes you to the New Harbour where you will arrive if you have come by ferry from Turkey.

Long distance buses arrive at the terminal on Bedrettin Demirel Caddesi at the junction with İnönü Caddesi (off map). If you arrive by car, bear right from Belediye Meydanı, turn left by St Andrew's Anglican Church then immediately right again and follow the road that leads downwards to the castle. You will find shaded street parking under the castle walls.

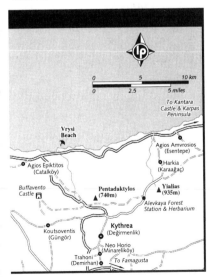

Maps
The NCTO produces a free *City Plan of Girne* in English and Turkish. While it is lacking in detail for the streets of the Old Town it does give a good overall view of Kyrenia and most of the main regional destinations on a smaller inset. Get your copy from the Kyrenia office of the NCTO.

INFORMATION
Tourist Offices
The NCTO office is on the Old Harbour. It's open 8 am to 6 pm daily. The British Resident's Association may be a good place to drop by to see if there are any worthwhile events taking place. Its office is behind the post office and there is usually someone there between 10 am and 12 noon daily. Otherwise its notice board will display details of upcoming events or excursions.

Money
There are two ATMs that take credit cards. The KOOP Bank is on Hürriyet Caddesi near Belediye Meydanı and farther west along Hürriyet Caddesi on the corner with Atatürk Caddesi is the İş Bankası. There are also several efficient money exchange offices along Hürriyet Caddesi. Look out for Yazgın Döviz, or the Kıbrıs Iktisat Bankası at Kordon Boyu 45A, opposite the Dome Hotel.

Post & Communications
The main post office is along Mustafa Çağatay Caddesi, about 150m east of Belediye Meydanı. The telephone communications office is directly opposite the post office. You can make overseas calls at the Dialog Telefon Konturlu bureau on Hürriyet Caddesi.

There are at least two Internet cafes in town. The best is C@fe Net (☎ 815 9259, ℮ cafenet-girne@hotmail.com) on Efeler Sokak. It is open 10 am to midnight daily. Access to one of the six terminals is TL1 million an hour. English-speaking owner Mehmet Chavuz serves up hot and cold drinks, jacket potatoes and runs a small book exchange. Mehmet can also arrange for you to take out an Internet account in

KYRENIA & THE NORTH COAST

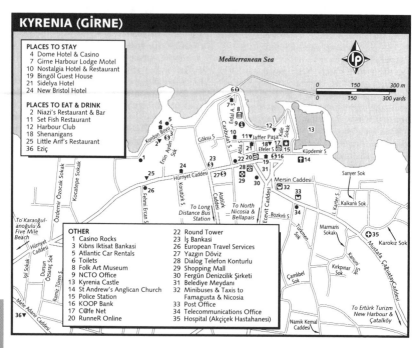

KYRENIA (GİRNE)

PLACES TO STAY
4 Dome Hotel & Casino
7 Girne Harbour Lodge Motel
10 Nostalgia Hotel & Restaurant
19 Bingöl Guest House
21 Sidelya Hotel
24 New Bristol Hotel

PLACES TO EAT & DRINK
2 Niazi's Restaurant & Bar
11 Set Fish Restaurant
12 Harbour Club
18 Shenanigans
25 Little Arif's Restaurant
36 Eziç

OTHER
1 Casino Rocks
3 Kıbrıs İktisat Bankası
5 Atlantic Car Rentals
6 Toilets
8 Folk Art Museum
9 NCTO Office
13 Kyrenia Castle
14 St Andrew's Anglican Church
15 Police Station
16 KOOP Bank
17 C@fe Net
20 RunneR Online
22 Round Tower
23 İş Bankası
26 European Travel Services
27 Yazgın Döviz
28 Dialog Telefon Konturlu
29 Shopping Mall
30 Fergün Denizcilik Şirketi
31 Belediye Meydanı
32 Minibuses & Taxis to Famagusta & Nicosia
33 Post Office
34 Telecommunications Office
35 Hospital (Akçiçek Hastanesi)

Mediterranean Sea

Northern Cyprus if you plan to stay any length of time.

The other Internet cafe is RunneR Online (☎ 815 6642, ✉ runnercafe@usa.net) just off Belediye Meydanı. This smaller centre is open 10 am to 11 pm daily, also has six terminals and charges TL1 million per hour for access.

Travel Agencies
Two agencies issue tickets for ferries to Turkey. Fergün Denizcilik Şirketi (☎ 815 3866) at Cumhüriyet Caddesi 2c and Ertürk Turizm (☎ 815 2308, fax 815 1808; off map) at İskenderum Caddesi towards the New Harbour. Ferry tickets are also issued at the New Harbour.

Toilets
There are public toilets on the breakwater, on the east side of the Old Harbour. Otherwise use the toilets in your hotel, restaurant or cafe.

Medical Services
Kyrenia's local hospital is the Akçiçek Hastanesi (☎ 815 2254). It is on Mustafa Çağatay Caddesi, about 500m east of the post office.

Emergency
In an emergency ring ☎ 112 for the hospital, ☎ 155 for the police or ☎ 199 for the fire station.

KYRENIA CASTLE & SHIPWRECK MUSEUM
The looming hulk of Kyrenia Castle effectively dominates the scene in Kyrenia. It sits protectively overlooking the Old Harbour on the east side with a further bay to the east of the castle. The castle was built by the Byzantines and, while it could in theory have staved off the Ottoman invasion of 1570, the Venetians quickly capitulated and surrendered the castle when they saw how quickly Nicosia had been overrun.

KYRENIA & THE NORTH COAST

A visit to Kyrenia would be incomplete without a trip to the castle. In the complex is a small museum containing the Kyrenia Shipwreck, possibly the oldest shipwreck in the world ever recovered. The castle comprises a large rectangular structure punctuated with four fortified bastions at each corner. Visitors are guided around the ramparts via routes marked by handrails. You are advised to stick to the marked routes since some sections are rather precipitous. The views to the west overlooking the harbour are totally picturesque. Photographers should get there before 10 am to take advantage of the angled light.

Within and off the central courtyard are the rooms and chambers that made up the living quarters and former prison sections of the castle. On the east side of the courtyard you can enter the temperature-controlled chamber containing the Kyrenia Shipwreck. This wooden-hulled cargo boat sank just off Kyrenia in approximately 300 BC and was discovered in 1967 by a local diver. Based on the freight found in the boat, which consisted mainly of almonds, grain, wine and millstones from Kos, the crew most likely traded along the coast of Anatolia as far as the islands of the Dodecanese in Greece.

Antechambers display samples of the boat's cargo and photographs detailing the delicate salvage operation that was carried out in a controlled way to prevent the disintegration of the Aleppo pine wood from which the boat was constructed. The boat is displayed in a dim chamber where you can examine in considerable detail the structure and layout of this remarkable marine archaeological find.

Both the castle and Shipwreck Museum are open 8 am to 5 pm daily. Admission is a fairly steep TL2.5 million.

FOLK ART MUSEUM
This small collection along the harbourfront contains a predictable but interesting collection of household utensils, furniture and fabrics. Look out for the impressive wooden wine press on the ground floor. Opening times are nominally 9 am to 5 pm in summer only and entry is TL750,000.

SCUBA DIVING
Scuba diving is well organised in Kyrenia with Scuba Cyprus (☎ 822 3430) offering PADI and BSAC diving courses. It is based at the Santoria Holiday Village 2km west of Kyrenia at Karaoğlanoğlu. The Kyrenia Diving Centre (☎ 815 6087) offers CMAS diving courses, in addition to the PADI and BSAC courses. It is at 21 Philecia Court.

AQUA FUN
Children and parents will be pleased to know that there is water-based fun to be had at Octopus Aqua Park (☎ 853 9674) at Çatalköy, 4km east of Kyrenia. Here young visitors can climb, swing, slide and bounce on watery and dry apparatus while their parents can relax at the pool bar or restaurant. Octopus Aqua Park is open 8 am to 5 pm daily and is at Beşparmak Caddesi, Çatalköy.

GO-KARTING
Children and adults who still aspire to be children can enjoy Go-Karting at Tazkarts (☎ 851 0439), also at Çatalköy. There is a snack bar, pool table, arcade games and a large-screen satellite TV so you can catch up on the news from home. Tazkarts is on Hazreti Omer Caddesi near the soccer ground and is open 5 pm to midnight daily. A Go-Kart ride will cost you TL3 million for 10 minutes karting.

ORGANISED PICNICS
If you want to do some hiking and perhaps enjoy a picnic, but can't be bothered to organise it yourself, get in touch with Personal Picnics (☎/fax 815 2820, ✆ deirdre mairi@ yahoo.com). Professional picnickers Deidre and Justin have a series of wonderful trips around Kyrenia combining hiking and enjoying a picnic lunch. Rates vary depending on clients' requests. Call or email for details.

PLACES TO STAY
Kyrenia is well supplied with high-quality accommodation, though much of it is to the west and east of the town centre. The following options are more central. First up though there is a basic camp site out of Kyrenia at Karaoğlanoğlu called *Riviera*

Mocamp (☎ *815 3369*). In Kyrenia, the *Bingöl Guest House* (☎ *815 2749, Ziya Rızkı Caddesi 6a*) on the main roundabout is reasonable and central and costs US$8/13 for singles/doubles with bathroom and breakfast. The owners didn't seem to know much English so communication may be a problem here.

A better choice might be *Sidelya Hotel* (☎ *815 605, fax 815 6052, Nasır Güneş Sokak 7*) where owner Yusuf Atman does speak good English and offers very neat and tidy rooms for US$18/25 which includes breakfast. *New Bristol Hotel* (☎ *815 6570, fax 815 7365, Hürriyet Caddesi 114*) is a really pleasant place to stay. Rooms go for US$20/25.

In a narrow street parallel to the harbour-front is the *Nostalgia Hotel* (☎ *815 3079, fax 815 1376, Cafer Paşa Sokak 7*), a tastefully designed hotel with rooms all bearing names of Turkish Cypriot historical figures. One room even has a four-poster bed. All rooms have TV, phone and air-conditioning. Rates are US$27/40.

Around to the west side of the harbour is the old-fashioned but spacious and airy *Girne Harbour Lodge Motel* (☎ *815 7392, fax 815 3744, Canbulat Sokak 46*) which charges US$26/42 with bathroom and breakfast.

One of Kyrenia's best and longer-standing hotels is the *Dome Hotel* (☎ *815 2453, fax 815 2772, Kordon Boyu Sokak*). Room rates with all facilities and breakfast are US$70/90.

PLACES TO EAT

Kyrenia is equally well supplied with restaurants and you could happily eat at a different place each night on a two-week holiday and still not get through them all. The most obvious choices are those on the harbourfront, but with perhaps one exception they tend to be uniformly bland and pitch their menus at the passing tourist crowd. British staples such as steak and chips or hamburgers are common offerings. Still, the view is pleasant and there is hardly a better place in town to while away a lunch hour, or partake of a romantic evening meal with a bottle of wine and a plate of kebabs.

Serious diners tend to head out towards Karaoğlanoğlu. LP lists here a few places closer to town that will not require you to take a taxi or pot luck, plus a couple of places west of town that you could try.

Eziç (*Mete Adanir Caddesi*) is really a fast-food joint, but it is far enough away from the centre to be overlooked by most travellers and is popular with locals who come to sit down to eat. Chicken dishes and sandwiches are the best meals and prices are cheap.

Little Arif's Restaurant close to the New Bristol Hotel is excellent value. Pitched almost exclusively at a local clientele, this eatery is no-nonsense, unpretentious and cheap. It's in a side street off Hürriyet Caddesi opposite European Travel Services.

Niazi's Restaurant & Bar (☎ *815 2160, Kordon Boyu Sokak*), diagonally opposite the Dome Hotel, has achieved something approaching cult status among kebab lovers. Most clients would claim that Niazi's does the best kebabs. Certainly the big centrally positioned kebab rotisserie looks very professional and the food is definitely top notch. It charges a reasonable TL3 million for a set kebab meze course.

Of the harbourfront restaurants, *Set Fish Restaurant* (☎ *815 2336*) is one of the few that gets the locals' approval. Fish predominates and, although prices are a little higher than elsewhere, the ambience is unmatched, especially on a warm balmy evening.

If you do decide to head out towards Karaoğlanoğlu look out for *The Address Restaurant & Brasserie* (☎ *822 3537, Ali Aktas 13*) where for TL3 million you can get a filling set kebab feast and enjoy the sea view. Farther west still is the *Altınkaya II* (☎ *821 8341*) overlooking Çikartma Beach on the way to Lapithos (Lapta). This is one of the more established restaurants in the region and fish and meze are its specialities. It's a good place to come for a lazy after-swim lunch. Prices are mid-range; count on around TL3.5 million per head for a meal.

For a meal or a drink drop into cosy *Shenanigans* (☎ *815 4521, Cafer Paşa Sokak*) – yet another Irish pub – which, while it cannot yet serve draught Guinness, does sell the near-perfect, canned and widgeted variety. Irish stew or scampi and chips sell for TL3 million. The **Harbour Club** on the harbourfront serves both diners and imbibers, the downstairs part being more suited for the latter. Sup on a beer or a designer drink and watch other people for DIY entertainment.

ENTERTAINMENT

If you want to dispose of surplus cash before you head home there is an oversupply of casinos in Kyrenia. These are not necessarily the black tie and tux establishments you might imagine, but glorified gaming machine, get-rich-quick dens of iniquity for gambling-deprived Turkish mainlanders. Still, if you want to try your luck at black jack, chemin de fer or roulette, or simply exercise your finger on the gaming machines try the **Dome Casino** (☎ *815 9283*) for starters, or if that doesn't pull you a pile, move to the **Casino Rocks** (☎ *815 9333*) where a tie and tux are not out of place.

For a little more active nightlife or for somewhere to spend your winnings, most major hotels will have some kind of disco and there is always a sprinkling of good to indifferent bars that kick on until the wee hours.

SHOPPING

There is a small shopping mall with boutiques and brand-name imported goods off Hürriyet Caddesi as well as a wide range of tourist shops that sell everything from snorkelling gear to leather goods. The Round Tower is a small art and crafts shop with a selection of tasteful goods such as pottery, rugs and paintings. It is in the restored Lusignan-era Round Tower in the central area of Kyrenia.

GETTING THERE & AWAY

The long distance bus station is on Ecevit Caddesi in the south of the New Town. Minibuses to Famagusta (UK£0.90) and North Nicosia (UK£0.50), as well as shared taxis to North Nicosia (UK£0.50), all depart from Belediye Meydanı.

There are express boats to Taşucu in Turkey at 9.30 am daily, taking three hours. There's also a daily ferry that takes about seven hours. One-way tickets cost UK£21 and UK£15.60 respectively and can be bought from the passenger lounge at the port or from Fergün Shipping Co Ltd (☎ 815 2344) on Belediye Meydanı. During peak season there is sometimes a ferry to Alanya in Turkey.

GETTING AROUND

Kyrenia is small enough for visitors to get around on foot. Should you need to travel farther afield there is a large number of car hire outlets. Try Atlantic Car Rentals (☎ 815 3053, fax 815 5673, ✆ mchavush@ yahoo.co.uk) based in a wing of the Dome Hotel complex. Its rates range from UK£10 per day for a small Renault to UK£45 per day for a Suzuki Trooper.

The North Coast

Given its northern and central position, Kyrenia is ideal for day trips to any part of Northern Cyprus. The distances are generally manageable and with only one or two exceptions can all be covered easily by conventional vehicle. There is great variety on offer with excellent beaches, mountain-top castles, Kyrenia Range foothills villages and the desolate stretches of the north-west corner of Northern Cyprus.

BEACHES

Kyrenia's best swimming beach lies to the west of the town and is known as **Five Mile Beach**, though in today's metric Cyprus it should strictly speaking be 'eight kilometre beach'. Known in Turkish as both Beşinci Mil and Yavuz Çıkartma, the beach is a pleasant spot and is protected from the open sea by a rocky islet easily reached by paddling. Watch out for tricky currents on the open water side. A few bathers have been caught out and swept away. There are water sports available and umbrellas and sun loungers for hire, though there is not much natural shade. The rather phallic-looking monument on the road overlooking the beach is a monument to the Turkish army that used this beach to launch their invasion/rescue operation in 1974. There is a handy restaurant overlooking the beach (see Kyrenia Places to Eat section earlier in the chapter).

East of Kyrenia you will find more beaches starting with **Karakoumi Beach** (Karakum) at 3km and **Vrysi Beach,** farther out at 11 km, just past the inland turn-off to the Pentadaktylos (Beşparmak) Pass. Both are reasonable spots for a dip, though you will need your own transport to get there, unless you are prepared to hang around for passing taxis to get back.

HIKING

The NCTO produces a small brochure called *Mountain Trails,* available free from NCTO offices. It describes at least two walks in the Kyrenia Ranges that you may want to investigate. However, the brochure is not detailed enough for serious hikers, so you are advised to seek local advice and use a good map.

St Hilarion to Ağirdağ-Geçitköy

This is a fairly long hike that would need to be taken in sections and perhaps broken over a few days, or taken as discrete hiking sections altogether. The hike runs along the southern flank of the Kyrenia Range starting from the village of Ağirdağ on the Nicosia-Kyrenia road and ending up at Geçitköy on the Kyrenia-Morfou road. The trail can be broken or joined at Lapta. Most sections are of two- to three-hour lengths.

BELLAPAIS (Beylerbeyi)

The greater majority of visitors on day trips out of Kyrenia will head for the beautiful hillside village of Bellapais, signposted as Beylerbeyi off the main Kyrenia road. The village is the site of an impressive but quite incongruous-looking **Augustinian Monastery** and is the former home of British writer Lawrence Durrell who lived here prior to and during the EOKA uprising against British rule in Cyprus.

Near the end of the 12th century the Augustinian monks who had fled Palestine

following the fall of Jerusalem to the Saracen Selahaddin Eyyubi in 1187, came to Bellapais. They established a monastery by the name of *Abbaye de la Paix* (Abbey of Peace) from which the corrupted version of the name Bellapais evolved. The original structure was built between 1198 and 1205, yet the major construction work of the monastery that we see today was undertaken between 1267 and 1284 during the reign of King Hugh III. The cloisters and the large refectory were added in the reign of King Hugh IV (1324–59).

When Cyprus was taken by the Ottomans the monastery was put under the protection of the Orthodox Church – a gesture which apparently wasn't enough to prevent villagers and later the British overlords from using the stone for other purposes.

What is left today is a mixture of completion and destruction with some parts of the monastery in an excellent state of preserve. The **refectory** to the north side of the cloister is frequently used for gatherings and events. From here there are splendid views across to the sea and the sea plains below. Less well-preserved is the **kitchen court** on the west side where little remains other than a few walls and a rather precarious section of wall onto which the more daring can scramble for a better view. The now dim and dank church is in generally good condition and remains much as it was in 1976 when the last Greek Orthodox faithful were obliged to leave.

The cypress-lined 14th-century **cloister** is the monastery's most poignant section and is almost complete, apart from the western side where it has fallen down or been pulled apart and now looks out onto a restaurant (see the following Places to Stay & Eat section) where diners can now gaze over meze onto the open cloister courtyard.

The monastery is open 8.30 am to 5 pm daily and entry costs TL1.5 million. Get your entry ticket from the not so obvious ticket booth set back a little to the left as you enter. You may exit the way you came, or directly into the restaurant forecourt.

Bellapais is now almost equally famous for its literary son, Lawrence Durrell, who

MARTIN HARRIS

Lawrence Durrell, author of *Bitter Lemons of Cyprus*, lived in Bellapais in the 1950s.

lived in the village from 1953 to 1956. The near-idyllic, mixed community days described in *Bitter Lemons of Cyprus* have long since gone, but the novel has become almost *de rigueur* reading for visitors to Cyprus. The **Tree of Idleness** under which Durrell's characters spent many an indolent hour still remains, these days more likely shading tourists clutching cold beers than idle villagers. Durrell's house is a private residence, but a yellow plaque over the main door marks the spot where he spent his bohemian days. To reach the house, head inland along the street to the right of the Tree of Idleness and walk about 200m more or less straight and upwards. You will come across the house on your left. Ask if you lose your way – not difficult in the windy, narrow alleyways.

Drivers should note that there is a large car park 70m past the monastery down to the left. Try to avoid parking in the already cluttered main street.

ST HILARION (Agios Ilarion)

Children will love exploring the almost magical fairytale remains of the castle of Saint Hilarion. It has just enough hidden rooms, tunnels, overgrown gardens and steep staircases and paths to leave parents gasping for breath and the children asking for more. It is rumoured that the view of the castle as you approach it from the Kyrenia road was the inspiration for Walt Disney's magic castle in the Disneyland corporate logo image.

This lofty aerie is named after a monk called Hilarion, who fled in persecution from the Holy Land. He lived and died in a cave on the mountain that overlooks the plain of Kyrenia and protects the pass between Kyrenia and Nicosia. During the 10th century the Byzantines built a church and monastery over the tomb of Hilarion, but the strategic position of the site called for its use mainly as a watch tower and beacon during the Arab raids of the 7th and 8th centuries. This was an important link in the communication chain between Buffavento and Kantara castles farther east. In 1191 Guy de Lusignan decided to take control of St Hilarion by besieging and dislodging the self-styled Byzantine emperor of Cyprus, Isaak Komninos. Over this time St Hilarion was extensively expanded and used both as a military outpost and a summer residence for the Lusignan court until the arrival of the Venetians.

The Venetians neglected the castle and it fell into disrepair. It only saw practical use again in 1964 when Turkish Cypriot TMT activists were able to take control of the castle and fend off EOKA-inspired attacks. It has been in Turkish Cypriot hands ever since and a covetously protected Turkish military base on the ridge below the castle is testament to its status once more as a militarily strategic location, guarding the key pass between Nicosia and Kyrenia.

The site is in three main parts and they are not immediately obvious to the eye of the visitor, so seamlessly do the stones and ruined buildings of the castle blend into the rocky landscape upon which it has been grafted. Visitors enter by the barbican and the main gate into a wide-open area which was used as the main garrison and stabling area. A meandering path leads you up to the second area which was originally protected and sealed off in time of need by a drawbridge. Here are the remains of a church, more barrack rooms and a four-storey royal apartment. There is also a large cistern for the storage of vital water.

Access to the upper section of the castle is via a windy and steep track, thankfully paved and renovated in recent years with the assistance of a London boys' home. You enter the upper castle via a Lusignan gate guarded by a Byzantine tower and reach an overgrown central courtyard. Around the courtyard are more royal apartments, kitchens and ancillary chambers. A final breath-sapping climb takes you to **Prince John's tower** where, as legend has it, Prince John of Antioch had two Bulgarian bodyguards thrown over the steep cliff to their death, having been convinced they were planning to kill him.

The view from the top is stunning and on a clear day you can see the **Taurus Mountains** in Turkey, more than 100km away. To the west you can look down on the village of Karmi. Kyrenia to the north, some 730m lower in elevation and several kilometres away, looks very small and insignificant.

St Hilarion is open 9 am to 5 pm daily and entry costs TL1.5 million. Come early if you can; the climb to the top is tiring and can be quite difficult on a hot day. There is a small snack bar in the car park.

BUFFAVENTO CASTLE

This lofty fortress, whose name meaning 'Buffeted by the winds' is appropriately descriptive, perches precariously 940m above the sea overlooking the Mesarya Plain to the south. In medieval times it was known as the Castle of the Lion, but its origins are less prosaic and little is known about its early history. It dates back at least to 1191 when Richard the Lionheart took it over from the daughter of the Byzantine emperor Isaak Komninos. The Lusignans used the castle as a prison and beacon tower as it was in line of sight with both Kantara Castle to the east and St Hilarion Castle to the west.

The attraction of the castle is its remoteness and the views afforded the visitor from the ruins which are in rather poor condition. However, Buffavento takes a bit more of an effort to get to, perhaps because access to it is not explicitly encouraged by the military

who have extensive holdings in the area. You may also be better off with an off-road vehicle since the access road is rather rough. From a poorly marked turn-off on the Pentadaktylos pass you can drive west along the unsealed approach road following a ridge for about 6.5km. From here you must walk the remaining distance (30 to 40 minutes) to the castle itself. Entry is free and there are no set opening times.

ALEVKAYA HERBARIUM

A worthwhile trip can be made along the back road of the Pentadaktylos spur of the Kyrenia Range where you can visit the **Alevkaya Herbarium**, a forest station on the mountain ridge between Esentepe and Değirmenlik. The herbarium is home to samples of most of the endemic Cypriot flora and includes some 1250 native plant species. On display are many dried and preserved specimens as well as the fresh and natural variety. The display developed out of an original collection made by English botanist Deryck Viney, whose book *Illustrated Flora of Cyprus* documented the country's varied botanical treasure trove.

The herbarium is normally open 8 am to 4 pm daily, though if you arrive outside of these times someone will normally let you in. Entry is free. To get there you can approach along a signposted forest road off the south side of Pentadaktylos Pass, or from the northern coastal road signposted via Karaağaç or Esentepe.

LAPITHOS (Lapta)

The beautiful village of Lapithos (Lapta) is popular as a day trip for its proximity to Kyrenia as well as its views, fine restaurants and cool, leafy atmosphere. Forest fires devastated much of the Kyrenia Range escarpment in the mid-1990s, but fortunately Lapithos managed to escape much of the ruination and still retains an old-world charm. Lapithos was one of the original city kingdoms of Cyprus and was a regional capital under Roman rule. Its abundant water and protected position has made it a favourite choice for foreign residents over many years. Greeks and Turks lived here in harmony until 1974. Today it is home to a scattering of expats, mainland Turks and original Turkish Cypriot villagers. The village is spread out and is best visited on foot, only if you have time to walk its leafy lanes.

KORMAKITIS PENINSULA
(Koruçam Burnu)

The bare north-western tip of Northern Cyprus is known as the Kormakitis Peninsula and, apart from being yet another 'land's end' in the same sense as Cape Greco and Cape Arnaoutis in the South, or Cape Apostolos Andreas in the North, it is also home to one of Cyprus' least known religious communities. The Maronites are an ancient Christian sect from the Middle East. They split from the prevailing Orthodox theory of Christianity that God was both Man and God. The Maronites, in contrast, followed a Monophysite religious line where God could only be viewed as one spiritual persona. Persecuted by the Orthodox, they first sought refuge in Lebanon and Syria and came to Cyprus in the 12th century in the wake of the Crusaders whom they had helped as auxiliaries in the Holy Land campaign.

Today they cling to a tenuous existence in the main town of Kormakitis (Koruçam) where they still maintain a church. Over the years the once vigorous congregation has gradually left and barely one hundred Maronites remain to keep the old traditions and religion alive. While primarily Greek speakers, they have managed to tread the fine line between political and religious allegiances with some degree of success. For that they are able to move between North and South with a greater degree of freedom that the few Greeks remaining in the Karpas Peninsula to the east.

A visit to the Kormakitis Peninsula should perhaps include a drive out to the cape at the tip of the peninsula. The road is not good and there isn't much to see, but it is Cyprus' closest point to Turkey, which lies 60km across the sea.

PLACES TO STAY & EAT

A great base for a few days is the village of Bellapais (Beylerbeyi) in the Kyrenia Range escarpment. It is close enough to Kyrenia to be easily accessible, yet far enough away to feel like somewhere different. *Hotel Bellapais Gardens (☎ 815 6066, fax 815 7667, ✆ bellapais@cypronet.net)* is the best place to stay. The hotel has a great view, is very homely and has well-appointed singles/doubles for US$39/79, breakfast is US$7 extra.

Huzur Ağaç Hotel (☎ 815 9444, fax 815 9446), close to Bellapais Monastery, is another good option. It's run by the same owners as the Tree of Idleness Restaurant (Huzur Ağaç means 'Tree of Idleness'). Room rates are US$29/38.

There are a couple of restaurants in Bellapais worth checking out also. The one with most atmosphere is *Kybele (☎ 815 7531),* right next to the Abbey and commanding the best views. While the food is good and service very attentive, you can also just enjoy a drink in the cool welcoming gardens. Prices are mid-range – bank on around UK£13 per person for a substantial meal.

Across the road is the *Huzur Ağaç Restaurant (☎ 815 3380)* serving food and drink. Most patrons seem to prefer a cool beer under the famous tree, but the food is pretty decent too.

In Lapithos three restaurants are worth checking out. *Başpınar (☎ 821 8661)* has the best view at the top of the village and offers cool, shaded dining under plane trees. There are a la carte dishes and ready-made local dishes of the day. Look for the prominent signs as you enter the village. Prices are mid-range. The *Hill Top* restaurant and *Belediye Restaurant* are also prominently signposted and easy to find. They are great places for a Sunday lunch excursion.

GETTING AROUND

No public transport serves the area around Kyrenia so it will have to be taxis, a hire car or pedal power. The area does provides for some of the best cycling in Northern Cyprus. Other than some climbing in the Kyrenia Range escarpment, the east-west routes are generally flat and well serviced by facilities such as places to eat and beaches to swim at.

KYRENIA & THE NORTH COAST

Famagusta & the Karpas Peninsula

The wide sweep of Famagusta Bay and the sprawling flat Mesarya hinterland were the home to some of Cyprus' most important ancient settlements. A bronze age city existed during the 17th century BC, while Mycenaean tombs from the 9th century BC support the description of a flourishing culture detailed by Homer in the Iliad, and the illustrious kingdom of Salamis prospered in the 6th century BC. In addition to these early civilisations, the Venetian city of Famagusta was perhaps the most opulent and wealthy in the eastern Mediterranean with almost as many churches as days in the year. In post-independence Cyprus and until 1974, Famagusta was the jewel in the crown of the country's tourist industry, its golden beaches attracting sun-starved visitors from all over Europe. Famagusta today is a quiet town for people who like it that way. Sunseekers head for the beaches in the north because those to the south have been out of bounds since 1974, thanks to regional politics.

Like a finger pointing searchingly to the Asian mainland, the Karpas Peninsula is the quietest and most undeveloped part of the country. Beyond the scattered village of Rizokarpaso (Dipkarpaz in Turkish) travellers will be hard pressed to find electricity, yet the island's most exquisite beach lies here. At the tip of the peninsula is a monastery that is dear to the hearts of the Greek Orthodox population of Cyprus. Many make the twice-yearly pilgrimage from the Republic to the monastery; a small glimmer of hope that, despite the politics of division on the island, allows Cypriots from both sides to mingle for a fleeting few hours. The region is wild and inviting, and its villages are scattered and unfamiliar with mass tourism. If time moves slowly elsewhere in Cyprus, here in Famagusta and the Karpas Peninsula it has almost stood still.

HIGHLIGHTS

- Admire the Gothic architecture of the imposing Lala Mustafa Paşa mosque.
- Reflect on the grandeur of the ancient kingdom of Salamis.
- Bathe at the most beautiful beach in Cyprus on the isolated Karpas panhandle.

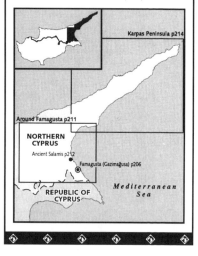

Karpas Peninsula p214

Around Famagusta p211

NORTHERN CYPRUS

Ancient Salamis p212

Famagusta (Gazimağusa) p206

REPUBLIC OF CYPRUS

Mediterranean Sea

Famagusta (Gazimağusa)

pop 27,742

Famagusta's booming tourist industry of the 1960s and early 1970s came to an end in August 1974 when the Turkish army swept into the city and the vast tourist enclave of Varosha (Maraş in Turkish) – Famagusta's Miami Beach – was closed down. It has remained closed to this day. Despite such an obvious setback the citizens of Famagusta (known in Turkish more commonly as Mağusa rather than the official

Gazimağusa) have picked themselves up, dusted off the debris of a bitter conflict and once more welcome visitors to this lively town on the far east coast of Northern Cyprus.

For most people Famagusta means Old Famagusta – the original walled city that has existed since its founding and now within the large Venetian Walls that surround and protect it. New Famagusta, once home to its Greek population, has expanded considerably. While it carries the hallmarks of any modern town, such as housing, supermarkets, petrol stations and lived-in suburbs, it offers little to attract the casual visitor.

The Old Town of Famagusta presents a curious cityscape to the first-time visitor. From the top of the Venetian Walls the Old Town looks almost bombed out or unfinished – an image not altogether untrue, since much of the damage from its turbulent past has never been repaired and, in some cases, buildings never were finished. It is however a pleasant place to spend a day or two. Famagustans are very welcoming of visitors, there are enough sites to keep the culturally attuned fascinated and there are good quality hotels and restaurants to support a low-key tourist presence.

HISTORY
For a long time Famagusta played second fiddle to Salamis, Cyprus' illustrious city kingdom just to the north. Famagusta was founded by Ptolemy Philadelphus of Egypt in the 3rd century BC. The city's original and Greek name was Ammohostos, which means 'buried in the sand'. Despite an increase in population after the abandonment of Salamis in 648 AD, Famagusta remained obscure and unimportant until the fall of Acre in 1291 when Christians fleeing the Holy Land took refuge in the city. From this sudden demographic boost Famagusta grew exponentially and became one of the richest and most lavish cities in the eastern Mediterranean. Many religious communities built churches and it is said at one stage there were as many churches in Famagusta as there were days in the year.

Famagusta's fortunes took a tumble in 1372 when the Venetians and the Genoese had a dispute which resulted in the seizure of Famagusta by the Genoese. This provoked an exodus of the city's wealthy and more illustrious citizens. The fortunes were never regained even after Famagusta was recaptured by the Venetians 117 years later. It was after this time that the huge walls and bastions were constructed, but even this belated measure did not prevent the capture of Famagusta by the Ottomans in 1571 following a bloody 10-month siege. Much of the damage caused during that siege is what you see today. The Turks have remained in residence of the Old Town – known as the Kaleici in Turkish – ever since.

ORIENTATION
Famagusta is not a difficult town to navigate since most of your movements will be within the Old Town. Buses and taxis all arrive on the southern side of the Old Town outside the Venetian Walls. Long distance buses arrive at the Otobüs Terminali on Gazi Mustafa Kemal Bulvarı, on the west side of the Old Town. Minibuses and service taxis arrive at a small parking lot, 100m farther south-east. In between both is Yirmisekiz Ocak Meydanı – a large square capped by an enormous black statue of Atatürk – the major landmark in the New Town and impossible to miss. Across from Yirmisekiz Ocak Meydanı is the Land Gate, the easiest way into the Old Town. İstiklal Caddesi is the main thoroughfare running through the Old Town to Namık Kemal Meydanı, the square in front of Lala Mustafa Paşa Cami.

Running due south from Yirmisekiz Ocak Meydanı is Fazıl Polat Paşa Bulvarı. One block east of this street is İlker S Körler where you will find the post office and the telecommunications office. Arrivals by ferry from Turkey will dock at the port outside the Venetian Walls to the east of the Old Town.

Maps
The NCTO produces a free *City Plan of Gazimağusa* in English and Turkish. While

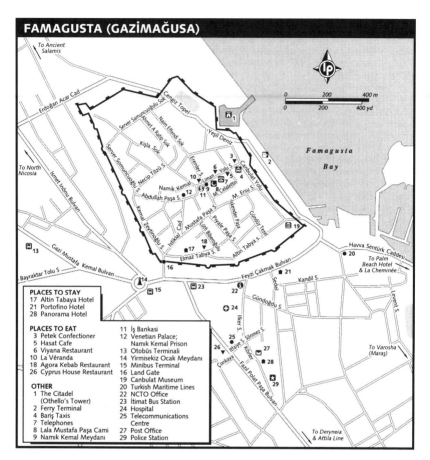

FAMAGUSTA (GAZİMAĞUSA)

PLACES TO STAY
17 Altin Tabaya Hotel
21 Portofino Hotel
28 Panorama Hotel

PLACES TO EAT
3 Petek Confectioner
5 Hasat Cafe
6 Viyana Restaurant
10 La Véranda
18 Agora Kebab Restaurant
26 Cyprus House Restaurant

OTHER
1 The Citadel
   (Othello's Tower)
2 Ferry Terminal
4 Barış Taxis
7 Telephones
8 Lala Mustafa Paşa Cami
9 Namık Kemal Meydanı

11 İş Bankası
12 Venetian Palace;
    Namık Kemal Prison
13 Otobüs Terminali
14 Yirmisekiz Ocak Meydanı
15 Minibus Terminal
16 Land Gate
19 Canbulat Museum
20 Turkish Maritime Lines
22 NCTO Office
23 İtimat Bus Station
24 Hospital
25 Telecommunications
    Centre
27 Post Office
29 Police Station

it's lacking in detail for the streets of the Old Town it does give a good overall view of the city of Famagusta. Most of the main regional destinations are included on a smaller inset. You can get a copy from the NCTO office in Famagusta or any other office of the NCTO.

INFORMATION
Tourist Office
The local NCTO office (☎ 366 2864) is just south of the city walls on Fevzi Çakmak Bulvarı and is open 9 am to 5 pm every day except Sunday.

Money
Inside the Old Town the İş Bankası on the main square opposite Lala Mustafa Paşa Cami has an ATM that accepts major credit cards. Money exchange offices nearby on İstiklal Caddesi keep extended office hours to service visitors.

Post & Communications
There is a clutch of phonecard telephones on Liman Yolu Sokak adjacent to the Lala Mustafa Paşa Cami and the main Telecommunications Centre is on Fazıl Polat Paşa Bulvarı, south of the Old Town. Private

phone offices are scattered through the Old Town, though mainly close to the small commercial centre on İstaklil Caddesi.

Emergency

In an emergency ring ☎ 112 for the hospital, ☎ 155 for the police or ☎ 199 for the fire station. The hospital is south of the Old Town on Fazıl Polat Paşa Bulvarı and the main police station is on İlker Körler Caddesi, also south of the Old Town.

THINGS TO SEE

When viewed from the roof of Othello's Tower on the north-eastern corner of the Venetian Walls you could be excused for thinking that Famagusta's Old Town sights consist solely of modern ruins. Indeed much of Famagusta's heritage has been ruined and never restored, and at first glimpse the cityscape looks much like bombed out cities must have done in Germany and England during WWII. Broken churches and other medieval buildings stud the skyline, while low houses and winding streets make up the rest of this laid-back and crumbling sector of what was once Cyprus's most lavish and important city. A full day, with a break for lunch, is recommended to take in the city in a leisurely way on foot. We list here some of the more important sites only.

The Venetian Walls

These squat, sprawling defence walls are what defines the extent of the **Old Town**. The walls were built to their present size in the early 16th century and cover a surprising amount of territory resolutely encircling the city on all four sides. The walls seem quite low – in reality 15m high and up to 8m thick in parts – an image perhaps exaggerated by their length. While they were built for defence purposes to keep out the marauding Ottomans, they ultimately failed to keep them at bay. The Ottomans took Famagusta in 1571 and, despite wreaking considerable havoc and damage within, the walls themselves escaped relatively unscathed.

Like their counterparts in North Nicosia the Famagusta walls were punctuated with 15 **bastions** around the roughly rectangular layout. While it is impossible to walk the length of the walls due to the existence of the military at various points, you can get a decent enough feel for them at the southern end near the **Land Gate** on the Ravelin or Rivettina Bastion. It was at this point that the Turks first breached the fortifications and captured the city.

From the Ravelin Bastion the walls head northwards passing four minor bastions, the **Diocare**, **Moratto** and **Pulacazara** culminating in the steeply pitched **Martinengo** bastion. This in turn leads seawards passing the **Del Mezzo**, **Diamante** and **Signoria** bastions where it cedes into the impressive Citadel, or Othello's Tower.

Farther along, the **Sea Gate** on the eastern side originally opened directly to the sea, but today the wharfs of the modern port have extended the land bridge considerably. At the south-east extremity you will come across the **Canbulat** bastion, in which a Turkish hero General Canbulat Bey died in the siege of Famagusta. This corner of the walls now houses the Canbulat Museum before looping back to the Land Gate via the **Composanto**, **Andruzzi** and **Santa Napa** bastions.

The Citadel (Othello's Tower)

This rather grandly but perhaps mistakenly named citadel was built as an extension to the main walls of the Old Town on the north-east seaward side of Famagusta. It was constructed in the 12th century during Lusignan rule in order to protect the harbour and the Sea Gate entrance farther south along the main walls. In 1492, during the time of Venetian rule, the citadel was further reinforced by its transformation into an artillery stronghold in much the same way Kyrenia Castle was fortified. Above the impressive entrance to the citadel you can spot the **Venetian Lion** inscribed with the name of the architect, Nicolò Foscarini. It is believed that Leonardo da Vinci gave advice on the refurbishment when he visited Cyprus in 1481.

The citadel consists of various towers and corridors leading to the artillery chambers, a large courtyard bordered on one side by a refectory and above that living quarters, both dating back to the Lusignans. The connection between the citadel and Othello is derived from the time of the British rule in Cyprus. Shakespeare's play of the same name is set 'in a seaport in Cyprus' and the 'moor' connection may be a misunderstanding of the name of the then Venetian governor of Cyprus Cristoforo Moro (1506–08), whose name means Moor. It was thus convenient for the British to put two and one together and call the citadel by its present name. It has since stuck permanently.

Other than wandering around the dusty corridors and the corroded sandstone walls where there is not all that much to see, the main attraction is climbing up to the ramparts and sampling the good views over Famagusta which are best enjoyed in the early morning or evening.

The citadel is open 10 am to 5 pm and entry costs TL1.2 million.

Lala Mustafa Paşa Cami

This enormous structure that dominates the skyline of the Old Town was formerly the **Cathedral of St Nicholas**, built between 1298 and 1326. It is the finest example of Lusignan Gothic architecture in Cyprus and was modelled on the Cathedral of Rheims in France. Many believe it outshines its sister church in North Nicosia, the Agia Sophia. The Cathedral of St Nicholas was the centrepiece of Famagusta's Lusignan heyday and the last Lusignan king, Jacques II, and his infant son Jacques III were buried here.

The church was damaged considerably during the siege of Famagusta by the Ottomans and during this time the twin towers of the church were destroyed. The Ottomans added a rather incongruous minaret, emptied the floor tombs and stripped the innards of all Christian accoutrements and turned it into the Lala Mustafa Paşa mosque, a role which it serves to this day.

The west-facing facade is particularly impressive and easier to admire in totality now that the area in front of the mosque is a pedestrian zone. Three gracious portals point towards a six-paned window which is

decorated with a circular rose. The inside has been whitewashed in typical Islamic fashion, but the soaring architectural lines are easy to follow. Visits are allowed when prayers are not being conducted. Entry costs TL750,000.

Venetian Palace & Namık

There is actually very little left of what was once a Venetian Palace in the area immediately to the east of Namık Kemal Meydanı. Known originally as the Palazzo del Provveditore, the remains of the palace today consist of some desultory cannon balls and a few arches supported by columns removed from Salamis. The one remaining whole structure is the once prison of Namık Kemal (1840–88) who was one of Turkey's best known poets and playwrights. He was imprisoned here for six years after writing a play that was considered offensive to the Sultan of the time. The square between the prison and the Lala Mustafa Paşa Cami is named in his honour. The prison is open 9 am to 5 pm daily and entry costs TL500,000.

Canbulat Museum

The tomb of **Canbulat Bey,** who was an Ottomon hero, contains a small museum at the south-eastern corner of the Venetian Walls. During the siege of Famagusta, he ran his horse and himself into a gruesome protective device consisting of a wheel with spikes. He destroyed the device and both himself and his horse in the process, thus precipitating the downfall of the Venetian-held city of Famagusta.

The museum is a rather tired collection of cultural and historical artefacts and a display detailing the 1974 campaign to liberate the enclaved Turks of the Old Town of Famagusta. It is on Canbulat Yolu and is open 9 am to 5 pm daily, except Sunday. Entry is TL750,000.

Varosha (Maraş)

The sight of the barricaded Varosha district (known as Maraş in Turkish) in southern Famagusta is one of this city's more haunting legacies and is a lingering reminder of the dark days of the summer of 1974. Prior to that time, Varosha was a thriving community of Greeks who also owned and ran most of the hotels in what was Famagusta's Riviera and that overlooked some of the island's best resort beaches. Panic-stricken by Turkish advances into the north in July and August 1974, Varosha's residents fled in fear, taking with them little more than the clothes they wore. Most of them believed that they would be returning within a few days when the emergency was over. As it happened the Turkish army just walked in unimpeded and took an abandoned city. To this day Varosha has remained uninhabited and abandoned.

Visitors to Famagusta cannot enter the area and are indiscreetly discouraged from entering by barbed wire fences and metal drums blocking the streets. Inside, shops, houses and hotels have lain untouched for 25 years. A Toyota car dealership still has models from the early 1970s, frozen in time, locked in the showroom windows. Visitors with their own cars can drive down the western side of Varosha, alongside the fence and peer into the past. You are not supposed to stop and stare and photography is not allowed. The perimeter road will take you almost as far as the Deryneia checkpoint. Here you encounter a military zone just before the checkpoint and it is probably advisable to turn around before you go too far.

PLACES TO STAY

Inside the city walls is the pleasant *Altın Tabaya Hotel* (☎ *366 5363, Altın Tabya Sokak)*, with singles/doubles with a private bathroom and breakfast for US$20/30. Follow the signs from the gate east of the Victory Monument. In a run-down section of the New Town (not far from the tourist office) is the friendly *Panorama Hotel* (☎ *366 5880, fax 366 5990, İlker S Körler)* where cosy rooms cost US$20/28 without breakfast.

On the south side of the Old Town outside the city walls is *Portofino Hotel* (☎ *366 4392, fax 366 2949, Fevzi Çakmak Bulvarı 9)* which was radically renovated in 1999 and offers comfortable accommodation for US$25/30 for bed and breakfast.

Home Sweet Home

Irwin was a lecturer in communication studies at a British university and was visiting Northern Cyprus on holiday. His curiosity about the events of 1974 had taken him in his hire car, with its distinctive black on red plates, to the Turkish-held but otherwise abandoned Varosha (Maraş). Slowly skirting the eerie ghost town with its bullet-ridden houses and prickly pear-infested streets, he remembered that his former Greek Cypriot colleagues once lived in Varosha and had on many occasions talked about the home they had left under such painful circumstances 25 years previously. They now lived in Larnaka on the south side of the island. How ironical it was that he who had never been to Varosha before was allowed to approach the forbidden territory, yet its former residents could only stare at their long-lost home from atop an observation post at Deryneia, in Greek Cyprus, just a few kilometres farther south.

Remembering his friends' pain and nostalgia for their lost home, he retuned his mobile phone from the Turkish Cypriot to the Greek Cypriot mobile phone network and called Larnaka. Stalla answered the phone. She could not believe her ears when Irwin told her where he was calling from. While driving back along the rusting fences and barrels that border Varosha, Irwin gave Stalla a blow-by-blow account of how her former home now looked. In turn Stalla guided Irwin, as if she was reliving the streets and lanes of her old home herself. She led him to the closest point to her old house which now lay abandoned and forlorn, visible but inaccessible, across barbed wire fences.

Having almost abandoned all hope of ever seeing Varosha again Stalla was once again able to 'see' her beloved home through the eyes of Irwin, who sat transfixed, staring across dusty desolation at a house that had had no human inhabitant for 25 years and whose former owner could only see it in her dreams ... until now.

Top of the lot is *Palm Beach Hotel (☎ 366 2000, fax 366 2002, ❷ bilfer@manage ment.emu.edu.tr, Deve Limanı)*, hard up to the Maraş dead zone and one of the few hotels to escape the sealing off of the ghost city immediately to the south. This well-appointed five-star hotel has most facilities you would expect from a top-class establishment. Prices are US$80/100, without breakfast.

PLACES TO EAT

For a cool beer and a quick snack make for *La Véranda* on the north side of the square in front of Lala Mustafa Paşa Cami, or walk east towards the port from Le Véranda along Liman Yolu Sokak and look for the cool and leafy *Hasat Cafe* on your right.

In the same street and diagonally opposite the Hasat Cafe is *Viyana Restaurant (☎ 366 6037, Liman Yolu Sokak 19)* where you can get excellent food served attentively in a vine-covered courtyard. A scrumptious *köfte* (grilled meatballs) meal with salad and beer wil cost you around TL3 million. At the eastern end of Liman Yolu Sokak is the wonderful *Petek Confectioner* where you can drink tea and eat cake and Turkish delight. On the south side of the Old Town is the unassuming *Agora Kebab Restaurant (☎ 366 53 64, Elmas Tabya Sokak 1)* that specialises in oven-cooked kebabs, done in the oven that is prominent at the front of the restaurant. A set kebab meal costs a reasonable TL1.5 million.

In the New Town there's *Cyprus House Restaurant (☎ 366 4845, Fazıl Polat Paşa Bulvarı)* which also has a beautiful outside dining area. It's about 400m down the first turn right to the east of the Yirmisekiz Ocak Meydanı. Kebab dishes are highly recommended and at night you might get a belly dancer thrown in for good measure. Hard up against the ugly road blocks of the Varosha area and very close to the Palm Beach Hotel is *La Cheminée (☎ 366 46 24, Kemal Server Sokak 17)*. Discreet French cuisine is the order of the day here, and you will find prices are mid-range to somewhat more expensive than many other places.

GETTING THERE & AWAY
Sea

Ferries to Mersin in Turkey leave from the port behind Canbulat Yolu on Tuesday, Thursday and Sunday. They depart from Famagusta at 10 pm and the trip takes eight hours. One-way tickets cost US$27.50 (students US$22). The ticket agents are Turkish Maritime Lines (☎ 366 5786, fax 366 7840) and are on Bulent Ecevit Bulvarı.

Bus

The main bus terminal is Otobüs Terminali on Gazi Mustafa Kemal Bulvarı. Minibuses to North Nicosia (TL600,000) go frequently from the İtimat bus station on the south side of Yirmisekiz Ocak Meydanı and from the small bus terminus on Lefkoşa Yolu, west of the roundabout. Also from here minibuses for Kyrenia leave every half hour or so (TL700,000).

GETTING AROUND

There are a few private taxi companies that operate in and around Famagusta. Bariş Taxis (☎ 366 2349) operates a fleet of modern air-conditioned Mercedes taxis around the city and farther afield. Tariffs are generally fixed, but make sure you know what you are about to pay before accepting a ride.

There is no public bus service within the city of Famagusta, but all the major sights are within walking distance so this is no particular disadvantage.

Around Famagusta

Most of the sites around Famagusta are conveniently clustered within a 9 to 10km radius from the town. This makes it feasible to hire a taxi and get around economically. The sites are also all immediately north of Famagusta, though if you have a car you can strike out farther north and west to the rarely visited northern Mesaoria villages of Lefkoniko (Geçitkale) and Trikomo (İskele). You can base yourself at any one of a scattering of hotels north of Famagusta, or at the little low-key resort of Bogazi (Boğaz in Turkish).

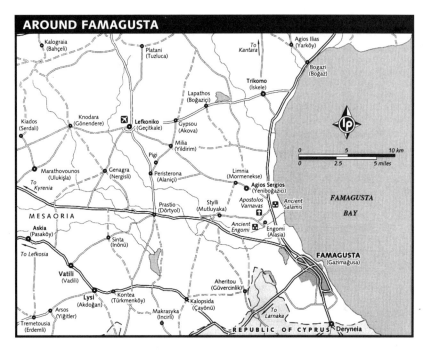

AROUND FAMAGUSTA

BEACHES

The best and most convenient beach in Famagusta is in front of Palm Beach Hotel (see the following Places to Stay section) where non-guests can use the beach. Look for the little 'To the Beach Club' sign south of the hotel, hard up against the Varosha barricades. There is also a decent beach with restaurant facilities at the Ancient Salamis site north of Famagusta. From there on are some excellent beaches all the way to the Karpas Peninsula at Bogazi to the north of Famagusta Bay (Gazimağusa Körfezi).

ANCIENT SALAMIS

Salamis is one of Cyprus' prime archaeological sites and should not be missed by visitors to the North. It is an extensive site and a minimum of half a day should be allowed for a visit. Salamis is 9km north of Famagusta and is signposted – not very prominently – to the seaward side of the Famagusta- Bogazi highway.

Ancient Salamis was one of the 10 city kingdoms of Cyprus and was first mentioned on an Assyrian stele in 709 BC where it was listed as paying a tribute to Assyrian ruler Sargon II. Its period of major importance came during the 6th century BC under kings Evalthon and Evagoras when Salamis issued its own money and nurtured a thriving philosophical and literary scene, with Greek poets as regular visitors to the royal court.

The Persians destroyed Salamis in 306 BC and it was placed under Ptolemaic rule from 294 BC until 58 BC at which point the Romans took control and Salamis flourished once again. For three centuries the city's fortunes waxed and waned and in AD 350 the city was renamed Constantia and declared an episcopal see. Constantia suffered the same depredation of the 7th- and 8th-century Arab raids as the rest of Cyprus, and remained largely abandoned and forgotten from that time onwards.

ANCIENT SALAMIS

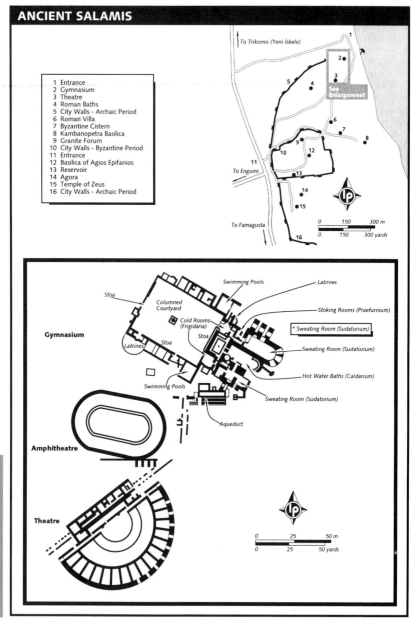

To Trikomo (Yeni İskele)

1 Entrance
2 Gymnasium
3 Theatre
4 Roman Baths
5 City Walls - Archaic Period
6 Roman Villa
7 Byzantine Cistern
8 Kambanopetra Basilica
9 Granite Forum
10 City Walls - Byzantine Period
11 Entrance
12 Basilica of Agios Epifanios
13 Reservoir
14 Agora
15 Temple of Zeus
16 City Walls - Archaic Period

See Enlargement

To Engomi

To Famagusta

0   150   300 m
0   150   300 yards

Swimming Pools   Latrines
Stoa
Columned Courtyard   Stoking Rooms (Praefurnium)
Cold Rooms (Frigidaria)   Sweating Room (Sudatorium)
Gymnasium
Stoa   Stoa   Sweating Room (Sudatorium)
Latrines
Hot Water Baths (Caldarium)
Swimming Pools   Sweating Room (Sudatorium)
Aqueduct

Amphitheatre

Theatre

0   25   50 m
0   25   50 yards

FAMAGUSTA & KARPAS PENINSULA

Much of the stone from the ancient city was carted away by Famagustans to help build their own city. Archaeological explorations of the ancient site started in 1880 and are still continuing.

Today visitors can see a fair amount of walls and columns though you will need a map to make much sense of the initially jumbled layout. Look out for the gymnasium and the baths that served as an exercise ground and were built close by the columned courtyard, and which today provides most of the visual clues of the glory days of Salamis. The **theatre,** dating from the time of Augustus (31 BC–AD 14), could hold 15,000 spectators in its day. Earthquakes in the 4th century destroyed much of the theatre and its stone was removed for building projects elsewhere. Today it has been restored to some degree and occasionally hosts summer events. The **Roman Villa,** originally a two-storey structure south of the theatre, was made up of a reception hall and central inner courtyard with columned portico. The nearby **Kambanopetra Basilica** was built in the 4th century and consisted of a columned courtyard. A mosaic floor is visible inside the basilica. The **Basilica of Agios Epifanios** was the largest basilica in Cyprus and was built during the episcopacy of Epifanios (386–403).

The extensive site is open 8 am to 6 pm daily in summer and entry is TL2.5 million. There are no buses to Salamis and a return taxi will cost UK£8. There is a decent beach nearby and a handy restaurant for lunch after you have explored the site.

CHURCH OF APOSTOLOS VARNAVAS

While the Turks have been accused of a fair amount of desecration of Orthodox religious sites – and justifiably so in many cases – they have at least made an effort to maintain an air of solemnity and normality with this important Orthodox church. It is in the Mesarya hinterland, 9km north-west of Famagusta and very close to Salamis.

The church of Apostolos Varnavas is dedicated to one of St Paul's good friends. Despite his name, Varnavas (Barnabas) was

never an official apostle, but he is mentioned for his missionary work in the Acts of the Apostles. He was born in Cyprus and carried out his missionary work here. The original church was built over the site of his tomb which was discovered by Anthemios the bishop of Constantia (Salamis), following a revelationary dream. The current structure dates from the 18th century, though it does incorporate parts of the 5th-century original church.

The church is used as an **icon museum** today and has a wide selection of well preserved Orthodox icons. There is also a small **archaeological museum** in the courtyard buildings containing an extensive selection of finds from Salamis and Engomi.

The church and museum are open 9 am to 5 pm daily and entry costs TL1.5 million.

ROYAL TOMBS

Close to Salamis are a couple of sights worth seeing that won't cause you to detour too much. The grandly titled Royal Tombs are a scattering of 150 graves spread out over a wide area. The relevance of this historic cemetery dating back to the 7th and 8th centuries BC is that the finds confirm the account of Mycenaean tombs described by Homer in *The Iliad.* Kings and various other nobles were buried with all their favourite worldly goods, food and drink, even favourite slaves, in order to make their afterlife a little easier. In one particularly gruesome reminder of the practices, two hapless horses were sacrificed after transporting a king to his tomb (No 79), where their agonised skeletons have been exposed to the public gaze. Most tombs have been looted over the years by unknown grave robbers, though at least three did yield enough treasure to make it to the Cyprus Museum in Lefkosia.

The tombs are south of Salamis on the road to the Monastery of Agios Varnavas and are open 9 am to 5 pm daily. Entry is TL750,000.

ENGOMI (ALASIA)

Heading farther west from the Royal tombs you will come across the ancient Bronze

Age city of Engomi which dates back as far as 1600 BC. It is thought that this city may have been the ancient capital of Cyprus and is referred to in some historical documents as Alasia. The Pedieos (Kanlı) River that runs through North Nicosia once reached as far as Engomi, since evidence of river harbour structures have been identified. For the casual visitor, Engomi is not very interesting and there is little information about the settlement at the site itself.

The site is open 9 am to 5 pm and entry costs TL500,000.

BOGAZI (BOĞAZ)

Bogazi makes a convenient stop for travellers around the Karpas Peninsula. It is a small fishing village about 24km north of Famagusta and the last beach halt before the now excellent sealed road heads inland to the peninsula proper. There is a little harbour, south of which is a stretch of developed beach with straw beach umbrellas and sun loungers for those few tourists on package holidays that base themselves in the low-key hotels in the village. For some reason Russians seem to have taken a shine to Bogazi and you are just as likely to hear Russian spoken in any of the beachside tavernas as German, since Germans make up the bulk of the remaining clientele. It is a pleasant enough place to stay for a day or two though there is little to do other than swim, read and eat.

The Karpas Peninsula

The long swathe of the Karpas Peninsula was virtually untouched by the traumatic events of 1974 and remains a timeless land of rolling fields, vast beaches, scattered settlements and the best sunsets in Cyprus. The Karpas is Cyprus' panhandle and it

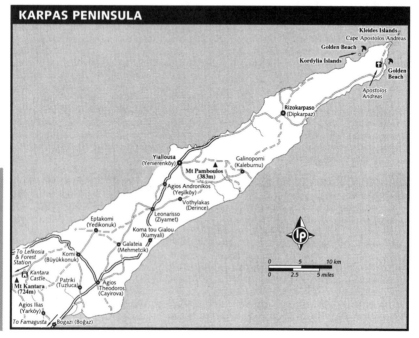

KARPAS PENINSULA

reaches eastwards to Syria as if seeking to look elsewhere. It is little visited, under-developed but exquisitely remote and un-touched by mass tourism. The government has plans to turn the area into a vast nature reserve, which is just as well since colonies of turtles nest on the broad expanse of its southern beaches. In any case, electricity has not yet reached beyond the village of **Rizokarpaso (Dipkarpaz)**. Those adventur-ous travellers that do stay on the panhandle make do with oil lamps or battery-powered lighting.

Twice a year Greek Cypriot pilgrims from the South are allowed to make the long trip to the tip of the panhandle to visit the Monastery of Apostolos Andreas while, in return, Turkish Cypriots are allowed to visit the Hala Sultan Tekkesi in the South (see Around Larnaka in the Larnaka and the East chapter).

Other than the village of Rizokarpaso, which was once home to a thriving Greek Cypriot community and now home to only a few score elderly Greeks, the only other vil-lage of any size if **Yiallousa (Yenierenköy)**. This is another village once populated by Greeks and now resettled with the former residents of Kokkina (Erenköy) in the South's Tylliria region (see Around Pafos in the Pafos and the West chapter). The NCTO is opening a tourist office in Yiallousa in the hope of generating a greater number of trav-ellers to visit the region and it also has plans afoot to establish a network of Agrotourist Pensions. However, it may well be a few years before this low-key green approach sees the light of day. Meantime, the area is ideal for cyclists, ramblers and lovers of wild flowers. The displays of wild flowers in the spring are magic.

BEACHES

The island's best beaches are on the Karpas Peninsula and if you visit the Karpas for only one reason then it should be to feast your eyes on the vast expanse of sand and dunes at **Golden Beach**, a duo of postcard fantastic swathes of golden yellow sand with not a hotel in sight. About 5km short of Cape Apostolos Andreas (Zafer Burnu),

KATE NOLAN

The habitat of the endangered Mediterranean Loggerhead turtle is now protected.

the twin beaches sit on either side of a scrubby headland and stretch for several kilometres. Reached by quite passable roads, the beaches sport only minimal fa-cilities – a couple of beach restaurants, both with fairly basic shack-like huts for accom-modation. If you want to get away from it all and you love sand and rolling dunes, then this is the place.

It is unlikely that Golden Beach is going to see any development in the future since a new nature reserve is on the drawing board. This is good news for the **Mediterranean Loggerhead turtles** or *caretta caretta* that nest on these two beaches and on other beaches on the north side of the Karpas pan-handle and for fans of nature who like it just the way it was.

HIKING

The NCTO produces a small brochure called *Mountain Trails*, available free from NCTO offices. This is the second of the two walks in the Kyrenia Range that you may care to investigate. However, the brochure is not detailed enough for serious hikers, so you are advised to seek local advice and use a good map.

Kantara to Alevkaya

This hike is fairly long, over 40km, linking Kantara Castle and the Alevkaya Forest Station and herbarium (see Around Kyrenia in the Kyrenia and the North Coast chapter). The hike follows mainly forest trails along the spine of the Beşparmak (Pentadaktylos) Range. It passes through or near a number of villages along the way and can be taken in sections.

FAMAGUSTA & KARPAS PENINSULA

Orthodoxy & Islam

While Turkish and Greek Cypriots may be separated by physical, man-induced barriers they at least share the same God – even if they worship Him via two different religions.

Cyprus is home to two major religious faiths: Eastern Orthodoxy and Sunni Islam. Smaller religious groups like the Maronites and the Jews also practise their faith on the island. Orthodoxy came to Cyprus with St Barnabus, companion and cotraveller of Apostle Paul in AD 45, while Islam arrived with the Ottoman conquerors of Cyprus in 1570.

Eastern Orthodoxy is a community of Christian churches that arose when the Greek-speaking Eastern section of the Latin-speaking Church of Rome split from Rome in what was known as the Great Schism in 1054. Orthodoxy means 'the right belief' and its adherents do not recognise the jurisdiction of the Catholic Pope. They recognise only the Patriarch of Constantinople as their leader. Other than dogmatic differences and an entrenched sense of separateness from Rome, the Eastern Orthodox Church is in many ways similar to the Catholic Church with which it has most in common.

However, much of the church liturgy is steeped in tradition and conservatism and little has changed since the Schism. Church services are redolent with formality and ceremony and often last up to three hours. Yet at the same time they are informal family affairs, with participants wandering in and out of the service at will, often exchanging small talk and gossip with other churchgoers. This is in stark contrast to the strict observances of behaviour in the Catholic Church, yet it has a more liberal approach to liturgy.

Islam is a monotheistic religion that came out of what is today's Saudi Arabia in the early 7th century. Islam is an Arabic word meaning 'submission to God' and Muslims are believers who strive to submit their individual wills to the will of God alone. The religion of Islam was named in honour of its final prophet Mohammed, after he was witness to a series of revelations about the one true God, Allah. These revelations are written up in the Islamic holy book, the Quran, and the dictates of the Quran constitute the basis for Islamic beliefs today.

Turkish Cypriots and mainland Turks who have settled in Northern Cyprus follow the Sunni branch of Islam – the traditional 'Orthodox' Islam that constitutes the majority in the Islamic world. However, Islamic life in Cyprus is far from the *chador*-shrouded world of Saudi Arabia or the strictures of Afghan Taliban Islam. Most Turkish Cypriots, while taking their religion seriously enough, are fairly liberal in the implementation of Islamic laws. Women dress much more freely than their Islamic sisters elsewhere and alcohol is commonly available. Mosques can be seen in both Northern Cyprus and the Republic, while previously Christian churches have been recycled into mosques – a solution that is both practical yet occasionally bizarre.

KANTARA CASTLE

The third of the trio of Cyprus' Lusignan Gothic castles Kantara Castle is the farthest east, the lowest in elevation and the best preserved. Its documented history dates back to 1191 when Richard the Lionheart seized it from Isaak Komninos, the Byzantine emperor of Cyprus. Kantara was used as a beacon station to communicate with Buffavento to the east. But its significance faded in the 16th century when Venetian military strategists began to depend more on firepower than elevation for protection and the ports of Famagusta, Larnaka and Kyrenia gained importance at the expense of the once crucial mountain fortresses.

Today you can see a quiet well-preserved northern section of the castle with towers and walls still resolutely standing. Inside the castle you are able to make out the garrison, latrines, a cistern and a postern gate used to catch would-be attackers by surprise.

You can see the sea on both sides of the Karpas Peninsula and on a good clear day the coast of Turkey or even Syria. Kantara is best reached from Bogazi and is at least a 45-minute drive. There is no public transport that reaches the castle. The site is open during daylight hours every day and there is no entry fee.

MONASTERY OF APOSTOLOS ANDREAS

Twice a year, August 15 and November 30, coachloads of Greek Cypriots cross the Green Line at the Ledra Palace Hotel in Lefkosia in order to make the long trek to the Monastery of Apostolos Andreas (St Andrew) at the farthest point east along the Karpas Peninsula. This is the only time when the Turkish Cypriot authorities allow any large numbers of Greeks to their side of the island and the visit is undertaken with great fanfare and seriousness. The object of their politically laden pilgrimage is to visit the site of a monastery where miracles are reputed to take place.

The monastery gained a reputation for miracle-making as far back as the time of St Andrew – the patron saint of sailors – who reputedly restored the sight of a ship's captain after arriving here from Palestine. The current main church dates from 1740, though additions have been made in later years to the whole monastery complex. Attested miracles range from curing blindness, lameness and epilepsy to granting personal wishes. In the years prior to 1974 the monastery made a good living out of the pilgrims' (monetary) votive offerings. Today, with mass visits taking place only twice a year, the revenue is down and the monastery's fortunes look ever bleaker, operating as it does under the watchful eye of the Turkish Cypriot administration and with only a couple of Greek caretakers to look after the place.

In between pilgrimages visitors may still come to the monastery during the day to be guided by one of the caretakers and after being signed in by a Turkish Cypriot guardian. Your contribution to the upkeep of the church will always be appreciated. There are no set opening times.

PLACES TO STAY & EAT

Choices are limited to a couple of centres – one with electricity and one without. At Bogazi you have the option of staying at the comfortable three-star *Boğaz Hotel* (☎ *371 2559, fax 371 2659,* ❿ *bogazhotel@cc.emu .edu.tr*) with good value singles/doubles for US28/40, breakfast is US$2 extra. Alternatively, you can move closer to Famagusta to stay at the more luxurious five-star *Salamis Bay Hotel* (☎ *378 8201, fax 366 2002)* which underwent renovation in 1999. Rooms cost US$80/100, slightly cheaper for rooms without a sea view. The hotel is between Famagusta and Bogazi.

Boğaz Hotel also has a handy beach *restaurant* which serves all the usual Cypriot specialities as well as superb fresh fish. The restaurant is immediately to the right of the approach road to the little harbour.

On the Karpas Peninsula choices come down to basic shacks at Golden Beach, one of which is the *Turtle Beach Restaurant & Cafe* that also serves good food. There are at least two other signposted places to stay nearby. Bring your own torch for the evenings since there is no mains electricity.

GETTING AROUND

Your own transport is necessary to get around this region, unless you are prepared to pay for taxis. The main road into the peninsula as far as Yiallousa is excellent, though signs to some of the sites are lacking in clarity and prominence and could do with replacing. A taxi shared between two or three people on a day basis may work out much the same as hiring a car and if you are on a day trip from the South you may have already hired a taxi in the first place.

Distances on the Karpas Peninsula are quite long and you will need to plan your time carefully if you want to get around to all sights. If you are coming from the South on a day trip, you will need to make a very early start. Be at the Ledra Palace Hotel crossing in Lefkosia by at least 8 am.

Language

GREEK

Greek spoken in Cyprus differs from mainland Greek in its pronunciation – much like Scots English differs from Estuarine English in the UK, or Alabama English from New York English in the US. The vocabulary can also differ quite considerably, though standard (ie mainland) Greek words are understood by all.

Most Cypriots in the Republic speak English and nearly all road signs are in Greek and English. Since mid-1995 the Republic has converted all place names into Latin characters according to the official system of Greek transliteration, which has resulted in some place names being changed (see the boxed text 'What's in a Name?' on page 29). Greek may still be spoken by some Turkish Cypriots who formerly lived in the South, though they may be understandably reluctant to speak it in public. Greek is also spoken by small numbers of Greeks enclaved in villages in the Karpas Peninsula and by Maronites living on the Kormakitis Peninsula in the North.

If you'd like a more in-depth guide to the language, get a copy of Lonely Planet's *Greek phrasebook*.

Pronunciation

The letters of the Greek alphabet generally have a consistent pronunciation and are reasonably easy to master, once you've learned the few rules described in the alphabet table. There are only five basic vowel sounds and there are only really two sounds that could be conceived as tricky for a native English speaker. Cypriot Greek pronunciation treats some consonants differently with κ and χ being pronounced as 'tch' and 'sh' respectively (see the boxed text 'Talking Cypriot' on page 31). Greek Cypriots tend to talk slower than their mainland brethren, but speech modulation and word syncopation, especially in rural areas, may make understanding Cypriot Greek difficult. The Pafos region is well known for the difficulty of its local accent.

The Greek Alphabet

The Greek alphabet consists of 24 letters of which about one-third resemble their Latin alphabet equivalents (and have similar sound values). Another third look the same but have different sound values. The remaining third bear no relation to letters or sounds common to English. The alphabet is easy to learn and it's worth putting in the effort to at least learn to read signs. The table below shows the letters of the alphabet with their approximate phonetic equivalents using the Roman system.

A α	**a**	as in 'father'
B β	**v**	as in 'vine'
Γ γ	**gh**	like a rough 'g'
	y	as in 'yes'
Δ δ	**dh**	as the 'th' in 'then'
E ε	**e**	as in 'egg'
Z ζ	**z**	as in 'zoo'
H η	**i**	as the 'ee' in 'feet'
Θ θ	**th**	as in 'throw'
I ι	**i**	as the 'ee' in 'feet'
K κ	**k**	as in 'kite'
Λ λ	**l**	as in 'leg'
M μ	**m**	as in 'man'
N ν	**n**	as in 'net'
Ξ ξ	**x**	as in 'ox'
O o	**o**	as in 'hot'
Π π	**p**	as in 'pup'
P ρ	**r**	as in 'road' (but trilled)
Σ σ/ς	**s**	as in 'sand'
T τ	**t**	as in 'tap'
Y υ	**i/y**	as the 'ee' in 'feet'
Φ φ	**f**	as in 'find'
X χ	**ch**	as 'ch' in Scottish *loch*
	h	as as a rough 'h'
Ψ ψ	**ps**	as in 'lapse'
Ω ω	**o**	as in 'hot'

The Greek question mark is represented by the English equivalent of a semicolon ';'.

Diphthongs

While the pronunciation of simple vowels is easy enough, when they are combined into diphthongs things get a little more complicated. Look at the following vowel pairs and make a note of their pronunciation:

αι	e	as in 'then'
οι	i	as in 'pin'
ει	i	as in 'pin'
υι	i	as in 'pin'
ου	oo	as in 'moon'
αυ	av, af	as in 'avow' or 'after' ('av' if following vowel is voiced, 'af' if it is unvoiced)
ευ	ev, ef	as in 'seven' or 'left' ('ev' if following vowel is voiced, 'ef' if it is unvoiced)

Consonant clusters

There are also some consonant clusters that have their own pronunciation. Make a note of the following:

μπ	b/mb	as in 'bed'/as in 'lumber'
ντ	d/nd	as in 'dog'/as in 'thunder'
γκ	g	as in 'go'
γγ	ng	as in 'finger'
γχ	nch	as in 'bronchial'
τσ	ts	as in 'hats'
τζ	dz	as in 'adze'

Essentials

Hello.
yasas Γειά σας.
yasu (informal) Γειά σου.
Goodbye.
andio Αντίο.
Yes.
ne Ναι.
No.
ohi Οχι.
Please.
parakalo Παρακαλώ.
Thank you.
efharisto Ευχαριστώ.
Excuse me. (before a request)
me synhorite Με συγχωρείτε.
How much is it?
poso kani? Πόσο κάνει;

Language Difficulties

Do you speak English?
milate anglika?
Μιλάτε Αγγλικά;
Does anyone here speak English?
milaee kanis anglika?
Μιλάει κανείς Αγγλικά;
I (don't) understand.
(dhen) katalaveno
(Δεν) καταλαβαίνω.
Please write that down.
parakalo grapste mou to
Παρακαλώ, γράψτε μου το.

Getting Around

Where is the bus stop?
pou ine i stasi tou leoforiou?
Που είναι η στάση του λεωφορείου;
Where is the taxi stand?
pou ine i stasi tou taxi?
Που είναι η στάση του ταξί;
I want to go to (Agia Napa).
thelo na pao stin Ayia Napa
Θέλω να πάω στην Αγία Νάπα.
Can you show me on the map?
borite na mou to dhixete sto harti?
Μπορείτε να μου το δείξετε στο χάρτη;
Go straight ahead.
piyenete efthia
Πηγαίνετε. ευθεία.
Turn left.
stripste aristera
Στρίψτε αριστερά.
Turn right.
stripste dexia
Στρίψτε δεξιά.
near/far
konda/makrya
κοντά/μακρυά

When does the ... leave/arrive?
pote fevyi/ftanee to ...?
Πότε φεύγει/φτάνει το ...;

ferry/boat	*ferribot*	φερρυμπώτ
city bus	*to astiko*	το αστικό
intercity bus	*leoforeeo*	λεωφορείο

next	*epomeno*	επόμενο
first	*proto*	πρώτο
last	*telefteo*	τελευταίο

Signs

ΕΙΣΟΔΟΣ	ENTRY
ΕΞΟΔΟΣ	EXIT
ΩΘΗΣΑΤΕ	PUSH
ΣΥΡΑΤΕ	PULL
ΓΥΝΑΙΚΩΝ	WOMEN (toilets)
ΑΝΔΡΩΝ	MEN (toilets)
ΝΟΣΟΚΟΜΕΙΟ	HOSPITAL
ΙΑΤΡΕΙΟ	SURGERY
ΑΣΤΥΝΟΜΙΑ	POLICE
ΤΡΟΧΑΙΑ	TRAFFIC POLICE
ΑΠΑΓΟΡΕΥΕΤΑΙ	PROHIBITED
ΕΙΣΙΤΗΡΙΑ	TICKETS
ΝΕΚΡΗ ΖΩΝΗ	BUFFER ZONE

I'd like a ... ticket.
tha ithela ena isitirio ...
θα ήθελα ένα εισιτήριο ...
one-way
   mono μονό
return
   me epsitrofi με επιστροφή
1st class
   protis thesis πρώτης θέσης
2nd class
   dhefteris thesis δεύτερης θέσης

Accommodation

I'd like ...
   thelo ena ... Θέλω ένα ...
a cheap hotel
   ftino xenodohio φτηνό ξενοδοχείο
a clean room
   katharo dhomatio καθαρό δωμάτιο
a good hotel
   kalo xenodohio καλό ξενοδοχείο
a camp site
   kamping κάμπιγκ

single	*mono*	μονό
double	*dhiplo*	διπλό
room with a	*dhomatio*	δωμάτιο
bathroom	*me banio*	με μπάνιο
key	*klidhi*	κλειδί

How much is it ...?
   poso kani ...? Πόσο κάνει ...;

per night
   ti vradhya τη βραδυά
for ... nights
   ya ... vradhyez για ... βραδυές

May I see it?
   boro na to dho? Μπορώ να το δω;
Where is the
bathroom?
   pou ine to banio? Πού είναι το μπάνιο;

Around Town

I'm looking for ...
   psahno ya ... Ψάχνω για ...

the bank
   tin trapeza την τράπεζα
the city centre
   to kendro tis το κέντρο της
   polis πόλης
the ... embassy
   tin ... presveea την ... πρεσβεία
a hotel
   ena xenodoheeo ένα ξενοδοχείο
a market (vegetable)
   ti laeekee aghora τη λαϊκή αγορά
the police
   tin astynomeea την αστυνομία
the post office
   to tahydhromeeo το ταχυδρομείο
a public toilet
   mia toualetta μια τουαλέττα
a telephone
   ena tilefono ένα τηλέφωνο
the tourist office
   to touristiko το τουριστικό
   grafeeo γραφείο

the beach
   tin plaz την πλαζ
the bridge
   ti yefyra τη γέφυρα
the castle
   to kastro το κάστρο
the church
   tin ekkliseea την εκκλησία
the hospital
   to nosokomeeo το νοσοκομείο
the lake
   ti limni τη λίμνη

the mosque
to dzamee   το τζαμί
the old city
tin palya poli   την παλαιά πόλη
palace
to palati   το παλάτι
the ruins
ta arhea   τα αρχαία
the square
tin plateea   την πλατεία
tower
ton byrgo   τον πύργο

Food

breakfast
proeeno   πρωινό
lunch
mesimvrino   μεσημβρινό
dinner
vradhino   βραδυνό

May I see the menu, please?
boro na dho to menou parakalo?
Μπορώ να δω το μενού, παρακαλώ;
Is service included in the bill?
symberilamvanete kai to servis?
Σψμπεριλαμβάνεται και το σέρβις;
I'm a vegetarian.
ime horotofagos
Είμαι χορτοφάγος.

Health

I'm ...
ime ...   Είμαι ...
diabetic
dhiavitikos/dhiavitiki (m/f)
διαβητικός/διαβητική
epileptic
epiliptikos/epiliptiki (m/f)
επιληπτικός/επιληπτική
asthmatic
asthmatikos/asthmatiki (m/f)
ασθματικός/ασθματική

I'm allergic ...
ime alergikos/alergiki ... (m/f)
Είμαι αλλεργικός/αλλεργική ...
to antibiotics
sta andiviotika   στα αντιβιωτικά
to penicillin
sthn penikillini   στην πενικιλλίνη

Emergencies	
Help!/Emergency!	
voithya!	Βοήθεια!
Call a doctor!	
fonaxte ena yatro!	Φωνάξτε ένα ιατρό!
Call the police!	
fonaxte tin astynomia!	Φωνάξτε την αστυνομία!
Go away!	
fiye!	Φύγε!

antiseptic
andisiptiko   αντισηπτικό
aspirin
aspirini   ασπιρίνη
condom
profylakatiko/ kapota   προφυλακτικό/ καπότα
contraceptive
andisylliptiko   αντισυλληπτικό
diarrhoea
dheeareea   διάρροια
medicine
farmako   φάρμακο
nausea
nafteea   ναυτία
sunblock cream
andieeliakee krema   αντιηλιακή κρέμα
tampon
tambon   ταμπόν

Time & Dates

What time is it?
ti ora ine?   Τι ώρα είναι;

It's ...	*ine ...*	Είναι ...
1 o'clock	*mia i ora*	μία η ώρα
2 o'clock	*dhio i ora*	δύο η ώρα
7.30	*efta ke misi*	εφτά και μισή
am	*to pro-i*	το πρωί
pm	*to apoyevma*	το απόγευμα
Sunday	*kyriaki*	Κυριακή
Monday	*dheftera*	Δευτέρα
Tuesday	*triti*	Τρίτη

Wednesday	*tetarti*	Τετάρτη
Thursday	*pempti*	Πέμπτη
Friday	*paraskevi*	Παρασκευή
Saturday	*savato*	Σάββατο

January	*ianouarios*	Ιανουάριος
February	*fevrouarios*	Φεβρουάριος
March	*martios*	Μάρτιος
April	*aprilios*	Απρίλιος
May	*maïos*	Μάιος
June	*iounios*	Ιούνιος
July	*ioulios*	Ιούλιος
August	*avghoustos*	Αύγουστος
September	*septemvrios*	Σεπτέμβριος
October	*oktovrios*	Οκτώβριος
November	*noemvrios*	Νοέμβριος
December	*dhekemvrios*	Δεκέμβριος

Numbers

0	*midhen*	μηδέν
1	*enas*	ένας (m)
	mia	μία (f)
	ena	ένα (n)
2	*dhio*	δύο
3	*tris*	τρεις (m & f)
	tria	τρία (n)
4	*teseris*	τέσσερεις (m & f)
	tesera	τέσσερα (n)
5	*pende*	πέντε
6	*exi*	έξη
7	*epta*	επτά
8	*ohto*	οχτώ
9	*enea*	εννέα
10	*dheka*	δέκα
20	*ikosi*	είκοσι
30	*trianda*	τριάντα
40	*saranda*	σαράντα
50	*peninda*	πενήντα
60	*exinda*	εξήντα
70	*evdhominda*	εβδομήντα
80	*oghdhonda*	ογδόντα
90	*eneninda*	ενενήντα
100	*ekato*	εκατό
1000	*hilii*	χίλιοι (m)
	hiliez	χίλιες (f)
	hilia	χίλια (n)

one million
ena ekatomyrio   ένα εκατομμύριο

TURKISH

Ottoman Turkish was written in Arabic script, but this was phased out when Atatürk decreed the introduction of Latin script in 1928. The Turkish spoken in Cyprus differs somewhat from that spoken on the mainland, both in pronunciation and vocabulary. In big cities and tourist areas, many locals know at least some English and/or German. For a more in-depth look at the language, get a copy of the new edition of Lonely Planet's *Turkish phrasebook*.

Pronunciation

The letters of the new Turkish alphabet have a consistent pronunciation; they're reasonably easy to master, once you've learned a few basic rules. All letters except ğ (which is silent) are pronounced, and there are no diphthongs.

Vowels

A a	as in 'shah'
E e	as in 'fell'
İ i	as 'ee'
I ı	as 'uh'
O o	as in 'hot'
U u	as the 'oo' in 'moo'
Ö ö	as the 'ur' in 'fur' (with pursed lips)
Ü ü	as the 'ew' in 'few' (with pursed lips)

Consonants

Most consonants are pronounced as in English, but there are a few exceptions:

Ç ç	as the 'ch' in 'church'
C c	as English 'j'
Ğ ğ	not pronounced – it draws out the preceding vowel
G g	as in 'go'
H h	as in 'half'
J j	as the 's' in 'measure'
S s	as in 'stress'
Ş ş	as the 'sh' in 'shoe'
V v	as the 'w' in 'weather'

Basics

Hello.	*Merhaba.*
Goodbye/ Bon Voyage.	*Allaha ısmarladık/ Güle güle.*
Yes.	*Evet.*
No.	*Hayır.*

Please. *Lütfen.*
Thank you. *Teşekkür ederim.*
That's fine/ *Bir şey değil.*
  You're welcome.
Excuse me. *Affedersiniz.*
Sorry. (Excuse me/ *Pardon.*
  Forgive me.)
How much is it? *Ne kadar?*

Language Difficulties

Do you speak *Ingilizce biliyor*
  English? *musunuz?*
Does anyone here *Kimse Ingilizce biliyor*
  speak English? *mu?*
I don't understand. *Anlamiyorum.*
Please write that *Lütfen yazın.*
  down.

Getting Around

Where is the bus *Otobüs durağınerede?*
  stop?
I want to go to *(Lefkoşa)'e gitmek*
  (Lefkoşa). *istiyorum.*
Can you show me *Haritada gösterebilir*
  on the map? *misiniz?*
Go straight ahead. *Doğru gidin.*
Turn left. *Sola dönün.*
Turn right. *Sağa dönün.*
far/near *uzak/yakın*

When does the ... *... ne zaman kalkar/*
leave/arrive? *gelir?*
  ferry/boat *feribot/vapur*
  city bus *şehir otobüsü*
  intercity bus *otobüs*

next *gelecek*
first *birinci/ilk*
last *son*

I'd like a ... ticket. *... bileti istiyorum.*
  one-way *gidiş*
  return *gidiş-dönüş*
  1st class *birincısınıf*
  2nd class *ikincısınıf*

Accommodation

Where is a cheap *Ucuz bir otel nerede?*
  hotel?
What is the *Adres ne?*
  address?

Signs

AÇİK	OPEN
KAPALİ	CLOSED
KAMPING	CAMPING GROUND
GIRIŞ	ENTRANCE
ÇİKİŞ	EXIT
DOLU	FULL
PANSIYON	GUESTHOUSE
OTEL(I)	HOTEL
DANIŞMA	INFORMATION
POLIS/EMNIYET	POLICE
POLIS KARAKOLU	POLICE STATION
YASAK(TİR)	PROHIBITED
BOŞ ODA VAR	ROOMS AVAILABLE
TUVALET	TOILET
ÖĞRENCİYURDU	STUDENT HOSTEL
YEŞİL HAT	BUFFER ZONE
PIKNIK ALANI	PICNIC GROUND

Please write down *Adresıyazar mısınız?*
  the address.
Do you have any *Boş oda var mı?*
  rooms available?

I'd like ... *... istiyorum.*
  a single room *tek kişilik oda*
  a double room *Ikıkişilik oda*
  a room with a *banyolu oda*
    bathroom
  to share a dorm *yatakhanede bir*
    yatak
  a bed *bir yatak*

How much is it *Bir gecelik nekadar?*
  per night?
May I see it? *Görebilir miyim?*
Where is the *Banyo nerede?*
  bathroom?

Around Town

I'm looking for *... arıyorum*
the/a ...
  bank *bir banka*
  city centre *şehir merkezi*
  ... embassy *... büyükelçiliğini*
  hotel *otelimi*
  market *çarşıyı*

police	polis
post office	postane
public toilet	tuvalet
telephone centre	telefon merkezi
tourist office	turizm danışma bürosu

beach	plaj
bridge	köprü
castle	kale/hisar
church	kilise
hospital	hastane
island	ada
lake	göl
mosque	cami(i)
old city	tarihışehir merkezi
palace	saray
ruins	harabeler/kalıntılar
square	meydan
tower	kule

Food

breakfast	kahvaltı
lunch	öğleyemeği
dinner	akşamyemeği

I'd like the set menu, please.	Fiks menü istiyorum, lütfen.
Is service included in the bill?	Servis ücretıdahil mi?
I don't eat meat.	Hiç et yemiyorum.

Health

I'm ...	Ben ...
diabetic	şeker hastasıyım
epileptic	saralıyım
asthmatic	astımlıyım

I'm allergic to ...	... alerjim var.
antibiotics	antibiyotiğe
penicillin	penisiline

antiseptic	antiseptik
aspirin	aspirin
condom	prezervatif
contraceptive	gebeliğıönleyici
diarrhoea	ishal/diyare
medicine	ilaç
nausea	bulantı
sunblock cream	güneş blok kremi
tampon	tampon

Emergencies

Help!/Emergency!	İmdat!
Call a doctor!	Doktor çağırın!
Call the police!	Polis çağırın!
Go away!	Git!/Defol!

Time & Dates

What time is it?	Saat kaç?
today	bugün
tomorrow	yarın
in the morning	sabahleyin
in the afternoon	öğleden sonra
in the evening	akşamda

Monday	Pazartesi
Tuesday	Salı
Wednesday	Çarşamba
Thursday	Perşembe
Friday	Cuma
Saturday	Cumartesi
Sunday	Pazar

January	Ocak
February	Şubat
March	Mart
April	Nisan
May	Mayıs
June	Haziran
July	Temmuz
August	Ağustos
September	Eylül
October	Ekim
November	Kasım
December	Aralık

Numbers

0	sıfır
1	bir
2	iki
3	üç
4	dört
5	beş
6	altı
7	yedi
8	sekiz
9	dokuz
10	on

LANGUAGE

11	*on bir*	40	*kırk*
12	*on iki*	50	*elli*
13	*on üç*	60	*altmış*
14	*on dört*	70	*yetmiş*
15	*on beş*	80	*seksen*
16	*on altı*	90	*doksan*
17	*on yedi*	100	*yüz*
18	*on sekiz*	200	*ikıyüz*
19	*on dokuz*	1000	*bin*
20	*yirmi*	2000	*ikıbin*
21	*yirmıbir*		
22	*yirmıiki*	one million	*bir milyon*
30	*otuz*		

Glossary

Gr = Greek Tr = Turkish

afelia – pork cooked in red wine and crushed coriander seeds (Gr)
agios (m), agia (f) – saint (Gr)
AKEL – Anorthotiko Komma Ergazomenou Laou (Cyprus Communist Party) (Gr)
ano – upper, eg, Ano Pafos (Gr)
Attila Line – the farthest point of advancement of the Turkish army following their 1974 invasion of Cyprus

baglam/baglamas – very small, bouzouki-like stringed instrument (Tr/Gr)
bankesi – bank (Tr)
bedesten – covered market (Tr)
belediye – town hall (Tr)
bouzouki – stringed lute-like instrument associated with rembetika music (Gr/Tr)
burnu – peninsula (Tr)
bulvari – boulevard, avenue (Tr)
Byzantine Empire – Hellenistic, Christian empire lasting from AD 395 to 1453, centred on Constantinople (İstanbul)

caddesi – road (Tr)
cami – mosque (Tr)
Commandaria – fortified red wine produced originally by the Knights Hospitaller at Kolossi castle
CTO – Cyprus Tourism Organisation, The South's official tourism promotion body
CTP – Cumhuriyetçi Türk Partisi (Republican Turkish Party) (Tr)

Cypriot syllabary – a writing system based on symbols representing syllables. Used in Cyprus from the 6th to the 3rd centuries BC
CYTA – Cyprus Telecommunications Authority (South)

DIKO – Dimokratiko Komma (Democratic Party) (Gr)
DISY – Dimokratikos Synaspismos (Democratic Coalition) (Gr)
dolmuş – shared (lit. 'stuffed') taxi (Tr)

DP – Demokrat Partisi (Democratic Party) (Tr)

EDEK – Eniea Dimokratiki Enosi Kyprou (United Democratic Union of Cyprus), socialist party (Gr)
enosis – union (with Greece); the frequent demand by Greek Cypriots prior to 1974 (Gr)
EOKA – Ethniki Organosi tou Kypriakou Agona (National Organisation for the Cypriot Struggle), nationalist guerilla movement that fought for independence from Britain
EOKA B – later reincarnation of EOKA, post-independence
EU – European Union
euro – unified European currency
exohiko kentro – country tavern; large restaurant specialising in catering for diners usually from the city (Gr)

feta – salty white goat's cheese (Gr)
foo-koo – Cypriot BBQ, usually low and designed for rotating spit. Name derives from sound made while blowing on the charcoal to get it to light. (Gr)
frescoes – painting made on fresh lime plaster so as to absorb the pigments

Genoese – residents of Genoa in Italy, once an occupying power in Famagusta from 1374 to 1774
Green Line – the section of the Attila Line dividing North Nicosia from Lefkosia

haloumi – firm goat's or ewe's milk cheese (Gr)
hammam – public bathhouse (Tr)
hastanesi – hospital (Tr)

kafenio – coffee shop (Gr)
kalamari – squid (Gr)
KKTC – Kuzey Kıbrıs Türk Cumuriyeti; Turkish Republic of Northern Cyprus
kleftiko ofto – lamb or goat wrapped in foil with herbs and baked in a sealed oven (Gr)

kontosouvli – large chunks of lamb cooked on a spit (see also *souvla*) (Gr)
KOT – Kypriakos Organismos Tourismou (CTO); the official tourist organisation of the South
körfezi – bay (Tr)
Kypriako – the 'Cyprus issue'; politically sensitive and never forgotten by Greek Cypriots and Greeks alike (Gr)

Lefkara lace – exquisite filigreed lace produced in the villages of Ano and Kato Lefkara in the Republic of Cyprus
leoforos – avenue (Gr)
Lusignan – Cypriot dynasty founded by French nobleman Guy de Lusignan in 1187 and which lasted until 1489

Mesaoria – the large plain between the Kyrenia and Troödos Mountains (Gr)
Mesarya – (see *Mesaoria*) (Tr)
meydanı – square (Tr)
mezes(s), mezedes(pl) – literally 'appetiser'; used in Cyprus to mean dining on lots of small plates of appetisers
meze – (see *mezes*) (Tr)
moni – monastery or convent (Gr)
moufflon – indigenous wild sheep of Cyprus, now an endangered species
mousakas – baked dish made from layers of minced meat, aubergines, spices and a cheese topping (Gr)
musaka – (see *mousakas*) (Tr)

neos, -a, -o – new; common prefix to placenames (Gr)
NCTO North Cyprus Tourist Organisation. The North's official tourism promotion body

odos – street (Gr)
Ottomans – subjects of the Turkish Empire that was founded in the 11th century ADthat ruled Cyprus from 1570 to 1878. The Ottoman Empire was abolished in 1922.

panigyri – feast or festival (Gr)
paşa – Ottoman title roughly equivalent to 'Lord' (Tr)
pide – flat, unleavened bread (Tr)

pitta – flat, unleavened bread (Gr)
plateia – square (Gr)

raki strong distilled spirit made from grape leftovers (Gr/Tr)
retsina – resinated white wine (Gr)

saz/sazi – long necked stringed instrument (Tr/Gr)
sheftalia – minced pork and herb rissole (Gr)
sokaki – street (Tr)
souvla – large chunks of lamb cooked on a spit (Gr)
stifado – rich beef and onion stew (Gr)
sufi – adherent of the Sufi variant of Islam (Tr)

taksim – partition (of Cyprus); demanded by Turkish Cypriots in response to Greek Cypriots' calls for 'enosis' (Tr)
taverna – traditional restaurant which serves food and wine (Gr)
tekkesi – gathering place of the Sufi; mosque (Tr)
TKP – Toplumcu Kurtuluş Partisi (Communal Liberation Party) (Tr)
TMT – Turk Müdafaa Teskilati, Turkish (underground) defence organisation (Tr)
TRNC – Turkish Republic of Northern Cyprus (see *KKTC*)

UBP – Ulusal Birlik Partisi (National Unity Party) (Tr)
Unesco – United Nations Educational, Scientific and Cultural Organisation
UNFICYP – United Nations Forces in Cyprus, UN body responsible for peace-keeping in Cyprus

Venetians – residents of Venice, commercial and military power in the 16th century. Venetian were the rulers of Cyprus from 1489 to 1570

yeni – new; common prefix to place names (Tr)

zivania – strong Cypriot spirit made from the leftovers of grapes after crushing (see also *raki*) (Gr)

LONELY PLANET

Phrasebooks

L onely Planet phrasebooks are packed with essential words and phrases to help travellers communicate with the locals. With colour tabs for quick reference, an extensive vocabulary and use of script, these handy pocket-sized language guides cover day-to-day travel situations.

- handy pocket-sized books
- easy to understand Pronunciation chapter
- clear & comprehensive Grammar chapter
- romanisation alongside script to allow ease of pronunciation
- script throughout so users can point to phrases for every situation
- full of cultural information and tips for the traveller

'... vital for a real DIY spirit and attitude in language learning'
– Backpacker

'the phrasebooks have good cultural backgrounders and offer solid advice for challenging situations in remote locations'
– San Francisco Examiner

Arabic (Egyptian) • Arabic (Moroccan) • Australian *(Australian English, Aboriginal and Torres Strait languages)* • Baltic States *(Estonian, Latvian, Lithuanian)* • Bengali • Brazilian • British • Burmese • Cantonese • Central Asia (Uyghur, Uzbek, Kyrghiz, Kazak, Pashto, Tadjik • Central Europe *(Czech, French, German, Hungarian, Italian, Slovak)* • Eastern Europe *(Bulgarian, Czech, Hungarian, Polish, Romanian, Slovak)* • Ethiopian (Amharic) • Fijian • French • German • Greek • Hebrew • Hill Tribes • Hindi & Urdu • Indonesian • Italian • Japanese • Korean • Lao • Latin American Spanish • Malay • Mandarin • Mediterranean Europe *(Albanian, Croatian, Greek, Italian, Macedonian, Maltese, Serbian, Slovene)* • Mongolian • Nepali • Pidgin • Pilipino (Tagalog) • Quechua • Russian • Scandinavian Europe *(Danish, Finnish, Icelandic, Norwegian, Swedish)* • South-East Asia *(Burmese, Indonesian, Khmer, Lao, Malay, Tagalog Pilipino, Thai, Vietnamese)* • South Pacific Languages • Spanish (Castilian) *(also includes Catalan, Galician and Basque)* • Sri Lanka • Swahili • Thai • Tibetan • Turkish • Ukrainian • USA *(US English, Vernacular, Native American languages, Hawaiian)* • Vietnamese • Western Europe *(Basque, Catalan, Dutch, French, German, Greek, Irish, Italian, Portuguese, Scottish Gaelic, Spanish (Castilian), Welsh)*

LONELY PLANET

Lonely Planet Journeys

Journeys is a unique collection of travel writing – published by the company that understands travel better than anyone else. It is a series for anyone who has ever experienced – or dreamed of – the magical moment when they encountered a strange culture or saw a place for the first time. They are tales to read while you're planning a trip, while you're on the road or while you're in an armchair in front of a fire.

These outstanding titles explore our planet through the eyes of a diverse group of international writers. JOURNEYS books catch the spirit of a place, illuminate a culture, recount a crazy adventure or introduce a fascinating way of life. They always entertain, and always enrich the experience of travel.

MALI BLUES
Traveling to an African Beat
Lieve Joris (translated by Sam Garrett)

Drought, rebel uprisings, ethnic conflict: these are the predominant images of West Africa. But as Lieve Joris travels in Senegal, Mauritania and Mali, she meets survivors, fascinating individuals charting new ways of living between tradition and modernity. With her remarkable gift for drawing out people's stories, Joris brilliantly captures the rhythms of a world that refuses to give in.

THE GATES OF DAMASCUS
Lieve Joris (translated by Sam Garrett)

This best-selling book is a beautifully drawn portrait of day-to-day life in modern Syria. Through her intimate contact with local people, Lieve Joris draws us into the fascinating world that lies behind the gates of Damascus. Hala's husband is a political prisoner, jailed for his opposition to the Assad regime; through the author's friendship with Hala we see how Syrian politics impacts on the lives of ordinary people.

THE OLIVE GROVE
Travels in Greece
Katherine Kizilos

Katherine Kizilos travels to fabled islands, troubled border zones and her family's village deep in the mountains. She vividly evokes breathtaking landscapes, generous people and passionate politics, capturing the complexities of a country she loves.

'beautifully captures the real tensions of Greece' – *Sunday Times*

KINGDOM OF THE FILM STARS
Journey into Jordan
Annie Caulfield

Kingdom of the Film Stars is a travel book and a love story. With honesty and humour, Annie Caulfield writes of travelling in Jordan and falling in love with a Bedouin with film-star looks.

She offers fascinating insights into the country – from the tent life of traditional women to the hustle of downtown Amman – and unpicks tight-woven western myths about the Arab world.

Lonely Planet Travel Atlases

L onely Planet has long been famous for the number and quality of its guidebook maps. Now we've gone one step further and produced a handy companion series: Lonely Planet travel atlases – maps of a country produced in book form.

Unlike other maps, which look good but lead travellers astray, our travel atlases have been researched on the road by Lonely Planet's experienced team of writers. All details are carefully checked to ensure the atlas corresponds with the equivalent Lonely Planet guidebook.

- full-colour throughout
- maps researched and checked by Lonely Planet authors
- place names correspond with Lonely Planet guidebooks
- no confusing spelling differences
- legend and travelling information in English, French, German, Japanese and Spanish
- size: 230 x 160 mm

Available now: Chile & Easter Island • Egypt • India & Bangladesh • Israel & the Palestinian Territories • Jordan, Syria & Lebanon • Kenya • Laos • Portugal • South Africa, Lesotho & Swaziland • Thailand • Turkey • Vietnam • Zimbabwe, Botswana & Namibia

---

Lonely Planet TV Series & Videos

L onely Planet travel guides have been brought to life on television screens around the world. Like our guides, the programs are based on the joy of independent travel and look honestly at some of the most exciting, picturesque and frustrating places in the world. Each show is presented by one of three travellers from Australia, England or the USA and combines an innovative mixture of video, Super-8 film, atmospheric soundscapes and original music.

Videos of each episode – containing additional footage not shown on television – are available from good book and video shops, but the availability of individual videos varies with regional screening schedules.

Video destinations include: Alaska • American Rockies • Argentina • Australia – The South-East • Baja California & the Copper Canyon • Brazil • Central Asia • Chile & Easter Island • Corsica, Sicily & Sardinia – The Mediterranean Islands • East Africa (Tanzania & Zanzibar) • Cuba • Ecuador & the Galapagos Islands • Ethiopia • Greenland & Iceland • Hungary & Romania • Indonesia • Israel & the Sinai Desert • Jamaica • Japan • La Ruta Maya • London • The Middle East (Syria, Jordan & Lebanon • Morocco • New York City • Northern Spain • North India • Outback Australia • Pacific Islands (Fiji, Solomon Islands & Vanuatu) • Pakistan • Peru • The Philippines • South Africa & Lesotho • South India • South West China • South West USA • Trekking in Uganda & Congo • Turkey • Vietnam • West Africa • Zimbabwe, Botswana & Namibia

The Lonely Planet TV series is produced by: Pilot Productions
The Old Studio
18 Middle Row
London W10 5AT, UK

LONELY PLANET

Guides by Region

Lonely Planet is known worldwide for publishing practical, reliable and no-nonsense travel information in our guides and on our Web site. The Lonely Planet list covers just about every accessible part of the world. Currently there are thirteen series: travel guides, shoestring guides, walking guides, city guides, phrasebooks, audio packs, city maps, travel atlases, diving & snorkeling guides, restaurant guides, first-time travel guides, healthy travel and travel literature.

AFRICA Africa on a shoestring ● Africa – the South ● Arabic (Egyptian) phrasebook ● Arabic (Moroccan) phrasebook ● Cairo ● Cape Town ● Cape Town city map● Central Africa ● East Africa ● Egypt ● Egypt travel atlas ● Ethiopian (Amharic) phrasebook ● The Gambia & Senegal ● Healthy Travel Africa ● Kenya ● Kenya travel atlas ● Malawi, Mozambique & Zambia ● Morocco ● North Africa ● South Africa, Lesotho & Swaziland ● South Africa, Lesotho & Swaziland travel atlas ● Swahili phrasebook ● Tanzania, Zanzibar & Pemba ● Trekking in East Africa ● Tunisia ● West Africa ● Zimbabwe, Botswana & Namibia ● Zimbabwe, Botswana & Namibia travel atlas
Travel Literature: The Rainbird: A Central African Journey ● Songs to an African Sunset: A Zimbabwean Story ● Mali Blues: Traveling to an African Beat

AUSTRALIA & THE PACIFIC Auckland ● Australia ● Australian phrasebook ● Bushwalking in Australia ● Bushwalking in Papua New Guinea ● Fiji ● Fijian phrasebook ● Healthy Travel Australia, NZ and the Pacific ● Islands of Australia's Great Barrier Reef ● Melbourne ● Melbourne city map ● Micronesia ● New Caledonia ● New South Wales & the ACT ● New Zealand ● Northern Territory ● Outback Australia ● Out To Eat – Melbourne ● Out to Eat – Sydney ● Papua New Guinea ● Pidgin phrasebook ● Queensland ● Rarotonga & the Cook Islands ● Samoa ● Solomon Islands ● South Australia ● South Pacific Languages phrasebook ● Sydney ● Sydney city map ● Sydney Condensed ● Tahiti & French Polynesia ● Tasmania ● Tonga ● Tramping in New Zealand ● Vanuatu ● Victoria ● Western Australia
Travel Literature: Islands in the Clouds ● Kiwi Tracks: A New Zealand Journey ● Sean & David's Long Drive

CENTRAL AMERICA & THE CARIBBEAN Bahamas, Turks & Caicos ● Bermuda ● Central America on a shoestring ● Costa Rica ● Cuba ● Dominican Republic & Haiti ● Eastern Caribbean ● Guatemala, Belize & Yucatán: La Ruta Maya ● Jamaica ● Mexico ● Mexico City ● Panama ● Puerto Rico
Travel Literature: Green Dreams: Travels in Central America

EUROPE Amsterdam ● Amsterdam city map ● Andalucía ● Austria ● Baltic States phrasebook ● Barcelona ● Berlin ● Berlin city map ● Britain ● British phrasebook ● Brussels, Bruges & Antwerp ● Budapest city map ● Canary Islands ● Central Europe ● Central Europe phrasebook ● Corsica ● Croatia ● Czech & Slovak Republics ● Denmark ● Dublin ● Eastern Europe ● Eastern Europe phrasebook ● Edinburgh ● Estonia, Latvia & Lithuania ● Europe on a shoestring ● Finland ● France ● French phrasebook ● Germany ● German phrasebook ● Greece ● Greek Islands ● Greek phrasebook ● Hungary ● Iceland, Greenland & the Faroe Islands ● Ireland ● Italian phrasebook ● Italy ● Krakow ● Lisbon ● London ● London city map ● London Condensed ● Mediterranean Europe ● Mediterranean Europe phrasebook ● Norway ● Paris ● Paris city map ● Poland ● Portugal ● Portugal travel atlas ● Prague ● Prague city map ● Provence & the Côte d'Azur ● Romania & Moldova ● Rome ● Russia, Ukraine & Belarus ● Russian phrasebook ● Scandinavian & Baltic Europe ● Scandinavian Europe phrasebook ● Scotland ● Slovenia ● Spain ● Spanish phrasebook ● St Petersburg ● Switzerland ● Trekking in Spain ● Ukrainian phrasebook ● Vienna ● Walking in Britain ● Walking in Ireland ● Walking in Italy ● Walking in Spain ● Walking in Switzerland ● Western Europe ● Western Europe phrasebook
Travel Literature: The Olive Grove: Travels in Greece

INDIAN SUBCONTINENT Bangladesh ● Bengali phrasebook ● Bhutan ● Delhi ● Goa ● Hindi & Urdu phrasebook ● India ● India & Bangladesh travel atlas ● Indian Himalaya ● Karakoram Highway ● Kerala ● Mumbai (Bombay) ● Nepal ● Nepali phrasebook ● Pakistan ● Rajasthan ● Read This First: Asia & India ● South India ● Sri Lanka ● Sri Lanka phrasebook ● Trekking in the Indian Himalaya ● Trekking in the Karakoram & Hindukush ● Trekking in the Nepal Himalaya
Travel Literature: In Rajasthan ● Shopping for Buddhas

Lonely Planet Online

Whether you've just begun planning your next trip, or you're chasing down specific info on currency regulations or visa requirements, check out Lonely Planet Online for up-to-the-minute travel information.

As well as miniguides to more than 250 destinations, you'll find maps, photos, travel news, health and visa updates, travel advisories and discussion of the ecological and political issues you need to be aware of as you travel. You'll also find timely upgrades to popular guidebooks that you can print out and stick in the back of your book.

There's an online travellers' forum (The Thorn Tree) where you can share your experience of life on the road, meet travel companions and ask other travellers for their recommendations and advice.

There's also a complete and up-to-date list of all Lonely Planet travel products including travel guides, diving and snorkeling guides, phrasebooks, atlases, travel literature and videos, and a simple online ordering facility if you can't find the book you want elsewhere.

Lonely Planet Diving & Snorkeling Guides

Beautifully illustrated with full-colour photos throughout, Lonely Planet's Pisces books explore the world's best diving and snorkeling areas and prepare divers for what to expect when they get there, both topside and underwater.

Dive sites are described in detail with specifics on depths, visibility, level of difficulty, special conditions, underwater photography tips and common and unusual marine life present. You'll also find practical logistical information and coverage on topside activities and attractions, sections on diving health and safety, plus listings for diving services, live-aboards, dive resorts and tourist offices.

FREE Lonely Planet Newsletters

We love hearing from you and think you'd like to hear from us.

Planet Talk

Our FREE quarterly printed newsletter is full of tips from travellers and anecdotes from Lonely Planet guidebook authors. Every issue is packed with up-to-date travel news and advice, and includes:

- a postcard from Lonely Planet co-founder Tony Wheeler
- a swag of mail from travellers
- a look at life on the road through the eyes of a Lonely Planet author
- topical health advice
- prizes for the best travel yarn
- news about forthcoming Lonely Planet events
- a complete list of Lonely Planet books and other titles

To join our mailing list, residents of the UK, Europe and Africa can email us at go@lonelyplanet.co.uk; residents of North and South America can email us at info@lonelyplanet.com; the rest of the world can email us at talk2us@lonelyplanet.com.au, or contact any Lonely Planet office.

Comet

Our FREE monthly email newsletter brings you all the latest travel news, features, interviews, competitions, destination ideas, travellers' tips & tales, Q&As, raging debates and related links. Find out what's new on the Lonely Planet Web site and which books are about to hit the shelves.

Subscribe from your desktop: www.lonelyplanet.com/comet

Index

Text

Bold indicates maps.

Bold indicates maps.

Boxed Text

MAP LEGEND

CITY ROUTES

Freeway .... Freeway
Highway .... Primary Road
Road .... Secondary Road
Street .... Street
Lane .... Lane
.... On/Off Ramp
= = = = ... Unsealed Road
.... One Way Street
.... Pedestrian Street
.... Stepped Street
= = ... Tunnel
.... Footbridge

REGIONAL ROUTES

...... Tollway, Freeway
.... Primary Road
..... Secondary Road
.... Minor Road

BOUNDARIES

.... International
.... State
.... Disputed
.... Fortified Wall

HYDROGRAPHY

.... River, Creek
.... Canal
.... Lake
...Dry Lake; Salt Lake
.... Spring; Rapids
.... Waterfalls

TRANSPORT ROUTES & STATIONS

.... Train
.. Underground Train
.... Metro
.... Tramway
... Cable Car, Chairlift
.... Ferry
.... Walking Trail
.... Walking Tour
.... Path
.... Pier or Jetty

AREA FEATURES

.... Building
.... Park, Gardens
.... Market
.... Sports Ground
.... Beach
.... Cemetery
.... Campus
.... Plaza

POPULATION SYMBOLS

○ **CAPITAL** .... National Capital
◉ **CAPITAL** .... State Capital
● **CITY** .... City
● **Town** .... Town
● Village .... Village
.... Urban Area

MAP SYMBOLS

☨ .... Place to Stay
▼ .... Place to Eat
● .... Point of Interest

✈ .... Airport
⚑ .. Archaeological Site
⊖ .... Bank
🚍 .... Bus Terminal
⛺ .... Camping Area
🏰 ...... Castle, Chateau
✝ 🕆 ....Church, Cathedral

🎬 .... Cinema
✚ .... Hospital
📱 .... Internet Cafe
☀ .... Lookout
⛏ .... Mine
🏛 .... Monument
☪ .... Mosque

🏛 .... Museum
🏞 .... National Park
🅿 .... Parking
🎡 .... Picnic Area
🚔 .... Police Station
✉ .... Post Office
🛍 ..... Shopping Centre

🏊 ...... Swimming Pool
🚕 .... Taxi Rank
☎ .... Telephone
🏺 .... Tomb
ℹ .. Tourist Information
🚏 .... Transport
🦁 .... Zoo

Note: not all symbols displayed above appear in this book

LONELY PLANET OFFICES

Australia
PO Box 617, Hawthorn, Victoria 3122
☎ 03 9819 1877 fax 03 9819 6459
email: talk2us@lonelyplanet.com.au

UK
10a Spring Place, London NW5 3BH
☎ 020 7428 4800 fax 020 7428 4828
email: go@lonelyplanet.co.uk

USA
150 Linden St, Oakland, CA 94607
☎ 510 893 8555 TOLL FREE: 800 275 8555
fax 510 893 8572
email: info@lonelyplanet.com

France
1 rue du Dahomey, 75011 Paris
☎ 01 55 25 33 00 fax 01 55 25 33 01
email: bip@lonelyplanet.fr
www.lonelyplanet.fr

World Wide Web: www.lonelyplanet.com *or* AOL keyword: lp
Lonely Planet Images: lpi@lonelyplanet.com.au